Poverty in America

Poverty in America

An Encyclopedia

RUSSELL M. LAWSON and
BENJAMIN A. LAWSON

GREENWOOD PRESS
Westport, Connecticut • London

Library of Congress Cataloging-in-Publication Data

Lawson, Russell M., 1957–
   Poverty in America : an encyclopedia / Russell M. Lawson and Benjamin A. Lawson.
     p. cm.
   Includes bibliographical references and index.
   ISBN 978-0-313-33398-9 (alk. paper)
   1. Poverty—United States—Encyclopedias. 2. Poor—United States—Encyclopedias. 3. Public welfare—United States—Encyclopedias. 4. United States—Social policy—Encyclopedias. 5. United States—Social conditions—Encyclopedias. I. Lawson, Benjamin A. II. Title.
HC110.P6L375   2008
305.5'69097303—dc22   2008009023

British Library Cataloguing in Publication Data is available.

Library of Congress Catalog Card Number: 2008009023
ISBN: 978–0–313–33398–9

First published in 2008

Greenwood Press, 88 Post Road West, Westport, CT 06881
An imprint of Greenwood Publishing Group, Inc.
www.greenwood.com

Printed in the United States of America

The paper used in this book complies with the
Permanent Paper Standard issued by the National
Information Standards Organization (Z39.48-1984).

10 9 8 7 6 5 4 3 2 1

This Book is Affectionately Dedicated to

Those We Love

Contents

List of Entries

Guide to Related Topics

Early American Poor Relief

British Poor and the Origins of Colonialism

Convict Transportation

Indentured Servitude

Poor Laws in England and America

Redemptioners

Spirits and Newlanders

Warning Out

Federal Relief Programs, Policies, and Agencies

Administration for Children and Families

Affirmative Action

Aid to Families with Dependent Children

Children's Bureau

Civilian Conservation Corps

Clinton Welfare Reform

Community Action Program

Department of Housing and Urban Development

Department of Labor

Economic Opportunity Act

Elementary and Secondary School Act

Equal Employment Opportunity Commission

Family Assistance Plan

Federal Housing Administration

Food Stamps

Head Start

Job Corps

Medicaid

Medicare

Minimum Wage

New Deal

No Child Left Behind

Office of Economic Opportunity

Public Works Administration

Social Security

VISTA

Works Progress Administration

Poverty of Specific Groups

African Americans and Poverty

Hispanic Americans and Poverty

Immigrants

Impoverished Children

Panhandlers

Urban Poor

Poverty Trends and Phenomena

Christianity and Poverty

Crime and Imprisonment

Disease and the Poor

Drugs, Alcohol, and the Poor

Education

Great Depression

Homelessness

Hoovervilles

Institutionalization of the Poor

Labor

Protest Movements

Pruitt–Igoe

Public Housing

Racism

Slavery

War and Poverty

War on Poverty

"Welfare Moms"

Welfare State

Reformers

Addams, Jane

Children's Aid Society

Progressives

Relief Organizations

Children's Defense Fund

Children's Health Insurance Program

National Center for Children in Poverty

Theories of Poverty

Culture of Poverty

Environmental Theory of Poverty

Race and Ethnicity

Writings on and Studies of American Poverty

The Grapes of Wrath by John Steinbeck

How the Other Half Lives by Jacob Riis

KIDS COUNT

Literature and Poverty

Measurement of Inequality

The Other America by Michael Harrington

Wealth and Income Inequality

Preface

Poverty has been part of the human experience for millennia. In one respect, poverty is a static experience for humans across space and time: in each human society, past and present, some portion of the population lives with insufficient food, shelter, and clothing to maintain strength, warmth, protection, and health. This experience of poverty transcends societal bounds; an individual is poor by lacking basic human needs. At the same time, poverty is in flux over time, for each society has particular standards for what is sufficient wealth to meet status, lifestyle, and material needs. This experience of poverty is highly dependent upon society, meaning that poverty is a comparative social experience. Static poverty has a transcendent component that encompasses all human experience; comprehension of it requires philosophy and theory. Questions that philosophers and theoreticians ask include: What is the nature of poverty? How is poverty experienced emotionally, mentally, and physically for each human? Why is poverty a normative condition of human existence? Poverty in flux, on the other hand, has a relative component that is of limited impact on particular human groups; comprehending it requires social scientific and historical study of individual groups in a specific time and place. Questions that social scientists and historians ask include: How has poverty changed over time? What are the historical trends of poverty for the population as a whole and for individual groups? What are the causes and consequences of poverty in a given time and place? How can poverty someday be reduced or eliminated in a given place?

Poverty in America is a reference book providing discrete entries describing the major phenomena in the history of American poverty from the sixteenth century to the twenty-first. The geographical parameter of this book is North America—particularly the region that became the United States of America. The book features alphabetized entries dealing with significant people, places, events, phenomena, theories, processes, and programs that have to do with the many possible answers to the basic questions that philosophers, theoreticians, social scientists, and historians ask about the nature and experience of poverty. Each entry has cross references to related topics. Appendices of the encyclopedia include documents illustrative of the history and experience of poverty in America, as well as a chronology of the major events in American poverty over time and a list of sources consulted by the authors, including published and unpublished documents, periodical literature, and books.

Introduction

The phenomenon of poverty in America and the intellectual and scientific response to it have changed over the centuries, from the colonial period to the onset of the Industrial Revolution in the nineteenth century to the global economy of the twentieth and twenty-first centuries. The poor have always been viewed with suspicion by educated middle- and upper-class people who, having rarely experienced poverty, assume that poverty is partly a matter of choice. Nevertheless, there is a strong tradition in America of caring for destitute members of the community. The sense of obligation toward the poor, however, coincides with mistrust. The American experience of poverty has been dominated by questions such as the following: Who are the deserving poor? How should the treatment of the deserving poor differ from that of the undeserving poor? How can society make the poor, especially those who have no clear physical or mental limitations, fulfill their obligation of contributing to society? Can poverty be eliminated and, if so, how?

Poverty has been a ubiquitous human experience. As recorded in the Gospel of John, Jesus of Nazareth, when questioned by one of his disciples about why he allowed expensive ointment to be used to anoint him when the sale of the ointment would have brought money to feed the poor, responded: "The poor you always have with you; but you do not always have me." Over the course of human existence, the mass of humanity has experienced poverty: limited and insufficient material resources to maintain an adequate existence of food, shelter, and clothing. There is an absolute state of poverty: for all times and places, a basic diet is required for adequate health and nutrition; clothes are required to protect the body from the elements; a rudimentary shelter is needed to survive changes in the climate. A diet of 500 calories per day, for example, is insufficient at any time, at any place. Relative poverty varies according to the time and place, the dietary standards of a particular society, clothing, and shelter. Hence, what constitutes poverty in a wealthy society, such as that of the United States, is different than in an impoverished society, such as Somalia. In this study, poverty is defined by the contemporaries of time and place. The poor of colonial Jamestown had a different material condition than the poor of modern Boston, yet each time and place has had contemporary standards that define poverty, which are disclosed in contemporary documents. The consequences and response to poverty also vary according to time, place, and individual circumstance. The community response to poverty was different in 1700 than in 1900 or 2000, depending on citizen expectations of the role of government and the common theories about poverty's causes. The individual response to poverty varies from action and movement for self-betterment or passivity, the sinking into disillusionment and dependence. Most difficult to determine are the emotional responses to poverty, which range among individuals from acceptance to resistance, from pride to embarrassment, from confidence to despair.

COLONIAL POVERTY

The English experience of poverty informed colonial Americans in their attitudes toward the poor and their response to poverty. The Statute of Artificers of 1562 and the Poor Law of 1601, both enacted under Elizabeth I, required that, in the words of Carl Bridenbaugh

> dependent classes should be maintained by general taxation, that the local group should provide for its own poor through its own officers, that 'sturdy and valiant beggars' were a species of criminal, and that workhouses should be set up wherein paupers might be segregated in groups from the rest of society.

The experience of Bostonians dealing with their growing problem of poverty in the late 1600s and early 1700s is instructive. At the same time that various charitable organizations provided for food, shelter, and medicine for selective groups of the poor, the town built an "almshouse" to provide an institutional basis for maintaining the poor. Unfortunately the almshouse brought together the deserving poor with the "sturdy" poor—the ne'er-do-wells who refused to engage in honest labor. The almshouses were, therefore, frequently places of loose morals, abuse, and criminal influence. Children were those most affected, usually to their detriment. During the eighteenth century, Boston, like other towns, no longer provided for the poor in the almshouse, but rather the "workhouse," the change in name reflecting a change in attitude toward the poor: regardless of age or sex, unless they were physically or mentally disabled, the poor should work for their keep.

Boston's experience was echoed by that of many other towns throughout America, especially in the north. As towns grew in population, they grew in number of dependents, often because of migration of the poor from one town to another as they sought help or handouts. New England towns adopted the practice of "warning out," which involved informing indigent newcomers that they were not welcome to the town and would not be cared for if they became ill or unable to find food and shelter. As towns grew larger after 1700, the poor were able to blend more effectively into the general populace. Private charity and warning out no longer sufficed "to save the towne harmless," in the words of the Portsmouth New Hampshire town records, from the expense of the poor. The citizens of towns responded by building more workhouses, by appointing town officials ("overseers") to oversee the poor relief system, by instituting mandatory indentures of apprenticeship for indigent children, and by hiring physicians to administer to the needs of the sick poor. During these centuries, the attitude of town officials and therefore the society at large was altered by the economic demands of poverty, which burdened taxpayers and overseers of the poor alike and convinced people that the poor were poor through sin, in particular the sin of indolence. In apparent contrast to the teachings of the Gospel, Puritan clergymen such as Cotton Mather believed, in the words of Louis B. Wright, that "the very fact that the poor had not prospered was indicative of their failure to live in accordance with Christian injunctions, and it was doubtful whether charity toward them was a virtue."

Approaching the time of the American Revolution, as colonial society grew in sophistication, the poor became a greater burden on towns and cities, whose citizens responded by imposing more Draconian methods to confront what seemed to be an insoluble problem. Houses of Correction were opened in the latter half of the eighteenth century to provide correction for criminals, poor, orphans, widows, the disabled, and the insane—all were housed together in one institution with little segregation.

INDUSTRIAL REVOLUTION

Industrialization, which began in America at the end of the eighteenth and beginning of the nineteenth centuries, led to dramatic changes in American society. Most important were the movement of people from the countryside to the city; urbanization; the rise of a wage-earning, blue-collar class; and negative changes to the family. The family was forced to adapt to inner-city living conditions; to endure long work hours in dangerous factory settings to earn inequitable wages; and to engage all members of the family, even children, in the vain attempt to earn enough money to live a decent life. Industrialization, which brought greater production and expanding national capital, ironically brought greater poverty to a greater number of people. Many cities inaugurated institutions to reform the criminal (penitentiaries), to house the insane (insane asylums), and to care for the orphaned and elderly. Nevertheless, the numbers of homeless people grew in American cities. Increasing immigration led to greater competition for jobs and to the displacement of workers who were unwilling to accept the dangerous working conditions and low wages. Eastern cities were hard-pressed to accommodate the great numbers of eastern European immigrants arriving on American shores. Increasingly, cities developed neighborhoods that were distinct according to race, class, ethnicity, and poverty.

The American middle class of the nineteenth century responded to the growing crisis in poverty with programs to change the behavior and beliefs of the working class. The temperance movement and evangelical Christianity sent volunteers, often women, into the developing inner city to distribute pamphlets and spread the good news of alcohol abstinence and Christ. Organizations such as the Children's Aid Society and the Young Men's Christian Association (YMCA) developed in the latter part of the century to help poor children. Charles Loring Brace created the Children's Aid Society to take poor boys and girls from the city to spend summers in the wide-open spaces of the countryside. The YMCA likewise addressed the needs of inner-city children. Jacob Riis, a Danish immigrant, author, and photographer, portrayed the plight of the homeless and poor, many of whom were children, in *How the Other Half Lives* (1890). Toward the turn of the century, Reformers such as Riis worked for reforms in working conditions, child labor, wages and hours, and workers' benefits. Notable among these progressives was Jane Addams, who opened Hull House in Chicago in 1889 to help the poor (children, single mothers, immigrants, and the ill, aged, orphaned, disabled, or unemployed). She began the settlement house movement, in which middle-class reformers opened institutions where the poor could find loving help and charity rather than condemnation and punishment.

From 1890 to 1920 the Progressives represented a growing liberal response to poverty, as opposed to a more conservative view. The conservatives, represented by the Republican party, continued to entertain the old idea that people were poor because of their own actions, not because of the environment in which they lived. They embraced the ideas of Social Darwinism—that the fittest adapt to their environment and the weak die off—and laissez-faire politics—that the government should keep its "hands off" the economy and allow the rhythms of the marketplace to determine whether or not society and the individual thrived. Liberals, particularly in the Democratic party, believed in social justice and civic responsibility, in the duty of the community to take care of those less fortunate. They believed that poverty was the product of circumstances rather than character and personality and that, if the environment in which a person lived was altered, the conditions leading to impoverishment would also alter.

THE GREAT DEPRESSION

The number of poor increased dramatically during the Great Depression of the 1930s, caused in part by the agricultural depression of the 1920s. Overproduction of farm products had resulted in declining prices, so many farmers had to quit the land and move to the city. In the Oklahoma and Texas panhandles, the Dust Bowl occurred because of erosion, drought, and high winds. The unemployment rate in American cities peaked at 25 percent in 1932. With limited government welfare programs, the unemployed, homeless, and hungry had to rely on the infrequent generosity of private charities and churches. The numbers of homeless increased, many took to the road, and the "Hobo" became an icon of the wandering good-for-nothing resembling the sturdy beggar of the colonial period. Also symbolic of the Depression and overwhelming poverty were "Hoovervilles," shantytowns at the edge of cities where families lived in makeshift box shelters. The Republican Hoover administration was saddled with blame for the Depression, which opened political office and opportunity to the Democrats. Franklin Delano Roosevelt won a landslide victory against Hoover, on the promise of a New Deal for America. The New Deal was the beginning of active federal government involvement in the economy, in protecting the rights of the poor and wage earners, in restricting business exploitation of workers, in providing for the security of the aged, in restoring the farm economy, and in helping put Americans back to work and reducing the unemployment rate. Government programs, labeled "Alphabet Soup" by wits, included the Banking Act, which created the Federal Deposit Insurance Corporation (FDIC), protecting deposits from bank closings; the Civilian Conservation Corps (CCC), which put young men to work on environmental programs and gave them food, shelter, and a small wage; the Public Works Administration (PWA) and Works Progress Administration (WPA), which employed workers in government public works programs; the Agricultural Adjustment Act (AAA), which gave subsidies to farmers and encouraged decreased production leading to rising prices; and the Social Security Act (SSA), which created the Social Security Administration, guaranteeing retirement benefits for America's elderly. Although the New Deal had limited success in easing some of the most serious problems of the Great Depression, it helped bring about greater hope for impoverished Americans and established a system of government that hinted at the possibilities of a socialist welfare state.

THE WAR ON POVERTY

The battle against poverty continued during subsequent Democratic presidential administrations: Truman's Fair Deal, Kennedy's New Frontier, and Johnson's Great Society. Particularly in the 1960s, the government waged a "war on poverty" across America. The battle lines were drawn in the inner city, among minority groups, the uneducated, and the unemployed. The weapons included the raising of the minimum wage for an hour's work; programs such as Head Start to help educate children in their early years; and welfare programs that targeted families with young children, such as food stamps and Women Infant Children (WIC). At the end of the 1960s the poverty rate had dropped significantly. People who were once poor could now maintain a "decent standard of living" and meet their common needs.

Although during the 1960s welfare programs were thought to be the best way to combat poverty, the increasing cost of such entitlement programs led to a scaledown of welfare programs in the Republican-dominated 1970s and 1980s. During the Clinton administration, however, from 1993 to 2001, the emphasis was on helping those caught in the welfare system to learn skills and gain education, which would allow the poor to achieve well-paying jobs and to help them break away from government dependence. The Clinton Welfare Reform Act reorganized government assistance; for example, the Administration for Children and Families, which included Temporary Assistance for Needy Families, replaced the much larger Aid to Families with Dependent Children. The Republican Bush administration from 2001 to 2008 addressed concerns about the poor with the No Child Left Behind Act. At the same time, however, the rising cost of living and lagging wages has kept the poverty rate surprisingly high. During the first decade of the twenty-first century, poverty continues to be a perplexing phenomenon in America. According to the U.S. Census Bureau, those living in poverty amount to almost 13 percent of the population. However, 25 percent of African Americans and more than one in five Hispanic Americans live in poverty. Sadly, the rate of children in poverty is much higher than the overall rate; 19 percent of children in America are poor, despite federal and state programs that work to the contrary.

Chronology

1691	Law under William III requires that newcomers to English towns have property or employment or else return to their parishes of birth
1705	Portsmouth, New Hampshire, builds its first almshouse
1717	Parliament grants felons convicted of capital crimes the option of transportation to the colonies
1724	The Episcopal Charitable Society is founded
1732	Philadelphia builds its first almshouse
1736	New York builds its first almshouse
1737	The Charitable Irish Society is founded in Boston
1752	Pennsylvania Hospital opens in Philadelphia to care for the sick poor
1764	Richard Burn publishes *The History of the Poor Laws: With Observations*
1797	Frederic Eden publishes the three-volume *The State of the Poor,* describing poverty in England
1804	The Portsmouth Female Asylum is founded in Portsmouth, New Hampshire
1809	Elizabeth Ann Seton founds the Sisters of Charity in Emmitsburg, Maryland
1814	The Female Benevolent Society is established in Lynn, Massachusetts
1814	The Cambridge Female Humane Society is established in Cambridge, Massachusetts
1842	Edwin Chadwick publishes *Report on the Sanitary Condition of the Labouring Population of Great Britain*, blaming the spread of disease in England on poor sanitation
1843	The Association for Improving the Condition of the Poor is founded in New York
1845	Dr. John Griscom publishes *The Sanitary Condition of the Laboring Population of New York*, in which he argues that environment plays a role in causing poverty
1852	Massachusetts enacts the nation's first compulsory education law
1853	Charles Loring Brace founds the Children's Aid Society
1862	Morrill Act establishes "Land Grant" colleges—state-run public institutions that expand college education to new, more practical areas of study such as agriculture, mechanical arts, and home economics
1863	The New York City Draft/Race Riot
1869	The Sisters of Charity of St. Peter's Convent is founded to care for foundlings in New York
1872	Charles Loring Brace publishes *The Dangerous Classes of New York*, describing the work of the Children's Aid Society in New York
1880	The Salvation Army comes to America from England

1882	Congress implements the Chinese Exclusion Act of 1882 to curtail immigration from Asia
1886	The Haymarket Square Riot in Chicago
1889	Reformer Jane Addams founds Hull House in Chicago
1890	Jacob Riis publishes *How the Other Half Lives: Studies among the Tenements of New York*, a description of the poor of New York
1890s	Beginning of mass migration, lasting for decades, of African Americans from the South to industrial cities in the North
1894	The Pullman Strike
1896	Republican William McKinley defeats Democrat-Populist William Jennings Bryan, guaranteeing the continuation of laissez-faire economics
1896	Stephen Crane publishes *Maggie: A Girl of the Streets*, illustrating poverty in the Bowery of New York
1904	The National Child Labor Committee established
1910	Jane Addams publishes *Twenty Years at Hull House*
1911	The National Housing Association, led by Lawrence Veiller, held its first meeting to discuss ways to correct poor housing conditions in America's cities
1912	The Federal Children's Bureau established
1916	The first federal child labor legislation is passed by Congress
1917	In an effort to restrict immigration, Congress votes to require new immigrants to pass a literacy test
1919	Violent race riot in south Chicago
1920s	The Harlem Renaissance leads to the formation of African American cultural identity
1924	Congress passes the National Origins Quota Act to restrict immigration to 3 percent of the number of that group living in the United States in 1914
1929	The Stock Market Crash in October begins Great Depression
1932	Hoover establishes the Reconstruction Finance Corporation in a belated attempt to limit the economic effects of the depression
1932	Franklin Delano Roosevelt is elected president
1933	Franklin Delano Roosevelt's New Deal begins, and Congress approves programs such as the Civilian Conservation Corps, National Recovery Administration, Agricultural Adjustment Act during the First Hundred Days
1934	The National Housing Act establishes the Federal Housing Administration
1935	Congress passes the Social Security Act, establishing the Aid to Dependent Children program
1935	The Works Progress Administration begins

1935	New York Senator Robert Wagner proposes the 1935 National Labor Relations Act (also called the Wagner Act) in an attempt to strengthen the federal government's support of unions
1935	Congress passes the Social Security Act
1936	Bolstered by the Wagner Act, organized labor wins concessions from General Motors
1937	Organized labor wins concessions from U.S. Steel
1937	The United States Housing Act leads to the popularity of big-box public housing
1938	Congress passes the Fair Labor Standards Act
1939	John Steinbeck publishes *The Grapes of Wrath*, a fictional account of the migration of Okies to California during the Great Depression
1941	Support for the New Deal dwindles as the economy begins to revive because of increased military production
1942	The United States enters World War II, making New Deal work–relief programs unnecessary
1951	The Schutz Index of Inequality is created by economist Robert Schutz
1954	The *Brown v. Board of Education* Supreme Court decision ends legal segregation
1956	John Kenneth Galbraith publishes *The Affluent Society*
1959	The Labor-Management Reporting and Disclosure Act
1962	The Public Welfare Amendments Law renames the Aid to Dependent Children program (established during the New Deal) as Aid to Families with Dependent Children
1963	Michael Harrington popularizes the concept of a "culture of poverty" in *The Other America: Poverty in the United States*
1964	President Lyndon B. Johnson declares the "War on Poverty" as part of his Great Society program
1964	Congress passes the Economic Opportunity Act, establishing many programs, such as the Community Action Program, in hopes of eliminating poverty in America
1964	Congress passes the Civil Rights Act, establishing the Equal Employment Opportunity Commission
1965	Race riot in Watts, a predominately African American section of southern Los Angeles
1965	The Department of Housing and Urban Development is established
1965	Congress passes the Elementary and Secondary Education Act
1965	Congress amends the Social Security Act, establishing Medicare and Medicaid
1965	Congress passes the Immigration Act of 1965

1967   Race riots occur in cities across the United States, worst of all in Detroit and Newark; President Lyndon B. Johnson appoints the Kerner Commission to investigate the cause of the "ghetto" riots

1967   Congress approves amendments to the Social Security Act, such as limiting Aid to Families with Dependent Children benefits and establishing the Work Incentive program

1968   Congress passes the *Bilingual Education Act,* allocating federal aid to school districts with significant numbers of non–English-speaking students

1969   Office of Management and Budget adopts the first federal threshold of poverty

1972   Congress gives the Equal Employment Opportunity Commission litigation authority

1972   St. Louis dynamites the infamous Pruitt–Igoe public housing project

1973   The Children's Defense Fund is founded

1973   The Nixon administration officially discontinues the Office of Employment Opportunity, an integral part of Johnson's War on Poverty

1977   Congress passes the Social Security Amendments and the Food Stamp Act

1978   The Supreme Court, in *Regents of the University of California v. Bakke,* is a setback for Affirmative Action, as the decision upholds race-conscious policy

1983   National Commission on Excellence in Education issues the report "A Nation at Risk"

1983   Supreme Court, in *Bob Jones University v. United States,* outlaws racial discrimination on the basis of religion and places limits on race-conscious policy

1984   Supreme Court, in *Firefighters v. Stotts,* upholds race-conscious policy, another apparent setback for Affirmative Action

1986   Two court decisions, *Firefighters v. City of Cleveland* and *Local 28 v. Equal Employment Opportunity Commission*, uphold Affirmative Action and call for clear statistical equivalence between the hiring and promotion of whites and minorities

1989   KIDS COUNT is founded

1989   National Center for Children in Poverty is founded at Columbia University

1993   Housing and Urban Development's HOPE VI program begins in an effort to revitalize public housing

1996   Clinton Welfare Reform ends the Aid to Families with Dependent Children and implements Temporary Assistance to Needy Families

1998   Congress passes significant amendments to the Elementary and Secondary Education Act of 1965

2001   The No Child Left Behind Act revises public education standards

2001   Congress gives Housing and Urban Development more power in the Appropriations Act

2005   Congress passes the Deficit Reduction Act in an effort to reduce Medicare and
             Medicaid

2006–   Hispanics across the nation stage demonstrations protesting strict
2007   anti-immigration laws

2007–   Housing crisis in America as foreclosures on delinquent mortgages rise in
2008   American cities

A

ADDAMS, JANE (1860–1935). Jane Addams was a progressive reformer famous for opening the first successful settlement house, Hull House, in 1889 in a poor Chicago neighborhood. Hull House was a community center that taught immigrant women how to adapt to life in an American city, where children played, learned music, and learned to read, where the hungry were fed, and where social reformers met for discussion.

Jane Addams grew up in the small Illinois town of Cedarville. Her father was a local leader and businessman. In her autobiography, *Twenty Years at Hull House*, Addams described her lifelong ambition to help the poor. She remembered that when she was seven years old in 1867 her father took her to the city of Freeport, Illinois, on a business trip. During the trip they visited one of his factories, located in a poverty-stricken neighborhood. Struck by the squalor of the city, she asked her father "why people live in horrid little houses so close together." His answer apparently did not satisfy her, for she declared that when she grew up she would have "a large house, but it would not be built among the other large houses, but right in the midst of horrid little houses like these." She attended a college for women at Rockford, Illinois, but upon graduating was unsure what course to follow. She did not wish to be a teacher, a nurse, or a housewife—the traditional occupations for women of the late nineteenth century. Her interest in helping the poor remained active. After the death of her father, Addams, now independently wealthy, felt the strong call of the nineteenth-century Christian American middle class to help the less fortunate. Uncertain precisely what her role in society would be, she traveled to Europe. At a bullfight in Spain, as she described it in *Twenty Years at Hull House*, she had a sudden revelation that she should pursue her latent ambition to help the poor adapt to city life. She returned to America and, with several friends, including Ellen Starr, rented a large tenement house in Chicago called Hull House. Surrounding Hull House were the tenement houses of thousands of immigrants, largely from eastern and southern Europe.

Because Jane Addams believed in the promise of America, *Twenty Years at Hull House* provided an optimistic assessment of industrialization and urbanization. Despite the poverty in America, the values of hard work, sacrifice, and freedom would ultimately help poor immigrants thrive in their adopted country. To assist them, Jane Addams worked for child labor laws, changes to urban housing, laws against sweatshops, better factory working conditions, the promotion of literacy, and programs to help immigrants adjust to life in urban America. Addams believed that such institutions as Hull House could help regenerate communities within the big city. A community of friends sharing common ideals was her solution to many of the problems of urbanization.

By 1900 Addams had become the spokesperson for progressive reform in issues directly affecting families: housing, education, women's rights, children's rights, thriving neighborhoods, assistance to the poor. She promoted her agenda in speeches, magazine articles, and books, which included *Democracy and Social Ethics* (1902), *The Spirit of Youth and the City Streets* (1909), and *Twenty Years at Hull House* (1910).

See also: Environmental Theory of Poverty; Progressives; Urban Poor

Sources: Addams, Jane, *Twenty Years at Hull House* (Chicago: Macmillan, 1910); Davis, Allen, *American Heroine: The Life and Legend of Jane Addams* (New York: Oxford, 1973).

ADMINISTRATION FOR CHILDREN AND FAMILIES (ACF). The Administration for Children and Families (ACF) is a federal agency that provides funding to public and private organizations that provide assistance to low-income families. In particular, the ACF funds local, state, and tribal organizations that provide child care and support programs. The general aim of most ACF-funded programs is to instill lifelong values of education and self-enrichment in an attempt to keep low-income youth off the street and constructively occupied. ACF programs are instrumental in the present-day fight against social ills such as crime, drugs, and disregard for education that keep low-income children from improving their social and material status.

A division of the Department of Health and Human Services (HHS), the primary goal of the ACF is to promote social and economic growth among families with children by instituting programs intended to increase these families' self-sufficiency. ACF programs strive for the following goals: helping families increase their economic independence, building supportive communities in which low-income families can safely live, and empowering groups such as Native Americans, migrant workers, and the developmentally disabled to meet their own needs. The ACF has established initiatives such as the Campaign to Rescue & Restore Victims of Human Trafficking (which works to keep children safe from predators), the Faith-Based and Community Initiative (which focuses on creating beneficial environments for families), the Healthy Marriage Initiative (which works to keep families together), and a comprehensive plan to improve Head Start (which was established by the Johnson administration in the 1964 Economic Opportunity Act but has undergone a series of changes since then). As the scope of these initiatives shows, the ACF focuses on creating positive environments where individuals and families can learn to address their own needs as an alternative to direct federal welfare.

Many ACF programs were part of the Clinton administration's 1996 Welfare Reform Act. Sponsored by conservatives, the 1996 reform initiatives drastically cut back programs such as the Aid to Families with Dependent Children (AFDC) program—the largest and most expensive welfare program at the time. In brief, the 1996 reforms emphasized the conservative belief in individual responsibility (replacing reliance upon government with self-reliance) and marked a shift away from long-term welfare relief toward short-term relief aimed at promoting the individual's role in the work force. The ACF-administered Temporary Assistance for Needy Families (TANF) program is a good example of this policy switch. TANF, successor of the AFDC, imposed strict employment requirements for recipients of aid. Unlike the AFDC, the TANF required mothers to work as well. TANF used precise definitions of work to determine continuing eligibility for aid, defining "work experience" as "a work activity, performed in return for welfare, which provides an individual with an opportunity to acquire the general skills, training, knowledge, and work habits necessary to obtain employment." In addition, TANF credit for such work required daily supervision by an employer or other "responsible party" to make sure undeserving recipients did not receive aid. But TANF is not merely a welfare relief program; it also oversees the WIC (Women, Infants, and Children) temporary food stamp program and programs to improve child nutrition.

The ACF provides services via state, county, city, and tribal governments, as well as through local private agencies. The ACF supports agencies (such as the Children's Bureau) that help low-income and neglected children. Similar ACF programs include Abandoned Infants Assistance and Adoption Opportunities (which helps abandoned infants and facilitates adoption), Mentoring Children of Prisoners (which helps educate and support the children of prison inmates), and Child Abuse and Neglect Prevention, the Child Care and Development Fund, and Runaway and Homeless Youth (which are intended to prevent child abuse and neglect and to provide assistance for youth without a stable family or home). The ACF also supports programs to educate parents, among which are Community-Based Abstinence Education, Family Violence Prevention and Services Discretionary Grants, and the Healthy Marriage Initiative. The ACF provides assistance with and education about community and individual economic development with programs such as the Community Economic Development Discretionary Grant Program, the Community Services Block Grant Program, the Compassion Capital Fund, the Low-Income Home Energy Assistance Program, and the Rural Community Development Activities Program. The ACF also funds programs intended to assist needy individuals, including the developmentally disabled and refugees, and providing assistance to Native American tribal organizations that operate separately from state and federal programs.

See also: Aid to Families with Dependent Children; Children's Bureau; Clinton Welfare Reform; Food Stamps and WIC; Head Start

Sources: Administration for Children and Families (ACF) (http://www.acf.hhs.gov/index.html); Haveman, Robert H., and John Karl Scholz, "The Clinton Welfare Reform Plan: Will It End Poverty as We Know It?" Institute for Research on Poverty Discussion, Paper no. 1037-94 (1994); Trattner, Walter I., *From Poor Law to Welfare State,* 6th ed. (New York: Simon & Schuster, 1999); U.S. Department of Health and Human Services (www.hhs.gov/children/index.shtml).

AFFIRMATIVE ACTION. Affirmative Action is based on the belief that the only way to overcome the racial prejudice ingrained in American society is—in the words of Supreme Court Justice Thurgood Marshall—"to take heed of race," no longer ignoring racial prejudice but allotting minorities temporary preferential treatment to help disadvantaged groups transition into mainstream society. Though Marshall focused on the situation of blacks, Affirmative Action is not limited to African Americans but includes diverse ethnic, religious, and social groups. In its broader sense, Affirmative Action attempts to lessen discrimination of all types in government, schools, and workplaces. The Johnson administration's Great Society advocated Affirmative Action policies, as well as economic, educational, and social reforms, as part of its attempt to wage an all-out "war" on poverty. Associated with liberal Democratic programs such as Johnson's, Affirmative Action remains a central issue in the controversy over the American welfare state and has in recent decades borne the brunt of attacks from the New Right.

Affirmative Action's attempt to make up for past discrimination toward certain select groups—such as African Americans and Native Americans—has angered other, more established ethnic groups (such as immigrants from Europe) who faced discrimination during the nineteenth and early twentieth centuries but have mostly assimilated into the American mainstream. These groups, remembering their families' struggles, opposed Affirmative Action policies that "took away their hard-earned advantages" and redistributed them among others. Many white conservatives continue to view Affirmative Action as an affront or threat; conservatives in general question whether the government has either the right or the responsibility to interfere in private lives, redistributing the private earnings of one group to help another. These "conservative egalitarians" have opposed any type of racial preference in government policies, arguing that Affirmative Action condones "reverse discrimination" against whites. Instead of government programs such as Affirmative Action, which give direct support to minorities, white conservatives have emphasized "self-discipline, education, hard work, and personal responsibility" as the means to get ahead. Reagan tapped into this discontent while campaigning for office in 1980—and these sentiments remain strong today.

Several Supreme Court decisions have affected Affirmative Action policies. In the 1978 *Regents of the University of California v. Bakke* and the 1984 *Firefighters v. Stotts* decisions, the Court upheld race-conscious policies, which appeared to be a setback for minorities. However, other decisions—such as *Bob Jones University v. United States* in 1983, which outlawed religiously motivated racial discrimination—placed limits on race-conscious policy and delivered a strong statement in support of Affirmative Action's race-based policies, as did the 1986 *Firefighters v. City of Cleveland* decision. This decision—along with another significant 1986 decision, *Local 28 v. Equal Employment Opportunity Commission*—called for clear statistical equivalence between the hiring and promotion of whites and minorities. As the difference between these cases shows, the Supreme Court has not held a strong position on either side, and has made decisions for and against Affirmative Action over time and in specific circumstances.

Despite the controversial status of Affirmative Action policies, since the 1960s more African Americans have entered the middle class. The extent of Affirmative Action's role in this transition is unclear, but Affirmative Action policies have at the least made it harder for corporations and colleges to justify excluding minorities. Because increased employment, education and promotion opportunities can be stepping-stones to improved financial status, Affirmative Action can be considered to have facilitated, to a certain extent, the social advancement of some minorities.

See also: African Americans and Poverty; Race and Ethnicity, War on Poverty

Sources: Atkins, Jacqueline M., ed., *Encyclopedia of Social Work,* 18th ed., 2 vols. (Silver Spring, MD: NASW, 1987); Bremner, Robert H., Gary W. Reichard, and Richard Hopkins, eds., *American Choices: Social Dilemma and Public Policy since 1960* (Columbus: Ohio State University Press, 1986); Patterson, James T., *America's Struggle Against Poverty in the Twentieth Century* (Cambridge, MA: Harvard University Press, 2000).

AFRICAN AMERICANS AND POVERTY (POST-SLAVERY). After being out-voted in the 1973 *Bakke v. Board of Regents of the University of California* decision, Supreme Court Justice Thurgood Marshall challenged the view that African Americans are just one of many minority groups, emphasizing that racism toward blacks has been so strong throughout the nation's history that the "experience of Negroes in America has been different in kind, not just in degree, from that of other ethnic groups." According to Marshall and Justice Harry Blackmun, who concurred with Marshall's dissenting minority opinion, the only way America would be able to advance beyond the confines of racism would be "to take heed of race," no longer ignoring or condoning prejudice. These justices asserted a need to give blacks temporary preferential treatment (as is the case with Affirmative Action) to make up for past damage.

Though Affirmative Action remained a controversial issue, Marshall and Blackmun had a wealth of historical evidence to support their view; no other racial or ethnic group in America—with the possible exception of Native Americans—had experienced racial hatred comparable in length or fervor to that borne by African Americans. After the end of the Civil War, although slavery was no longer legal, blacks continued to experience social and economic exploitation in both the North and South. Many African Americans in the post–Civil War South remained in rural areas as sharecroppers, performing work little different from their employment before the war. High interest rates on the loans they needed to obtain farm supplies and continuing racism combined to ensure that most Southern blacks remained very poor. In the late nineteenth and early twentieth centuries, many rural African Americans migrated to Northern cities looking for work. Faced with racism in the North as well, blacks often congregated in run-down areas isolated from the white areas of the city—but close enough to cause confrontations over jobs and racial prejudice. One of the worst race riots occurred in south Chicago in 1919 when the burgeoning black population infringed upon a white neighborhood. The violence erupted near Lake Michigan when a black youth floating on the white side of the segregated beach area drowned after being hit by a thrown rock. Afterward, whites invaded nearby black neighborhoods, leading to a riot in which 15 whites and 23 blacks died and 1,000 houses burned. The black communities bore the brunt of the damage and continued to face exclusion from white areas of the city.

Inequality also existed in the workplace, with blacks employed in the lowest unskilled jobs, and hostile whites and immigrants ensuring their exclusion from unions. White laborers feared loss of status if blacks had skilled jobs; the result was a stereotype that blacks could not do skilled work. Blacks rarely obtained an education, and white artisans rarely accepted black youths as apprentices. In addition, Irish and Chinese immigration led to blacks losing even unskilled jobs, which destined them to live in the worst areas of most northern cities. One short-lived exception was the Harlem Renaissance in the 1920s, when New York blacks found a nationwide cultural voice that was accepted in white society; however, high rental rates, continuing white prejudice, and internal divisions prevented Harlem from enjoying its elevated status for long.

Civil rights for African Americans began to expand during the New Deal of the 1930s, though with few tangible results. The New Deal, however, helped to instill hope among blacks, many of whom began to believe they had the power to change their situation. Programs such as the Civilian Conservation Corps (CCC) and the National Youth Administration (NYA) benefited black youths: blacks constituted 11 percent of the CCC and 10 percent of the NYA. Other signs of progress included a decline in the mortality rate of blacks, as their average standard of living and prospects for housing, nutrition, literacy, and education improved. African American intellectuals also participated in the New Deal; for example, Richard Wright, author of *Native Son,* a black protest novel of the 1930s, worked under the Federal Writers' Project. New Deal politicians such as New York Senator Robert Wagner supported black rights, urban renewal, and low-cost housing projects. Aubrey Williams, assistant director of the Works Progress Administration (WPA), worked with the NYA to provide blacks with better education; the NYA gave blacks the same wages as whites, and provided them with job training. However, many urban blacks failed to obtain meaningful employment and remained isolated in ghettos.

The landmark Supreme Court decision of *Brown v. Board of Education* in 1954 provided African Americans with a legal initiative for ending segregation. In the following decade African Americans made significant strides toward integration into mainstream American society, but poverty remained a serious problem for many blacks. In the mid-1960s, angry African Americans vented their frustration in a series of "ghetto" riots across the nation; the most serious took place in Watts (1965), Detroit (1967), and Newark (1967). In the wake of these riots President Johnson appointed the Kerner Commission to determine their cause. In 1967 the Kerner Commission reported that the widespread poverty and segregation of African Americans in impoverished urban ghettos was the cause of the riots and proposed a comprehensive plan to lessen the racial basis for the concentration of poverty in the inner city; Johnson rejected the commission's plan, however, and the concentration of impoverished blacks in the urban core remains a serious problem in many American cities today.

See also: Affirmative Action; New Deal

Sources: Atkins, Jacqueline M., ed., *Encyclopedia of Social Work,* 18th ed., 2 vols. (Silver Spring, MD: NASW, 1987); Bremner, Robert H., Gary W. Reichard, and Richard Hopkins, eds., *American Choices: Social Dilemma and Public Policy since 1960* (Columbus: Ohio State University Press, 1986); Goldfield, David R., and Blaine A. Brownell, *Urban America: From Downtown to No Town* (Boston: Houghton Mifflin, 1979); Kerner Commission, *Report of the National Advisory Commission on Civil Disorders* (Washington, DC: 1968); Litwack, Leon, *North of Slavery: The Negro in the Free States, 1790–1860* (Chicago: Chicago University Press, 1971); Patterson, James T., *America's Struggle Against Poverty in the Twentieth Century*

(Cambridge, MA: Harvard University Press, 2000); Sitkoff, Harvard, *New Deal for Blacks: The Emergence of Civil Rights as a National Issue* (New York: Oxford University Press, 1981).

AIDS. *See* Disease and the Poor

AID TO FAMILIES WITH DEPENDENT CHILDREN (AFDC). The much-maligned and now defunct program Aid to Dependent Children (ADC)—renamed Aid to Families with Dependent Children (AFDC) in 1962—was for several decades the federal government's largest program of direct welfare relief to the poor. The AFDC program drew significant criticism because of its supposed negative impact on American society. Liberals argued that AFDC broke up families because it denied aid to mothers with able-bodied male relations. Most AFDC aid recipients were African American, so the program drew the ire of whites unwilling to support impoverished blacks. And as the largest manifestation of federal welfare, AFDC was subject to criticism from conservatives, who believed welfare encouraged laziness and eroded recipients' work ethics.

The AFDC program did not remain static; Congress has repeatedly reformed its measures. The program began during the Great Depression as Aid to Dependent Children, part of the New Deal's campaign to aid impoverished children. The 1935 Social Security Act set up ADC on a matching-funds basis, in which the federal government agreed to match the amount each state allocated to the program. From the start, the ADC failed to provide equal relief to all states, and significant geographical differences emerged. States in the deep South, such as Mississippi and Alabama, were especially stingy in allocating funds—due to both smaller budgets and reluctance to aid impoverished blacks—and states in the North (Wisconsin and Massachusetts) and large states such as California and New York allocated more money and thus received more federal funds.

In the early 1960s, President John F. Kennedy signed the Public Welfare Amendments Law, which changed the ADC program to incorporate a more family-oriented approach, reflected in the name change to Aid to Families with Dependent Children. This act changed the funding system from matching funds to 25 percent state-funded and 75 percent federally funded. In the 1967 amendments to the Social Security Act, Congress approved additional significant changes to AFDC, limiting the program's benefits. Among the new provisions were the WIN work incentive program, which disqualified work-eligible minors (under 21 years of age) who did not obtain employment and set strict limits for the number of benefit recipients in a family. These amendments signified the federal government's reluctance to continue the AFDC program, and though Congress was unsuccessful at ending it until over two decades later, the late 1960s began the switch away from welfare toward work incentives.

The Nixon administration's Family Assistance Plan (FAP) was the most significant of the unsuccessful plans to reform AFDC. The congressional debate over FAP reforms reflected the traditional ideological split between liberals and conservatives on welfare policy and also clearly demonstrated that neither side approved of the AFDC. Liberals argued that it denigrated the poor because its entrenched bureaucracy reinforced the harsh stigma of welfare. In contrast, conservatives thought the AFDC was too expensive and unnecessary. Interestingly, both liberals—such as Daniel P. Moynihan, who advised presidents Kennedy, Johnson, and Nixon on urban welfare policy—and conservatives argued that AFDC was harmful to American society. Specifically, Moynihan lamented the breakdown of the family among impoverished African Americans, and conservatives emphasized a policy pushing work instead of welfare relief.

Congress finally discontinued the AFDC in 1996. Stating that the existing welfare system—of which AFDC was the largest and most visible aspect—was "broken beyond repair," Democratic President Bill Clinton approved the Republican-sponsored reform bill that ended AFDC and emphasized the need to find work rather than welfare for all able-bodied Americans. In place of the AFDC, the Welfare Reform Act of 1996 established the Temporary Assistance for Needy Families (TANF) program, a division of the Office of Family Assistance (OFA), which provides limited assistance to low-income families.

See also: Clinton Welfare Reform; Family Assistance Plan (FAP); Welfare State

Sources: Axinn, June, and Mark J. Stern, *Social Welfare: A History of the American Response to Need,* 5th ed. (Boston: Allyn and Bacon, 2001); Bremner, Robert H., Gary W. Reichard, and Richard Hopkins, eds., *American Choices: Social Dilemma and Public Policy since 1960* (Columbus: Ohio State University Press, 1986); Haveman, Robert H., and John Karl Scholz, "The Clinton Welfare Reform Plan: Will It End *Poverty* as We Know It?" Institute for Research on Poverty Discussion Paper no. 1037-94 (1994); Moynihan, Daniel P., ed., *Toward a National Urban Policy* (New York: Basic Books, 1970); Office of Family Assistance (http://www.acf.hhs.gov/programs/ofa/); Patterson, James T., *America's Struggle Against Poverty in the Twentieth Century* (Cambridge, MA: Harvard University Press, 2000); Transcript of President Clinton's 1997 State of the Union speech, CNN (http://edition.cnn.com/2005/ALLPOLITICS/01/31/sotu.clinton1997/index.html); Trattner, Walter I., *From Poor Law to Welfare State,* 6th ed. (New York: Simon & Schuster, 1999).

AMERICAN INDIANS AND POVERTY. For centuries poverty has been a consistent economic and social experience for the American Indian. Prior to the coming of the Europeans to America, and for several subsequent centuries during the European colonial period, American Indians were commonly unable to achieve a subsistence level of existence. In more recent centuries, in the wake of the development of a money economy among American Indians, poverty, as defined by falling below an acceptable societal standard of living, has continued.

European and American observers from the sixteenth to the nineteenth centuries commented frequently on the recurrent struggle of American Indians to survive. In the late 1600s, for example, John Gyles, a Maine colonist captured by and forced to live for several years with the Abenaki Indians, experienced firsthand the impoverishment of the Indians during the winter, when they were forced to travel through the Maine forest attempting to satisfy the needs of basic existence. Very often they went for days without eating; food was acquired more by chance than by intention. When the hunters made a kill, such as a moose or bear, the party would stay and feast for several days, the Indian women crying out, "Wegage Oh Nelo Who!" ("Fat is my eating!"). More days of privation would, however, follow the infrequent feasting. Lacking sufficient nutrition and shelter from the harsh Maine winter, the Abenakis experienced physical disabilities and sickness. They spent winter days waiting for spring, when they could return to the rich fertile valleys of the Maine coast to plant maize.

Reports from other American observers of the eighteenth and nineteenth centuries indicate that the Abenakis' experience was hardly unique. Jeremy Belknap and Jedidiah Morse, two missionaries for the Scots Society for Propagating Christian Knowledge, journeyed to upstate New York in 1796 to investigate and report on the situation of the Oneida and Mohekunuh Indians. Belknap and Morse discovered that these tribes of the Iroquois, particularly the Oneida, lived in terrible poverty, in part because of the dislocation brought about by the American War for Independence. The Oneida village had been destroyed during the war, and the people, almost two decades later, were slow to recover. Oneida males did not adapt well to the farming lifestyle, and according to the missionary John Kirkland, all save one turned to alcohol for solace. Belknap, who was sympathetic to the struggle of the Native Americans to confront and adapt to white civilization, countered the argument that civilization had brought about the present dire state of the Indians; rather, "an idle and desultory mode of life is more likely to have been the cause of their present undistinguishable situation." Meriwether Lewis and William Clark, in their journey up the Missouri River, across the Continental Divide, and down the Columbia River from 1804 to 1805, met with a variety of Indian tribes, some of whom lived in dire poverty. When Lewis and Clark in August 1805, crossing the Continental Divide in what is today Montana, met with a tribe of the Shoshone Indians, they discovered that the tribe had only berries to eat. Indeed, so famished were the men, women, and children of the tribe that when it was announced that one of the American hunters had killed a deer more than a mile away, hunger drove the people to immediately run or, for those so lucky to have a horse, ride in the direction of the kill. Upon arriving at the feast, Lewis was astonished to find the Indians not only tearing the deer apart and eating it raw, but fighting over the offal; one person gorged on the deer's stomach and its contents; another ate the kidneys; another ate the intestines, pressing the internal contents out as he merrily ate.

Few American Indians escaped the consequences of the expansion of the United States west across the Appalachian Mountains, Mississippi River, and Rocky Mountains. Whether or not Indians resisted the invasion of their lands, they often suffered the general consequences of resistance, which was the restriction to reservations established by the U.S. government. The Navahos, for example, who today reside on the largest reservation, were defeated by American troops in the 1860s and restricted to a reservation in Arizona. The massive Navaho reservation, covering 24,000 square miles of unfertile desert land, supports 110,000 people, who live in abject poverty. In addition to the establishment of reservations, federal policies toward American Indians have typically had a negative economic and social impact. An example is the Dawes General Allotment Act of 1887, in which reservation lands were to be divided up into small farms; the idea was to allow Indians to become self-sufficient farmers. The reality, however, was that many Indians could not adapt to a farm lifestyle; others simply lost their land. By 1932 the 187 million acres owned by Indians in 1887 had been reduced by two thirds. During the New Deal of the 1930s, the Dawes Act was discontinued with the institution of the Indian Reorganization Act of 1934, which brought some reforms to federal policies respecting reservations. Such federal policies were based, however, on Indians' willingness to assimilate into the larger white society; Indians who were slow or reluctant to assimilate were often left behind in a rapidly changing capitalist society. During the 1960s, as part of Lyndon Johnson's overall war on poverty, federal programs were increasingly devoted to the education and health care of American Indians living on reservations. The Capital Conference on Indian Poverty of 1964 led to the Office of Economic Opportunity's providing oversight of Indian anti-poverty programs. Such programs helped many American Indians in their fight against poverty. Reservations continued, however, to be centers of impoverishment compared with the larger society. In the late 1960s, Indians, increasingly aware of their comparative poverty, became more active and vocal in soliciting government support. The activities of groups such as the American Indian Movement (AIM) led to more federal reforms during the 1970s, such as the Indian Health Care Improvement Act of 1976 and the Indian Child Welfare Act of 1978. This progress was stifled during the 1980s, when Reagan's policies of deregulation were extended to federal aid to Indian tribes, who were encouraged to become more self-sufficient. Consequently, the unemployment rate skyrocketed, along with alcohol and drug abuse. Welfare reform during the Clinton years was extended to American Indians, who were part of the change that replaced Aid to Families with Dependent Children (AFDC) with Temporary Assistance for Needy Families (TANF). Moreover, the Native Employment Works (NEW) program was instituted to address the needs of American Indians. Even so, during the first few years of the twenty-first century, poverty among Native Americans has remained high, at close to 25 percent. Clearly the goal of reducing poverty in Native American communities will require more than just welfare reform.

Sources: Belknap, Jeremy, and Jedidiah Morse, "The Report of a Committee of the Board of Correspondents of the Scots Society for Propagating Christian Knowledge, Who Visited the Oneida and Mohekunuh Indians in 1796," in *Collections of the Massachusetts Historical Society,* ser. 1, vol. 5 (Boston: Massachusetts Historical Society, 1799); De Voto, Bernard, ed., *The Journals of Lewis and Clark* (Boston: Houghton Mifflin, 1953); Golden, Olivia A., "Statement on Welfare Reform and Implementation," presented before the Senate Indian Affairs Committee, April 14, 1999, accessed at: http://www.hhs.gov/asl/testify/t990414a.html; Gyles, John, *Memoirs of Odd Adventures, Strange Deliverances, &c. in the Captivity of John Gyles, Esq., Commander of the Garrison on St. George's River* (Boston: S. Knesland and T. Green, 1736); Josephy, Alvin M., Jr., *The Indian Heritage of America* (Boston: Houghton, Mifflin, 1991).

APPRENTICESHIP. *See* Children and Poverty

ASIAN AMERICANS AND POVERTY. *See* Immigrants; Race and Ethnicity

B

BRITISH POOR AND THE ORIGINS OF COLONIALISM. The founding of the British colonies of North America in the 1600s and 1700s took place at a time when the countries of western Europe were aggressively competing to conquer and claim the riches of the New World. The Spanish conquest of much of Central and South America catapulted Spain, under Charles V, into world power, leaving the English and French to compete for the spoils of North America. The gold and silver of the Aztecs and Incas were not, however, found among the poor tribes of North America. British sovereigns such as Elizabeth I, intent on expanding English power by expanding British wealth, encouraged trade and the establishment of colonies. The English were slow to realize that colonial wealth would result from settlements of people willing to work hard, exploiting the resources of the land. Such promoters of colonization as Richard Hakluyt and Captain John Smith convinced Tudor and Stuart English men and women that empire, wealth, and power awaited England in the colonization of North America.

The arguments of the promoters of colonization were more convincing because of the apparent overpopulation of the British Isles and the poverty that ensued. English observers in the late 1500s and early 1600s, such as Robert Johnson, in *Nova Britannica,* believed that "we need not doubt our land abounding with swarmes of idle persons." William Jones, in *The Planters Plea,* also commented on the "over-flowing multitudes" in England. The author of the pamphlet *A True and Sincere Declaration* wrote in 1609 that colonies will allow for the

> transplanting the rancknesse and multitude of increase in our people; of which there is left no vent, but age; and evident danger that the number . . . of them . . . shall infest and become a burthen to another. But by this provision they may be seated as a Bulworke of defense in a place of advantage.

But England only appeared to be overpopulated during the late Tudor and early Stuart years. Economic and social changes resulted in the displacement of freeholders from the land, growing numbers of wage earners in the cities, and greater demand for agricultural products and consequent inflation. A primary cause of these problems was the English enclosure movement, which began in earnest under the Tudors. Enclosure was intended to make England more agriculturally productive by bringing wastelands under cultivation and improving crop yields with new farming techniques. Large landowners bought up fens and forests once used by the poor to put food on the table. Demand for land increased its price, which benefited large—rather than small—landowners. As a consequence, many small farmers lost their lands and had to hire themselves out as farm laborers or tenants, or fled to the city in search of a living. Wages of farm and city laborers failed to keep up with rising prices, and tenant farmers found their rents increasing faster than the price of produce. The impact of inflation on the English economy was as little understood as was the enclosure movement. There were manifold causes of rising prices, such as war and trade disruptions, debasement of the currency, competition over land, and increasing proletariat representation in the cities. Justices of the peace, themselves landowners, set low wages for agricultural workers. Urban laborers discovered that their wages remained the same while prices rose. Between 1583 and 1702, according to the calculations of James Rogers (*A History of Agriculture and Prices in England*), the price of wheat rose over 200 percent. According to George Beer, agricultural laborers in mid-seventeenth-century England earned a paltry £16 per year—and it required over £20 to prevent a family from starving.

As the wealthy prospered, therefore, the poor grew in numbers. Poverty under a toiling economy could only be caused, reasoned thinkers of the Tudor–Stuart period, by an uncontrolled growth in population. The same thinkers also developed theories about how to enrich England at the expense of other countries. Mercantilists envisioned colonies employing the poor and criminal, transplanted from England and made productive and virtuous. These English immigrants would labor on the great plantations of Southern farmers, growing tobacco and sugar; fish the banks off the coast of New England; cut and transport products from the great forests of America—all for the benefit of the mother country. Mercantilist Josiah Gee, writing in 1729, claimed that colonies benefited England by

> raising and producing great Plenty of Materials in our Plantations for setting the Poor to Work, the several Employments arising from Hemp, Flax, Silk, &c. will afford such Variety, that there will be enough, not only for the robust and strong, but for the weakly, and even for Children; and doubtless a good Example and Perseverance in the Rules of Industry will change the very Inclinations of those idle vagrant Persons, who now run about the Kingdom, and spend their Time and what Money they can any Way come at upon their Debauches.

See also: Convict Transportation; Indentured Servitude; Poor Laws in England and Early America

Sources: Beer, George Louis, *The Old Colonial System: 1660–1754* (New York: Peter Smith, 1958); Brown, Alexander, *The Genesis of the United States* (London: Boston and New York: Houghton Mifflin, 1890); Clarkson, L. A., *The Pre-Industrial Economy in England, 1500–1750* (New York: Schocken Books, 1972); Knorr, Klaus, *British Colonial Theories, 1570–1850* (Toronto: University of Toronto Press, 1968): Rogers, James, *A History of Agriculture and Prices in England*, 6 vols. (Oxford: Clarendon Press, 1887).

C

CCC (CIVILIAN CONSERVATION CORPS). Part of the New Deal's plan to lower the nation's high unemployment level, the Civilian Conservation Corps (CCC)—implemented in the spring of 1933—relocated young urban male workers to the countryside for employment. The focus of the CCC was not so much on the importance of the work performed as it was on providing occupation, shelter, and food to its members, who could then send a little money to their families. Consequently, the CCC—similar to New Deal programs such as the Works Progress Administration (WPA)—was a direct federal relief program thinly disguised as employment to allow Americans to retain their self-esteem.

President Roosevelt took a personal interest in the CCC; the action of relocating young men from the impoverished cities and providing them with work, food, and lodging in a rustic setting appealed to his environmental ideals. Even so, relief assistance was the program's most important goal. Many of the projects undertaken were related to conservation and planned land use; for example, the CCC planted nearly 3 billion trees to renew America's forests and prevent soil erosion.

The highly structured CCC was based on a military model. The basic plan of the CCC was to set up camps in the countryside that could accommodate a large group of men; overseers directed the work. CCC camps were modeled on military barracks, and strict discipline was emphasized. The Army, Coast Guard, Marine Corps, and Navy helped with the logistics of setting up the program, especially in transporting men from cities to camps, which were located in isolated regions.

The CCC was generally popular among the public, and many young men enrolled. By 1935 the CCC employed 500,000 men; by 1942 when the program ended, over 2.75 million men had served in the CCC. Politicians also realized the benefits of supporting the CCC and sought to locate CCC camps in home states to serve their constituencies: by 1935 there were about 2,650 CCC camps across the country. As the CCC matured, the original plans changed to accommodate diverse groups: an amendment in 1933 allowed impoverished Native Americans to join; by

1941 nearly 80,000 Native Americans had participated. Another change was the inclusion of older local men with the experience and skills necessary to train young urban workers for the particular work of rural and uninhabited regions.

In 1936 Congress authorized additional funding for the CCC, allowing for a total of 600,000 workers. However, other programs, such as the WPA, began to gain popularity at the expense of the CCC. Harry Hopkins, director of the WPA and one of Roosevelt's top advisors for the New Deal, established new procedures for CCC recruiting that lessened the program's total enrollment. Roosevelt's unsuccessful attempt to establish the CCC as a permanent government organization in 1937 also led to dwindling support in Congress. This decision was part of the larger breakdown of congressional support for the New Deal in 1937 after Roosevelt's battle with the Supreme Court and the renewed economic recession. From 1937 to 1942, the last years of the New Deal and the Great Depression, the CCC steadily dwindled in size and resources. Congress officially ended the CCC in 1942 after America's entry into World War II negated the need for federal work-relief programs.

See also: New Deal; WPA (Works Progress Administration)

Sources: Civilian Conservation Corps (arcweb.sos.state.or.us/50th/ccc/cccintro.html); Link, Arthur S., and William B. Catton, *American Epoch: A History of the United States Since 1900, Volume II 1921–1945,* 4th ed. (New York: Alfred E. Knopf, 1973); Patterson, James T., *America's Struggle against Poverty in the Twentieth Century* (Cambridge: Harvard University Press, 2000); The Civilian Conservation Corps and the National Park Service (http://www.nps.gov/history/history/online_books/ccc/).

CHILDREN AND POVERTY. Children have historically been the most anonymous yet the most vulnerable of America's poor. Even today, when the United States is the richest country in the world, the largest block—19 percent—of the poor is made up of persons under the age of eighteen. In 1960 impoverished children made up 25 percent of the poor in America. For minority groups such as African Americans, Native Americans, and Hispanic Americans, the numbers are even grimmer. And the number of children in poverty has risen since the new millennium by well over a million. Children who live in poverty are vulnerable to disease, both physical and mental, are often malnourished, tend to struggle to learn in school, and often become entrenched in a way of life that carries them into adulthood. Notwithstanding the increased understanding of the causes and consequences of child poverty, social and behavioral scientists and government planners and researchers have been unable to reverse its continuing prevalence in American society.

Emigrants and Apprentices. From the beginning of English settlements in America, there were impoverished children, who made up a significant portion of the poor in Tudor–Stuart England. Leaders in government and religion were at a loss as to how to halt the rising tide of poverty or what to do with orphans and child vagabonds. Feeble attempts were made during the long reign of Elizabeth I. The 1562 Statute of Artificers laid the foundation for the laws of apprenticeship. Legislation in 1597 directed parish overseers of the poor to make provision for the care and employment of poor youth. These laws continued in force during the reigns of the Stuart kings, when the first English colonies were established. With the successful establishment of the Jamestown colony in Virginia, a solution for ongoing child poverty dawned on English entrepreneurs with profit more than compassion on their minds. The plan involved gathering up orphaned and impoverished children and transporting them to the colonies—to labor there until age twenty-one, when they would be set up with land that they could own or rent. In 1619, for example, 100 children were transported to the Jamestown colony on the condition that, on reaching the proper age, they would be freed and presented with fifty acres of land to farm, holding the land in fee simple with a modest rent to pay. A year later another shipment of youthful cargo arrived in Jamestown, this group having less favorable terms, because the novelty of the experiment had worn off: they were to receive twenty-five acres of land, holding it in fee simple as before, but not until seven years after they reached their majority. In other words, after serving as apprentices until the age of twenty-one, followed by seven further years of bound servitude, they would begrudgingly be given the chance to make it on their own in the new world. This harsh, sometimes cruel system continued for many decades, during which rich Englanders believed that they were doing their Christian duty by supporting the mass transport of children to the colonies. One London noteworthy, Anthony Abde, provided funds in his will "to be disposed and bestowed by my Executors upon twenty poore Boyes and Girles to be taken up out of the streets of London as vagrants for the Cloathing and transporting of them either to Virginia New England or any other of the Western Plantations there to be placed." On the other hand, it was all too easy for spirits to kidnap orphans and put them on board a ship bound for America. In 1660, the case of the ship *Seven Brothers* was hardly unique. This ship was bound for Virginia; included in its cargo were youths who had been "deceived and inticed away Cryinge and Mourning for Redemption from their Slavery." In 1664 during the reign of Charles II, an act attempted to curtail the abuses incumbent on such manipulation of children, providing that no child under the age of twelve could be transported to America without the permission of a relative or close friend. And in 1670 Parliament attempted, without success, to end the practice of spiriting children by condemning to the gallows those spirits who were captured and found guilty.

Apprenticeship. During the colonial period, the apprenticeship of impoverished children bound to a master generally followed the pattern set forth in England by the Statute of Artificers of 1562 and the Elizabethan Poor Law of 1601. The English system of apprenticeship involved the binding of a child to a master for at least seven years, until he or she reached the age of twenty-one or twenty-four, in return for which the master contracted to teach the child a craft and serve as surrogate parent during the time of the child's minority. Apprenticeship was an option for poor parents who struggled to feed their children or who could provide little education in skills that would help the child earn an independent living as an adult. At other times, to prevent an impoverished or orphaned child from becoming a public charge, the local parish bound the child to a master without the child's consent. In such a case, the object was more to find employment for a pauper than to teach a trade to a deserving person. The indenture of apprenticeship was similar to the indenture of servitude respecting the servant's responsibilities and master's obligations, save that the former called for a specific educational and technical component—the servant was to learn a craft and, sometimes, grammar, spelling, and arithmetic. A typical indenture of apprenticeship from 1718 New York reads:

> This Indenture Wittnesseth that I, William Mathews . . . doth voluntarily and of his own free Will and Accord and by the Consent of his . . . Mother put himself Apprentice to Thomas Windover . . . Cordwiner with him to live and to serve . . . untill the full Term of seven years be Compleat and Ended. During all which Term the said Apprentice his said Master Thomas Windover faithfully shall serve his secrets keep, his lawfull Commands gladly every where Obey, he shall do no damage . . . to his said Master, he shall not waste his said Masters Goods, nor lend them unlawfully to any, he shall not Committ fornication nor Contract Matrimony with the said Term. . . . He shall not absent himself day or night from his Masters service without his leave, nor haunt Alehouses, Taverns or Playhouses, but in all things as a faithful apprentice he shall behave himself towards his said Master and all his during the said Term. And the said Master during the said Term shall, by the best means or Method that he can Teach or Cause the said Apprentice to be taught the Art or Mystery of a Cordwiner, and shall find and provide unto the said Apprentice sufficient Meat, Drink, Apparel, Lodging and washing fitting for an Apprentice, and shall during the said Term every winter at Nights give him one Quarters schooling, and at the Expiration of the said Term to provide for the said Apprentice a sufficient New Suit of Apparell four shirts and two Necletts, for the true Performance of all and every the said Covenants and agreements Either of the said parties bind themselves unto the Other by these Presents.

Other than apprenticeship, early American communities provided for orphaned and impoverished children through all of the typical means of poor relief: direct relief, the almshouse, the workhouse, and the asylum. Colonial Boston provided education for orphans, apprentices, and other young paupers. Children were part of the overall system of poor relief, subject to the direction of the overseers of the poor. In Portsmouth, New Hampshire, selectmen and overseers of the poor routinely placed orphaned children in homes until the children reached adulthood. For example, the town clerk recorded that in 1678 an orphaned girl, age five, was bound to a man until she was twenty, during which time he was "to find her with sufficient meate, drinke, clothing washing and Lodging and to teach her to reade." With the maturation of society in such cities as Portsmouth, more sophisticated institutions were developed to provide for the care of the poor, including impoverished children. Most significant eighteenth-century seaport cities built almshouses and workhouses in which, regardless of age or gender, the poor were put to work to earn their keep and reform their morals. Some institutions were exclusively for children. For example, concerned citizens of Portsmouth established the Portsmouth Female Asylum in 1804 to care for orphans, as well as girls whose parents could not provide the necessary support. The girls received education in reading, personal care, religion, and the domestic arts. Governesses read from the Bible daily "to inculcate the principles of religion." Children rose at six in morning, washed in cold water, combed their hair, ate at eight, played until nine, attended school until noon when they dined, studied from two to five, when they had an hour to play, supped at six, and went to bed at eight.

The trend toward the institutionalization of impoverished children and the poor in general continued into the nineteenth century. The almshouse and workhouse combined to become the poorhouse, an institution with neither beauty nor gentleness, the exclusive goal of which was work and moral reform. Unfortunately for the poor inmate, the poorhouse itself needed institutional reform. For example, the poorhouse of Erie County, in western New York, which housed the children of many adult paupers, was a place of suffering and death during the first half of the 1800s. One observer wrote that "the whole policy of the Poorhouse is niggardly and mean. Cheap provisions, cheap doctors, cheap nurses, cheap medicines, cheapness everywhere is the rule." The food, care, and accommodations of the poor were terrible and disgusting. Meals consisted of gristly pork, half-baked bread, coffee, and tea. For months at a time, the inmates received no vegetables, causing some to develop scurvy. The ventilation was bad, the air foul, and the stench incredible. The poorhouse, in short, spawned suffering and death.

> Lying-in women have died of fever, leaving their children, and the numerous foundlings brought to the house, to die of starvation together. Brought there as bright, healthy infants, these little offsprings of misfortune and crime have scarcely an average of four weeks of [life] in this great lazar house. Older children become idiotic, dwarfed, inanimate; and men and women die from a hundred diseases, written down upon the casebook with Latin names, but which might be better called starvation.

Equally dramatic was Jacob Riis's description of children on the city streets of New York in *How the Other Half Lives*. Riis, a journalist and reformer who probed the existence of the poor and forgotten in New York, found astonishing the number of poor children without apparent home or family; equally astonishing were the numbers who ostensibly had a family that had abandoned them to find their own food, care, and love on the filthy streets of the city. Riis researched an East Side tenement that had two-score families with, he estimated, 170 children. Most were hungry and ignorant, few went to school, and their family life consisted of "running for beer for their elders"—they found it safer to spend their nights on the streets rather than with their drunken, violent parents. Riis realized that such children were not inherently evil or savage—their environment made them ignorant and engaged in a constant search for survival. The children knew little of religion or culture, yet Riis claimed that so rare was even the sight of the beauty of a flower that the waifs forgot all else if presented with a bouquet. New York authorities were sufficiently aware of the problem that, according to Riis

> in the last fifteen years of this tireless battle for the safety of the State the intervention of the Society for the Prevention of Cruelty to Children has been invoked for 138,891 little ones; it has thrown its protection around more than twenty-five thousand helpless children, and has convicted nearly sixteen thousand wretches of child-beating and abuse. Add to this the standing army of fifteen thousand dependent children in New York's asylums and institutions, and some idea is gained of the crop that is garnered day by day in the tenements, of the enormous force employed to check their inroads on our social life, and of the cause for apprehension that would exist did their efforts flag for ever so brief a time.

Most perplexing for the reformer was the street arab, a child who roamed the streets in a Darwinian survival of the fittest. "Vagabond that he is," wrote Riis

> acknowledging no authority and owing no allegiance to anybody or anything, with his grimy fist raised against society whenever it tries to coerce him, he is as bright and sharp as the weasel, which, among all the predatory beasts, he most resembles His sturdy independence, love of freedom and absolute self-reliance, together with his rude

sense of justice that enables him to govern his little community, not always in accordance with municipal law or city ordinances, but often a good deal closer to the saving line of "doing to others as one would be done by."

Riis noted the many private institutions that intervened on behalf of the impoverished children of New York: the most significant were the Foundling Asylum of the Sisters of Charity (New York Foundling Hospital) and the Children's Aid Society. Children who were found by the police and became wards of the city ended up at Randall's Island Hospital, where the mortality rate for young children was more than 60 percent. Children had a much better chance if they were picked up by the Sisters of Charity. Sister Mary Irene, a nun at the Sisters of Charity of St. Peter's Convent, opened the foundling asylum in 1869. Over the years, an "Adoption Department," a "Maternity Pavilion," and St. John's Hospital for Children were founded. "The Children's Aid Society," wrote Riis

> came into existence as an emphatic protest against the tenement corruption of the young, has sheltered quite three hundred thousand outcast, homeless, and orphaned children in its lodging-houses, and has found homes in the West for seventy thousand that had none.

Charles Loring Brace, a Christian minister who founded the Children's Aid Society in 1853, wrote of his experiences and acquired knowledge in *The Dangerous Classes of New York*. Brace argued that ignorance, illiteracy, broken marriages, immigration, lack of training in a trade, overcrowding, and alcoholism are prime causes of criminal activity among the young poor. Brace sought solutions for the problems of the city, advocating education of children as

> a better preventive of pauperism than charity. The best police and the most complete form of government are nothing if the individual morality be not there. But Christianity is the highest education of character. Give the poor that, and only seldom will either alms or punishment be necessary.

Believing impoverished children to be particularly susceptible to the temptations and corrupting influences of the city, Brace described the "temptations which beset the class of unfortunate children and similar classes," including

> the inducements to sharpness, deception, roguery, lying, fraud, coarseness, vice in many forms, besides toward open offenses against the law; the few restraining influences in social opinion, good example, or inherited self-control; the forces without and the organization within impelling to crime. There are thousands on thousands in New York who have no assignable home, and 'flit' from attic to attic, and cellar to cellar; there are other thousands more or less connected with criminal enterprises; and still other tens of thousands, poor, hard-pressed, and depending for daily bread on the day's earnings, swarming in tenement-houses, who behold the gilded rewards of toil all about them, but are never permitted to touch them. All these great masses of destitute, miserable, and criminal persons believe that for ages the rich have had all the good things of life, while to them have been left the evil things. Capital to them is the tyrant.

A literary example of the experiences of poor children in New York comes from the writings of Stephen Crane, who wrote novels and short stories at the turn of the century. In fictional works such as *Maggie: A Girl of the Streets* and

An Experiment in Misery, Crane provided a realistic, horrifying, and depressing portrait of the lives of children and young adults in the Bowery of Manhattan in New York. Jimmy and Maggie, brother and sister of drunken parents living in a broken down tenement in the Bowery, live a brutal life, seeking to survive amid violence and poverty on the streets as well as at home: "Eventually they entered a dark region where," Crane wrote

> from a careening building, a dozen gruesome doorways gave up loads of babies to the street and the gutter. A wind of early autumn raised yellow dust from cobbles and swirled it against a hundred windows. Long streamers of garments fluttered from fire-escapes. In all unhandy places there were buckets, brooms, rags, and bottles. In the street infants played or fought with other infants or sat stupidly in the way of vehicles. Formidable women, with uncombed hair and disordered dress, gossiped while leaning on railings, or screamed in frantic quarrels. Withered persons, in curious postures of submission to something, sat smoking pipes in obscure corners. A thousand odours of cooking food came forth to the street. The building quivered and creaked from the weight of humanity stamping about in its bowels.

The characters in Crane's fiction are lost in the city—spiritually, morally dispossessed from society, family, and self. Meaning, such as it is, comes from the experience of the city rather from a sense of self-worth, which has been destroyed by poverty. The poor were forgotten, anonymous. Maggie, in Crane's words, who was "attired in tatters and grime . . . went unseen."

Poverty among children was alleviated, although not removed, during the twentieth century. During the first two decades, impoverished children and their families were helped by the Progressives: under President Taft, the Children's Bureau was established in 1912 and Congress passed child labor legislation in 1916. During the New Deal of the 1930s and 1940s and subsequent liberal programs inspired by the New Deal, such as Lyndon Johnson's Great Society program, the federal government increased its actions on behalf of children. Because of the misery that the Great Depression brought to families with children, in 1935 Congress passed the Social Security Act, which included the Aid to Dependent Children. In this program, the federal government reimbursed states for part of the funds spent on impoverished children. After 1950 the program was extended to parents of dependent children and the name was changed to Aid to Families with Dependent Children. The program included the availability of food stamps for poor families and money for medical care (a precursor to Medicaid). More recent attempts to help children include the creation of Head Start during the 1960s, the founding of the nonprofit Children's Defense Fund in 1973, and a host of congressional laws directed toward helping children, such as the Adoption Assistance and Child Welfare Act (1980) and the Family Support Act (1988).

Notwithstanding the wealth of America, child poverty still stands at 19 percent— an improvement, at least, over the poverty rate of children from 1996 compared to that of 1990 and 1987 to that of 1981, when it was more than 20 percent, or an improvement in the face of an astonishing fact: according to the U.S. Census Bureau, one in four of the poor from 1959 to 1962 was a child under the age of eighteen. These figures rise when the population is restricted to African Americans, American Indians, or Hispanic Americans. Today, impoverished Caucasian children make up 11 percent, but 36 percent of African American children, 32 percent of American Indian children, and 29 percent of Hispanic American children live in poverty.

See also: Administration for Children and Families; Aid to Families with Dependent Children (AFDC); Children's Bureau; Poor Laws in England and Early America; Spirits (Crimps) and Newlanders

Sources: Brace, Charles Loring, *The Dangerous Classes of New York, and Twenty Years' Work Among Them* (New York: Wynkoop and Hallenbeck, 1872); Bridenbaugh, Carl, *Cities in Revolt* (New York: Oxford, 1955); Crane, Stephen, *Maggie: A Girl of the Streets* (New York: Appleton, 1896); Herrick, Cheesman A., *White Servitude in Pennsylvania, Indentured and Redemption Labor in Colony and Commonwealth* (Philadelphia: McVey, 1926); Katz, Michael B., *Poverty and Policy in American History* (New York: Academic Press, 1983); Kids Count (http://www.kidscount.org); Morse, Richard B., *Government and Labor in Early America* (New York: Harper & Row, 1965); *Portsmouth New Hampshire Town Records,* typescript, Portsmouth Public Library; Riis, Jacob A., *How the Other Half Lives: Studies among the Tenements of New York* (New York: Charles Scribner's Sons, 1890); Smith, Abbot Emerson, *Colonists in Bondage: White Servitude and Convict Labor in America, 1607–1776* (New York: Norton, 1971); *The Rules, Regulations, & c. of the Portsmouth Female Asylum, with the Act of Incorporation* (1815).

CHILDREN'S AID SOCIETY. Founded by Charles Loring Brace in 1853 in New York City as a mission and shelter for homeless children, the Children's Aid Society was a significant alternative to institutionalized care and housing for abandoned and orphaned children. For almost forty years, Brace served as director of the Children's Aid Society, focusing on issues facing low-income urban children, such as homelessness, vagrancy, and destitution. Brace particularly emphasized child welfare. In addition to his role in social reform, Brace was a writer and a minister. He had his first contact with New York's poor while serving as a minister in one of the city's prisons and further contact while serving as a missionary in the city. The latter role placed Brace in contact with influential, concerned citizens who supported him in establishing the Children's Aid Society as a mission for children in New York. The services offered in the Society's early years included free children's shelters, industrial schools and night schools, reading rooms, summer camps, and classes for handicapped children. As these programs show, the Society's focus was on instilling middle-class values in low-income children, to help them adapt better to society and thus become more affluent and conscientious adult citizens.

The Children's Aid Society offered an unconventional approach to providing foster care to accommodate the new urban society, which Brace recognized was constantly changing. In an effort to combat the constant cycle of fragmentation that led to standardization and institutionalized reform, Brace hoped to preserve the beneficial organic and spontaneous relationships, which were impossible in urban society. Brace did not think that the traditional, organic institutions of family and church were working in New York, so he developed the Children's Aid Society in an attempt to mirror the old organic institutions and thus achieve the stability needed to create a haven for low-income urban children.

An interesting aspect of Brace's plan was to remove urban children without suitable parental care from the city and place them in rural farm homes where, theoretically, the beneficial influence of family and community would help them turn their lives around. Sending unattached children to the West, Brace argued, freed the city from their presence, gave the children a chance to escape lives of poverty, and even benefited the foster families who took in the children because they gained an extra labor source in exchange for providing shelter. Like other nineteenth-century reformers, Brace emphasized the evil influence of city life, and his policy of relocating New York's children to the West is a classic, if extreme, example of this anti-urban view.

Brace's ideas did not meet with universal acclaim from other reformers or society at large. For example, the Catholic Church portrayed Brace's relocation scheme as a Protestant scheme to draw children away from their Catholic heritage; some poor families lamented having to give up their children, despite their inability to provide for them; and some Western states opposed Brace's plan to transfer misfit urban children there. Nevertheless, under Brace's direction, the Children's Aid Society developed into one of the most significant nineteenth-century efforts to provide for unattached and potentially deviant urban children.

See also: Children and Poverty

Sources: Atkins, Jacqueline M., ed., *Encyclopedia of Social Work,* 18th ed., 2 vols. (Silver Spring, MD: NASW, 1987); Brace, Charles Loring, *The Dangerous Classes of New York, and Twenty Years' Work Among Them* (New York: Wynkoop and Hallenbeck, 1872); Patterson, James T., *America's Struggle Against Poverty in the Twentieth Century* (Cambridge, MA: Harvard University Press, 2000).

CHILDREN'S BUREAU. Established in 1912 by President William Howard Taft, the Children's Bureau is a federally sponsored program that seeks to provide for the well-being of children through leadership, planning, and partnerships with state-run, tribal, and community organizations. Currently a part of the Administration for Children, Youth, and Families (ACYF), the Children's Bureau works with state and local agencies to develop programs intended to prevent the abuse of children living in troubled families and to find alternative arrangements for children who cannot safely return to their homes. Like the other programs of the ACYF, the Children's Bureau emphasizes the creation of beneficial living environments for children as the primary means to keep them from harm.

When the Children's Bureau was created in 1912, its primary task was to investigate and report on the state of low-income children, infant mortality rates and birth rates, and orphanages and juvenile courts. Julia Lathrop, a former settlement house worker, was the first director of the Bureau. Lathrop had previously led reform efforts in Illinois and worked at Jane Addams's Hull House in the 1880s. Before she headed the Children's Bureau, Lathrop founded the nation's first mental hygiene clinic for children—the Juvenile Psychopathic Institute—in 1909. Lathrop's background influenced the setup of the Children's Bureau, which she headed for twelve years: under her direction, the Bureau investigated and analyzed the relation of social and economic background to children's health and social aptitude.

As a federal government agency, the Children's Bureau has been instrumental in federal legislation regarding the social and economic status of children. Soon after its founding, the Bureau prepared a report on the dangerous labor that children performed in the workplace. These findings led to legislation—such as the 1916 Keating–Owen bill—that outlawed unregulated child labor. Although this particular bill was struck down as unconstitutional two years later, child labor decreased significantly—from 18 percent in 1900 to 5 percent in 1930—a change that was caused, in part, by the efforts of the Children's Bureau to increase awareness of the plight of America's impoverished children. Despite the Children's Bureau's research, the government has not always responded with the appropriate legislation. For example, in 1954 the Children's Bureau initiated a conference on juvenile delinquency in depressed urban areas: although President Dwight D. Eisenhower requested $5 million to research this problem, Congress failed to allocate the money.

At present, the Children's Bureau has an annual budget of more than $7 billion, and its primary function is to recommend legislative and budgetary proposals, develop initiatives to benefit low-income children, and compile research and evaluate existing programs. Thus, the Children's Bureau focuses on evaluating and planning, and it works actively with other ACYF programs to implement interagency projects for children and families. The Children's Bureau also coordinates many programs and activities that have been undertaken by other components of the ACYF.

See also: Administration for Children and Families (ACF); Children and Poverty

Sources: Atkins, Jacqueline M., ed., *Encyclopedia of Social Work*, 18th ed., 2 vols. (Silver Spring, MD: NASW, 1987); Children's Bureau (http://www.acf.hhs.gov); Patterson, James T., *America's Struggle Against Poverty in the Twentieth Century* (Cambridge, MA: Harvard University Press, 2000).

CHILDREN'S DEFENSE FUND. The Children's Defense Fund (CDF) is a nonprofit advocacy and research organization, founded in 1973, that works to ensure that all children—regardless of race, creed, or income—have an equal chance to succeed under the American political and economic system. The Civil Rights movement of the 1960s formed the ideological basis of the CDF, in that the organization focuses on providing a political voice for young low-income and minority children. The CDF receives funding from various sources—corporate grants, foundations, and individual donations—but not from the federal government. Founded by Marian Wright Edelman, the CDF also works to provide benefits such as health care, child care, and education programs to help disadvantaged children overcome poverty.

The CDF has focused on various social aspects of poverty, depending on what issues seemed most pressing at the time. In its first decade, the CDF focused on research and on influencing public policy. Some of these early programs included a project to define the "critical child needs" for all income and racial groups and to determine the effectiveness of various policies designed to correct these needs. Another project analyzed the effectiveness of "early intervention" and "early child development" programs such as Head Start, which is designed to facilitate low-income children's entrance to grade school. The CDF also has helped organize child advocacy programs to protect children.

In the next decade, the CDF focused more on advocacy and improving public awareness of the importance of education. The CDF-sponsored "Child Watch" coalitions worked to build strong community and political ties with local and state policymakers. In an effort to reach both policymakers and the general public, the CDF began publishing yearly reports on the status of children in its annual "State of America's Children Yearbook" and held national conferences to promote child advocacy programs. Recently, the CDF has continued its focus on promoting advocacy, education, and awareness of the status of children in America.

The CDF also works to affect federal policy. Some examples of federal initiatives that the CDF influenced through research or advocacy include the passage of the 1975 Education for All Handicapped Children Act, the 1980 Adoption Assistance and Child Welfare Act, the implementation of the Children's Mental Health Program in 1982, the 1988 Family Support Act, and the reorganization and improvement of the Head Start program in 1994. As these policies show, the CDF has successfully helped America's disadvantaged children.

See also: Children and Poverty; Head Start

Sources: Administration for Children and Families (ACF) (http://www.acf.hhs.gov/index.html); Children's Defense Fund (www.childrensdefense.org); Children's Defense Fund Action Council (http://www.cdfactioncouncil.org/stateandlocal/default.asp); Trattner, Walter I., *From Poor Law to Welfare State*, 6th ed. (New York: Simon and Schuster, 1999); US Department of Health and Human Services (www.hhs.gov/children/index.shtml).

CHILDREN'S HEALTH INSURANCE PROGRAM (CHIP). Federal low-income health insurance programs like Medicaid only provide for a specific portion of the population; they neglect individuals and families living just above the official poverty line (which varies by state and geographic region). Some states have implemented state and local programs to provide insurance to needy families who do not qualify for Medicaid but cannot purchase private insurance. Texas's Children's Health Insurance Program (CHIP) is one of the most comprehensive. For those who qualify, CHIP covers health services for children—including preventative checkups and immunizations, access to hospitals, labs, and specialized clinics—and helps procure prescription drugs.

A state government program run by the Health and Human Services Commission (HHSC), CHIP has strict eligibility requirements and standards for professional care. The basic guidelines for eligibility are simple. Any adult Texas resident who provides care for a child or youth under age nineteen may apply for CHIP coverage: thus, grandparents, relatives, step-parents, legal guardians, and adult siblings can apply for coverage as well as the child's parents. This is significant, because many past welfare-relief programs—such as Aid to Families with Dependent Children (AFDC)—attempted to deny aid to children born out of wedlock; CHIP, however, allows any caregiving adult to apply for coverage. In addition, CHIP does not exclude immigrants—of which Texas has a substantial number—and the parent's immigration or citizenship status does not affect the child's eligibility for CHIP.

The income levels for eligibility in CHIP are substantially higher than those required for Children's Medicaid. To qualify for Children's Medicaid coverage, a family of two needs an average income less than $1,141 per month and less than $13,690 per year; for CHIP eligibility, the same family could average as much as $2,282 per month and $27,380 per year. Likewise, to qualify for Medicaid, a family of five needs an average income of less than $2,011 per month and less than $24,130 per year but could have as much as $4,022 per month and $48,260 per year to qualify for CHIP coverage. As these figures show, CHIP coverage allows nearly double the average income compared to Medicaid. In addition to average income, Medicaid and CHIP also assess each family's assets but do not include home ownership or private property in these calculations.

CHIP coverage is very similar to that of Children's Medicaid. Both programs allow participants to choose their own doctors, pay for regular preventative check-ups and immunizations, provide for basic dental care, provide prescription drug coverage, cover hospital and emergency care, and allow coverage of preexisting conditions. However, despite programs such as CHIP and Children's Medicaid, a substantial proportion of America's children remain without health insurance coverage. In 2005, 11.2 percent of all Americans under the age of eighteen (8.3 million persons) lacked coverage. Low-income Americans comprised a disproportionate percentage of the uninsured: 19 percent of children whom the Census Bureau defined as "living in poverty" were uninsured, compared to only 11.2 percent of the nation's total children. Children from minority groups were especially likely to lack coverage: nearly 22 percent of Hispanic children, 12.5 percent of African American children, and 12.2 percent of Asian children, but only 7.2 percent of white non-Hispanic children. State-administered programs such as CHIP provide important state and local coverage, but more states need to implement similar programs if the national problems are to lessen.

See also: Medicaid

Sources: Children's Health Insurance Program, "2006 Status Report" Texas Health and Human Services Commission (2006); CHIP (http://www.cms.hhs.gov); DeNavas-Walt, Carmen, Bernadette D. Proctor, and Cheryl Hill Lee, "Income, Poverty, and Health Insurance Coverage in the United States: 2005," U.S. Census Bureau (2006); Patterson, James T., *America's Struggle Against Poverty in the Twentieth Century* (Cambridge, MA: Harvard University Press, 2000).

CHRISTIANITY AND POVERTY. Since the beginnings of Christianity almost 2,000 years ago, there has been a close relationship between Christian beliefs and practices and the experience of poverty. This relationship has been no less true in America. Influenced by Christian teachings, Americans have long felt a duty to care for the impoverished, especially the deserving poor. English colonial promoters pictured America as a place where the destitute and criminal could find redemption. More secular thinkers have seen America as an asylum of liberty, where the opportunity to succeed could hasten material redemption. Indeed, Americans have long struggled with the contradictions between the material abundance of America and the teachings of Jesus of Nazareth. Although Jesus clearly taught that poverty is a blessing rather than a curse, Americans have, over the course of American history, viewed poverty as a curse to rid the land of, to bring prosperity to all people.

The Gospel of Luke records Jesus, in the Beatitudes, saying, "Blessed are the poor, because yours is the kingdom of God"; "Blessed are the ones hungering now, for you will be satisfied"; and "Blessed are those weeping now, for they shall laugh." Luke's gospel, more than the other three, stresses the message of woe to the wealthy, the full, the happy, and the self-satisfied. The Apostle Paul of Tarsus, in his second letter to the Corinthians, echoed the teachings of Jesus in Luke, proclaiming that God's power is perfected in weakness. "For whenever I am weak, then powerful I am." Paul's writings complemented Jesus's stress on poverty rather than wealth, touting weakness rather than strength. The message of the New Testament is that God blesses not the rich, happy, and beautiful, but rather the hungry, sick, suffering, ugly, insecure, and frightened. Jesus also said, "you will always have the poor," predicting that poverty will always exist, notwithstanding the plans of countless utopian thinkers and many modern government agencies.

The response to poverty among Christians in American society has had many dimensions, ranging from condemnation to concern. Under the influence of European Protestantism, particularly Calvinism, early American communities emphasized the virtue of one's calling: that God wished people to have set vocations by which they contributed to the community. Work and the acquisition of material goods was not a sin, as Medieval Catholicism sometimes portrayed it, but a virtue. German sociologist Max Weber called this virtue of moneymaking "the Protestant Ethic." During the seventeenth century, many Christians believed that God required a new exodus of the chosen people to go on an errand into the wilderness to spread the Gospel and to establish a New Jerusalem in America. Puritans of New England, in particular, brought their Protestant ideas of hard work and personal sacrifice to bear on the problem of poverty, concluding that God rewarded dedicated servants but allowed the impoverishment of the idle. The poor were the cause of their own suffering by means of idleness. "A 'Diligent' man is very rarely an 'Indigent' man," declared Cotton Mather in his 1701 essay, *A Christian at His Calling*. Mather argued that God wished each human to have a distinct calling that resulted in work, which was the only way to defend oneself against the temptations of Satan. Old Testament writings such as Proverbs provided clear support for this point of view. Widows and orphans, of course, were poor by chance rather than by choice, and the Puritans cared for them accordingly, even if they assigned their unfortunate condition to God's will.

The Puritan approach to poverty continued to influence America long after the days of Cotton Mather. For example, one of Mather's descendants, Jeremy Belknap, who was a minister in Dover, New Hampshire, during the years before and after the Revolutionary War, continued to preach sermons against idleness even after he had rejected the Calvinist teachings of his fathers. On a journey to upstate New York in 1796, accompanied by his friend and fellow minister Jedidiah Morse of Charlestown, Massachusetts, Belknap condemned the Oneida Indians for choosing idleness and poverty over diligence and prosperity. "Idleness is the sin that easily besets them," he wrote, "and is the parent of many other vices." The men thought that their role was to fight and hunt, so they refused to engage in agriculture, leaving it to the women. The Indians were also beset by alcoholism.

Belknap and Morse traveled among the Indians and others in North America as representatives of the Society for Propagating the Gospel, one of the first American missionary societies, founded in 1649. A few years later, in 1657, the Scots' Charitable Society was founded at Boston to help poor and sick Scots, many of whom had been sent to New England as servants after the English Civil War. Other such societies included the Charitable Irish Society, founded in 1737, also in Boston, and the Episcopal Charitable Society, founded in 1724.

These early American charitable societies had a long-lasting influence on the orphaned, widowed, and worthy destitute. An example is the patient work and care of missionaries—from the Society for Propagating the Gospel—among the Indians and others in North America in the small town of Gosport, New Hampshire.

Gosport was a fishing village situated at the Isles of Shoals, eight tiny islands several miles off the coast of Maine and New Hampshire. The Isles, near the best fishing grounds in North America, were used by sixteenth- and seventeenth-century European fishermen as a temporary way station where they could cut, dry, and salt their catch. There were several small fishing villages on the islands, the last of which was Gosport on Star Island. The fishers and fishwives of Gosport were rarely comfortable, and they knew poverty more than wealth, particularly in the years of economic chaos during and after the Revolutionary War. In 1800 the Society for Propagating the Gospel, being informed of the dire circumstances of the Gosport fishers, sent a succession of missionaries to help them. Jedidiah Morse, who again played a central role, journeyed to Gosport on August 6, 1800, where he baptized, catechized, preached, and performed marriages. He gave the islanders "6 Bibles, 12 Testaments, 24 Spelling books, 12 Primers, 12 Little Truths, 8 Wall Catechisms, 6 Doddridge's Sermons to young people, 4 Doddridge's Rise and Progress . . . 3 Psalm books," and a copy of his *Elements of Geography*. Morse helped the Gosport citizens found a new parish; the meetinghouse, which was quickly constructed, was a one-room stone building that was serviceable if not ornate. In November 1800 Rev. Morse dedicated the meetinghouse and prepared articles of agreement for the fishers, prefaced with the following comment:

> Whereas the islands now commonly called the *Isles of Shoals*, but heretofore named *Smith's Islands*, in honour of the renowned Capt. John Smith, who first discovered them, have fallen into a lamentable state of decay, since the revolution war; and the inhabitants, from their extreme poverty, and other unhappy circumstances, have long been destitute of the means of religious and moral instruction; and whereas some pious and charitable persons have generously erected a commodious and durable building, to be solely appropriated to the public instruction of the inhabitants, and the Massachusetts Society for propagating the gospel have appointed a missionary to reside at the said islands, as a religious and moral teacher to the inhabitants, and an instructor of the youth; and whereas there is ground to hope for further charities from the said society, and other humane and benevolent persons, should the good effects of their present bounty be visible in the improvement of the morals, manners, and conversation of the inhabitants; and whereas from the local situation of the said islands, it is very difficult to resort to the laws for the decision of disputes which unavoidably arise.

Such organizations as the Society for Propagating the Gospel were middle class in membership, temperament, belief, and morality. Early nineteenth-century evangelical Christian groups retained the colonial view toward the poor: that immorality and vice resulted in poverty. Yet colonial attempts, centered on the almshouse and workhouse, had failed. What was needed, these reformers thought, was direct intervention by religious activists in the area where poverty flourished—the city. This required a shift in viewpoint: from seeing poverty as an exclusively moral issue to adopting the view that an impoverished urban environment provided a negative influence, especially on youth, that could encourage sinfulness. This recognition required that the answer to poverty was not locking up and isolating the poor, but rather reforming their ideas, habits, and environment.

During the 1800s urban population expanded, and with it came the negative consequences of city life—prostitution, alcoholism, crime. Christian reformers responded with a variety of approaches and organizations aimed at changing the lifestyles and morality of the urban poor. One approach was the religious tract movement, in which middle-class Protestant women went to poor urban neighborhoods to distribute pamphlets directed toward moral and religious reform. Another approach was the Sunday School movement in Protestant churches, the aim of which was to bring poor children to a caring, religious, middle-class moral environment, to help them break from the patterns of poverty. Some of the most notorious slums in New York City succumbed to the efforts of middle-class Christian missionaries. Protestant women set up a mission—Murderer's Alley and Den of Thieves—right in the heart of the New York slum.

Indeed, nineteenth-century New York was a center of middle-class efforts to curb poverty. For example, the New York Tract Society spawned the Association for Improving the Condition of the Poor (AICP) in 1843. The AICP, led by Robert Hartley, advocated active intervention, both morally and environmentally, in New York slums. Another example was the Children's Aid Society, founded by Charles Loring Brace in 1853, which provided numerous services for New York children, ranging from classes—to teach occupational skills and reading—to summer camps. Brace believed that removing children from the city and taking them to the country was a justifiable environmental shift that could hasten moral reformation and break the cycle of poverty. Orphans from the city boarded Orphan Trains that took them West, where they would work as indentured servants for farm families until they reached adulthood. Orphan Trains brought thousands of children to the western United States from the 1850s to the 1920s. In *The Dangerous Classes of New York* (1872), Brace wrote that "Christianity is the highest education of character. Give the poor that, and only seldom will either alms or punishment be necessary." Boston minister and missionary Joseph Tuckerman advocated single-family dwellings as the means of achieving Christian moral reform. The Young Men's Christian Association (YMCA), which was founded in England and arrived in New York and other American cities in the 1850s, was committed to helping prevent newcomers to the city from falling into sin. During times of economic crisis, such as the Great Depression, YMCAs provided direct relief to the urban poor. Another charitable institution founded in Great Britain, the Salvation Army, arrived in New York in 1880; henceforth the Salvation Army spread throughout America, bringing its combination of evangelical Christianity and work on behalf of the poor. With the increase of Catholic immigration to America in the mid- to late nineteenth century, the Roman Catholic Church became significantly involved in helping the poor, especially the young, through orphanages. For example, in 1809 Elizabeth Ann Seton founded the Sisters of Charity at Emmitsburg, outside Baltimore; the Sisters devoted their lives to helping the poor.

By the end of the nineteenth century, at the beginning of the Progressive movement, the middle class viewed the poor as different—not quite equal, yet deserving of Christian social justice. This was the attitude of reformers such as Jane Addams, founder of Hull House. Addams was wealthy and educated, completely unlike the poor that she helped. Nevertheless, she felt a calling to use her resources and energies to help the impoverished of Chicago. During the Progressive Era, Christian poor relief continued to be met by private individuals or organizations because the federal government had not yet taken a large role in poor relief. But this changed with the Great Depression, which brought about such suffering that the federal government, centered on the New Deal of the 1930s, became an active participant in helping the poor, eclipsing private and religious charities.

Even as the federal government becomes more involved in issues of poverty, private Christian charities continue to work to help the poor, answering Christ's call to his followers to imitate His concern for the impoverished. Soup kitchens, which became a symbol of private charity during the Great Depression, have continued in better economic times to be a symbol of the Christian concern to feed the hungry. The main soup kitchens across America include the Holy Apostles Soup Kitchen in Manhattan, which has served meals for the homeless and hungry since 1982; the Trenton Area Soup Kitchen, sponsored by local churches, also in operation since 1982; the Open Door Community of Atlanta, which has served meals for over a decade; and the Iron Gate soup kitchen of Trinity Episcopal Church in Tulsa, Oklahoma, which has served more than 300 meals daily to the hungry for over twenty years.

John Kenneth Galbraith argued in *The Affluent Society* (1956) that poverty is essentially a premodern phenomenon and that, in the age of modern industry poverty, if it has not been eliminated, is less dominating over a society and economy than it once was in an agrarian, preindustrial society. However, the many antipoverty programs of Christian agencies—which call on Christians to make ending poverty a central social issue—as well as the continuing role that the issue of poverty plays in American politics, indicate that poverty is very much a contemporary issue in America.

See also: Addams, Jane

Sources: Boyer, Paul, *Urban Masses and Moral Order in America, 1820–1920* (Cambridge, MA: Harvard University Press, 1978); Brace, Charles Loring, *The Dangerous Classes of New York, and Twenty Years' Work among Them* (New York: Wynkoop and Hallenbeck, 1872); Bushman, Richard L., *From Puritan to Yankee: Character and the Social Order in Connecticut, 1690–1765* (Cambridge, MA: Harvard University Press, 1967); Christian Churches Together (www.christianchurchestogether.org); Lawson, Russell M., *The American Plutarch: Jeremy Belknap and the Historian's Dialogue with the Past* (Westport, CT: Praeger Publishers, 1998); *The Constitution and By-Laws of the Scots' Charitable Society of Boston* (Cambridge: Wilson, 1878); "The Town Records of Gosport, New Hampshire," *New England Historical and Genealogical Society* (1913–1914); Weber, Max, *The Protestant Ethic and the Spirit of Capitalism,* translated by Talcott Parsons (New York: Scribner's, 1958).

CLINTON WELFARE REFORM. Stating that the American welfare system was "broken beyond repair," President Bill Clinton signed welfare reform legislation into law that significantly reduced federal welfare programs in an effort to lower the welfare budget and encourage able-bodied Americans to work. The election of Clinton in 1992 had brought the Democrats back to the White House, but the Clinton Administration did not return to the liberal welfare policies of earlier Democrats like Lyndon B. Johnson and Franklin D. Roosevelt. Instead, Clinton signed a Republican-sponsored welfare reform bill in 1996 that was intended to "end welfare as we know it." The main idea of this reform bill was to change federal welfare from a direct form of aid given to the nation's poor to a program of financial aid for people in dire need of assistance—Clinton emphasized the need to get people off welfare and into jobs that would enable them to get out of poverty.

The welfare reform in 1996 was not a unique project of the Clinton Administration; in fact, Clinton's immediate predecessors, Republicans George H. W. Bush and Ronald Reagan, had worked to reduce the welfare state. Ironically, although the 1996 Welfare Reform Act was the most extensive welfare reform in decades, its motivating ideology was closer to Reagan's than Clinton's views. A former actor, fond of quasi-homespun phrases, Reagan adopted an extremely conservative stance on welfare. Reagan idealized the free enterprise system (closely allied with Social Darwinism) of the nineteenth century, in which the government did not interfere with business and there were no public relief programs. Such a conservative policy had not been pursued by any president since Herbert Hoover, whose presidency (1929–1933) was marred by the Great Depression; Franklin Roosevelt's New Deal—the beginning of the American welfare system—was a reaction against Hoover's unwillingness to involve the federal government in public relief. Because the 1980s were a time of general prosperity—compared to the recession years of the mid-1970s—many affluent Americans no longer felt the need for institutionalized welfare. This reluctance had racial, economic, and political motivations: the majority of welfare recipients were minorities, the disabled, or single parents. "Welfare moms"—a pejorative term for single, often black, mothers on welfare—drew some of the strongest criticisms because, according to conservatives, they symbolized the (supposed) connection between welfare, laziness, and immorality.

By the time that Clinton assumed the presidency in 1993, the overall attitude toward welfare—among more than just conservatives—was negative. Clinton's primary goal for reform was not reforming welfare but instituting universal health care. Nevertheless, the Democrat Clinton agreed to sign the conservative Republican-backed proposal to reform the welfare system. The 1996 welfare reform bill gave states more control over welfare, did not extend welfare assistance to non-U.S. citizens, and took steps to encourage welfare recipients to find alternative sources of income: the bill limited the maximum benefits to five years of support per family and required able-bodied adults to work after two years of support. In place of the Aid to Families with Dependent Children (AFDC) program—the largest welfare program at the time—the 1996 welfare reform established the Temporary Assistance for Needy Families (TANF) program, to provide limited assistance to low-income families. With the 1996 reform, Congress hoped to transform the welfare system into a temporary relief program: only those with documented medical conditions that prevented them from finding employment—the deserving poor—would receive long-term benefits. Clinton also allocated 4 billion dollars to continue the program to help single mothers on welfare—"welfare moms"—to pay for child care and health care, although the bill put the responsibility on states to provide these health care programs.

There were four main aspects of the 1996 welfare reform. Clinton wanted to "make work pay" by increasing the earned income tax credit; improve child support measures, such as renovating existing programs like Head Start and beginning similar new programs; implement programs to educate the poor and provide job training to facilitate employment opportunities; and limit the amount of time that people can receive welfare assistance. Clinton's reform measures drew some criticism—the measures to limit the timeframe and provide education were especially controversial. Even with the proposed education and training programs, which critics argued were too costly, few welfare recipients were able to obtain jobs with sufficiently high wages to improve their position significantly. Consequently, despite bipartisan support, the 1996 Clinton welfare reform bill generated controversy, especially among liberals, who argued that the bill was not realistic in its assessment of the needs of the poor.

See also: Aid to Families with Dependent Children (AFDC); Head Start; "Welfare Moms"

Sources: Divine, Robert A., T. H. Breen, et al., *The American Story*, 2nd ed. (New York, 2005); Haveman, Robert H., and John Karl Scholz, "The Clinton Welfare Reform Plan: Will It End Poverty as We Know It?", Institute for Research on Poverty Discussion Paper no. 1037-94 (1994); Patterson, James T., *America's Struggle Against Poverty in the Twentieth Century* (Cambridge, MA: Harvard University Press, 2000); Transcript of President Clinton's 1997 State of the Union speech. CNN article (http://edition.cnn.com/2005/ALLPOLITICS/01/31/sotu.clinton1997/index.html); Trattner, Walter I., *From Poor Law to Welfare State*, 6th ed. (New York: Simon and Schuster, 1999).

COMMUNITY ACTION PROGRAM. Instituted by Congress during the Johnson administration as part of the 1964 Economic Opportunity Act, the Community Action Program was intended to provide "services, assistance, and other activities of sufficient scope and size to give promise of progress toward elimination of poverty or a cause or causes of poverty through developing employment opportunities, improving human performance, motivation, and productivity, or bettering the conditions under which people live, learn, and work." In addition, Community Action emphasized the need to involve the poor directly in the development of the policies and programs conducted and administered; this policy of "maximum feasible participation" of the residents of the areas and groups served garnered much publicity for Community Action but angered existing elites and hampered its ability to accomplish its many goals.

Intended to allow more efficient coordination of local projects by bypassing federal red tape, the decentralized structure of Community Action—its insistence on the "maximum feasible participation" of the poor over direct governmental control—led to its becoming a "federally supported device for challenging the local political and welfare structure." In its attempt to involve the poor, Community Action encouraged questioning of local government authority; although its founders had envisioned it as a long-term planning tool to improve conditions with minimal federal spending, the program became a tool for antiestablishment protest. Cognizant of the growing civil rights movement, Community Action switched its focus in 1964—under the direction of Richard Boone and Sanford Kravitz, among others—from long-term planning and coordination to an all-out attempt to "shake up the establishment."

Community Action's policy of involving the poor in decisions affecting their status angered WASP elites, who protested the program's emphasis on conflict rather than cooperation. The urban unrest of the late 1960s, including the 1965 Watts riot, further alienated the white middle class from the aims of Johnson's War on Poverty. Ghetto uprisings led by minorities sparked a white backlash, and, rather than increasing efforts to improve ghetto living conditions, most white middle-class Americans chose to ignore the situation and withdraw to the suburbs. Ironically, minorities rioted in order to obtain assistance, but rather than leading to increased federal or local support, the violence ended the little funding that white voters had previously supported. As a result of its militant inclusion of the poor, Community Action was one of the biggest political failures of Johnson's War on Poverty because it symbolized everything that conservatives feared about liberal social reforms.

See also: Economic Opportunity Act; War on Poverty

Sources: Bremner, Robert H., Gary W. Reichard, and Richard Hopkins, eds., *American Choices: Social Dilemma and Public Policy since 1960* (Columbus: Ohio State University

Press, 1986); Patterson, James T., *America's Struggle against Poverty in the Twentieth Century* (Cambridge, MA: Harvard University Press, 2000); Trattner, Walter I., *From Poor Law to Welfare State*, 6th ed. (New York: Simon and Schuster, 1999).

CONVICT TRANSPORTATION. Many of the impoverished in early America were convicts who were transported to America to serve their sentence as servants to a master. Convict transportation was one of several forms of involuntary bound labor that existed in the thirteen American colonies. As many as 20,000 felons of all ages and sexes escaped the gallows at Tyburn in London by journeying to America as servants. Most of those transported died en route or during the first few months of "seasoning"—that is, adapting to the humid climate of the southern colonies. These transported felons generally lived short, impoverished lives. Poverty had driven them to steal in England, whereupon they were transported to America as paupers; while they served their extensive sentences, they earned little if any money. If they survived long enough to experience freedom, they were released penniless into an American society and economy wherein the proletariat were looked down on and excluded from polite society and deprived of many of the rights of citizens.

Sixteenth- and seventeenth-century English proponents of mercantilism believed that the American colonies served a dual purpose for England: sources of raw materials and markets for English goods. Furthermore, the colonies required labor to harvest the natural resources of America: England had an excess of people who could serve colonial labor needs. Although England prospered during the Tudor and Stuart dynasties of the sixteenth and seventeenth centuries, along with prosperity came income and wealth disparity, growing poverty, and increasing crime. The observant Spanish ambassador to the court of James I, Don Alonso de Velasco, in a letter to his sovereign Philip III in 1611, wrote that "their principal reason for colonizing these parts is to give an outlet to so many idle and wretched people as they have in England." Meanwhile Sir Thomas Dale of the Virginia Company complained of the troubles in procuring men for the colony:

> if it will please his majesty to banish hither all offenders condemned, betwixt this and then, to die, out of common Gaoles, and likewise so continue that grant for 3 yeres unto the Colony it would be a readie way to furnish us with men, and not always the worst kinde of men either for birth, spirits, or Bodie, and sutch who wold be right glad so to escape a just sentence to make this their new countrie.

The Lord Mayor of London in 1614 echoed these sentiments, calling for the "charitable and christian worke . . . by which meanes wee maybe disburthened of many idle and vagrant persons which otherwise are, and will be more and more, chargeable, dangerous and troublesome unto the state." Merchant Josiah Gee agreed in 1729, writing, "I am of Opinion" that transported convicts

> put upon raising and dressing Hemp and Flax . . . might not only find a most profitable Employment, but also those that are condemned for petty Larceny, or any other Crime less than the Penalty of Death, being sent thither might be rendered useful.

Some, he predicted, would repent of their past and become useful citizens.

Convict transportation began with the founding of the American colonies. John Popham, the promoter of the colony at Sagadahoc, Maine, that was founded in 1607 (but subsequently abandoned), believed that the Popham colony could use convicts as laborers. Jamestown, Virginia, also used convicts to alleviate the labor shortage. In 1617 prisoners arrived from Oxford, in 1618 from the notorious Newgate gaol. A hundred poor children arrived in Virginia the next year, along with "certain vile and dissolute persons who swarmed the streets of London" and who had been "arrested and sent to Virginia." Under Charles II, after the English Restoration, in 1661, the Council of Foreign Plantations tried to uncover "the best ways of encouraging and furnishing people for the Plantations, and how felons condemned to death for small offenses and . . . sturdy beggars, may be disposed of for that use." This led in 1664 to a ruling requiring "all vagrants, rogues, and idle persons that can give no account of themselves, felons who have the benefit of clergy, such as are convicted of petty larceny, vagabonds, gypsies, and loose persons, making resort to unlicensed brothels," to be transported to the American colonies for four years, if they were over twenty years of age, and seven years, if they were under twenty. Although the most violent criminals were executed, the Crown commuted the sentences of an increasing number of the condemned. Those who could read and write could escape the gallows by claiming the "benefit of the clergy," a holdover from Medieval Europe, in which it was assumed that clergy alone were literate among the general population.

Close to 5,000 convicts were transported to the American colonies before 1700. Colonies receiving more than their share of transported convicts, such as Maryland and Virginia, complained of "the great number of Felons and other desperate villains sent hither from the several prisons of England," because of which "we are believed to be a place only fit to receive such base and lewd persons." These two colonies passed laws by 1670 restricting the importation of convicts. Virginia's law prevented the transports of "any jaile birds or such others, who for notorious offenses have deserved to dye in England." South Carolina passed a law in 1712, and Pennsylvania in 1722, restricting the importation of convicts. There were, overall, few convicts transported between 1670 and 1717, partly because of such colonial laws and partly because of war—male convicts were often impressed into the military.

Under George I, however, the English attempted to revive the system. In 1717 Parliament passed "An act for the further preventing robbery, burglary, and other felonies, and for the more effectual transportation of felons," in which literate persons convicted of noncapital crimes deserving corporal punishment (such as whipping) could, by pleading the benefit of the clergy, have the punishment commuted by a Justice of the Peace to seven years of servitude in America. Illiterates without benefit of the clergy received sentences of fourteen years if the King graced them with the option of transportation. Unlike those transported in the seventeenth century, these eighteenth-century transports included rapists and murderers. On completion of the term of service, the convict was pardoned and free. This act of Parliament superseded all colonial laws to the contrary, so that the transportation of convicts to America increased in earnest. The demand of tobacco planters in Maryland and Virginia ensured that most of these convicts, perhaps as many as 20,000 before the Revolution, were sent to the region of the Chesapeake Bay, Potomac, and James river valleys.

Many of the convicts transported to America were, like Daniel Defoe's title character in *Moll Flanders*, ne'er-do-wells, liars, cheats, and thieves, who were nevertheless nonviolent. By the beginning of the seventeenth century, the English penal system was inefficient and ineffectual, burdened by a growing number of capital crimes for relatively minor offenses. "Never were severe laws issued in greater abundance nor executed more rigorously," wrote Frederic Eden in 1797, "and never did the unrelenting vengeances of justice prove more ineffectual." Notwithstanding the English poor laws, the numbers of poor increased, and, out of desperation, many people turned to petty thievery to provide food in order to stave off starvation. The Draconian English criminal justice system, however, brooked no straying from the letter of the law, and those who stole even a trifling amount were locked up in a bridewell or other prison to await standing before a judge, who was more likely than not to pass the most severe sentence—ranging from death by hanging to scourging or branding. Some transported felons were religious prisoners. The Quakers, for example, after the 1664 Conventicle Act, could be transported to America after having violated the statute against meetings of the Society of Friends. Many prisoners of war found themselves transported to America as well. Scotch and Irish soldiers and rebels captured by the armies of Oliver Cromwell during the English Civil War were sometimes transported to America. Wars with the Scots during the reigns of Charles II and James II also resulted in Scottish prisoners being shipped to America as servants.

Convicts transported to the southern colonies often did not reach their destination, and those who did often succumbed to the harsh climate of heat, humidity, and disease. Prisoners bound to America were marched in chains from Newgate or Old Bailey prison to the nearest port, where they boarded a vessel in which they were kept under deck in chains. Contractors were paid as much as £25 per prisoner to transport them, but captain and crew were hardly concerned with the well-being of their charges. Generally the convicts were fed well, but the conditions in which they lived were nevertheless disgusting. "All the states of horror I ever had an idea of," wrote one eighteenth-century visitor to a convict ship, "are much short of what I saw this poor man in; chained to a board in a hold not above sixteen feet long, more than fifty with him; a collar and padlock about his neck, and chained to five of the most dreadful creatures I ever looked on." The mortality rate on board ship was significant, usually 15 to 20 percent. Smallpox and other communicable diseases passed unabated from prisoner to prisoner.

On arrival to an American port, the convicts were sold to the highest bidder. Potential buyers came on board ship and examined their prospective laborers. The convicts' seven- to fourteen-year term of service made them highly sought after, notwithstanding their reputation for malevolence. Literary evidence suggests that the crime rate rose in colonies such as Maryland and Virginia, where most convicts were transported. One Philadelphian wrote in frustration

> Our Mother knows what is best for us. What is a little House-breaking, Shoplifting, or Highway-robbing; what is a son now and then corrupted and hanged, a Daughter debached, and Pox'd, a wife stabbed, a Husband's throat cut, or a child's brains beat out with an Axe, compared with this "Improvement and Well peopling of the Colonies."

Benjamin Franklin thought a fit recompense for the transport of convicts to America was a shipment of serpents to England. In 1670 Virginia punctuated its law restricting the importation of convicts with the following comment: "we are believed to be a place only fit to receive such base and lewd persons." At the same time Dr. Samuel Johnson, the English lexicographer and wit, wrote of the American colonies: "Sir, they are a race of convicts and ought to be content with anything we may allow them short of hanging."

Even so, planters continued to import the prisoners. George Washington, for example, purchased the labor of convicts to work on his Mount Vernon plantation. The numbers of convicts brought to Maryland was consistent from the end of King George's War in 1748 to the beginning of the Revolutionary War in 1775. During these years, more than 9,000 convicts were shipped to Maryland, in any given year, between 200 and 500. These numbers were almost equal to the thousands of indentured servants who also immigrated to the colony. The number of convicts shipped from London between 1718 to 1772, according to public records, was 17,470. Convicts were, of course, shipped from other ports as well, such as Bristol. The combination of American labor needs, English mercantilist thought, and soaring numbers of the poor and criminal activities in England ensured that convict transportation thrived throughout the colonial period. The system ended only with the Revolutionary War, which forced the English to find another location—Australia—to receive their excess felons.

See also: British Poor and the Origins of Colonialism; Indentured Servitude; Poor Laws in England and Early America

Sources: Brown, Alexander, *The Genesis of the United States* (London: Boston and New York: Houghton Mifflin, 1890); Butler, James D., "British Convicts Shipped to American Colonies." *American Historical Review* 2 (1896); Eden, Frederic, *The State of the Poor,* 3 vols. (London: Davis, 1797); Ford, Worthington C., *Washington as an Employer and Importer of Labor* (Brooklyn: by the author, 1889); Gillian, Charles E., "Jail Bird Immigrants to Virginia," *Virginia Historical Magazine* Vol. 52 (1944); Herrick, Cheesman A., *White Servitude in Pennsylvania, Indentured and Redemption Labor in Colony and Commonwealth* (Philadelphia: McVey, 1926); Hofstadter, Richard, *America at 1750: A Social Portrait* (New York: Random House, 1971); McCormac, E. I., *White Servitude in Maryland, 1634–1820* (Baltimore: Johns Hopkins, 1904); Morse, Richard B., *Government and Labor in Early America* (New York: Harper & Row, 1965); Smith, Abbot Emerson, *Colonists in Bondage: White Servitude and Convict Labor in America, 1607–1776* (New York: Norton, 1971).

CRIME AND IMPRISONMENT. Throughout American history, it has been a common perception that the poor have a higher propensity toward crime than the middle class. Although there is some basis to this belief—because the poor have less lawful options to obtain material goods and, if unemployed, have less constructive pursuits with which to occupy their time—the poor are not by nature more inclined to crime than are the more affluent classes. Nevertheless, the poor—especially minorities—are more likely to be in prison. Whether this is a result of increased crime levels or a sign of greater police presence in poor and minority areas is a point of contention among scholars. Most mainstream and conservative scholars argue that the higher proportion of minorities and the poor is caused by the higher incidence of crime in poor areas; however, liberal historian Howard Zinn argues that the authorities are to blame for the unequal prison system, which he sees as an example of America's bias against minorities and the poor.

The relationship between the poor, crime, and imprisonment was present in Tudor-Stuart England, and perceptions and behaviors followed the English to America. Thousands of impoverished English men and women who had turned to crime, been apprehended, tried, and condemned to the gallows, escaped their fate by transportation to the colonies, to serve fourteen years as bound servants. Colonials such as Ben Franklin feared that England used the colonies as dumping grounds for poor ne'er-do-wells. Upright colonials considered immigrant servants to be little better than criminals, a view that would continue for centuries to haunt immigrants who sought asylum in America. The pauper in early America was not only unwanted but sometimes jailed for vagrancy or other petty crimes. Creditors by law could demand the incarceration of debtors until the debt was paid. The Dominion of New England in 1679, for example, required that jailed debtors not be allowed even the most temporary furlough to earn money. In 1716 a pauper petitioned the General Court for mercy, complaining that he had been incarcerated for four years, "which Is the Cause of my poverty." He admitted his debt but added that he had "not . . . one farthing In this world wherewith to pay itt, nor wherewithall to Subsist my Self, my wife, and three young Children who Cry for Bread." Eventually in 1767 the colony took action to help imprisoned debtors who, "when they are capable of Labour thier [sic] detention becomes a Publick loss & the Confining Prisoner for Debt with Criminals is not Expedient or any way Suitable to their different Circumstances." New Hampshire legislators resolved by law that, if a debtor swore an oath that his property was not above £3, he would earn release (although not forgiveness of the debt). The proclamation of the Declaration of Independence of freedom and equality did little to mitigate the evil of debtor's prison. Some reformers realized the absurdity of a system that imprisoned the very person who could work to pay the debt. But not until the 1830s did states finally outlaw debtor's prison. But debts, and resulting poverty, could not be legislated out of existence.

In his 1890 book, *How the Other Half Lives*, Jacob Riis clearly demonstrated the perceived connection between the poor and crime. In his introduction he wrote of the tenements:

> The story is dark enough, drawn from the plain public records, to send a chill to any heart. If it shall appear that the sufferings and the sins of the 'other half,' and the evil they breed, are but as a just punishment upon the community that gave it no other choice, it will be because that is the truth.

Riis identified crime as a condition of the poor, but he also laid blame on the city's middle class and elites for not taking steps to fix the problem. Specifically, Riis identified the tenements as the "boundary line" between the peaceful middle-class neighborhoods and the crime-filled poor neighborhoods, arguing that in

> the tenements all the influences make for evil; because they are the hot-beds of the epidemics that carry death to rich and poor alike; the nurseries of pauperism and crime that fill our jails and police courts; that throw off a scum of forty thousand human wrecks to the island asylums and workhouses year by year; that turned out in the last eight years a round half million beggars to prey upon our charities; that maintain a standing army of ten thousand tramps with all that that implies; because, above all, they touch the family life with deadly moral contagion.

Riis qualified his denouncement of the tenements, however, by noting that the prevalence of crime in New York was just as much the fault of the "top half" of society who only cared about profits and thus forced the poor to live in wretched conditions. Riis wrote:

> There had been tenant-houses before, but they were not built for the purpose. Nothing would probably have shocked their original owners more than the idea of their

harboring a promiscuous crowd; for they were the decorous homes of the old Knickerbockers, the proud aristocracy of Manhattan in the early days. It was the stir and bustle of trade, together with the tremendous immigration that followed upon the war of 1812 that dislodged them. In thirty-five years the city of less than a hundred thousand came to harbor half a million souls, for whom homes had to be found.

The movement of the affluent—out of the central city toward the outskirts—led to the conversion of "once fashionable streets along the East River" into tenements under the direction of shady proprietors and real estate speculators. According to the report of the New York Legislature of 1857, cited by Riis,

> in its beginning, the tenant-house became a real blessing to that class of industrious poor whose small earnings limited their expenses, and whose employment in workshops, stores, or about the warehouses and thoroughfares, render a near residence of much importance.

However, business increased soon afterward, leading to exponential population growth; large, old houses suddenly become valuable for their capacity to house large numbers of people. Of the general structure of tenement housing, Riis wrote: the

> *large* rooms were partitioned into *several smaller ones*, without regard to light or ventilation, the rate of rent being lower in proportion to space or height from the street; and they soon became filled from cellar to garret with a class of tenantry living from hand to mouth, loose in morals, improvident in habits, degraded, and squalid as beggary itself.

Middle-class New Yorkers, like Riis, saw these tenement dwellings, which were "prolific of untold depravities," as both the scene and cause of the city's high crime levels. Within the "dark bedroom" of the tenement house, Riis wrote—echoing the beliefs of Progressive reformers—the immigrant poor reveled in "evils more destructive than wars." The proprietors did little to correct this situation; instead, they sought to protect their own interests by fixing rents high enough to cover the "damage and abuse" of the residents. Moreover, the tenement was no place for the middle-class conception of "neatness, order, cleanliness," as by nature the tenements encouraged "slovenliness, discontent, privation, and ignorance," engulfed by general "dilapidation, containing, but sheltering not, the miserable hordes that crowded beneath smoldering, water-rotted roofs or burrowed among the rats of clammy cellars." Yet the real object of Riis's anger was the proprietors, who cited the "filthy habits of the tenants as an excuse for the condition of their property" rather that take steps to improve their properties; according to Riis, the proprietor's tolerance of the tenement-dwellers' habits was the "real evil."

Similar conceptions of crime as a companion of poverty are evident in twentieth-century America. Particularly illustrative are the poor's perception of the police and the connection between police brutality and minority unrest. The situation in St. Louis's Pruitt–Igoe public housing complex provides insight. A series of surveys of the complex residents conducted in the 1960s clearly illustrated their distrust of authority and belief that city officials were not concerned with their needs. In general, the residents tolerated welfare workers more than police. These surveys demonstrated that men (66 percent dissatisfaction) serving as "Head of Household" were more critical of welfare workers than women (17 percent dissatisfaction) serving in the same capacity. Common complaints about the welfare system (represented by the experience of residents with individual welfare workers) were that the system was too inflexible and unjust—many residents thought the welfare system promoted inequality. The police, however, were a more prominent symbol of authority, and they tended to elicit more poignant responses.

Despite the fact that many residents welcomed police presence as a counter for youth violence and the drug trade within the complex—which was out-of-hand because of poor upkeep and frustrated residents—the overwhelming perception of the police was negative. Although 91 percent of the respondents (88 percent of the men and 92 percent of the women) agreed that Pruitt–Igoe needed more policemen (whereas only 3 percent thought the complex needed fewer policemen), many respondents complained that the police (both the St. Louis police and the project's police force) took too long to respond and acted disrespectfully. Only 31 percent of the respondents agreed that the St. Louis police did a "good job of providing protection" for the residents of Pruitt–Igoe; 78 percent complained that the St. Louis police were "never around and take too long to come when you call them"; likewise, only 40 percent thought that the project police did a good job providing protection, and 65 percent complained that the project police were never around and did not come when called. Two typical quotes illustrate this perception: "the (city police) threw me behind bars and took all my money and the ring off my hand . . . they talk to you like a dog"; and "three fourths of the time they (the project police) don't come."

Statistically, the poor are more likely to be incarcerated, which superficially seems to justify their distrust of the police and the prison system. In particular, urban blacks and Hispanics are overrepresented in U.S. prisons: in the 1980s, although blacks comprised only 12 of the nation's population, they represented 48 percent of all prison inmates; 51 percent of black males in large urban areas had been arrested at least once for an "index crime—murder, aggravated assault, forcible rape, robbery, car theft—compared to only 14 percent of white males in the same areas. Likewise, in the 1980s Hispanics comprised only 6 percent of the population but represented 12 percent of all arrests, and Hispanic males represented 11 percent of the nation's male prison population. Scholars disagree on the effect of racism in this statistical discrepancy, but it is not a coincidence that these groups also represent a significant portion of America's poor. Although America no longer explicitly incarcerates the poor in debtor's prisons, poverty remains an indicator of social infirmity because of the continued perception that poverty and crime are irrevocably joined.

See also: Convict Transportation; Poor Laws in England and Early America; Pruitt–Igoe

Sources: Atkins, Jacqueline M., ed., *Encyclopedia of Social Work,* 18th ed., 2 vols. (Silver Spring, MD: NASW, 1987); Riis, Jacob, *How the Other Half Lives* (New York: Charles Scribner's Sons, 1890); Stromberg, Jerome S., "Private Problems in Public Housing: A Further Report on the Pruitt-Igoe Project." Occasional Paper no. 39 (1968); Zinn, Howard, "Surprises," *A People's History of the United States,* rev. ed. (New York: Harper Collins, 1995: 493–528).

CULTURE OF POVERTY. The notion of a "culture" of poverty refers to the idea that poverty is not merely a result of economic forces, but a structural, ongoing cycle. Like its opposite—the environmental view of poverty, which emphasizes the impact of place—the idea of a culture of poverty is an oversimplification, employed primarily by activists and politicians pushing for social change. The theory of cultural poverty has several major characteristics. First, it assumes that the majority of the poor are from poor families and that poverty transfers from generation to generation. Second, it assumes that the poor are complacent and either unwilling or unable to take the initiative to rise above poverty; thus their disorganized and miserable lifestyle displays the specific trends of "cultural" poverty. The theory also assumes the preponderance of maladjusted groups among America's poor: rural whites in Appalachia; urban blacks; and, more recently, Hispanic immigrants. These assumptions are, however, oversimplified half-truths; none is entirely accurate.

Michael Harrington popularized the concept of a culture of poverty in his 1963 book *The Other America*. Harrington emphasized the defeated attitude of the poor, arguing that the poor can and will not raise themselves up but required the intervention of more affluent Americans. The poor are isolated from mainstream society. The "new" poor of the twentieth century are entirely different from the nineteenth-century poor because fewer opportunities exist for advancement.

The growing acceptance among liberals of the 1960s that a culture of poverty existed influenced the social policies of the Kennedy and Johnson administrations. During the 1960s the government waged a war on poverty: before his death, Kennedy focused on the plight of rural Appalachian whites, and his advisors—many of whom Johnson retained, at least temporarily—set up the basic political structure needed to combat poverty in the United States. After 1964, when Johnson was elected in his own right, the government officially declared a "war on poverty," in which Johnson focused primarily on minorities in the inner city. According to U.S. Census data, the poverty rates in the late 1950s and early 1960s were more than 18 percent, but by the end of the 1960s the rates had lowered dramatically. During the 1960s, the minimum wage could maintain a person above the poverty line, so people with a full-time or steady job were not considered to be in poverty by government standards. Because the poor of the 1960s—made visible by activists like Harrington and the War on Poverty—were mostly unemployed, uneducated, and unskilled, more than 30 percent of Americans viewed poverty as the fault of the poor, who could easily be lumped into stereotypical groups, such as urban blacks and Appalachian whites. Statistical data did not always uphold such assertions, however, according to the Council of Economic Advisors (CEA) report "What is Poverty": no specific area of the country or social group has drastically higher poverty rates. In fact, the factor that contributes greatly to poverty in families is the number of children—not race or geographical area. The CEA notes that a family with four or five children has a higher chance of being in poverty than a family with one or two children. In short, the theory of a culture of poverty is an oversimplification that does not provide significant insight into America's poor.

See also: The Other America; War on Poverty

Sources: Council of Economic Advisors, "What is Poverty" www.whitehouse.gov/cea; Harrington, Michael, *The Other America: Poverty in the United States* (Baltimore: Penguin, 1963); Patterson, James T., *America's Struggle Against Poverty in the Twentieth Century* (Cambridge, MA: Harvard University Press, 2000).

D

DEPARTMENT OF HOUSING AND URBAN DEVELOPMENT (HUD). The federal agency in charge of administering programs and policies to alleviate America's housing needs is the Department of Housing and Urban Development (HUD). Established in 1965 by the Department of Housing and Urban Development Act, and passed during President Lyndon B. Johnson's War on Poverty, HUD subsumed existing agencies such as the Federal Housing Administration (FHA). Since the mid-1960s, HUD has helped low-income and working-class Americans obtain suitable homes.

HUD works with local organizations to foster community development and to diminish discriminatory practices that limit the availability of homes to minority groups; in particular, HUD offers a variety of grants and low-interest mortgages to needy communities and individuals. For example, HUD works with the PIH (Public and Indian Housing) to provide funds for rental vouchers and to assist local PHA (public housing agencies) in developing healthy communities. Likewise, HUD works with the Office of Community Planning and Development (CPD) to provide funds to state and local government and nonprofit organizations to assist the homeless. These HUD funds help local administrators remove the homeless from the streets to temporary shelters and, eventually, to public or low-cost housing.

Public and subsidized housing is a major aspect of HUD. HUD oversees programs that help provide low-cost public housing, but its focus has recently switched to rent subsidies and vouchers that give tenants greater freedom to choose where they want to live. For example, the Section 8 certificate program allocates rent subsidies to pay landlords the difference between the rent and what the tenants can pay, thus allowing low-income individuals and families (who otherwise would be without adequate homes) to afford housing. Another HUD-assisted program is Homeownership and Opportunity for People Everywhere (HOPE), which is an attempt to phase out dilapidated and crime-ridden public housing developments. HOPE improves troubled public housing developments, provides low-interest FHA mortgages and insurance and vouchers to help low-income households meet rent payments, assists local and nonprofit programs in addressing the problems of homelessness, and allocates Community Development Block Grants (CDBG) to help communities improve available housing, construct or improve public facilities such as sewers, and stimulate general economic growth. Since HOPE began in 1993, HUD has allocated over $4 billion to improve public housing by integrating low-income residents into the larger community and setting up programs to help residents obtain skills. In particular, HOPE funds have eased the transition from large-scale public housing complexes (such as Pruitt–Igoe in St. Louis and the Robert Taylor Homes in Chicago) to lower-density units. Such architectural distinctions make a large difference in the quality of life, and the HOPE program is a concerted attempt to improve the structural elements of public housing while supporting the self-sufficiency of residents.

Another significant HUD program is the CDBG, which began in 1974 as a way to help states and local organizations build strong communities; since then, CDBG grants have provided over $95 billion. CDBG funds are restricted to three uses: to aid low- and moderate-income households, to address the problems of slums or blight, and to correct threats to safety and health. Local officials have primary responsibility for how they spend CDBG funds, but at least 70 percent must benefit low- and moderate-income individuals or households, and HUD has the authority to determine that local officials spend the funds in an appropriate manner. HUD follows a strict plan when allocating CDBG grants: 70 percent of the funds go to cities with more than 50,000 residents and 30 percent go to smaller communities. As these programs show, HUD works to improve the availability of adequate housing to low- and moderate-income Americans, and its primary focus is on allocating funds to state and local organizations that engage in the hands-on work. Overall, HUD programs have improved the housing choices that are available to Americans living in near-poverty conditions. However, it does little for those at the very bottom of the social and economic spectrum, and homelessness and inadequate housing remain serious problems across the nation.

See also: Federal Housing Administration (FHA); Homelessness

Sources: Bauman, John F., Roger Biles, and Kristin M. Szylvian, eds., *From the Tenements to the Taylor Homes: In Search of an Urban Housing Policy in Twentieth-Century America* (University Park: The Pennsylvania State University Press, 2000); HUD (http://www.hud.gov); Patterson, James T., *America's Struggle against Poverty in the Twentieth Century* (Cambridge, MA: Harvard University Press, 2000).

DEPARTMENT OF LABOR. The Department of Labor (DOL) is the federal government agency that administers employment policy. Created at the end of the Taft presidency in 1913, the DOL built on the success of previous federal labor programs, such as the Bureau of Labor, which was created in 1884. DOL programs provide assistance to job seekers, wage earners, and retirees in both an informational and an administrative and legal capacity. An example of the DOL's informative role is the annual publication of an occupational handbook that outlines the expected salary range, educational requirements, and general working conditions of most major occupations in America. In its administrative and legal capacity, the

DOL works to ensure that all employees have safe working conditions and are paid at least the minimum wage. The DOL works with employers to ensure that employees have access to retirement and health care benefits, and it monitors nationwide economic changes that may affect employment patterns and lessen unemployment.

Some branches of the DOL are the Employees' Compensation Appeals Board, the Bureau of Labor Statistics, the Employment and Training Administration, the Employee Benefits Security Administration, the Occupational Safety and Health Administration, the Women's Bureau, and the Office of Public Affairs. All of these agencies perform in research, legal-enforcement, or policymaking capacities. The Office of the Job Corps, a holdover from Lyndon B. Johnson's War on Poverty and previously administered by the Office of Economic Opportunity (OEO), is also part of the DOL.

A primary task of the DOL is to oversee and enforce federal employment and labor laws: the DOL currently monitors more than 180 federal laws that affect nearly 125 million U.S. workers and 10 million employers. Some of the most significant of these are as follows. The Fair Labor Standards Act (FLSA), which sets standards for wages (all employees must receive at least the minimum wage) and overtime pay (at least one and one-half the normal pay rate) for both public and private employment. The FLSA also limits the maximum number of hours that children under the age of sixteen may work outside of the family and outlaws children less than eighteen years of age from working in "dangerous" jobs. The Occupational Safety and Health (OSH) Act establishes standards for safe and healthy work environments. The Occupational Safety and Health Administration (OSHA) oversees OSH regulations in private and public employment; the OSHA requires employers to provide employees with a working environment that is free from significant health hazards. When employees are hurt on the job, the Federal Employees' Compensation Act (FECA), administered by the Office of Workers Compensation Programs (OWCP), gives workers the right to medical care and disability compensation. Likewise, the Employee Retirement Income Security Act (ERISA) ensures that employers offer sufficient pension or welfare benefit plans for eligible employees. The DOL also regulates labor unions. The 1959 Labor-Management Reporting and Disclosure Act ensures that no union can take unfair advantage of its members. The Act requires labor unions to file financial reports annually and to establish fair standards for electing union officers.

The DOL also administers programs that protect the rights of wage earners and immigrant workers. The Migrant and Seasonal Agricultural Worker Protection Act, part of the Wage and Hour Division, oversees the employment of migrant and seasonal agricultural workers, many of whom are of Hispanic descent. This act sets standards for wages and for the housing and transportation of these workers and requires employers to disclose specifics about whom they hire. The FLSA also sets standards for the employment of migrant and seasonal agricultural workers. The FLSA does not require employers to pay migrant workers overtime, but it does require employers to pay at least minimum wage if at least seven full-time workers are employed. In addition, the Immigration and Nationality Act limits employers' ability to hire temporary workers from outside the United States unless they can obtain official certification from the Employment and Training Administration that American workers are not able, willing, or of sufficient number to perform the work.

See also: Immigrants

Sources: DOL (www.dol.gov); Department of Labor (DOL) (http://www.usa.gov/Agencies/Federal/Executive/Labor.shtml); Patterson, James T., *America's Struggle against Poverty in the Twentieth Century* (Cambridge, MA: Harvard University Press, 2000).

DISEASE AND THE POOR. The rising costs of health care in the United States have spawned a national debate about whether or not health care, especially as manifested by health insurance, is a right or a privilege. In twenty-first century America, as in previous centuries, the very poor suffer the most from disease because of squalid living conditions, inadequate diet, ignorance about health issues, and insufficient funds to pay for care. Federal programs such as Medicare and Medicaid, in place since the 1960s, provide some relief for the poor, although such relief is rarely adequate to meet the costs of prescription drugs, lab results, surgery, and extended hospital stays.

Colonial America. Although status and wealth have always had an impact on disease and health, the rich and poor in colonial America, compared to today, tended to be more equal in respect to health care. Colonial America had no medical schools and few trained physicians. Health care was usually the domain of the amateur practitioner—the barber surgeon, chirurgeon, midwife, pastor, master, or parent. Books such as John Tennent's *Every Man his own Doctor: Or The Poor Planter's Physician* (1734) provided common sense, traditional, and Native American remedies for ailments ranging from the common cold to cancer. The seemingly unlimited botanical resources of America encouraged amateur botanists to treat themselves and others with a variety of folk remedies. The ability to collect herbs in a forest or garden did not depend on personal wealth and status. Such *ad hoc* medical treatment explains in part the mortality rate of colonial children. On average, one in ten children in New England died in infancy—although the percentage increased during epidemics. Only 50 percent of Chesapeake youth made it to adulthood during the colonial period. Children, especially of the poor, were struck down by smallpox, diphtheria, yellow fever, and malaria; intestinal complaints caused by worms were all too common.

From the beginning, Americans have felt an obligation to care for the unfortunate physically or mentally ill members of the community. The earliest cities, such as Boston, remunerated local physicians who cared for impoverished townspeople. In 1731 Boston appointed a physician whose sole task was to treat the city's poor. Towns such as Portsmouth, New Hampshire, paid physicians to inoculate the poor for smallpox. New Hampshire in 1680 passed a law requiring that medical expenses generated by the care of the poor be passed on to the town of the poor person's origin. Townspeople were paid to care for sick or mentally ill poor. In the eighteenth century, the impoverished mentally and physically ill were increasingly placed in almshouses with the sane and well. Benevolent physicians sometimes treated the inmates of the almshouse for no charge. The institutionalization of the poor took a different turn (for the better) with the creation of hospitals to care for the sick poor. Of early significance was the Pennsylvania Hospital, opened in Philadelphia in 1752. Founded in part by Benjamin Franklin and consistent with his beliefs in the practice of charity and benevolence toward the downtrodden, the Pennsylvania

Hospital initially treated the sick poor, especially those with terminal illnesses who had nowhere to go to suffer through their final illnesses and die. Philadelphia physicians who practiced at the Pennsylvania Hospital treated their poor charges for free. Franklin's promotional tract, *Some Account of the Pennsylvania Hospital* (1754), brought early notoriety to the institution. From the beginning, the Pennsylvania Hospital practiced the "reception and cure of lunaticks"; such treatment and care of the impoverished mentally ill became a trademark for late eighteenth- and early nineteenth-century American physicians. Benjamin Rush, for example, America's most famous physician, was also one of the first to study "diseases of the mind," recording his insights in the 1812 book *Medical Inquiries and Observations upon the Diseases of the Mind.*

Another early American institution that housed the impoverished sick was the pesthouse, which was a place, usually on a secluded island, where those who were ill with deadly diseases, such as smallpox, were quarantined from the rest of the population. Sick servants, redemptioners, and convicts arriving from England and Europe often had to wait aboard ship for their illness to mitigate unless local authorities had already whisked them away to the pesthouse. The eighteenth-century medical technique to prevent smallpox epidemics was inoculation, which involved taking the blood or tissue of a person who was ill with smallpox and purposely transposing it to a well person; the inoculated person, it was hoped, would develop a less virulent form of the disease that would make them forever immune. Because the inoculated person was contagious, he or she was quarantined at the pesthouse. During the Revolutionary War, inoculation was practiced widely and sometimes administered to the poor for free, as a public health measure. Boston's pesthouse was at Spectacle Island; Newport's pesthouse was at Coaster's Harbor Island; Philadelphia's pesthouse was at Province Island. "As Christians and men," wrote a Philadelphian in 1738, referring to those redemptioners awaiting aboard ship for admission to the city, "we are obliged to make a charitable provision for the sick stranger, and not by confining him to a ship, inhumanly expose him to fresh miseries when he hopes that his sufferings are soon to be mitigated."

Nineteenth-Century Reforms. During the 1800s scientists and physicians in America and Europe made important discoveries in public health and in understanding how disease occurs and is spread. Scientists realized that the increasing population of American cities led to unhealthy conditions. They had learned that microorganisms are the cause of contagious disease and that disease-causing microorganisms thrive in certain environments. Increasing awareness of the causes and contagion of disease resulted in the continuation of some practices directed toward the sick poor, such as the quarantine system, as well as the development of sanitary commissions directed toward bettering public health.

American public health advocates worked in the wake of the publication of Edwin Chadwick's *Report on the Sanitary Condition of the Labouring Population of Great Britain* in 1842. Chadwick argued that poor sanitation led to the spread of disease through densely populated areas. He was an advocate of the standard medical theory of the time (before the discoveries of Louis Pasteur)—that miasmic air, caused by rotting organic filth, resulted in disease. At the same time, cities such as New York were experiencing a dramatic increase in population that included impoverished neighborhoods exuding physical and moral filth, which inspired the City Inspector of New York, Dr. John Griscom, to publish *The Sanitary Condition of the Laboring Population of New York* in 1845. In the words of Alexander Von Hoffman, Griscom argued that "when applied to the urban poor . . . the physical disorder and dilapidation of the shabby residential districts determined, or helped to determine, the physical and moral conditions of their inhabitants." Robert Hartley, a founder of the New York Association for Improving the Condition of the Poor (AICP), argued for the presence of "miasmatic air" as a cause of immorality and disease in crowded New York neighborhoods. The AICP declared in 1847 that the poor "suffer from sickness and premature mortality; their ability for self-maintenance is thereby destroyed; social habits and morals are debased, and a vast amount of wretchedness, pauperism, and crime is produced."

Other mid- to late nineteenth-century reformers advocated altering the physical environment to produce important social, moral, and emotional results, thus breaking from the cycle of poverty. Charles Loring Brace was a minister and missionary who worked for the AICP and founded the Children's Aid Society in 1853, which provided children with a host of services, ranging from medical care to education to direct relief. Noteworthy was Brace's implementation of the orphan trains, which brought thousands of children from the East Coast to the West, where they lived in foster homes until they reached majority. Dorothea Dix was a mental health reformer who investigated the vile treatment of the poor and criminal insane in prisons, almshouses, and asylums. She tirelessly lobbied state and federal government for reforms, including the opening of mental hospitals to treat the insane. Julia Lathrop also worked for the care and support of poor children with mental illnesses. Lathrop was involved with Hull House, the Chicago United Charities, and the U.S. Children's Bureau. Lillian Wald of Ohio, who was similarly involved in child health issues, opened the Henry Street Settlement among the poor of New York and, as a nurse, offered care to indigent children.

Advances in knowledge about the causes and spread of disease in the late nineteenth into the twentieth centuries resulted in commensurate developments for the prevention and treatment of disease in the poor. Understanding of infectious disease and contagion—as well as the development of antibiotics and vaccinations, particularly to treat and prevent cholera, diphtheria, polio scarlet fever, tetanus, tuberculosis, whooping cough, and yellow fever—resulted in a decline in child mortality rates, even as urban population grew. Hospitals, once the domain of the dying pauper, were, by the twentieth century, on the forefront of treatment and prevention; the numbers of hospitals grew from hundreds in the nineteenth century to more than 6,000 by the end of the twentieth century.

From the late nineteenth to the twentieth centuries, the federal government increasingly took the lead in health care for the poor. Federal involvement was instigated because of cholera and yellow fever epidemics in the 1870s, which led to the creation of the National Board of Health. Local, state, and federal public health officials worked to alleviate the problems, such as inadequate plumbing and sewage, unsanitary public venues (such as restaurants), and air and water pollution, causing poor public health, especially among the poor. Federal agencies created during the twentieth century that directly or indirectly affected health care and the poor include the Food and Drug Administration, the National Institutes of Health (NIH), and the Centers for Disease Control, all organized under the executive office of the Department of Health and Human Services. At the close of World War II, the Hill-Burton Act (1946) was passed by Congress, authorizing the federal government to sponsor the erection of hospitals in rural America. During the

1960s, Lyndon Johnson's Great Society program created Medicare, a program to provide health care for the elderly poor.

Despite government involvement and programs such as Medicaid that help the disadvantaged, the United States has no universal health care program. At the beginning of the twenty-first century, 40,000,000 Americans, mostly the poor, lack health insurance, even as the costs of health care skyrocket. Minority groups are at a higher risk for obesity, cancer, low birth weight, and infant mortality. According to the National Institute of Child Health and Human Development, one in four African American children live in poverty, with consequent health risks. The NIH reports that African Americans have a 25 percent higher cancer mortality rate compared to the overall population. The NIH also reports that diabetes has grown to become a serious illness (four to eight times greater than in the overall population) for Native Americans, who traditionally have high poverty rates as well; Native Americans also have a higher rate of dependency on tobacco than the general population.

See also: Institutionalization of the Poor; Medicaid; Medicare; Redemptioners

Sources: Bridenbaugh, Carl, *Cities in Revolt* (New York: Oxford, 1955); Bridenbaugh, Carl, *Cities in the Wilderness* (New York: Oxford, 1938); Grob, Gerald N., *The Deadly Truth: A History of Disease in America* (Cambridge, MA: Harvard University Press, 2002); Hoffman, Alexander von, "The Origins of American Housing Reform." Joint Center for Housing Studies, Harvard University (1998); Hofstadter, Richard, *America in 1750: A Social Portrait* (New York: Random House, 1971); Mazzari, Louis, "Child Health" in *Encyclopedia of New England* (New Haven: Yale University Press, 2005); National Institute of Health (www.nih.gov); Rosen, George, *A History of Public Health* (Baltimore: Johns Hopkins University Press, 1993); Stevens, Rosemary, *In Sickness and Wealth: American Hospitals in the Twentieth Century* (Baltimore: Johns Hopkins University Press, 1999).

DRUGS, ALCOHOL, AND THE POOR. The idea that the poor are impoverished because of their immoral lifestyle—such as addiction to drugs and alcohol—is a basic tenet of the pathological view of poverty; this view led to the notion that there was a "culture of poverty." One of the basic assumptions of the pathological view is that the majority of society's most impoverished persons are unemployed and "undeserving" because of substance abuse—that addiction to drugs and alcohol undermines their ability to hold a job. The pathological view also maintains that there is a direct connection between substance abuse and crime: that addicts—whether panhandlers, beggars, inner-city blacks, or the homeless—become violent because of a need to obtain the money to support their addiction.

Alcohol has played a mixed role in American culture. In the 1700s and early 1800s, taverns served as social gathering places for diverse social classes in cities such as Philadelphia and Boston. The mixing of social classes ceased in the early nineteenth century after the rise of industrialization, but taverns continued to serve as centers of urban politics throughout the nineteenth century. Likewise, the immigrant experience in large urban centers such as Chicago and New York revolved around neighborhood taverns, where working-class men met and socialized after work. In part, the temperance movement of the late nineteenth century—that led to Prohibition—was motivated by anti-immigrant fervor; outlawing alcohol disrupted the patterns of immigrant life and targeted the immorality that the reformers believed taverns condoned.

The anti-immigrant aspect of the temperance movement is a good example of how images of substance abuse are inseparable from racial and ethnic constructs. Today, images of impoverished African Americans in inner-city ghettos flood the media; similarly, the "myth" of the largely ethnic "underclass" (the most impoverished and ostracized element of society) is associated with pathologic drug use and immorality. The debate over Eugene Richards's photos of "the front lines of violence, drug addiction, poverty, racism, and cancer," in *Cocaine True Cocaine Blue* (1994) illustrates this assumption. Filled with close-up images of shockingly brutal and self-destructive behavior, this book associated hard-core drug use with African Americans. "Why are nearly all of the people in these photographs black?" asked the *New York Times*. "Why is the white aspect of drug addiction so consistently invisible?" To this charge, Richards replied: "the last thing I noticed about the pregnant women smoking crack, the addicts dying after shooting up, the young girls prostituting themselves, the drug boys with automatic weapons or the mothers grieving for their dead children was their skin color." Instead, Richards sought to force the viewer "to be horrified by . . . the waste of life" inherent in hard-core drug addiction; he argued that it was only coincidence that the gruesome images were of blacks.

According to the 2006 National Survey on Drug Use and Health, American Indians have the highest rate, at 13.7 percent, of illicit drug use. Next are African Americans at 9.8 percent; 8.9 percent of mixed-race individuals; 8.5 percent of whites; 6.9 percent of Hispanics; and 3.6 percent of Asians. The 2005 National Survey report reported that more than 20 percent of white and Hispanic high school students in the United States were current marijuana users; the report listed 14 percent of students from "other" race categories, including blacks, as current users of marijuana.

At the same time, the Bureau of Justice Statistics released data showing that, in 2004, more than 50 percent of blacks in federal and state prisons admitted using illegal drugs in the month prior to their arrest. In 2006, there were 1,376,792 arrests in the United States for drug abuse. Of those arrested, nearly 64 percent were white and 35 percent were black (the report did not consider Hispanics as a separate race). At the end of 2003, of the nearly 1.3 million prison inmates in the fifty states, 250,900 were imprisoned for drug-related offenses. Over half of these inmates, 133,100, were black, 64,800 were white, and 50,100 were Hispanic. As these data show, a racial aspect to the relation of drug use and incarceration, but it is not possible to claim that one race or ethnicity has a greater predisposition.

See also: African Americans and Poverty (post-slavery); American Indians and Poverty; Race and Ethnicity; Urban Poor

Sources: Callow, Alexander B. Jr., ed., *American Urban History: An Interpretive Reader with Commentaries,* 3rd ed. (New York: Oxford University Press, 1982); Office of National Drug Control Policy (http://www.ondcp.gov/); Patterson, James T., *America's Struggle against Poverty in the Twentieth Century* (Cambridge, MA: Harvard University Press, 2000); Richards, Eugene, *Cocaine True Cocaine Blue* (New York: Aperture, 1994); Richards, Eugene, "Cocaine True Cocaine Blue," Letter to the Editor, *New York Times* (March 6, 1994); Staples, Brent, "Coke Wars," *New York Times* (February 6, 1994).

E

ECONOMIC OPPORTUNITY ACT. The Economic Opportunity Act (EOA) was the first significant domestic legislation enacted by the Johnson Administration; the programs funded by this legislation formed the basis of the War on Poverty. Passed in August 1964, the EOA had the stated goal "to mobilize the human and financial resources of the Nation to combat poverty in the United States." The Johnson Administration described the reasons for this Act as follows: "Although the economic well-being and prosperity of the United States have progressed to a level surpassing any achieved in world history, and although these benefits are widely shared throughout the Nation, poverty continues to be the lot of a substantial number of our people." With the EOA, the Johnson Administration sought to guide the United States to "its full economic and social potential," emphasizing that "every individual," regardless of race and social or economic background, had the duty and the right to "contribute to the full extent of his capabilities and to participate in the workings of our society." Thus the EOA was Johnson's attempt to "eliminate the paradox of poverty in the midst of plenty in this Nation by opening to everyone the opportunity for education and training, the opportunity to work, and the opportunity to live in decency and dignity."

Designed to put into practice the domestic reforms promised by the Kennedy administration, the EOA gave power to the Office of Economic Opportunity (OEO), which set up federal programs such as the Job Corps, Head Start, VISTA, Neighborhood Youth Corps, and the Community Action Program (CAP). The purpose of the Job Corps was to prepare disadvantaged youth for "the responsibilities of citizenship and to increase the employability of young men and young women aged sixteen through twenty-one by providing them in rural and urban residential centers with education, vocational training, useful work experience, including work directed toward the conservation of natural resources, and other appropriate activities." Financial support for the Job Corps was low. The EOA authorized the program's director to make agreements with federal, state, and local public agencies—and also with private organizations—to establish new camps and to supply operational expenses, but these contributions proved inadequate. As a result, the Job Corps experienced great financial difficulties, had too many applicants, and never achieved its goals. In addition to the Job Corps, the EOA established programs to facilitate educational and vocational training among low-income youth. These additional programs included work-training programs to "provide useful work experience opportunities for unemployed young men and young women" and work-study programs to "stimulate and promote the part-time employment of students in institutions of higher education who are from low-income families."

In an additional effort to counteract racial and class division, the OEO implemented the Head Start program, which was designed to help underprivileged minority children adapt better to school and to prepare them for making well-informed decisions in later life (such as not joining gangs). Unfortunately, Head Start did not return long-term results, because, despite short-term improvements, most Head Start graduates did not perform better in secondary school.

The most infamous aspect of the EOA was the CAP, intended to provide

> services, assistance, and other activities of sufficient scope and size to give promise of progress toward elimination of poverty or a cause or causes of poverty through developing employment opportunities, improving human performance, motivation, and productivity, or bettering the conditions under which people live, learn, and work.

The CAP attempted to involve the poor in the development of its policies. This policy of "maximum feasible participation" of the poor received much publicity because it angered existing policymakers, which hampered the CAP's ability to pass significant legislation. Although the EOA intended the CAP to give the poor—a large proportion of whom were African American—"equal political opportunity" and greater control of their situation, it led to distrust in Johnson's War on Poverty and to an increase in the split between the wealthy and the poor.

Because of the Job Corps's lack of funding, Head Start's lack of significant results, and the CAP's controversial policies, the 1964 EOA failed to accomplish its primary goals. The EOA was the backbone of Johnson's War on Poverty and the Great Society program, so the EOA's lack of success placed in jeopardy Johnson's ambitious plans for domestic reform. When Republican Richard Nixon became president in 1968, he phased out the EOA and discontinued its liberal programs.

See also: Community Action Program; Head Start; Job Corps; Office of Economic Opportunity; VISTA; War on Poverty

Sources: Economic Opportunity Act (http://www2.volstate.edu/geades/FinalDocs/1960s/eoa.htm); Bremner, Robert H., Gary W. Reichard, and Richard Hopkins, eds., *American Choices: Social Dilemma and Public Policy since 1960* (Columbus: Ohio State University Press, 1986); Johnson, Lyndon B., "The War on Poverty" (1964), *Public Papers of the Presidents of the United States, Lyndon B. Johnson, Book II: 1965* (Washington, D.C.: Government Printing Office, 1966); Johnson, Lyndon B., "Great Society Speech" (1964), *Public Papers of the Presidents of the United States, Lyndon B. Johnson, Book I: 1963–1964* (Washington, D.C.: Government Printing Office, 1965), 704–707); Patterson, James T., *America's Struggle against Poverty in the Twentieth Century* (Cambridge, MA: Harvard University Press, 2000); Trattner, Walter I., *From Poor Law to Welfare State*, 6th ed. (New York: Simon and Schuster, 1999).

EDUCATION. According to a 2005 report of the U.S. Census Bureau, "educational attainment is the social variable that often displays the largest socioeconomic differential . . . because education affects income and occupation." This is not a new idea. Throughout American history, social reformers have realized that acquiring a skill, profession, or trade was the most common way to move "up" the social and economic scale. This realization led, among other things, to compulsory education of American youth, but the development of public schools is not the only result of such awareness. Education also has a direct relation to quality of life. As noted by the Census Bureau, there is a positive correlation between education level and health: more-educated people have increased "ability to understand public health messages" and more-educated people tend to have a greater awareness of their role and surroundings, and thus a higher sense of self-worth.

The role of education in colonial America was mixed. Most youths entered society through acquiring trade from their family or a tradesman who offered them an apprenticeship. Thus, liberal arts education—the foundation of most modern schools and colleges—was often limited to the very wealthy, as well as to those entering a profession such as law or the clergy, which required more extensive knowledge. The Massachusetts Bay Colony was the first to pass a "universal" education requirement, in 1642, but its function was not to educate the public in the modern sense, but rather to produce citizens cognizant of their social and religious duty. The first institutions of higher education, Harvard College and Yale College, focused largely on training young men for the clergy.

In the nineteenth century, the role of education changed significantly to fit new societal needs. Increased immigration altered the social makeup of the nation's major cities, many of which were overrun with impoverished and unskilled persons. Social workers such as Jane Addams set up settlement houses to provide life-skill education to impoverished wives, children, and immigrant men, but reform-minded persons—social workers and policymakers—soon realized that the problem was too large for isolated relief efforts to control. Compulsory education—first enacted by Massachusetts in 1852 and adopted soon after by other states—served to keep children and youth busy, off the streets, and out of dead-end and dangerous jobs and to open the doors of opportunity. Compulsory education served as a means to assimilate immigrants into the American way of life; policymakers and reformers used education as a tool to remake society. In striking contrast, late nineteenth and early twentieth-century Pragmatist John Dewey advocated a hands-on approach to education to engage students in studies that intrigued them as individuals: he viewed education as a means to self-realization rather than a social tool.

During the mid-nineteenth century, colleges and universities were founded throughout America. The 1862 Morrill Act established "Land Grant" colleges, state-run public institutions that expanded college education to new, more practical areas of study such as agriculture, mechanical arts, and home economics. Education at land grant colleges cost substantially less than at private liberal arts institutions, which allowed less-affluent Americans to obtain a college education. In the 1860s racial segregation negated the law's effect on African American educational opportunity, but, in the following decades, black-only institutions were established. Most state-run colleges in the South remained segregated until the 1960s and 1970s.

The 1954 *Brown v. the Board of Education* Supreme Court decision significantly altered American education. In its decision, the Court struck down the "separate but equal" clause that had enabled states to segregate schools into white and black.

Although nearly a decade passed before real changes began to occur (especially in the Deep South), the *Brown v. the Board* ruling that "separate educational facilities are inherently unequal" changed the way that public elementary, secondary, and universities approached their role. The continuing woes of the educational system in the late-twentieth century—after integration—demonstrated that, in many respects, the impact of poverty on the educational system was more considerable than that of race.

Part of Lyndon B. Johnson's War on Poverty, the Elementary and Secondary Education Act of 1965 (ESEA), gave financial support to low-income districts to help offset the unequal funding created by local subsidy of schools. This legislation did not solve the problem, however, because wealthy districts still received more funding, and most states did not put all of the tax revenue raised for education into a common fund for equal distribution. For this reason, the amount of funding that a school receives often provides insight into the wealthy and poor areas of a particular city: social class, not racial distinction, is the primary division of post-1960 urban areas. Though most if not all school districts were integrated by the end of the twentieth century, affluent school districts had noticeably better facilities and test scores than impoverished districts. In short, there is a direct correlation between funding resources and performance that has nothing to do with racial or ethnic makeup.

The philosophy that education is the primary means of economic and social advancement has remained popular through the twentieth century. Federally funded programs such as Head Start, which was designed to incorporate minorities and the poor into mainstream society, were the twentieth-century equivalent of settlement house life-skill education programs (for example, Hull House): the focus was on preparing low-income children to succeed as mainstream Americans. At times this approach has received harsh criticism. The 1983 "A Nation at Risk" report issued by the National Commission on Excellence in Education is a significant example. This report, designed to scare educators into approving substantial changes— notably an increased emphasis on math and science—decried America's declining role as a world leader in education; the report implied that Russia would soon—if it had not already done so—eclipse the United State's technological capacity. The report also indicated that "23 million American adults are functionally illiterate by the simplest test of everyday reading, writing, and comprehension," a finding that, if accurate, signified the failure of the public education system to help low-income persons advance socially and economically.

To address the findings of "A Nation at Risk," Congress approved a series of amendments to the ESEA that culminated in the 2001 "No Child Left Behind" (NCLB) program. Signed by George W. Bush, NCLB emphasized standardized tests as a way to determine school performance based on equality of race and income. The NCLB program explicitly singled out low-income areas, such as the inner city and depressed rural areas, in an effort to help all Americans—regardless of location, race, ethnicity, and income level—enjoy the lifestyle of mainstream middle-class America.

See also: War on Poverty

Sources: Bremner, Robert H., Gary W. Reichard, and Richard Hopkins, eds., *American Choices: Social Dilemma and Public Policy since 1960* (Columbus: Ohio State University Press, 1986); Elementary and Secondary School Act of 1965, Higher Education Act of 1965,

1998 Higher Education Act Amendments, at the History of American Education Web Project (http://www.nd.edu/~rbarger/www7/); National Education Association (http://www.nea.org/esea/index.html); No Child Left Behind, Public Law 107–110, 107th Congress; U.S. Department of Education (www.ed.gov/nclb/); The White House, Washington, D.C. (www.whitehouse.gov/news/reports/no-child-left-behind.html).

ELEMENTARY AND SECONDARY SCHOOL ACT. Implemented in 1965 as part of Lyndon B. Johnson's War on Poverty program, the Elementary and Secondary School Act (ESEA) emphasized the need to assist low-income and minority groups in public schools. Commissioner of Education Francis Keppel designed and introduced the bill, which allocated extensive resources—primarily federal grants—to fund elementary and secondary school programs for children of low-income families. Specifically, the Act enabled schools to extend library resources, buy more up-to-date textbooks and instructional materials; established supplemental educational services and centers; funded additional research into educational techniques; and strengthened state departments of education. The ESEA gave financial support to low-income districts to help offset the unequal funding created by local subsidy of schools, but the legislation did not solve the problem, because wealthy districts still received more funding than poorer districts. Most states do not put all of the tax revenue raised for education in a common fund and distribute it equally. For this reason, the amount of funding that a school district receives often mirrors the financial status of the residents of the area: in general, wealthier areas (such as the suburbs) tend to enjoy better-funded schools and higher scores in national standardized testing.

The ESEA explicitly acknowledged its focus on low-income and minority children. In Section 201 of the Act, Congress acknowledged that low-income families had "special educational needs" and laid out its plans to address the problems faced in areas with "concentrations of low-income families," where insufficient funding hindered the "ability of local educational agencies to support adequate educational programs." Thus, in 1965, as part of the War on Poverty, Congress determined to "provide financial assistance . . . to local educational agencies serving areas with concentrations of children from low-income families to expand and improve their educational programs by various means (including preschool programs) which contribute to meeting the special educational needs of educationally deprived children."

Soon after its implementation, the ESEA allocated $1 billion to address these aims. In a speech to Congress, Johnson said that the ESEA would soon "offer new hope to tens of thousands" of preschoolers from low-income families and would enable "five million grade-school children to overcome their greatest barrier to progress: poverty." Of the measures of the Act itself, Johnson stated that "every one of the billion dollars" spent on the program "will come back tenfold as school dropouts change to school graduates" and thus become functioning mainstream citizens. Johnson's comments reflected his belief that once structural barriers—lack of money, access to education, and the means of advancement—were overcome, the poor would learn to help themselves and thereby end the need for future welfare relief. Not all contemporaries agreed with Johnson's liberal outlook: for example, the 1966 Coleman Report argued that structural improvements, such as the quality of facilities and teachers and the provision of early-education programs such as Head Start, would affect the situation of the poor only slightly.

The subsequent years demonstrated that Johnson's ideals were unfounded. By the end of the 1960s, most War on Poverty programs had lost favor and been discontinued; the new president, Richard Nixon, did not share Johnson's liberal domestic policies, but he did not abruptly discontinue all of Johnson's programs. The ESEA, for example, remained in effect for several decades; conservatives also recognized that providing education to low-income children was a significant issue.

The ESEA has undergone several significant amendments. The first, the 1968 Bilingual Education Act, addressed the issue of non-English-speaking children—primarily Spanish-speaking students in the South and in large urban areas—by allocating federal aid to school districts with significant numbers of non-English-speaking students. Congress passed more significant amendments in 1998. One part of the 1998 bill was a renewed emphasis on children from families receiving welfare. The bill called for research to determine "the effectiveness of educational approaches (including vocational and post-secondary education approaches) and rapid employment approaches to helping welfare recipients and other low-income adults become employed and economically self-sufficient." This research would specifically focus on providing "a comparison of the effects of programs emphasizing a vocational or postsecondary educational approach to programs emphasizing a rapid employment approach," examining "the impact of postsecondary education on the educational attainment of the children of [welfare] recipients," and providing

> information regarding short and long-term employment, wages, duration of employment, poverty rates, sustainable economic self-sufficiency, prospects for career advancement or wage increases, access to quality child care, placement in employment with benefits including health care, life insurance and retirement, and related program outcomes.

The most substantial change to the ESEA was the 2002 implementation of the No Child Left Behind Act (NCLB), under the direction of President George W. Bush, which retained the basic ideals of the ESEA but significantly altered the federal government's approach to the issue.

See also: Education; No Child Left Behind; War on Poverty

Sources: Bremner, Robert H., Gary W. Reichard, and Richard Hopkins, eds., *American Choices: Social Dilemma and Public Policy since 1960* (Columbus: Ohio State University Press, 1986); U.S. Department of Education (www.ed.gov/nclb/); Elementary and Secondary School Act of 1966, at the History of American Education Web Project (http://www.nd.edu/~rbarger/www7/).

ENVIRONMENTAL THEORY OF POVERTY. The basic premise of the environmental theory of poverty is that the environment where a person lives and works is the primary shaper of the individual's social, economic, and moral outlook. This perspective has enjoyed various stages of both popularity and disrepute throughout the nineteenth and twentieth century in America; nevertheless, it has affected the way that social workers have approached reform and has greatly influenced America's response to the poor. Like its opposite perspective—the idea of a "culture" that sustains poverty from generation to generation—environmentalism is an oversimplified approach, but it does provide some insights into the causes and effects of poverty.

The environmental perspective was especially strong among Progressive reformers in the late nineteenth and early twentieth centuries. Reformers and settlement house activists such as Jane Addams and Jacob Riis publicized the environmental movement among social workers, who argued that poverty was caused by decrepit surroundings and moral failings, not by ingrained inferiority. The basic argument of environmentalists was that the provision of better housing and education would improve the condition of the poor. In *How the Other Half Lives* (1890), Jacob Riis described in great length the terrible living conditions of New York City's tenement districts, using photographs and illustrations to emphasize that the dilapidated conditions of the city's poor—most of whom were immigrants—was the primary cause of the high incidence of crime in New York.

Reformers and social workers came to realize that the best way to alter the environment was to implement comprehensive neighborhood reconstruction programs. Settlement houses, such as Addams's Hull House in Chicago, which opened in 1889, were one solution. Hull House was the nation's first successful settlement house; it served as a community center in an impoverished neighborhood, offering practical training to help immigrant women learn habits and skills to assist their adaptation to the American way of life. Hull House provided a place for children to play and receive a basic education, offered meals for the hungry, and served as a training ground for other social reformers, as well as a model for subsequent settlement homes.

A prominent example of environmentalism in the mid-twentieth century was the 1967 report of the Kerner Commission, which investigated the causes of the "ghetto" race riots in cities across the nation. The Kerner Commission reported that the riots were the result of America's ingrained inequality, especially the segregation of whites and blacks into two very distinct societies. The Commission emphasized the effect of the depressing conditions endured by African Americans and minorities in the decaying inner city, which were in direct contrast to the living conditions of the affluent middle class and elites. To prevent additional riots, the Commission proposed the implementation of a comprehensive plan to change the structure of American society—in effect, to alter the environment of the urban poor and thus pacify them. Although President Lyndon B. Johnson refused to accept the Commission's recommendations, the Commission's report illustrated the continuing impact of environment on the attitudes and perception of the poor.

The environmental theory has remained strong in recent years. Conservative welfare-reform policies, such as the now-defunct Welfare to Work program (which ended in 2004), imposed strict limits on welfare in an attempt to instill a stronger work ethic in the poor. The program bussed participants from impoverished areas to work in more affluent areas—thus the program identified poverty as a function of impoverished areas. The program's emphasis on work, not welfare, also connected to the environmental perspective, because the program's supporters hoped that persons who were formerly dependent on welfare and lived in depressed areas would learn to support themselves. This particular program failed because, among other reasons, the causes of poverty are too complicated to be simplified in terms of where a person lives. Like the cultural view of poverty, the environmental perspective is, at best, a partial explanation. Although environment obviously has some effect on the perceptions and attitudes of and toward the poor, it is not the only or the most significant cause of poverty. Nevertheless, the focus on the environment has greatly influenced the way that reformers attempted to aid the poor, because most reformers have not experienced firsthand the burdens of extreme poverty.

Environmentalism (and the culture of poverty) explain the complex causes and effects of poverty according to theory, not according to experience.

See also: Addams, Jane; African Americans and Poverty (post-slavery); Progressives

Sources: Atkins, Jacqueline M., ed., *Encyclopedia of Social Work*, 18th ed., 2 vols. (Silver Spring, MD: NASW, 1987); Goldfield, David R., and Blaine A. Brownell, *Urban America: From Downtown to No Town* (Boston: Oxford University Press, 1979); Kerner Commission, "Report of the National Advisory Commission on Civil Disorders" (Washington, D.C.: 1968); Patterson, James T., *America's Struggle against Poverty in the Twentieth Century* (Cambridge, MA: Harvard University Press, 2000); Riis, Jacob, *How the Other Half Lives* (New York: Charles Scribner's Sons, 1890).

EQUAL EMPLOYMENT OPPORTUNITY COMMISSION. Established by the 1964 Civil Rights Act, the Equal Employment Opportunity Commission (EEOC) is the federal agency responsible for limiting workplace discrimination. The Civil Rights Act of 1964 addressed discrimination in areas besides employment—such as education, voting, and public space—but the EEOC did not obtain real power until 1972, when Congress gave it litigation authority. Consequently, despite the early idealism that pervaded the Commission, the real significance of the EEOC is its ability to obtain legal—and thus practical—solutions to counteract discrimination in the workplace.

At its founding in 1964, the EEOC focused on policies of conciliation and education. Title VII of the Civil Rights Act prohibited discrimination based on race, color, national origin, sex, and religion, but the EEOC had little power to enforce employer compliance. At the time, the EEOC was a five-member bipartisan commission that only had authority to investigate complaints that it received about discrimination and to attempt to conciliate disputes between employers and employees. When the EEOC could not work out an agreement, the statute required that the affected individuals bring private lawsuits; if the EEOC discovered regular discrimination patterns by an employer, it could recommend that the Department of Justice initiate litigation.

Charges of discrimination increased every year between 1965 and 1971. In 1966 the EEOC handled 8,854 cases and by 1970 that number had risen to 20,310. To deal with the increase, the EEOC refined its practices and initiated a preventative program. Section 709(c) of Title VII of the 1964 Civil Rights Act gave the Commission the authority to require employers to keep records and to submit reports on the employment status of women and minorities. In 1966 the EEOC required large private companies to submit EEO-1 reports demonstrating the ratio of men and women from five racial or ethnic groups in nine job categories—ranging from low-level jobs such as laborers to high-level supervisory positions. These reports identified possible areas of employment discrimination; the data clearly demonstrated the demographic breakdown of the workforce across the nation. The EEOC was able to discern patterns of racial and gender exclusion and discrimination within job categories and geographic areas. Between 1967 and 1971, the EEOC sponsored public hearings that focused on discrimination in select industries, such as textile factories in the South, New York corporations; and the Los Angeles entertainment industry. These hearings increased public awareness of workplace discrimination, which contributed to Congress's decision to give the EEOC litigation authority in 1972.

The EEOC processed discrimination complaints in several areas. In 1966, for example, the Commission filed 3,254 cases of discrimination of race, 53.1 percent of the year's total cases; 87 cases of religious discrimination, 1.4 percent; 2,053 cases of sex discrimination, 33.5 percent; 131 cases of discrimination of National Origin, 2.1 percent; and 608 unspecified cases, 9.9 percent of the year's total cases. As these data show, the majority of the EEOC's charges were claims of race discrimination; claims of sex discrimination were second. In dealing with such charges, the EEOC followed the "Disparate Impact Theory of Discrimination," which held that discrimination took place not only through intentional acts of discrimination, but also through ostensibly neutral policies that had an adverse impact on minorities or women. Thus the EEOC attempted to delve beneath the surface of impartiality and attack the underlying prejudices that barred the advancement of women and minorities. In 1966 EEOC issued the "Guidelines on Employment Testing Procedures," which publicly stated that Title VII of the Civil Rights Act prohibited "neutral" employment and promotion practices that negatively affected women and minorities.

The Disparate Impact Theory of Discrimination allowed the EEOC to alter legal interpretations of discrimination significantly and thus work to benefit underprivileged groups. In the 1971 *Griggs v. Duke Power Co.* decision, the Supreme Court upheld the EEOC's position, declaring that an employer cannot require that applicants have a high school diploma or pass aptitude tests to be eligible for employment or promotion; such requirements had been used to restrict African Americans to low-level labor positions. In its decision the Court stated that the Civil Rights Act proscribed overt discrimination and also "practices that are fair in form but discriminatory in operation" that do not serve a "business necessity." Moreover, the Court placed the onus on the employer to prove that apparent discriminatory practices are related to job performance. Thus the EEOC successfully altered the legal interpretation of discrimination to a more inclusive definition, which allowed the Commission to obtain more concessions from employers for underprivileged minorities and women.

See also: Culture of Poverty; Race and Ethnicity

Sources: EEOC History: 35th Anniversary: 1965–2000 (http://www.eeoc.gov/abouteeoc/35th/index.html); US Equal Employment Opportunity Commission (EEOC) (www.eeoc.gov/).

F

FAMILY ASSISTANCE PLAN (FAP). Proposed during the Nixon administration as part of the plan to reform the old Aid to Families with Dependent Children (AFDC) program, the Family Assistance Plan (FAP) garnered controversy for its liberal features and was never enacted. The proposed FAP led to a bitter legislative struggle in Congress over the traditional debate between liberals and conservatives on whether the poor are to blame for their situation or whether all of society is at fault. Part of the problem was that the FAP did not satisfy either Republicans or Democrats: despite the early support of President Nixon, the FAP generated criticism from the same conservative Republicans who had criticized Johnson's Great Society, and many liberals criticized FAP as too limited or wrongly motivated. Thus the FAP was a compromise that did not satisfy either side, and the program died in Congress.

As part of his plan to curtail Johnson's liberal Great Society program, Richard Nixon emphasized economic and legal solutions over the welfare state, a switch away from Johnson's liberal "equal opportunity" plan. However, the FAP was in many ways similar to War on Poverty programs such as the Community Action Program (CAP) that confronted established authority; like the CAP, the FAP adopted a puffed-up rhetoric and confrontational style of including the poor on its panels. Although Nixon paid lip service to the FAP, he did not offer tangible support; in practice, the FAP was too liberal and too reminiscent of Johnson's plans. Nixon's plan for the FAP was to nationalize the AFDC program and to provide a minimum guarantee of $2,400 per family of four. The overall percentage that each family earned would have decreased under the FAP, and built-in work requirements would, theoretically, have limited the number of long-term able-bodied recipients.

Differing views between conservatives and liberals about the nature of poverty led to the debate in Congress that doomed the FAP. In general, conservatives viewed poverty as a result of "cultural deprivation" rather than "permanent physical misfortune," so they discontinued many of Johnson's welfare programs. Not surprisingly, many liberals criticized Nixon and the conservatives' rejection of these welfare policies and decried the Republican emphasis on the suburbs and corporate interest over the minorities in the inner city who, liberals believed, needed aid the most. Adopting a moderate view, Nixon promoted a "revenue sharing" plan that empowered local administrations in an attempt to lessen federal welfare, while at the same time he sought to influence and promote urban development. For this policy, Nixon relied on the advice of Daniel Patrick Moynihan, a former aide to Kennedy and Johnson and head of the Urban Affairs Council (UAC). Moynihan was a well-known scholar and the author of "The Negro Family," an analysis that followed the structuralist ideology that had motivated Kennedy's and Johnson's policies. The FAP was a good example of the ideological conflict within the Nixon administration's policy toward the poor: Nixon wanted to reduce federal welfare and allow local officials to make more decisions, but he did not disband all of the Johnson administration's programs thoughtlessly. The FAP was a failed compromise, and the debate over it exposed the ideological divide associated with poverty in the United States.

See also: Aid to Families with Dependent Children (AFDC); War on Poverty

Sources: Atkins, Jacqueline M., ed., *Encyclopedia of Social Work*, 18th ed., 2 vols. (Silver Spring, MD: NASW, 1987); Bremner, Robert H., Gary W. Reichard, and Richard Hopkins, eds., *American Choices: Social Dilemma and Public Policy since 1960* (Columbus: Ohio State University Press, 1986); Moynihan, Daniel P., ed., *Toward a National Urban Policy* (New York: Basic Books, 1970); Patterson, James T., *America's Struggle against Poverty in the Twentieth Century* (Cambridge, MA: Harvard University Press, 2000); Trattner, Walter I., *From Poor Law to Welfare State*, 6th ed. (New York: Simon and Schuster, 1999).

FEDERAL HOUSING ADMINISTRATION (FHA). A federally funded program intended to increase home ownership among low-income buyers, the Federal Housing Administration (FHA) has allowed many people who could not afford a conventional mortgage to purchase homes. Established by the 1934 National Housing Act, the FHA began as part of the New Deal program to restore Americans' faith in the economy and, specifically, in the nation's banking system. Self-funded, the FHA remains in effect today under the Department of Housing and Urban Development (HUD), of which it became a part in 1965.

Soon after the stock market crash in October 1929, banks across the United States failed—partly because of ill-advised stock market lending, as well as "bank runs" in which anxious patrons frantically rushed to withdraw the entirety of their holdings. As a result of the bank system's failure, many people lost their homes and fewer people obtained loans to buy homes. After the stock market collapse, many banks called for immediate repayment of all debt and foreclosed on many borrowers, who, unsurprisingly, were unable to make their mortgage payments. This practice caused the housing market to plunge downward. Even though banks attempted to use recently foreclosed property as loan collateral to prevent bankruptcy, the low value of property forestalled their efforts, and the banking system remained chaotic until 1933, when the newly elected president, Franklin D. Roosevelt, implemented the New Deal. Restoring the American faith in the economy was Roosevelt's primary goal for the New Deal; restructuring the banking system was one of his first significant steps. During his first three months in office, the "Hundred Days," Roosevelt declared a "Bank Holiday," in which he temporarily closed all of the nation's banks and only reopened the ones that did not have significant problems. He also proposed the Federal Deposit Insurance Corporation (FDIC), to prevent further bank runs by protecting investors' deposits.

The 1934 National Housing Act that created the FHA continued Roosevelt's plan to jump-start the nation's confidence in the economy: real estate comprised a significant part of the economy and contributed to the development of community, because people who owned their homes tended to take more pride in their surroundings. Specifically, the FHA facilitated home buying by regulating the interest rate and the terms of mortgages that it insured. This made it possible for a greater number of people to afford a down payment and monthly mortgage payments on a house and, in turn, stimulated the real estate market. By regulating mortgages and interest rates, the FHA successfully convinced banks to continue lending and consumers to take out loans. By 1938, four years after the implementation of the FHA, Americans could purchase a house with a down payment of 10 percent and a 25-year FHA-insured mortgage loan.

The FHA has continued to impact the nation's real estate market. After World War II, the FHA assisted returning veterans and their families in financing homes, which also stimulated the development of the suburbs. Whereas earlier FHA homes tended to be in central-city neighborhoods, post-World War II FHA homes facilitated the "white flight" to the suburbs. Although the FHA continued to assist low-income minorities in urban areas, the program's encouragement of suburban dwellings yielded mixed results for the nation's urban poor. Since its founding in 1934, including its years as part of HUD, the FHA has insured nearly 34 million home mortgages and over 47,000 multifamily project mortgages. Whereas in the 1930s only 40 percent of Americans owned their homes, by 2000 this figure increased to 70 percent. The FHA has clearly been successful in restoring faith in mortgage loans and facilitating home buying among lower-income Americans.

See also: Department of Housing and Urban Development (HUD); New Deal

Sources: Bauman, John F., Roger Biles, and Kristin M. Szylvian, eds., *From the Tenements to the Taylor Homes: In Search of an Urban Housing Policy in Twentieth-Century America* (University Park: The Pennsylvania State University Press, 2000); Department of Housing and Urban Development (www.hud.gov); Link, Arthur S., and William B. Catton, *American Epoch: A History of the United States Since 1900, Volume II 1921–1945,* 4th ed. (New York: Alfred E. Knopf, 1973).

FOOD STAMPS AND WIC. Established by the Food Stamp Act of 1977 as a means to "permit low-income households to obtain a more nutritious diet by increasing their purchasing power," the Food Stamp Program (FSP) is the largest federally funded program targeting the nutritional needs of low-income Americans. Administered nationally by the Food Nutrition Service (FNS) department of the USDA, the FSP helps low-income families and persons obtain needed food and supplies. The FSP grew out concern that welfare recipients did not spend their benefits on necessary food but wasted money on liquor or drugs. Thus the FSP does not provide cash; instead, it provides stamps or a card with a specific allocation for grocery products. In general, a household must have less than $2,000 in "resources," which includes money in the bank, cash, or personal property; households with a disabled person or a person over sixty years of age must have less than $3,000. Recipients of other welfare programs, such as the Supplemental Security Income (SSI) or Temporary Assistance for Needy Families (TANF), do not have to count benefits received under those programs as "resources" when applying for food stamps. Food Stamp programs vary slightly from state to state, because state officials determine the specifics of the program; in general, wealthier states provide better benefits than states with smaller budgets.

In 2005 nearly 26 million people and 11.2 million households received food stamp benefits each month. Contrary to stereotypical perceptions of the poor as a group primarily consisting of unemployed minorities, food stamp recipients come from diverse backgrounds. Children (under the age of eighteen) comprise 50 percent of all recipients, and the elderly (over sixty years of age) comprise 8 percent, which shows that the majority of food-stamp recipients are the "deserving" poor—those unable (not unwilling) to support themselves. Twenty-eight percent of recipients were working-age women and 13 percent were working-age men. Of these, many work at low-paying jobs; 29 percent of households receiving food stamps include at least one working adult whose earnings are the household's primary source of income. In addition, most households receiving food stamps do not receive other welfare benefits; 27 percent receive SSI benefits and 15 percent receive TANF benefits. Overall, recipients of food stamps are very poor; 82 percent have incomes below the federal poverty line. The average for households receiving food stamps is a gross income of only $648 a month, and so, with the food stamp allotment averaging $209 per month, food stamps comprise nearly 25 percent of recipients' monthly income.

Nutrition is a large aspect of food-stamp programs, especially in related programs such as the Women, Infants, Children (WIC) program. Unlike the more welfare-oriented FSP that constitutes a significant part of many recipients' total income, WIC is a temporary food-stamp program designed to help pregnant women and new parents provide adequate nutrition for their newborn child. WIC focuses on nutritional needs, not day-to-day sustenance. There are still some problems with the administration of food-stamp programs such as WIC. Vendors sometimes charge customers using WIC different amounts than they do for non-WIC customers, although this occurrence has lessened. In 1991 vendors overcharged 9.9 percent of WIC customers and undercharged 8.3 percent; in 2001 vendors overcharged 3.5 percent and undercharged 4.6 percent. Despite these relatively small problems, food-stamp programs— both the welfare-like FSP and temporary special-needs programs such as WIC—help ensure that less affluent Americans can obtain more nutritional foods than they would otherwise. Because recipients may only redeem food stamps for grocery items, food stamps are a pragmatic alternative to easily squandered cash benefits; consequently, food stamps are one of the more successful programs of direct federal relief.

See also: Administration for Children and Families (ACF); Social Security

Sources: *Characteristics of Food Stamp Households, Fiscal Year 2005.* U.S. Department of Agriculture, Food and Nutrition Service, Office of Analysis, Nutrition and Evaluation (2005); *Food Stamp Facts,* Social Security Administration (www.socialsecurity.gov); U.S. Department of Agriculture, Food and Nutrition Services, Office of Analysis, Nutrition, and Evaluation, *WIC Program Coverage: How Many Eligible Individuals Participated in the Special Supplemental Nutrition Program for Women, Infants, and Children (WIC): 1994 to 2003?;* U.S. Department of Agriculture, Food and Nutrition Service, Office of Analysis, Nutrition, and Evaluation, *WIC Participant and Program Characteristics 2004, WIC-04-PC,* Susan Bartlett, Ellen Bobronnikov, Nicole Pacheco, et al. and project officer Fred Lesnett (Alexandria, VA: 2006); Trattner, Walter I., *From Poor Law to Welfare State,* 6th ed. (New York: Simon and Schuster, 1999).

G

THE GRAPES OF WRATH BY JOHN STEINBECK. *The Grapes of Wrath* is a powerful novel set in the American South and West during the Great Depression. Native Californian John Steinbeck (1902–1968) won the Pulitzer Prize for the book, which evokes the lives of poor white tenant farmers driven from their land by the Dust Bowl and the Depression to become impoverished migrant farmers in California. Steinbeck's accurate portrayal of the Okies was disturbing, passionate, and empathetic. It portrayed hunger and despair in a land of plenty.

The Grapes of Wrath centers on the experience of the Joad family, tenant farmers in Oklahoma, who are forced off the land and who take to the road to find a better life. The Joads are, by middle-class standards, rough, coarse, uncouth, violent, hard-drinking, and immoral. They stick together in a large extended family and are tied to the land; farming is all they know. Forced to abandon their ramshackle home by an unscrupulous, anonymous corporate banking power, they load their few possessions onto an old jalopy converted into a truck and head west on Route 66. Rumor and promotional fliers convince the Joads that California is a promised land of abundant work and plentiful food. The vision of oranges, grapes, fertile farms, and full stomachs drives them west through Oklahoma, Texas, New Mexico, and Arizona to California. Along the way, they spend nights along the roadside or at the makeshift camps—Hoovervilles—of other desperate migrants and Okies. Here they find camaraderie among the poor. The anticipation and fear along the road builds to a climax, and the family arrives at California only to find that, rather than the promised land, they have come to a place of despair, hunger, and vanished dreams. Indeed, Californians treat the Okies as invaders, foreigners, and even slaves; the Okies have few rights when faced with the overwhelming economic and political power of big farmers and conservative law enforcement. The rich and powerful, however, are actually insecure and scared by the coming of thousands of hungry people who seek the most basic needs of humankind. Echoing the ideas of Karl Marx, Steinbeck portrayed the owners as selfish bourgeoisie, exploiting the poor for their own gain. Yet their power is fleeting, and the numbers of poor coming to

California presages the eclipse of the owners, who sense the desperation of their cause and react with violent oppression to stave off inevitable defeat.

In *The Grapes of Wrath*, Steinbeck creates a moving portrait of the dispossessed. The Joads—without succor, facing hunger, their sporadic work picking cotton and peaches hardly paying for the food they need—lose their possessions in a flood and end up weak, homeless, and on the run from man and nature, with no place to turn. It is at this point of utter defeat that they show the most perfect love and humanity. Arriving at an abandoned barn in the middle of a rainstorm, they find a young boy and his father, who is starving to death. Rose of Sharon, the eldest Joad daughter, recently delivered of a stillborn baby, offers the milk of her breasts to the starving man, keeping him alive. The novel ends with little hope for material and physical comfort, but the Joads have risen above their condition of abject poverty, spiritually and emotionally, to show the dignity and humanity of the poor.

The Grapes of Wrath continues to be an important statement of hope for the downcast, disenfranchised, and impoverished—for dignity, rights, and sufficient food and shelter. The experience of the poor during the Great Depression is vicariously reexperienced by the thousands of high school and college students who regularly read the book for English and literature classes. Steinbeck was castigated as a communist and a fomenter of revolution, and capitalists and advocates for the status quo decried *The Grapes of Wrath* for years after its writing. But Steinbeck's purpose, showing the simple dignity of all humans—even the poor and ignorant—is the source of the book's true significance.

See also: Great Depression; Literature and Poverty

Sources: Benson, Jackson, *John Steinbeck, Writer: A Biography* (New York: Penguin Books, 1990); Steinbeck, John, *The Grapes of Wrath* (New York: Viking Press, 1939).

GREAT DEPRESSION. The Great Depression began in October 1929 when the stock market crashed, causing economic chaos and forcing many businesses and banks to go bankrupt. The Great Depression increased America's awareness of the poor as more Americans lived in poverty, ceasing to take affluence for granted. In its most basic sense, the Great Depression arose from economic circumstances: during the Depression, the total national income fell from $90 million to $40 million; from 1929 to 1933 consumption levels declined 18 percent and investment levels declined by 98 percent. The American state of mind during the Great Depression also had an impact on the economy as businesspeople lost faith in the economy and refused to invest, which caused the Gross National Product (GNP) to decline. Although the economic effect of the Depression had ended by late 1941, when America entered World War II, some of the cultural, social, and political effects faded more slowly; some remain even today.

The causes of the Great Depression were more complicated than a simple stock market crash. Some long-term causes of the Great Depression were evident in the 1920s, notably overproduction of agricultural produce and commercial products, which led to low prices for farm produce, and a relative lack of demand for products in the 1930s that negatively impacted the economy. In the 1930s workers' wages lagged, plummeting many middle- to lower-class persons below the poverty line. This process began before the stock market crash: at the end of the 1920s, 60 percent of

Americans lived below the poverty line, and the top 1 percent owned 20 percent of the nation's wealth. The agricultural downturn of the 1920s also foreshadowed the Great Depression: production during World War I led to agricultural growth in the 1910s, but continued high-level production after the war flooded the market, driving profits down. This result was a crisis in American agriculture, and small-scale farms (sharecroppers, family farms) were affected the most. Large farms were able to outlast the downturn because of New Deal programs such as the 1933 Agricultural Adjustment Act (AAA), which limited production in an attempt to raise produce prices. Ironically, the AAA only helped large farmers and drove most remaining small (or dependent) farmers from their land. Such examples show that the nation was totally unprepared for the onset of the Great Depression, despite various warnings in the 1920s. The stock market crash affected all aspects of American life: society, politics, economy, and psychology.

The Official Response: Conflicting Ideologies. Herbert Hoover, a self-made Progressive Republican from Iowa, was president in 1929 when the stock market crashed. Although he was a capable leader and a successful businessman, Hoover did not know how to react, except to reassure business leaders and the public that the economy would soon recover. Ironically, the very traits that made Hoover a success—faith in individualism and optimism in the American capitalist system—led to his political downfall. Faced with America's largest economic crisis in recent memory, Hoover chose not to involve the federal government directly, hoping that the economy would correct itself. As the Depression continued and more and more people lost work, many Americans began to resent Hoover's inaction and policy of catering to large business. Impoverished Americans blamed the President for the high unemployment levels and bitterly referred to the makeshift shantytowns that developed across the nation as "Hoovervilles." The low point of Hoover's popularity was the so-called Bonus Army of World War I veterans, who gathered in Washington in 1932 to demand early payment of promised service benefits. After a riot broke out in late July, Hoover called for federal troops, led by General Douglas MacArthur, to disperse the Bonus Army. Hoover was not entirely unsympathetic, however, and he established a few programs in 1932 to aid the economy, such as the Reconstruction Finance Corporation (RFC), which was designed to prevent banks and insurance companies from bankruptcy. But his overall policy was to wait out the Depression rather than to engage the federal government in welfare-relief programs or superfluous spending.

The policies of Franklin D. Roosevelt, who decisively defeated Hoover in the 1932 election, were nearly opposite his predecessor's. Roosevelt's New Deal emphasized action over planning, and, although its economic results were mixed, the nation's morale improved after 1933. The New Deal began the American welfare state, but it retained many conservative elements: the New Deal used federal money to aid the unemployed and to restore economic prosperity, but Roosevelt never turned to the strategies of the political Far Left, such as the federalization of industry. Some historians think that the New Deal saved the American capitalist system. During the 1932 campaign, Roosevelt emphasized his willingness to act quickly, and his engaging personality and optimistic outlook helped him convince people that, under his guidance, America could overcome the Depression. Roosevelt's optimism was one of the most successful aspects of the New Deal: his public persona helped lessen the psychological effects of the Depression. After 1933, bankers lost some of their initial reluctance, and the economy improved slightly from 1933 to 1937, when a short-lived recession occurred. The election of 1936 was Roosevelt's high point, and the recession of 1937, along with disagreements with the Supreme Court, lessened congressional support for New Deal programs, which were less necessary in the late 1930s from an economic standpoint—the initial shock had faded somewhat.

Roosevelt's New Deal significantly changed the way that the federal government understood its role in controlling social and economic order. In general, the New Deal replaced the individualistic approach of the Progressives—like Herbert Hoover, who favored private business over federal control—with a more liberal and active federal government. Under the New Deal, federal agencies set up and over-saw relief and work programs such as the Civilian Conservation Corps (CCC) and the Works Progress Administration (WPA). Some historians have emphasized Roosevelt's left-leaning political orientation, but Roosevelt was primarily concerned with action, not ideology, and the New Deal did not mark a political shift to the Left but was rather the result of the economic, social, and political crisis that followed in the wake of the Great Depression.

Roosevelt's New Deal policies, though optimistic, were often poorly planned and inefficient. There were two main stages of the New Deal: in general, the first stage was more idealistic and depended primarily on Roosevelt's charisma for support; the second stage marked a switch away from blind action toward more moderate policies, such the 1935 Social Security Act, that addressed specific problems. The "Hundred Days," the first months of Roosevelt's first term, was an extraordinarily active period, in which Congress approved many New Deal programs despite the lack of a comprehensive plan. After the initial fervor wore off, in the still-active period from 1935 to 1936, Roosevelt considered more pragmatic solutions—such as Keynesian economics. The basic ideology of Keynesian economics, named after English economist John Maynard Keynes, states that the way a government can correct economic recession is to increase spending, which will jump-start investments and the buying power of consumers, which, in turn, will improve the economy. Keynesian economics thus supports deficit spending rather than balancing the budget or increasing taxes; Keynes argued that, once the government invests sufficient capital, the economy will correct itself. Roosevelt corresponded with Keynes but never officially adopted his strategy. However, the return to wartime production in the late 1930s mirrored Keynes's approach.

Changing Perceptions of Poverty. The Great Depression had a great impact on the way that Americans viewed themselves and their social role: the economic downturn bred psychological depression. Faced with plummeting prices for produce, small farmers—many of who were already poor before 1929—desperately sought to retain their livelihood: many withheld goods from the market, plowed under fields of crops, and slaughtered livestock in an attempt to increase demand and thus prices for agricultural goods. At the same time, many impoverished and unemployed urban dwellers went hungry—there was little cooperation between distinct areas. These conditions contributed to the development of survival attitudes: many Americans began hoarding goods, and many people relocated to other areas, such as California, hoping to obtain jobs.

The Great Depression and the New Deal affected minorities but did not lead to long-term improvement in their lives: the New Deal gave marginalized groups such as African Americans hope; because of the New Deal, many blacks began to believe that they had the power to alter their situation. Federally supported new Deal programs, such as the Civilian Conservation Corps (CCC) and the National Youth Administration (NYA), did not discriminate by race and thus benefited black and minority youths equally. Blacks compromised 11 percent of the CCC and 10 percent of the NYA. Like the NYA, most New Deal programs gave blacks the same wages as whites and provided unskilled workers with job training. During the 1930s the mortality rate of African Americans declined because of an increase in their average standard of living and increased education opportunities. New Deal politicians, such as New York Senator Robert Wagner, also supported workers' rights—which benefited many minorities. In 1937 Congress passed the United States Housing Act (USHA), which set up large-scale public housing complexes—such as the Red Hook and Queensbrough housing developments in Brooklyn—as sanitary and low-cost alternatives to tenement housing. Unfortunately, public housing failed to solve many problems of the urban poor, and the USHA plan for urban rejuvenation did not provide a long-term solution.

One of the most publicized aspects of the Great Depression was the plight of "Okies"—impoverished farmers and migrant workers who, because of drought and the extremely low produce prices, traveled to California searching for work. Novelist John Steinbeck portrayed the harsh life of Okies in his novel, *The Grapes of Wrath*, which followed the travels and trials of the Joad family. Steinbeck's portrayal, though somewhat sympathetic, illustrated the pessimistic outlook that the Great Depression spread throughout the country. The Joads reach California, but their hardships continue there, and Steinbeck gives little impression that their situation will ever significantly change. A work of fiction, *The Grapes of Wrath* nevertheless provides insight into the psychological and material impact of the Great Depression.

The collective impact of this pessimism—combined with bankers' financial struggles and reluctance to invest—was a general loss of faith in the American economic system. Brought up in the optimistic pre-Depression culture that stressed self-reliance and individualism as the means to obtain the "American Dream," unemployed men lost their self-respect because of their inability to provide for self and family; the Depression fomented significant ideological and social changes. The middle-class conception of society—the belief that hard work and determination ensured that one could overcome poverty—was one of the casualties of the 1930s; the economic depression had an especially hard impact on the middle class, which was ill equipped to deal with destitution after the opulence of the consumer-oriented 1920s. During the Great Depression, the middle class understood first-hand what it was like to be poor; thus public-relief programs enjoyed widespread support. In the long-term, however, the Great Depression had little lasting effect on the perception of the poor by affluent Americans. With the return of prosperity and the emphasis on national unity during World War II, many Americans fell back on the traditional perception that poverty is the consequence of personal inferiority or lack of effort.

See also: CCC (Civilian Conservation Corps); *The Grapes of Wrath*; Hoovervilles; New Deal; Panhandlers; Social Security; WPA (Works Progress Administration)

Sources: Conkin, Paul, *The New Deal,* 2nd ed. (Arlington Heights, Illinois: Harlan Davidson, 1975); Divine, Robert A., T. H. Breen, et al., *The American Story*, 2nd ed. (New York: Penguin Books, 2005); Link, Arthur S., and William B. Catton, *American Epoch: A History of the United States Since 1900, Volume II: 1921–1945*, 4th ed. (New York: Alfred E. Knopf, 1973); McElvaine, Robert S., *The Great Depression: America, 1929–1941* (New York: Three Rivers Press, 1993); Patterson, James T., *America's Struggle against Poverty in the Twentieth Century* (Cambridge, MA: Harvard University Press, 2000); Sitkoff, Harvard, *New Deal for Blacks: The Emergence of Civil Rights as a National Issue* (Oxford: University Press, 1981); Steinbeck, John, *The Grapes of Wrath* (New York: Viking Press, 1939).

H

HEAD START. Intended to facilitate low-income children's transition to grade school, Head Start is a federal program that seeks to provide a safe, healthy, and educational environment for disadvantaged children. Originally established by the Johnson Administration in the 1964 Economic Opportunity Act (EOA), under the authority of the Office of Economic Opportunity (OEO), Head Start has undergone structural changes, but its mission remains the same: to instill positive values in at-risk children, thus preparing them to make well-informed decisions in later life. The larger goal of Head Start is to reduce the problems of urban youth gangs and drug addiction through instilling values of individual achievement and self-sufficiency. To date, this larger goal has not been achieved, but the Head Start program remains in place. Unlike other EOA initiatives such as the Community Action Program (CAP) and the Job Corps, Head Start has not attracted much controversy, having rarely offended social elites.

Administered by the Office of Head Start (OHS), Head Start

> provides grants to local public and private non-profit and for-profit agencies to provide comprehensive child development services to economically disadvantaged children and families, with a special focus on helping preschoolers develop the early reading and math skills they need to be successful in school.

Head Start programs also emphasize the importance of the parental role in children's learning. Head Start educates parents about the importance of creating a home environment, such as good health and nutrition, that is conducive to children's educational goals. In 1995, in an effort to reach children at an even younger age, the Early Head Start program was established to include from newborns to children as old as three years of age.

Funding for local Head Start programs comes from grants awarded by the Administration for Children and Families (ACF). Most Head Start programs are run locally—through public and private organizations, American Indian tribes, and schools. Two nationwide programs run by Head Start are Early Childhood Development and Health and Family and Community Partnerships. The purpose of the Early Childhood Development and Health program is to provide a safe and secure learning environment for low-income children and to help them gain the confidence and social skills needed to succeed both in school and in adulthood. The focus is on instilling values of social responsibility and respect for differences at an early age; consequently, Early Childhood Development and Health programs target all aspects of low-income children's growth and development, working to improve the "physical, social, emotional, and cognitive development of each child."

The focus of the Family and Community Partnerships program is on the parents. Head Start recognizes that more children succeed if their home situations are secure and conducive to education. Family and Community Partnerships helps parents identify their own strengths and weaknesses and find their own solutions. Encouraging parents to strive for their own goals helps return the initiative to the local communities and thus lessens the commitment and intrusion of the federal government. In addition, local initiative allows children to develop in the context of their unique culture, ideally creating diverse communities supportive of other cultures. Finally, empowering communities helps build collaboration between parents and staff, which encourages parents to be involved in children's development and to share with and learn from one another.

Head Start has expanded since the 1960s to incorporate wellness programs in addition to preschool educational programs. Through the department of Child Health and Development Services, Head Start works to prepare and implement comprehensive health services for low-income children and families. Head Start focuses on the needs of both the individual and the community and has a more integrated approach than the 1964 EOA proscribed. This expansion of the program's influence demonstrates that it was one of the more successful of Johnson's Great Society initiatives—at least in terms of longevity. Head Start has been in existence long enough to adapt to the nation's changing policies and needs.

Head Start has played a prominent role in recent welfare-reform strategies. For example, President Clinton's 1996 Welfare Reform bill ended traditional welfare giants—such as the Aid to Families with Dependent Children program (which, until then, had been the largest and most expensive program)—and made substantial alterations to Head Start. In 2006 the ACF allocated $6,085,972,000 for Head Start programs across the nation and in U.S. territories; of this total, $38,202,000 was allocated for monitoring the program to help ensure that Head Start made as much impact as possible. The 1996 reform of Head Start implemented strict, quantifiable standards for Head Start—including both financial and administrative standards and program expectations—because of the program's escalating cost and questions about its long-term effectiveness. Although these reforms did not quiet all concerns, Head Start remains an important tool for providing low-income children support when they enter elementary school.

See also: Administration for Children and Families (ACF); Clinton Welfare Reform, Economic Opportunity Act; Office of Economic Opportunity; War on Poverty

Sources: ACF Head Start Office (http://eclkc.ohs.acf.hhs.gov/hslc/HeadStartOffices); Bremner, Robert H., Gary W. Reichard, and Richard Hopkins, eds., *American Choices: Social Dilemma and Public Policy since 1960* (Columbus: Ohio State University Press, 1986); Office of Head Start (www.acf.hhs.gov/programs/hsb/); Patterson, James T., *America's Struggle against Poverty in the Twentieth Century* (Cambridge, MA: Harvard University Press, 2000).

HISPANIC AMERICANS AND POVERTY. The rise of immigration from Spanish-speaking countries in the last decades of the twentieth century has profoundly affected the makeup of American society, bolstered especially by the large numbers of immigrants from Mexico in the Southwest and increasing immigration from the islands of the Caribbean to cities such as Miami and New York. The controversy over the porous border between the United States and Mexico has contributed to an increasingly negative perception of impoverished Hispanics in the United States: Hispanics have been accused of bringing competition for good jobs and a willingness to work at low-income jobs as migrant laborers, farm workers, and general laborers.

Although racism and ethnic prejudice have negatively influenced ethnic Mexicans in the United States, the discrimination that Mexican Americans have faced is more nuanced than that historically directed toward African Americans. The American annexation of territory from Mexico at the end of the Mexican American War in 1848 formally granted ethnic Mexicans the rights of citizenship, but Anglo prejudice often denied them the means to exercise these rights. Legally, ethnic Mexicans were "white," even though they enjoyed few of the privileges of whiteness. This remains an important issue today, because Spanish speakers continue to face social embarrassment—as shown by recent efforts to declare English as America's official language.

In the mid-twentieth century, the economic discrepancy between white middle-class Americans and Hispanics still existed: whites tended to monopolize professional jobs, whereas most Hispanic men worked as industrial or farm laborers and Hispanic women often held low-level clerical or service occupations. Most Hispanic Americans still resided in the Southwestern states: Colorado, New Mexico, Texas, Arizona, Utah, and California. One of the best examples of the intense changes and struggles endured by Hispanic Americans is what occurred in Los Angeles, California—the city with the largest number of Hispanics in America. As in cities across the nation, Los Angeles launched an extensive urban renewal program, which destroyed "blighted" ethnic and impoverished neighborhoods in an attempt to improve the city's image. As a result, many of the city's Hispanics lost their residences and, in the 1960s and 1970s, began organizing protests against the actions of city officials. In the early 2000s, similar protests have also occurred in Los Angeles, Detroit, and other cities across the nation in opposition to immigration policies.

In the 1960s many Hispanic Americans turned to protest as a means to voice their discontent. Mexican Americans—"Chicanos"—were the most visible of these groups, and, especially in the Southwest, several strong Chicano nationalist movements developed that emphasized the region's Spanish and Mexican heritage. Some Mexican American journalists—such as John F. Mendez of the Los Angeles *Eastside Sun*—identified Americans as the invaders, which was a confrontational stance to take during the Cold War. Chicano nationalists constructed their identity from Mexican history and used historical interpretation as a means to political power. The Mexican American Political Association (MAPA) supported John F. Kennedy's presidential campaign in 1960 but soon became dissatisfied with the Democrats and struck out on its own. An unsuccessful bid to make East Los Angeles an independent city in 1962, which would have ensured greater Mexican American voting power, lessened MAPA's power, and in 1964 the city of Los Angeles redrew its political boundaries and effectively excluded the Chicano vote in municipal elections. When Cesar Chávez and the United Farm Workers Association (UFWA) picketed MAPA in 1965—after MAPA's failure to take a strong stance on the Watts riots that left three Mexican Americans dead—MAPA lost its remaining credibility among Los Angeles's Chicano community.

Unlike later groups such as the La Raza Unida Party and the Brown Berets, earlier Chicano civil-rights organizations—such as the Community Service Organization (CSO) and Asociación Nacional México Americana (ANMA)—respected the American democratic system. Ethnic Mexicans often placed their faith in advancement in the process of Americanization; idolized America's famous men like Abraham Lincoln; and respected the traditions of freedom, equal opportunity, and progress. Prior to the 1960s, most Chicanos believed that advancement would be the consequence of immersion in the American way of life. Social inequality and continued violence on the part of the Los Angeles Police Department toward Mexican Americans—the most publicized occurrence was the arrest and beating of CSO chairman Anthony Rios in 1951—broke down moderate Chicano reform movements and led to more extreme resistance. In 1966, however, the Chicano movement took a more radical stance, and, for the first time, Mexican Americans blamed the American establishment for their woes. The Brown Berets, the Chicano equivalent of the Black Panthers, adopted khaki military-like clothing to fit their belligerent attitude and published their "Ten Point Program" in their newsletter, *La Causa*. This program emphasized the importance of upholding Mexican traditions and language, called for an end to urban renewal programs, and stressed the need for Mexican American officials to ensure that the city's ethnic Mexican population was not abused by municipal institutions such as the police and court systems. In 1972, after pursuing more radical policies, the Brown Berets fell apart because of internal discontent.

Illegal immigration from Mexico has contributed to the isolation of impoverished Hispanics in many U.S. cities. Hispanic "ghettos" differ in many ways from the structure of traditional African American ghettos, which have either been largely institutionalized through public housing, as Chicago's Robert Taylor Homes have been, or are crumbling through disrepair, as in central Detroit and Camden, New Jersey. Although some impoverished urban Hispanics live in similar surroundings in older cities in the Northeast or Midwest, most Hispanics live in the newer, sprawling cities of the South and West, such as Dallas and Los Angeles, that have less confined urban space. In general, ghettos in these Sunbelt cities are more energetic, dynamic, and open to change than the crumbling and institutionalized ghettos of the Northeast and Midwest. Language presents the strongest barrier to the residents of Hispanic ghettos: poor English communication skills ensure that Hispanic immigrants remain segregated in Spanish-speaking neighborhoods, limiting their ability to move up the social and economic ladder.

See also: Protest Movements

Sources: Atkins, Jacqueline M., ed., *Encyclopedia of Social Work*, 18th ed., 2 vols. (Silver Spring, MD: NASW, 1987); Callow, Alexander B. Jr., ed., *American Urban History: An Interpretive Reader with Commentaries,* 3rd ed. (New York: Oxford University Press, 1982); Chávez, Ernesto, *"¡Mi Raza Primero!": Nationalism, Identity, and Insurgency in the Chicano*

Movement in Los Angeles, 1966–1978 (Berkeley: University of California, 2002); Divine, Robert A., T. H. Breen, et al., *The American Story*, 2nd ed. (New York: Penguin Books, 2005); Gibson, Campbell, and Kay Jung, "Historical Census Statistics on Population Totals by Race, 1790 to 1990, and by Hispanic Origin, 1790 to 1990, for the United States, Regions, Divisions, and States." U.S. Census Bureau, Population Division Working Paper 87 no. 56 (2002); Goldfield, David R., and Blaine A. Brownell, *Urban America: From Downtown to No Town* (Boston, 1979); Riis, Jacob, *How the Other Half Lives* (New York: Charles Scribner's Sons, 1890); Vergara, Camillo, *The New American Ghetto* (New Brunswick, NJ: Rutgers University Press, 1995).

HOMELESSNESS. Among the most impoverished persons in the United States are the homeless—individuals and families without established residences. Throughout American history, the homeless have caused alarm among more affluent citizens because of middle-class reluctance to allocate town resources to care for the itinerant poor, who do not have a stake in the community, and because of the popular perceptions that the homeless are disorderly, have problems with substance abuse, and display little respect for authority. Perceptions of the homeless, often developed to fit a political or ideological position, include the view that the homeless are crafty, conscious manipulators of the system who have more assets then they let on, as well as the view that they are vulnerable persons who are poor because of individual weakness. These perceptions are at best half-truths, popularized by the affluent classes either to separate themselves from the itinerant poor or to push for political reform.

In the most basic sense, the homeless are those who must seek out shelter on a day-to-day basis; however, there are many categories of homelessness. Some homeless persons find temporary shelter with relations and acquaintances or at private shelters such as the Young Men's Christian Association (YMCA) and Salvation Army. Others, however, rely primarily on makeshift shelters—made of materials like cardboard—or find temporary shelter in automobiles, under bridges, in abandoned buildings, or wherever they happen to be for the night. In some cases, such as in the winter, they seek out jails for shelter, demonstrating the ability of some homeless persons to adapt to their situation, using whatever means necessary to survive. The demographic characteristics of the homeless do not fit a single stereotype. Although single men comprise the largest segment, homelessness affects diverse portions of the populace, including single women, families, teenagers—"street youth"—and children. Moreover, accurate demographic counts of the homeless are difficult to compile, because many homeless persons, especially street youth, do not rely on homeless shelters and are thus hard to account for.

In general, the homeless are a very vulnerable group. Medical records show that homeless persons are more likely to have serious health problems—ranging from diseases such as tuberculosis and HIV to mental illness—and are more likely to die prematurely than the general public. Part of the reason for this is that the homeless have less access to health care: those who do have health insurance coverage, such as through Medicaid, still face difficulties, such as paying for the inevitable costs of prescriptions and visits to the doctor, and many homeless persons lack even the means or self-awareness to seek medical help in the first place.

Life on the street or moving from shelter to shelter is hard—a fact that medical data illustrate. For example, homeless persons tend to age faster; forty- to fifty-year-old homeless persons can develop health conditions common to much older people, partly because homeless individuals often do not or cannot perform basic health duties—such as taking prescription drugs regularly, brushing teeth, and controlling diseases like diabetes that require continual maintenance. Mental illness and substance abuse are also commonly, if not always accurately, associated with the homeless. Recent medical data suggest that schizophrenia is not as widespread as stereotypes assert: schizophrenia rates among the U.S. homeless are about 10 to 13 percent. Alcoholism is, however, clearly a widespread problem among the homeless. Data on hard-drug usage—crack cocaine and marijuana—among the homeless are sparse, although some studies place the rate of drug use at 30 percent.

Middle-class Americans have often sought to distance themselves from the homeless. In colonial America, towns cared for their own poor but sent away ("warned out") most itinerant poor. In the nineteenth century, reform-minded social workers established settlement houses, and the government set up poorhouses for the itinerant poor. Homeless and orphaned children often found lodging in orphanages or aid societies, such as Charles Loring Brace's Children's Aid Society in New York. Similar practices continued throughout the twentieth century and up to the present. In modern cities such as Los Angeles and New York (and also in smaller industrial cities), rampant homelessness is a significant problem. According to leftist urban historian Mike Davis, the police and affluent citizens of Los Angeles are engaged in an explicit battle to marginalize the homeless. Davis pointed out the existence of law codes that outlaw temporary residences—such as cardboard shelters—in order to prevent visible homelessness in the city's public areas. Likewise, Davis points out that the city's purposeful commissioning of uncomfortable park benches and lack of public restrooms are part of a plan to oust the homeless from widely used public areas.

Homelessness remains a significant problem despite the economic resurgence of the 1990s and 2000s. In 1991 Congress passed the Department of Housing and Urban Development (HUD) Appropriations Act, which gave HUD the authority to collect data to assess problems of homelessness more accurately and determine what types of programs would be effective; HUD researched the characteristics of the homeless by age, disability, race, gender, and types of service or shelters requested. The 2001 HUD Appropriations Act updated these requirements and provided HUD with additional funding. Congress required HUD to collect data determining the extent of homelessness in America and develop a new Homeless Management Information System (HMIS) to determine the effectiveness of existing relief programs. According to HUD's *Annual Report to Congress* from 2007, about 335,000 homeless persons were housed in "emergency shelter or transitional housing" across the nation on a typical day in 2005; the range was from 235,000 and 434,000 people per day. Likewise, the number of unsheltered persons—defined as those who do not "use shelters and are on the streets, in abandoned buildings, or in other places not meant for human habitation"—peaked at 338,781 for a single day in January 2005. HUD's 2007 report also noted that homelessness occurs primarily in central cities; not surprisingly, there are more homeless shelters in central cities than in rural or suburban areas.

See also: Department of Housing and Urban Development (HUD); Disease and the Poor

Sources: Atkins, Jacqueline M., ed., *Encyclopedia of Social Work*, 18th ed., 2 vols. (Silver Spring, MD: NASW, 1987); Davis, Mike, *City of Quartz* (New York: Vintage Books, 1992); HUD, The Annual Homeless Assessment Report to Congress (February 2007)

(http://www.huduser.org/publications/povsoc/annual_assess.html); Hwang, Stephen W., "Homelessness and Health" *Canadian Medical Association Journal,* Vol. 164, No. 2 (January 23, 2001): 229–233; Patterson, James T., *America's Struggle against Poverty in the Twentieth Century* (Cambridge, MA: Harvard University Press, 2000); Trattner, Walter I., *From Poor Law to Welfare State*, 6th ed. (New York: Simon and Schuster, 1999).

HOOVERVILLES. Derisively named after President Herbert Hoover, "Hoovervilles" were makeshift camps that sprang up in the early years of the Great Depression. Often located near the edges of cities and towns, Hoovervilles—temporary gathering places where the newly homeless congregated—poignantly illustrated the economic and social effects of the stock market crash in October 1929.

The Great Depression affected more than America's economic system. Although the stock market crash caused the widespread panic that forced many banks and businesses to close, the 1920s had not been as prosperous as optimistic investors and politicians such as Hoover thought. Farmers and the rural poor were especially affected; overproduction in the 1910s had led to low prices for agricultural produce in the 1920s. However, most middle-class Americans enjoyed a real advance in the material standard of living in the 1920s; mass production and successful advertising led to the rise of a modern consumer culture. Consequently, the middle class began to expect a high standard of living, and people were very optimistic about the economy. In the 1920s many Americans began investing in the stock market, artificially stimulating both stock prices and optimism about the economy.

However, Americans' faith was unfounded. In late October 1929 it became clear that the stock market was artificially high, and a correction—a sharp fall in prices—was imminent. Because so few middle-class Americans, banks, and businesses were prepared for the sudden drop of the stock market, the correction—a normal occurrence that did not have to set off a decade-long depression—created widespread panic. In the last months of 1929 and through the early 1930s, many businesses went bankrupt or laid off substantial numbers of workers, leading to mass unemployment. Losing one's job often led to the loss of one's home, and homelessness sharply increased. The newly homeless had nowhere to go and no jobs, so they congregated in shantytowns, which they termed "Hoovervilles" after the President.

The Great Depression destroyed Herbert Hoover's reputation. A self-made businessman and engineer born in small-town Iowa, Hoover epitomized the American Dream. Prior to the Depression, Hoover's optimism was an asset. But his faith that the economy would correct itself and his belief that the government should remain aloof—except for moderate programs such as the Reconstruction Finance Corporation (RFC) to help businesses get back to normal—alienated those Americans who lost their jobs and homes. Consequently, they blamed Hoover for their plight, even though he was not personally to blame.

The election of Franklin D. Roosevelt as president in 1932 significantly changed the nation's attitude. Roosevelt's engaging personality and willingness to involve the federal government directly in work relief convinced many Americans that the government cared. Real changes were few, however, despite Roosevelt's New Deal. Although programs such as the Works Project Administration (WPA) provided work and the Federal Housing Administration (FHA) provided low-cost housing loans, homelessness remained a serious problem throughout the 1930s, declining only with the end of the Great Depression in the early 1940s, when World War II began.

See also: Great Depression; New Deal

Sources: Link, Arthur S., and William B. Catton, *American Epoch: A History of the United States since 1900, Volume II 1921–1945,* 4th ed. (New York: Alfred E. Knopf, 1973); Patterson, James T., *America's Struggle against Poverty in the Twentieth Century* (Cambridge, MA: Harvard University Press, 2000).

HOW THE OTHER HALF LIVES BY JACOB RIIS. One of the most influential exposés of the underside of nineteenth-century urban life, Jacob Riis's *How the Other Half Lives,* published in 1890, provides insight into the inner workings of the social, economic, and ethnic structure of New York City. Analyzing the city's decrepit tenement blocks—centers of crime, disease, and disorder—Riis argued that the area's crime was the fault of the city's elites—the top half of society—who cared only about profits and forced the poor to live in wretched conditions. Taking the environmental view of poverty, Riis argued that, although the poor often turned to criminal pursuits, the fault was just as much on the rich for condoning the oppressive system as on the perpetrators themselves. Riis mixed photographs and engravings with his text; his images are often more striking than his commentary. The documentary style of Riis's photographs and writing style lent an air of immediacy to his exposé of the underside of New York City; Riis's straightforward writing style—short chapters organized into subsections divided by bullet points—and grim illustrations contributed to the book's popularity both among his contemporaries and later twentieth-century reformers.

Riis began his treatise with the statement:

> Long ago it was said that "one half of the world does not know how the other half lives." That was true then. It did not know because it did not care. The half that was on top cared little for the struggles, and less for the fate of those who were underneath, so long as it was able to hold them there and keep its own seat. There came a time when the discomfort and crowding below were so great, and the consequent upheavals so violent, that it was no longer an easy thing to do, and then the upper half fell to inquiring what was the matter. Information on the subject has been accumulating rapidly since, and the whole world has had its hands full answering for its old ignorance.

Riis applied this general thesis to the conditions of New York (Manhattan), arguing that New York's problems came later than those of European cities because New York was younger and not until the early nineteenth century did the city experience the overcrowding that led to its social problems. "Greed and reckless selfishness," Riis asserted, "wrought like results here as in the cities of older lands."

Riis emphasized the immorality of the tenement system and proposed a call for action to New Yorkers to clean up the city. "The story is dark enough," he wrote, "drawn from the plain public records, to send a chill to any heart. If it shall appear that the sufferings and the sins of the 'other half,' and the evil they breed, are but as a just punishment upon the community that gave it no other choice, it will be because that is the truth." He blamed the tenements as the source of epidemic disease, crime, the deserving poor, and the beggars, those "human wrecks" sent to "asylums and workhouses year by year."

Despite Riis's cynical view of late nineteenth-century American urban society, *How the Other Half Lives* retains a hopeful tone; Riis emphasized the need for a call to action rather than a passive resignation that New York's problems were beyond hope. Riis placed the onus of responsibility to change the situation on affluent New Yorkers, who had a moral and civic responsibility to work for social reform.

Riis viewed the problems of the urban poor much as Progressives like Jane Addams did: he thought that alcohol was a primary cause of the poor's predicament, although Riis placed more blame on the "top half" for condoning the squalor through inaction and indifference. Citing legislative reports on urban crime, Riis noted that 40 percent of the poor's social problems were "due to drunkenness," leading to the conclusion "that certain conditions and associations of human life and habitation are the prolific parents of corresponding habits and morals." The solution was to change the environment of the tenements. Owners of the tenements, he argued, reap a large profit but make no return by investing in the property. In response to complaints of the dilapidated condition of the apartments, the landlords demanded prompt payment of rent rather than complaints, or the tenants would face ejection. The only remedy Riis saw to this overwhelming situation was for factory owners to build homes for their workers and for the tenements to be abandoned and torn down.

Riis was sympathetic to the Christian point of view, contrasting God-fearing and righteous religious reformers with the immigrant poor, little better than heathens. Fundamentally, he argued, more than a change in the environment, the poor required a moral as well as social conversion into law-abiding and conscientious citizens. But "how shall the love of God be understood by those who have been nurtured in sight only of the greed of man?"

How the Other Half Lives was very influential in its time, and it has influenced similar photojournalistic exposés in the twentieth century. Some noteworthy examples are José Camillo Vergara's photographic essays of late-twentieth century urban ghettos in *The New American Ghetto* (1995) and Eugene Richards's photos of the impact of poverty, drug addiction, and race in *Cocaine True Cocaine Blue* (1994). Riis's work was also a precursor for Michael Harrington's *The Other America*, which drew from the same moral indignity that such extreme poverty should exist in a nation as wealthy as America. A striking difference between Riis and Harrington, however, is Riis's assertion that the plight of the poor was obvious to any interested observer, whereas Harrington emphasized the ways in which the poor were "invisible" because they had no contact with middle-class America. Because of Riis's discerning eye, effective visuals, and provocative voice, *How the Other Half Lives* provides exceptional insight into the chaotic urban experience of late nineteenth-century America.

See also: Addams, Jane; Environment Theory of Poverty; Immigrants; *The Other America*; Progressives; Urban Poor

Sources: Harrington, Michael, *The Other America* (Baltimore: Penguin, 1963); Richards, Eugene, *Cocaine True Cocaine Blue* (New York: Aperture, 1994); Riis, Jacob, *How the Other Half Lives* (New York: Charles Scribner's Sons, 1890); Vergara, José Camillo, *The New American Ghetto* (Newark: Rutgers University Press, 1995).

I

IMMIGRANTS. Although a nation of immigrants, the United States of America has a history of marginalizing immigrant groups, especially those of non-Anglo ethnicity. When the first British colonists arrived in what is now the United States in the early seventeenth century, they were themselves immigrants who moved to a new land in search of economic and spiritual advancement. The new nation retained its Anglo-Saxon social and cultural roots after establishing independence, however, which laid the foundation for the common assumption that "white" Anglo-Saxon society was superior to the traditions of later immigrants. The idea of the "melting pot" was a variant of this idea, which also assumed that later immigrants needed to discard their old-world traditions to become "Americans." This proved unappealing, and many, though not all, immigrant groups have attempted to retain some elements of their heritage.

Because seaport cities were the main point of entry for most immigrants, these cities profoundly changed during each successive immigration wave. Early American cities, such as prerevolutionary Philadelphia and Boston, boasted a flourishing urban community in which residents mingled in public spaces such as the many taverns that lined city streets. This openness was not to last, however, and a crass spirit of dehumanization accompanied the rise of industry and technology. Cities became increasingly specialized, and neighborhoods separated along class lines; elites often lived in the center, leaving the poor to congregate near the city's edge. With better transportation—such as the streetcar and later the automobile—the white middle classes moved to outlying areas to separate themselves. Isolated in the older parts of the city, most immigrants lived in old, decrepit tenement houses amid rampant disease and unsanitary conditions. Jacob Riis's *How the Other Half Lives* (1890) is one of the best contemporary accounts of the poor conditions of New York's many immigrant groups.

As illustrated in *How the Other Half Lives,* mass immigration upset the Anglo-Saxon ideal: the Irish, Italians, Russian Jews, and Germans, among other groups, did not share the same faith in individual initiative, and they continued to adhere to their traditional cultures. Consequently, the white, native-born middle class and elites became increasingly fearful of urbanization, which they saw as a chaotic force that was typified by crime, bestiality, and allegiance to the Pope. Despite legislation intended to curtail nonwhite immigration in the late nineteenth century, such as the Chinese Exclusion Act of 1882, immigration remained a contentious issue. By 1890 two thirds of America's foreign born population lived in cities; by 1920 three fourths did. Not all immigrant groups remained in cities, however; many Germans and Scotch-Irish migrated to the Midwest and the rural South; many Hispanic immigrants also crossed over from Mexico, looking for work as farm laborers.

Although most nineteenth-century immigrants were from Europe, other ethnic and racial groups immigrated in significant numbers as well. For example, many West Indian immigrants relocated to Harlem in the early nineteenth century, and many Chinese and Japanese arrived in the mid-twentieth century after Congress lessened the strict quota previously imposed on Asian immigration. Recently, Hispanic immigrants, especially from Mexico, have posed the greatest problems, because local and federal officials have difficulty controlling the American–Mexican border. Likewise, cities in the North, such as New York, have large Spanish-speaking populations from Puerto Rico and the Dominican Republic. Sometimes, competition between ethnic groups becomes violent. The recent influx of Cuban immigrants in Miami has frustrated the city's impoverished African Americans, because Cubans accept lower wages and perform jobs that blacks have not wanted to do. This competition has led to violence between blacks and Cubans, both of whom are marginalized and not accepted in Miami's affluent white society; the effects of racial discrimination, as this scenario shows, can be very complicated.

In the early twentieth century, the federal government passed legislation to restrict immigration. In 1917, for example, Congress voted to enact a literacy test to restrict immigration, which, along with World War I, resulted in a decline from the 1900–1914 average of 1,000,000 immigrants per year to 110,000 in 1918. Congress also passed an anti-immigration bill in 1924, the National Origins Quota Act, which restricted immigration levels to 3 percent of the numbers of specific ethnicities of immigrants living in the United States in 1914. The choice of 1914 rather than 1924 allowed the United States to nullify immigration from Asia and to restrict most immigrants from countries other than Great Britain, Ireland, Germany, and Scandinavia. This openly biased Act remained in effect until the 1960s, when the Immigration Act of 1965 went into effect. Ironically, the 1924 National Origins Quota Act did not effectively block Mexican immigrants, who crossed the border in increasing numbers—about 100,000 per year—and it was not as successful as nativist groups wished.

The rise of immigration from Spanish-speaking countries in the last decades of the twentieth century has profoundly affected the makeup of American society, bolstered especially by the large numbers of immigrants from Mexico in the Southwest and increasing immigration from the islands of the Caribbean to cities such as Miami and New York. These new immigration trends have also altered traditional American perceptions of Hispanics. The controversy over the imperfect nature of the border with Mexico has contributed to an increasingly negative perception of impoverished Hispanics in the United States: many Americans associate the presence of Hispanics with poverty and ignorance.

An examination of the history of immigration and assimilation in the United States reveals a general trend. Most immigrant groups living in America—including the first Anglo-Saxon settlers—began in poverty and as outsiders in an unfamiliar land but eventually adapted and either formed their own niche or merged with the mainstream culture and society. In addition, each immigrant group has raised the ire of more established groups who had adopted the cultural outlook of "accepted" society. For example, Progressive reformers, such as Jane Addams, worked to assimilate immigrants into American society by educating them in the Anglo-Saxon tradition. Competition over jobs has also been a point of contention, especially among impoverished "outsider" groups—illustrated in the conflict between blacks and Cubans in Miami and Koreans and blacks in Los Angeles—because a group that is better established but still marginalized (the blacks in both of these examples) resents the intrusion of newer groups that threaten its already precarious position. Consequently, there seems to be a direct connection between recent immigrants and poverty. One of the primary reasons that people immigrate to the United States is to make a better life for themselves and their family. Although financial success is elusive for most recent immigrants, that does not seem to keep them from continuing to move to America; current immigration levels remain high.

See also: Hispanic Americans and Poverty; Race and Ethnicity; Urban Poor

Sources: Callow, Alexander B. Jr., ed., *American Urban History: An Interpretive Reader with Commentaries,* 3rd ed. (New York: Oxford University Press, 1982); Chávez, Ernesto, *"¡Mi Raza Primero!": Nationalism, Identity, and Insurgency in the Chicano Movement in Los Angeles, 1966–1978* (Berkeley: University of California, 2002); Divine, Robert A., T. H. Breen, et al., *The American Story,* 2nd ed. (New York: Penguin Books, 2005); Gibson, Campbell, and Kay Jung, "Historical Census Statistics on Population Totals by Race, 1790 to 1990, and by Hispanic Origin, 1790 to 1990, for the United States, Regions, Divisions, and States," U.S. Census Bureau, Population Division Working Paper 87 no. 56 (2002); Goldfield, David R., and Blaine A. Brownell, *Urban America: From Downtown to No Town* (Boston: Houghton Mifflin Co, 1979); Riis, Jacob, *How the Other Half Lives* (New York: Charles Scribner's Sons, 1890); Vergara, Camillo, *The New American Ghetto* (New Brunswick, NJ: Rutgers University Press, 1995).

INDENTURED SERVITUDE. Indentured servitude was one of several forms of voluntary bound labor in the thirteen American colonies. The institution involved a pauper signing a contract, or indenture, that provided for goods or services in return for a period of service in which the pauper was bound to a master for a set number of years. The typical form of indentured servitude granted an individual pauper or family of paupers passage by ship from England to America; on arrival, the captain of the vessel sold the indenture to the highest bidder, usually a planter in the American South. The contract bound the pauper to the master for a term usually ranging from four to seven years, at which point the servant would be set free; sometimes the indenture included a payment on release, "freedom dues," of clothing, money, or land. Most indentures read like the following:

> This Indenture made the 15th day of the 3rd moneth 1639 betweene George Richardson, mariner, and Michael Gabilloe, Frenchman, of the one parte, and Edmund James of Watertowne in New England, planter, of the other parte, Witnesseth that the said George Richardson for the summe of eight pounds to him in hand payd for the passage of the said Michael, by the said Edmund James, doth assigne and put over the said Michael, and the said Michael Doth put himselfe a servant unto the said Edmund

James, him his executors administrators and assignes truly and faithfully to serve the day of the Date of these presents for and During the space of seaven yeares thenceforth next ensuing fully to be compleat and ended. And the said Edmund James shall fine and provide to and for his said servant sufficient and reasonable meate drinke lodging and apparell during the said terme, and in the end of the said terme shall give his said servant double apparell and five pounds in money.

The increasing poverty and inadequate relief provided by the English poor laws of the 1600s made voluntary transportation to America for a new start a desperate yet doable option for English individuals and families who refused to give into the temptation of lawlessness to improve their economic condition. Some paupers appeared to have a full understanding of all that voluntary servitude entailed and believed that it was the best alternative to a host of evils. The chance for a new life was a real possibility, however remote; some indecisive paupers were initially attracted by promotional literature describing America as a land of freedom and plenty. Typical was the tract *Leah and Rachel, or the Two Fruitfull Sisters, Virginia and Mary-Land*, written by John Hammond in 1656:

> Thos Servants that will be industrious may in their time of service gain a competent estate before their Freedomes, which is usually done by many, and they gaine esteeme and assistance that appear so industrious: There is no Master almost but will allow his Servant a parcell of clear ground to plant some Tobacco in for himself, which he may husband at those many idle times he that allowed him and not prejudice but rejoyce his Master to see it. . . . And whereas it is rumoured that Servants have no lodging other then on boards, or by the Fire side, it is contrary to reason to believe it: First, as we are Christians; next as people living under a law, which compels as well the Master as the Servant to perform his duty; nor can true labour be either expected or exacted without sufficient cloathing, diet, and lodging; all which both their Indentures (which most inviolably be observed) and the Justice of the Country requires.

The reality was quite different from the rosy picture painted by promoters and recruiting agents. The paupers signed their rights away with the indenture, whereupon the indentured servants were gathered together by the agent or ship's captain into a holding area, awaiting the voyage to America. Following is an eyewitness account from 1704 of an agent and his recruits:

> We peep'd in at a Gateway, where we saw three or Four Blades well Drest, with Hawks Countenances, attended with half a Dozen Ragamuffinly Fellows, showing Poverty in their Rags, and Despair in their Faces, mixt with a parcel of Young Wild Striplings like Run-away Prentices . . . that House, says my Friend, which they are entring is an Office where Servants for the Plantations bind themselves.

Conditions in the vessel bound for America were usually deplorable. Servants were crowded together below the deck and rarely allowed topside. The quarters were damp, humid, and stifling with heat during summer or icy, frigid, bone-chilling cold in winter; the air was stagnant and the odors were repugnant. Disease easily spread in such places, and many of the servants died before they reached the object of their dreams and desires. The situation was little better on arriving at America, typically at a port in the South, where the captain sold the indenture to a planter who was seeking cheap and plentiful labor. William Eddis observed that the indentured servant was usually treated worse than the convict laborer or slave, simply because the planter had the former for a shorter time and hence wanted to get the most labor out of his investment with the least expense. The servants, "over whom the rigid planter exercises an inflexible severity," wrote Eddis, "are strained to the utmost to perform their allotted labour; and, from a prepossession in many cases too justly founded, they are supposed to be receiving only the just reward which is due to repeated offences. There are doubtless many exceptions to this observation, yet, generally speaking, they groan beneath a worse than Egyptian bondage."

Indeed, the mortality rate among servants was shocking. Colonial observers noted that it took usually a year of "seasoning" before a new servant, who was used to the cooler climates of the British Isles and northern Europe, adapted to the humidity, heat, disease, and hard work in the American South. Most servants worked as field hands on tobacco plantations alongside convict laborers and African slaves. Their quarters, diet, clothing, and general health were little better—and sometimes worse—than those of slaves. Because servants were white and of British heritage, they possessed more rights before the law than did slaves. Most colonies had laws, however unenforceable, preventing the abuse of servants by their masters. White servants could appear in court and testify against their masters. Servants could own property but could not trade or sell goods. They could serve in the colonial militia. In some colonies, masters were responsible for their servants' behavior and had to pay fines for servants' misdemeanors. Colonial courts respected the legality of the indenture, the term of service, and the freedom dues. Some servants, however, especially in the early seventeenth century, arrived in America without an indenture; courts judged the terms of their service according to the "custom of the country." During the course of the 1700s, colonies passed laws formalizing the customs by which servants served. Even so, the custom of the country was often the basis for freedom dues and was so stated in many indentures. In 1717 a South Carolina law granted to freed women a "Wast coat and Petticoat of new Half-thicks or Pennistone, a new Shift of white Linnen, a new Pair of shoes and stockings, a blue Apron and two Caps of white Linnen." By a law of 1640 Maryland granted to freed men "one good Cloth suite of Keirsy or broad cloth a Shift of white linen one new pair of stockins and Shoes two hoes one axe 3 barrells of Corne and fifty acres of land." When land was in great supply in the 1600s, freedom dues in South Carolina, North Carolina, Maryland, Pennsylvania, and New Jersey provided grants of land of as many as fifty acres for freed servants. Seventeenth-century colonies in the South, such as Virginia and Maryland, offered the fifty-acre "headright" to any person who brought a servant to the colony. Headrights could be exchanged, bought, and sold without regard to the interests or desires of the servant.

During the term of their service, servants were chattel, the property of the master, so they could be bought, sold, and inherited according to the terms of a master's will, used to pay a debt, or even gambled away. Husband, wife, and children could be sold separately. Courts punished misdemeanors and crimes by servants with additional terms of service. Runaways who were returned to their masters were given additional months or years of bondage. Masters could use corporal punishment on servants, as long as it was not cruel and beyond the bounds of decency. Whereas slaves could be stripped and whipped, whites could be whipped but not stripped. Marriage between servants was discouraged, because pregnancy and child rearing took time away from female servant's work. Sexuality outside of marriage was condemned outright, particularly if it led to the birth of a child out of wedlock, in which case male as well as female servants could be condemned to corporal punishment (whipping) and extra years of service. Such were also the punishments for escaping. If the master of an escaped servant could not be discovered, the servant would be auctioned to the highest bidder.

Most indentured servants in America worked on plantations, engaged in the toil of clearing the land of trees; plowing; planting and caring for tobacco, rice, or sugar; harvesting; and bringing the crop to market or on board a ship bound for England. Some servants had special training and skills, which were either recognized by their masters, who put their skills to work, or established in the indenture as the proper task of the servant. E. I. McCormac, in *White Servitude in Maryland*, argues that two thirds of teachers in colonial Maryland were servants. Servants in the northern colonies worked as masons, wagoners, bakers, carpenters, cooks, tailors, attorneys, and accountants. An example of the latter is Jacob Sandersz Glen, a servant in Dutch New Netherland in 1659, who was "very careful . . . and always properly transfers the accounts, for he is very neat and particular that things do not get mixed up." Glen even acted as executor of his master's estate upon the latter's death.

Indentured servitude as a system of providing labor for the colonies and relieving the numbers of poor in England thrived throughout the colonial period. More than 10,000 indentured servants arrived at Maryland from 1745 to 1775. Likewise, more than 10,000 servants departed London for the colonies from 1654 to 1686. Most servants went to the South; for example, of the 3,257 servants who shipped from London to the colonies from 1720 to 1732, 918 went to Maryland but only 32 went to New England.

See also: British Poor and the Origins of Colonialism; Convict Transportation; Poor Laws in England and Early America; Redemptioners; Spirits (Crimps) and Newlanders

Sources: Brown, Alexander, *The Genesis of the United States* (Boston: Houghton Mifflin, 1890); Herrick, Cheesman A., *White Servitude in Pennsylvania, Indentured and Redemption Labor in Colony and Commonwealth* (Philadelphia: McVey, 1926); Hofstadter, Richard, *America at 1750: A Social Portrait* (New York: Random House, 1971); McCormac, E. I., *White Servitude in Maryland, 1634–1820* (Baltimore: Johns Hopkins, 1904); Morse, Richard B., *Government and Labor in Early America* (New York: Harper & Row, 1965); Smith, Abbot Emerson, *Colonists in Bondage: White Servitude and Convict Labor in America, 1607–1776* (New York: Norton, 1971).

INSTITUTIONALIZATION OF THE POOR. Almshouses and other institutions to house and work the poor were established in the late 1600s and continued for the next two centuries in the colonies and early United States. As in other characteristics of early American poor relief, the American institutionalization of the poor mirrored English beginnings in the 1500s and 1600s.

The English system of poor relief, which began under Elizabeth I, originated the basic concepts that local government should care for its destitute, who must themselves contribute to the cost of relief whenever possible by work. English authorities often failed to distinguish between the deserving, innocent poor and the habitual beggar; both were categorized, economically and morally, as burdens and malefactors. It therefore seemed reasonable to create institutions that would exclusively house, work, and correct the poor. A statute in 1581 established such "houses of correction" in England. In 1597 an Elizabethan Act went further, creating the local parish office of Overseer of the Poor, part of whose job was to supervise the building of institutions to house and work the poor. Elizabeth's successor, James I, in 1610 reasserted the Crown's commitment to the Elizabethan statutes, demanding that more parishes build houses of correction. These institutions, which were also known as workhouses and "bridewells," after the notorious London hospital and prison, worked the able poor in the manufacture of cloth goods.

Seventeenth-century American communities established poor relief on the same English assumptions of community responsibility to aid the deserving poor and to work the undeserving poor. Initially American towns used private relief, paying members of the community to care for the aged, disabled, and orphaned; the town remunerated caregivers with in-kind grants, tax forgiveness, and, more rarely, cash payments. The able-bodied, deserving poor, such as widows with children and military veterans and their families, received direct grants as well.

The records of the town of Portsmouth, New Hampshire, during the 1600s and 1700s illustrate the varied experiences of community care for the poor. In March 1670 Portsmouth resident, the "Widdow Sheaves," who cared for her two children and had "nothing to releive them," was granted thirty-seven shillings by the town. In 1688 the "Selectmen" of the town, "being informed of the povertie of Jos. Atkeson see it meete to remit his rate of foure shillings." Over the course of several years in the 1690s, the Portsmouth selectmen paid various residents as much as £12 a year to shelter, feed, and nurse the aged, long-time resident "Father Lewes." Because towns usually accepted bids and bound the sick and disabled to the lowest bidder, the system sometimes resulted in abuse. A solution appeared, it seemed, in the more humane system of the almshouse.

A change in the institutionalization of the poor in colonial America first came about in 1685 with the creation of the Dominion of New England under King James II. Edmund Andros, governor under the Dominion, instructed the colonies of New Hampshire, Massachusetts, Rhode Island, and Connecticut to erect institutions "for the Imploying of poor and Indigent People" as well as to elect overseers of the poor, who were charged with erecting and managing institutions to house and work the poor. Overseers were town leaders, usually with sufficient wealth to contribute their own funds, by way of a loan, if town finances were insufficient; not surprisingly, only the most committed townsmen agreed to serve as overseers of the poor. Governor Andros instructed overseers to take charge of raising funds through taxation, to care for the poor, and to erect almshouses. The first almshouses were built in such towns as Boston and Portsmouth in the late 1600s and early 1700s. Boston's almshouse, erected in 1685, was at first a private concern but became public after the election of overseers of the poor in 1691. The Portsmouth almshouse, erected in 1705, provided food, drink, water for washing, lodging, and firewood. In the mid-eighteenth century, it cost the town £8 per person, part of the cost of which was to be satisfied by the work of paupers producing cloth goods. Although Portsmouth only had one almshouse, by 1706 Boston had eight, corresponding to eight wards for poor relief established in 1715. Philadelphia and New York did not erect almshouses until 1732 and 1736, respectively. Almshouses often combined the innocent poor with ne'er-do-wells, to the detriment of the former. Some colonial towns had three or four overseers, but Boston had twelve in 1735.

As colonial towns matured into the eighteenth century, so too did the numbers of poor. Larger urban populations allowed for more anonymity among town inhabitants, hence the increasing presence of sturdy beggars. The solution, again following the English model, was the creation of institutions that were designed not so much to care for, but to work the poor—to pay their keep and alleviate the town of the burden of poor relief. Boston constructed a workhouse in 1739 in which ten men, thirty-eight women, and seven children worked. Laws passed in the colonies to erect workhouses were similar to that of New Hampshire, which declared in 1718 that such institutions should "be used and employed, for the Keeping, Correcting, and Setting to Work of rogues, Vagabonds, and common Beggars, and other Lewd, idle and Disorderly Persons." When the town of Portsmouth passed a law in 1752 "Relative to the Establishment of a Workhouse . . . to accommodate and work the poor both for the poor's benefit and the towns," the town proclaimed its intention to keep the poor "under proper care and regulation" so that "in a Little time instead of being a Charge, become Serviceable." After the town raised money for the work-house by sponsoring a lottery, the overseers of the poor set to work "to purchase Necessaries for the Support of the poor & Purchasing Stock at the Whole Sale and Cheapest Rate to Employ any Poor Person Either in the Work House or Elsewhere in the Town." The cost of maintaining and working the poor continued to increase, however, during the 1760s. The town of Portsmouth declared "Whereby Numbers of poor Idle Persons that are now a burden to the public may be properly Employed and Become Examples of Industry and Good Morals as they are now Shameful Examples of Idleness & Vice." At the same time, the town empowered the overseers to "supply the Work house with Stock to Imploy the poor in the said house or any Others that Shall be put there by the overseers." The overseers often found them-selves "abused and Affronted" by the poor, "which is a very great Injury to those whose Office & Services gives them a right to be Treated with the greatest Respect." The townspeople finally grew so exasperated that they determined to erect a house of correction to keep, work, and punish the most idle and undeserving of the poor. The house of correction was built on the grounds of the workhouse, which, by the 1770s, contained a separate room for the insane, a school to educate children, and facilities for medical care. The poor were worked six days a week but enjoyed rest and religious services on the Sabbath. Over the years, the environs of the Portsmouth workhouse declined, however, leading town officials and concerned cit-izens in the nineteenth century to erect a new almshouse to provide for the indigent. The new institution was dedicated in 1835, featuring a sermon by the local Episcopal priest, Charles Burroughs, in the almshouse chapel. This institution existed for a half century, caring for the poor, disabled, orphaned, and insane, until a county structure was built in the 1880s.

Institutionalization of the sick poor was of varied quality. Eighteenth-century Philadelphia sponsored an institution for the poor that echoed the English Bridewell, the hospital that imprisoned and worked the sick poor. The Pennsylvania Hospital for the Sick Poor, which began in 1751, brought a more charitable, car-ing approach to the institutionalization of the poor. The hospital was founded by Dr. Thomas Bond and Benjamin Franklin, who wrote *Some Account of the Pennsylvania Hospital* in 1754. The hospital, inspired by Quaker values, received all who were sick—the rich and poor, lunatics and sane, Americans and Indians, even Tories during the Revolutionary War. The institution expanded from humble quarters as the eighteenth century progressed; the grounds included an area for the sick poor to work, exercise, and play.

Supplementing public institutions for the poor were varied private concerns, indi-viduals, associations, or organizations providing charity. Such institutions were a worthy alternative to the almshouse. Calamities, such as fire and epidemics, found the charitable hands of the rich coming to the aid of the poor. Such charity was always selective, of course, and usually focused on widows and orphans. The Female Benevolent Society in Lynn, Massachusetts, and the Cambridge Female Humane Society were both founded in 1814. The Portsmouth Female Asylum, founded in the early 1800s, is an example: its purpose, like others of its ilk, was "to rescue [children] from the accumulated misery of poverty and vice" and to educate young women in reading, sewing, religion, and personal health. The asylum cared for orphans, as well as for children whose parents could provide insufficient care and who bound their children to the asylum until age eighteen. Wealthy matrons of Portsmouth subscribed to provide money to found the society and maintain its support; a committee visited the asylum weekly to check on the quality of care. The live-in "Governess" in charge ensured their religious education—not only by punctual attendance at Sunday church services, but daily Scripture readings as well, "to inculcate the principles of religion." The daily schedule was as follows, according to *The Rules, Regulations, &c. of the Portsmouth Female Asylum, with the Act of Incorporation*, published in 1815:

> The Children Shall rise at six o'clock in the morning, say their prayers, wash themselves in cold water, and comb their heads; breakfast at eight, play until nine, attend school from this hour until twelve, dine at one, attend school from two o'clock to five, play until six, and retire for the night at eight o'clock.

Nineteenth-century Americans changed their understanding of the poor from the colonial view of a destitute group of unfortunate or immoral people, deservedly separated from the rest of society, to merely a segment of society having insufficient wealth and resources to maintain an adequate standard of living according to the larger society. Such a change in social philosophy took time, culminating only during the Progressive Movement. Before progressivism, the poorhouse, which evolved from the almshouse and workhouse of the eighteenth century, dominated the institutionalization of poor adults and children. Social reformers of the late 1800s and early 1900s, however, believed that poverty in an industrialized, scientific society could no longer be blamed on God's will or on individual depravity, but rather on the society at large. To cure society of the sickness of poverty required the action of the community as a whole, working to improve conditions in the economy, workplace, neighborhoods, schools, and cities. The poor, at least in theory, should be integrated into the larger society rather than segregated in institutions ultimately designed to keep them in their place.

See also: British Poor and the Origins of Colonialism; Disease and the Poor; Poor Laws in England and Early America

Sources: Bridenbaugh, Carl, *Cities in Revolt* (New York: Oxford, 1955); Bridenbaugh, Carl, *Cities in the Wilderness* (New York: Oxford, 1938); Burn, Richard, *The History of the Poor Laws: With Observations* (London: Woodfall and Strahan, 1764); Eden, Frederic, *The State of the Poor*, 3 vols. (London: Davis, 1797); Katz, Michael B., *Poverty and Policy in American History* (New York: Academic Press, 1983); *Portsmouth New Hampshire Town Records*, typescript, Portsmouth Public Library.

J

JOB CORPS. Established by the Office of Economic Opportunity (OEO) under the 1964 Economic Opportunity Act (EOA), the Job Corps was part of the Johnson administration's Great Society program. Dogged by insufficient funding and too many applicants, the Job Corps did not work as planned and did little to improve the situation of the poor. Along with other failed OEO programs, such as the Community Action Program, the Job Corps never accomplished anything of note and its financial and administration struggles attracted scathing criticism that undermined support for the War on Poverty.

As described in the EOA, the purpose of the Job Corps was to prepare low-income youth "for the responsibilities of citizenship and to increase the employability of young men and young women aged sixteen through twenty-one by providing them in rural and urban residential centers with education, vocational training, useful work experience, including work directed toward the conservation of natural resources, and other appropriate activities." As this description shows, the Job Corps had many similarities to New Deal programs such as the Civilian Conservation Corps (CCC), which was established by President Franklin Delano Roosevelt in 1933. Both programs relocated low-income youth from urban settings to the countryside, where they performed various conservation work and odd jobs. Both programs attempted to address two pressing issues at the same time: conserving America's endangered natural resources and keeping at-risk youth out of cities and thus out of trouble.

The Job Corps was not as successful as the CCC, however. The Johnson administration had implemented its program during a period of economic surplus, whereas Roosevelt implemented the CCC during the Great Depression. Consequently, Johnson's program was exposed to harsher criticism—especially from conservatives like Arizona Senator Barry Goldwater, who sarcastically accused the Job Corps of being good for little else than allowing its participants to get tans. Responses like Goldwater's underlined the increasing resistance of many Americans toward federal relief or work programs in the late 1960s. The most significant development, however, was the decline of congressional support for the Job Corps, which ensured that the program lacked sufficient funds to accomplish anything. The EOA had authorized the program's director to make agreements with federal, state, and local public agencies and also with private organizations to establish new camps and to supply operational expenses, but these contributions proved inadequate. Like the entire War on Poverty, the Job Corps failed, in part, because of loss of political support in the late 1960s. Despite the subsequent reorganization and discontinuation of many OEO welfare-relief programs, the Job Corps was not abolished. At present, the Office of Job Corps is one of many programs administered by the Department of Labor (DOL).

See also: CCC (Civilian Conservation Corps); Department of Labor; Economic Opportunity Act; Office of Economic Opportunity; War on Poverty

Sources: Bremner, Robert H., Gary W. Reichard, and Richard Hopkins, eds., *American Choices: Social Dilemma and Public Policy since 1960* (Columbus: Ohio State University Press, 1986); Department of Labor (www.dol.gov); Economic Opportunity Act (http://www2.volstate.edu/geades/FinalDocs/1960s/eoa.htm); Patterson, James T., *America's Struggle against Poverty in the Twentieth Century* (Cambridge, MA: Harvard University Press, 2000).

K

KIDS COUNT. KIDS COUNT is a national and state project, supported by the Casey Foundation, to document the status of children nationwide and to impress on policymakers the importance of providing adequate services for the nation's children. Founded in 1989, KIDS COUNT has a three-tiered approach: (1) collecting and publishing information, (2) organizing community mobilization efforts, and (3) working to influence public policy. As part of its programs to mobilize communities and influence policy, KIDS COUNT has developed an extensive media campaign to inform the public about the needs of children.

KIDS COUNT focuses on the local, state, and national levels; often these levels are interconnected—localized programs and data collection often affect statewide and national trends. Since 1990 the primary national focus of KIDS COUNT has been the annual publication of data books that measure the social, educational, physical, and economic status of children in each state. In general, KIDS COUNT data books illustrate what types of problems affect children as a way of seeking to influence state, local, and federal policies to find solutions. The information in the data books allows KIDS COUNT to increase public awareness and public accountability for the relative security of America's children.

In 1992 the KIDS COUNT data book began focusing on specific themes to help policymakers and the public interpret the significance of the data presented: for example, the 1993 book focused on "distressed communities." To define a "distressed area," the program relied on the census definition of "a tract which exhibits at least four of the five following characteristics: high poverty rate (more than 27.5 percent), high percentage of female-headed families (more than 39.6 percent), high percentage of high school dropouts (more than 23.3 percent), high percentage of males unattached to the labor force (more than 46.5 percent), and a high percentage of families receiving public assistance income (more than 17.0 percent)." The 1994 data book included a discussion section on the influence of "environmental factors" that negatively impact children and youth. KIDS COUNT suggested the appropriate solutions, such as the increased involvement of local community development programs in impoverished areas. The 2001 KIDS COUNT data book focused on ten areas: the percentage of low–birth-weight babies; the infant mortality rate; the child death rate; the rate of teenage deaths by accident, homicide, and suicide; the teen birth rate; the percentage of children living with parents without full-time year-round employment; the percentage of teens who are high school dropouts; the percentage of teens not attending school and not working; the percentage of children in poverty; and the percentage of families with children headed by a single parent. KIDS COUNT data books also provide information on demographic and family income data for each state, to help local reformers focus on their area's specific problems.

KIDS COUNT has generally succeeded in its aim of increasing awareness of the status of children. The data collected and published in the data books are well-researched and facilitate the efforts of child advocates, researchers, and policymakers to make well-informed decisions about how to provide for disadvantaged children. Overall, KIDS COUNT is one of the more successful social policy projects because of its combination of effective research, dissemination of data, and application of its findings to specific policies to help improve the social, economic, and educational condition of America's children.

See also: Children and Poverty

Sources: www.kidscount.org and accompanying databases: State Level Data Online, Census Data Online, CLIKS: Community-Level Information on Kids, and Right Start Data Online.

L

LABOR. Throughout American history, the workplace has greatly affected society. Prior to the development of heavy industry in the nineteenth century, most work was localized, often following the traditional master-and-apprentice system in which young workers learned a skill from a master tradesman. The master provided lodging and trained the apprentice; thus, a bond formed between employer and worker, and both parties had a stake in the well-being of the other. Industrialization and standardization eclipsed this system, however. The need for complex skills diminished because machines performed specialized functions. As noted by Lewis Mumford in *Technics and Civilization,* the specialized functions of early machines—which only performed one task and required other machines or workers to perform the other tasks in order to produce the finished product—diminished the role of workers to that of machines. Workers no longer functioned as tradesmen who produced a completed product. As a result of specialization and standardization, the business elite—company owners, employers—relied less on skilled workers, and the relationship between workers and employers deteriorated; by the late nineteenth century, an outright labor war was underway.

Labor Conflict. The late nineteenth century and early twentieth century were times of intense labor conflict. The popularity of Social Darwinism—the application of Charles Darwin's theory of natural selection (the "survival of the fittest") to society—among wealthy businessmen increased the conflict between the poor and the wealthy. Whereas pre-industrial employment had encouraged ties between master and apprentice, fostering a noticeable but innocuous class division, employer and employee relations in nineteenth-century industrial society became confrontational. Attempting to consolidate their position against employers, workers developed labor unions such as the Knights of Labor and the American Federation of Labor (AFL). Unions, whose success depended on the cooperation of a large percentage of workers, allowed laborers to voice their discontent by means of strikes, through which they hoped to force employers to provide better working conditions and higher pay.

At times, strikes degenerated into violence, an outright fight between the workers and the business elite. The government typically sided with the elites, so the labor movement became more radical over time. The Haymarket Square Riot in Chicago in 1886 and the Pullman Strike in 1894 are good examples: both led to increased federal measures to secure the position of American business and worker dissatisfaction with the American government. The pro-business stance of the government contributed to the spread of socialism among the urban poor as a means of escape from what they believed was an oppressive system. The popularity of socialism and communism among the urban poor of all races and ethnicities alarmed business and political elites; in response, the elites renewed their efforts to secure the position of individual initiative and free-market capitalism. It was not until the stock market crash of October 1929 and the unpopular response of President Herbert Hoover that the federal government—under the leadership of President Franklin D. Roosevelt—decided to pay attention to the demands of workers.

In general, labor unions benefited during the New Deal. The 1933 National Recovery Administration (NRA) was the first attempt to facilitate industrial recovery through coordinating labor and business with the government. The primary intent of the NRA was to decrease competition and thereby increase efficiency. To accomplish this, the NRA allowed businesses to draft codes of fair conduct and allowed labor leaders to establish a maximum number of work hours, a minimum wage, and collective bargaining. However, the NRA failed to give workers real improvements, and many companies ignored the collective bargaining clause, set minimum wages at starvation levels, and set up company-controlled unions to negate the power of worker-led unions. Despite this, labor received some benefits during the 1930s. The 1935 National Labor Relations Act (also called the Wagner Act), proposed by New York Senator Robert Wagner, strengthened the federal government's support for unions and allowed unions such as the AFL and Committee on Industrial Organization (CIO) to win concessions—bargaining rights, an end to company-sponsored unions, and wage-hour protection from large industrial corporations such as General Motors in 1936 and U.S. Steel in 1937. These successes were not direct results of New Deal programs but attributable to the willingness of government and labor leaders to work together. Roosevelt's "try anything" approach to the New Deal allowed workers to have a greater political voice; the Great Depression broke down the federal government's reluctance to oversee the issues of the workplace.

The Fair Labor Standards Act (FLSA), first passed in 1938 and administered by the Department of Labor, is one of the most significant contemporary labor laws. The FLSA sets standards for wages by requiring employers to pay all employees at least the minimum wage, and it sets standards for overtime pay—at least one-and one-half the normal pay rate. The FLSA also sets standards for the employment of migrant and seasonal agricultural workers. Under the FLSA, employers are not required to pay migrant workers overtime; however, the law does require employers to pay at least the minimum wage when they employ seven or more full-time workers. One of the most significant aspects of the FLSA is its regulation of child labor.

Child Labor. Child labor is another significant issue. Prior to the implementation of FLSA regulations that prohibited children from performing hard labor, many working-class American families relied on the wages of all family members, including children, to survive. The idea that the male is the bread winner and the wife stays home with the children is a middle-class ideal—a luxury that the working class could not afford. Employers often preferred women and children because they could pay them lower wages, justifying the practice with the spurious reasoning that the male was the primary wage earner of the family, which made the earnings of women and children secondary. Late nineteenth-century Progressives noted that working-class children had few opportunities for advancement under this system, so reformers pushed for mandatory education and restrictions on child labor. Laws passed in the twentieth century, such as FLSA, served two purposes: to limit children's exposure to hazardous employment and to encourage children to better their future prospects through education.

The FLSA prohibits children under age sixteen from working in dangerous or "hazardous" jobs or from working during times that preclude their ability to obtain an education. The FLSA specifically prohibits children under eighteen from working jobs involving explosives, driving a motor vehicle, coal mining, logging, working with power-driven machines, exposure to radioactive substances, meat packing or processing, or roofing. Compulsory education laws further ensure that more children grow up with the basic educational skills that will allow them to obtain jobs that are more satisfying and higher paying.

Department of Labor. Labor relations with business and government have grown increasingly amenable in the twentieth and twenty-first centuries compared to the controversies of the 1800s. Part of the reason for this is the increased role of the federal government. Since the creation of the Department of Labor (DOL) in 1913, influential unions like the AFL-CIO are more apt to treat the federal government as a friend rather than an enemy. The DOL has been successful in overseeing and implementing labor policy. Most laws administered by the DOL ensure that all employees receive at least the minimum wage and have safe working conditions. The DOL also requires employers to give employees access to retirement and health care benefits. A primary task of the DOL is to oversee and enforce federal employment and labor laws. At present, the DOL oversees 180 federal laws affecting about 10 million employers and 125 million employees.

See also: Children and Poverty; Department of Labor; New Deal

Sources: Conkin, Paul, *The New Deal*, 2nd ed. (Arlington Heights, IL: Harlan Davidson, 1975); Department of Labor (www.dol.gov); Divine, Robert A., T. H. Breen, et al., *The American Story*, 2nd ed. (New York: Penguin Books, 2005); Mumford, Lewis, *Technics and Civilization* (New York: Harcourt Brace, 1935, reprinted 1962); Patterson, James T., *America's Struggle against Poverty in the Twentieth Century* (Cambridge, MA: Harvard University Press, 2000).

LITERATURE AND POVERTY. Scholars differ in opinions as to whether art mimics life or life mimics art; either way, literature is full of allusions to poverty. Some of America's most acclaimed authors—including Jack Kerouac, John Steinbeck, William Faulkner, Langston Hughes, and Ralph Ellison—focused on the hardships and humanity of the poor. Although these authors presented diverse representations of poverty, some, such as Kerouac, romanticized individualism; others, such as Steinbeck, portrayed the poor as resilient but beaten-down victims of depression and unfeeling authorities; and still others, such as Ellison, emphasized the racial dimension of poverty. Fittingly, one of the primary themes of American literature—as in society as a whole—is the distinction between the "deserving" and the "undeserving" poor.

During the affluent 1920s, New York socialite and novelist F. Scott Fitzgerald remarked to fellow author Ernest Hemingway that the rich were "different" than the poor; meaning that the high-life and culture of the wealthy set them apart from the rest of society culturally as well as economically. To this assertion Hemingway replied: "Yes, they have money." These very different responses show the ongoing split between the economic and the cultural interpretation of poverty: whereas Fitzgerald focused on the cultural merits of the wealthy, Hemingway emphasized the financial distinction and downplayed the importance of lifestyle. Both interpretations have gained popularity in American literature.

Novelist John Steinbeck portrayed the harsh life of "Okies"—impoverished tenant farmers forced to migrate west to California in search of work— in his novel *The Grapes of Wrath*, which followed the trials of the Joad family. Steinbeck's portrayal illustrated the pessimistic outlook that the Great Depression spread throughout the country. The Joads reach California, but they find no end of hardship there; the book gives little impression that their situation will improve. Similarly, William Faulkner detailed the struggles of poor whites in the rural South in novels such as *As I Lay Dying*, in which he emphasized the humanity of the poor despite their lack of education and privilege. In *As I Lay Dying*, Faulkner wrote the entire book in dialect from the perspective of several characters, poignantly capturing the strong personalities of the characters and the depth of their feelings.

Jack Kerouac, one of the leaders of the Beat movement of the 1950s, presented a very different view of poverty in his novels *On the Road* and *The Dharma Bums*. In *On the Road*, a semiautobiographical account of youth rebellion and the intermingling of material and spiritual journeys, Kerouac captured the allure of the automobile and the drifter lifestyle of not being tied down by commitments. Kerouac thus romanticized the voluntary hobo lifestyle of the Beats, even though he dutifully captured the hardships—cold, heat, fatigue, police attempting to arrest bums, homeless riding freight trains into town—facing the itinerant poor. The beginning of *The Dharma Bums* focuses on the patience and quiet determination of hobos—Kerouac notes the saintliness of an elderly hobo he meets on a freight train in the opening chapter—a very different perspective than that typically held by middle-class Americans.

African American writers, including Ralph Ellison and Langston Hughes, focused on the impact of racial prejudice on poverty. In the novel *Invisible Man*, Ellison depicted the structural barriers barring blacks and minorities from advancement: impoverishment, according to Ellison's portrayal, was more than an economic situation. Likewise, Hughes emphasized the absurdity of race prejudice that prevented minorities from assimilating with the American mainstream: Hughes's work—such as *Brass Spittoons* (1927) and *Theme for English B* (1959)—emphasizes the idea that prejudice and ignorance, not economics, are the cause of social and cultural impoverishment.

The distinction between the "deserving" and the "undeserving" poor plays a central role in all of these works, but in very different forms. Steinbeck and Faulkner tended to emphasize the humanity of the poor through the use of dialect to capture the individuality of the characters. In both *Grapes of Wrath* and *As I Lay Dying*, the white rural poor are dignified by their struggle to survive, and, despite their lack of education, they demonstrate strength of character and the will to survive. In contrast, Ellison and Hughes emphasized the importance of noneconomic barriers, especially racial prejudice, and, even though their characters show no less individual strength, they are more concerned with acceptance than survival or material advancement. Kerouac's work is the most extreme; he depicts voluntary poverty, in the sense that his bohemian characters disdain steady work for the quick fulfillment of fast cars and spiritual searching. Whereas Steinbeck, Faulkner, Hughes, and Ellison depicted the "deserving" poor, Kerouac idealized the carefree nonattached lifestyle of the Beats. One significant point about Kerouac's work, however, is that his characters do not ask for public assistance or relief; they focus instead on their freedom and ability to fend for themselves: in that sense Kerouac's characters merely update the type of individualism required for the American Dream. In short, American literature, with few exceptions, tends to portray two sides of the poor: some authors emphasize the individualism and will to survive necessary for the American Dream, and others focus on the structural barriers that prevent all Americans from taking part in mainstream society.

See also: African Americans and Poverty (post-slavery); *The Grapes of Wrath*; Racism

Sources: Ellison, Ralph, *Invisible Man* (New York: Knopf, 1995); Ellman, Richard, and Robert O'Clair, eds., *The Norton Anthology of Modern Poetry,* 2nd ed. (New York: Norton, 1973); Faulkner, William, *As I Lay Dying* (New York: Vintage Books, 1990); Kerouac, Jack, *On the Road* (New York: Penguin, 1976); Kerouac, Jack, *The Dharma Bums* (New York: Penguin, 1971); Patterson, James T., *America's Struggle against Poverty in the Twentieth Century* (Cambridge, MA: Harvard University Press, 2000); Steinbeck, John, *The Grapes of Wrath* (New York: Viking Press, 1939).

M

MEASUREMENT OF INEQUALITY. Social scientists consider the measurement of changes in wealth inequality to be an important indicator of the extent of poverty, class distribution and conflict, and relative health of the economy. Conceptualizations of equality and inequality, of wealth and poverty, are served by the concrete analyses of wealth distribution over time. During the past half century, American social scientists have developed a variety of techniques to measure wealth inequality over time. These indices include measurements of frequency distribution and standard deviation from the mean, such as the Paredo Coefficient, the Lorenz Curve, the Size Share Top Ten (SSTT), the Gini Index, the Schutz Index, and the Atkinson Index. At the same time, the federal government has devised inequality standards to establish an official poverty level for use in aid programs and in determining tax rates.

Wealth inequality measurements rely on statistical analysis of change over time, as reflected in plots on a graph, frequency distributions, standard deviations, and the Lorenz Curve. The simplest and most comprehensible indices measure extremes in wealth or income distribution. The SSTT is a useful statistical device for determining wealth inequality at a particular time and place. The SSTT indicates the percentage of wealth or income held by the richest 10 percent of the population. If, for example, the upper 10 percent of the population holds 85 percent of the wealth, the remaining 90 percent of the population divide the remaining 15 percent of the wealth. It is not hard to imagine the kind of suffering experienced by the majority of the people under such circumstances.

Frequency distribution is the quantification of wealth distribution according to the average deviation from the mean, or the overall dispersion according to comparison of population and wealth. Most tests of inequality rely on simple graphing, with a range between 1 (total inequality, absolutely uneven distribution of wealth) and 0 (complete equality, absolutely even distribution of wealth). The earliest wealth inequality measurements were developed by the Italian economists Vilfredo Paredo and Max Lorenz in the early twentieth century. The Paredo Coefficient examined the relationship of income to population in an attempt to derive a standard measure that would become normative. The Lorenz Curve is based on a graph of income or wealth compared to population. The extremes are a straight line going from lower left to upper right (equality) or an extreme curve comparable to a right angle (inequality).

The Gini Coefficient of Concentration, one of the oldest and most frequently used measurements, is a ratio that describes the relationship between population and wealth distribution. Based on the Lorenz Curve, the Gini examines the area on the graph between the line of perfect equality and the actual curve indicating degree of inequality. The higher the Gini is, the greater the wealth inequality is. As Mary Jean Bowman noted in 1945, the Gini Coefficient "measures comparative degrees of inequality on the assumption that within any given distribution equal arithmetic differences in income are to be regarded as of equal importance, regardless of the size of the economy." Regardless of the monetary unit, the Gini provides a ratio of the deviation from the absolute rate of equality. Because of its lack of regard for intra-categorical dispersion, the Gini can give the same ratio for different curves. The Gini requires precise graphs with coordinates based on intervals, not ordinals based on deciles. Some have criticized the Gini for not being sensitive to societal change and social differences. It is possible to obtain the same Gini for two completely different societies in terms of standard of living, production, monetary system, and Gross Domestic Product (GDP). The strength of the Gini Index, however, is its use as an absolute measurement that is not subject to deviations of time and place.

Even so, in 1951 the American economist Robert Schutz sought to eliminate some of the limitations of the Gini Coefficient and devised the Schutz Index of inequality. Rather than look at wealth concentration, he examined the Lorenz Curve itself, arguing that "the direct comparison of the slopes at various points will give us a clear picture of inequality than is ordinarily derived from the Lorenz curve." Schutz was particularly interested in changes in the wealth distribution above and below that point on the curve where wealth or income is equally distributed—that is, where the population percentage equals the wealth percentage, called the Equal Share Point (ESPT). Schutz asserted that the sum of the slopes at various points on the curve above and below the ESPT would be numerically equivalent.

The Atkinson Index was formulated by the British economist Anthony Atkinson in 1970. Atkinson was heavily influenced by the work of Hugh Dalton, who argued in 1920 that inequality of income distribution is the same as "the ratio of the total economic welfare attainable under an equal distribution to the total economic welfare attained under the given distribution." The Atkinson Index centers around the "equally distributed equivalent level of income," which is "the level of income per head which if equally distributed would give the same level of social welfare as the present distribution." Social welfare to Atkinson is the same concept as economic welfare to Dalton: both refer to the entire national resources per capita of a country. The Atkinson Index is based on the assumption that increased inequality lessens the overall capability of the economy. Thus, the lower the index is, the less is the potential gain to social welfare by means of redistribution. Conversely, the higher the inequality is, the greater percentage of national income would be needed to achieve the same degree of social welfare.

The first federal government standard of poverty was developed in the 1960s as part of Johnson's War on Poverty. A statistician at the Social Security Administration, Mollie Orshansky, developed an absolute measure of poverty based on low-cost family food plans derived from the Department of Agriculture. In 1969 the Office of

Management and Budget adopted Orshansky's poverty threshold measure—the lowest level family income that allows for an adequate low-cost food plan. The poverty threshold does not change because of changing perceptions in the U.S. standard of living, but it does change according to consumption patterns.

Sources: Atkinson, Anthony R., "On the Measurement of Inequality," *Journal of Economic Theory,* Vol. 2 (1970); Bowman, Mary Jean, "A Graphical Analysis of Personal Income Distribution in the United States," *American Economic Review,* Vol. 35 (1945); Dalton, Hugh, "The Measurement of the Inequality of Incomes," *Economic Journal,* Vol. 30 (1920); Iceland, John, *Poverty in America: A Handbook*, 2nd ed. (Berkeley: University of California Press, 2006); Schutz, Robert R., "On the Measurement of Income Inequality," *American Economic Review,* Vol. 41 (1951); Smith, James D., *The Personal Distribution of Income and Wealth* (New York: National Bureau of Economic Research, 1975); Williamson, Jeffrey G., and Peter H. Lindert, *American Inequality: A Macroeconomic History* (New York: Academic Press, 1980).

MEDICAID. Established by Congress as part of the 1965 Social Security Act, Medicaid is a health insurance program for low-income Americans. Jointly funded by federal and state government, individual states administer Medicaid, so the specific features of the program vary. In general, Medicaid covers low-income families, children and parents, and disabled persons. Like Medicare—the federal health program for the elderly—Medicaid has generated controversy, because expanding expenses and its quasi-welfare status do not satisfy many conservatives, and some liberals think it insufficiently comprehensive.

On the federal level, the Centers for Medicare and Medicaid Services (CMS), part of the Department of Health and Human Services (HHS), administer Medicaid. Medicaid is an entitlement program—meaning that the federal government provides some funding, but states also contribute a large proportion—nearly half—of the program monies. Funding methods vary by state, and some states require each county to gather its own funds, but some basic guidelines are common in all states. Across the nation, eligibility for Medicaid is based on low-income status. All fifty states participate in the Medicaid program; some states subcontract with private insurance companies and others directly compensate providers: health clinics, hospitals, and individual doctors.

The United States has never instituted a program of universal health care; Medicaid and Medicare partially address the needs of specific parts of the population, but they do not provide access to health care for all Americans. In 2005, 27.4 percent of the population—over 80 million people—had government insurance (Medicare, Medicaid, and military-sponsored insurance). At the same time, 46.6 million Americans—15.9 percent of the total population—had no health insurance coverage. Although Medicaid covered over 38 million Americans in 2005—13 percent of the population—over 8 million (11.2 percent) children under age eighteen were without health insurance, and 19 percent of children living below the poverty line were uninsured. Consequently, Medicaid covers a significant portion of low-income Americans—many of whom would otherwise be without health insurance coverage—but it is far from a universal plan.

Funding Medicaid has become a problem in recent years; many states allocate a quarter of their yearly budget to support Medicaid programs. The federal government has adopted some changes in an attempt to streamline Medicaid funding. The 2005 Deficit Reduction Act (DRA) is one example of this. The DRA altered the rules for asset transfers and assessing the homes owned by nursing home residents and strengthened identification procedures to ensure that all enrollees are U.S. citizens or legal resident aliens. The specific future of Medicaid is uncertain, because new federal and state requirements and budgetary restraints will undoubtedly affect the program's coverage. Like Medicare, Medicaid is a dynamic political issue, and liberals and conservatives disagree over the specifics of its implementation. Regardless of political ideology, however, Medicaid has significantly improved the health insurance coverage of low-income Americans, and it is unlikely that Congress will phase out the program any time soon.

See also: Children and Poverty; Disease and the Poor; Medicare; Social Security; War on Poverty

Sources: Centers for Medicare & Medicaid Services (www.cms.hhs.gov/); DeNavas-Walt, Carmen, Bernadette D. Proctor, and Cheryl Hill Lee, "Income, Poverty, and Health Insurance Coverage in the United States: 2005" (U.S. Census Bureau: 2006); Patterson, James T., *America's Struggle against Poverty in the Twentieth Century* (Cambridge, MA: Harvard University Press, 2000); Social Security Online, Medicaid Information (www.socialsecurity.gov/disabilityresearch/wi/medicaid.htm).

MEDICARE. An insurance program for the elderly that is administered by the federal government, Medicare provides assistance to people age sixty-five or older and those with specific permanent disabilities. The Centers for Medicare and Medicaid Services (CMS)—a part of the Department of Health and Human Services (HHS)—administers Medicare. Established by Congress in 1965, Medicare has evolved over the years; although it has borne criticism from both liberals and conservatives, its impact increases nearly every year: in 2005, 42.6 million Americans received Medicare coverage, and some experts project that by 2031 Medicare will cover nearly 77 million Americans. Medicare has several major divisions: Hospital Insurance (Part A), which helps cover inpatient hospital care in hospitals and hospice care; Medical Insurance (Part B), which helps cover outpatient care and doctor's services; and, beginning in 2006, (Part D) Prescription Drug Coverage, in which Medicare beneficiaries may pay lower out-of-pocket expenses for medically necessary prescription drugs.

Unlike most other industrialized Western nations, the United States has never instituted a program of universal health care; Medicare and Medicaid are two halfway programs that address the needs of specialized portions of the population but do not provide health care to all Americans. Medicare developed from existing but inefficient or unsuccessful programs, such as the 1960 Kerr–Mills Act, which had established a program for the elderly in which the federal government matched funds spent on health care; this program failed because of the wide variations by state, among other things. Medicare, like Medicaid, sought to ease the financial burden placed on state and local government and to level geographical differences: poorer southern states could not bear the burden, and northern state governments grumbled about the large numbers of needy.

The passage of Medicare was not a large political issue in the 1960s. Most legislators did not realize that it would evolve into such a large and costly program (by 2000 Medicare costs were about $277 billion per year). The high cost of Medicare has caused controversy: conservatives balk at the idea of allocating nearly 15 percent of the federal budget on a quasi-welfare program like Medicare, and escalating costs—illustrated by the Medicare Board of Trustees 2006 report to Congress that Medicare's hospital insurance trust fund could run out of money by 2018—place the program in jeopardy. However, the elderly have very well-organized political lobbies—such as the American Association of Retired Persons (AARP). Like Social Security, Medicare is very unlikely to be dismantled by Congress anytime soon. One of the major controversies about Medicare is the projected increase in the number of baby boomer retirees drawing benefits at the same time as the number of workers paying taxes to support Medicare declines. Medicare depends on FICA (Federal Insurance Contributions Act) taxes—drawn directly from workers' paychecks, matched by the employer, and placed in a trust fund—to fund its services; consequently, the economic future of the program seems very bleak, and policymakers and experts are considering alternative means of funding.

The various parts of Medicare receive funding from different sources. In 2006 FICA taxes comprised 40 percent of the overall budget but 86 percent of Part A (Hospital Insurance) and 0 percent of all other parts. "General" revenue"—primarily from the federal government—comprised 41 percent of the total, 0 percent of Part A, 75 percent of Part B (Medical Insurance), and 78 percent of Part D (Prescription Drug Coverage). Beneficiary premiums comprised 11 percent of the total, 1 percent of Part A, 24 percent of Part B, and 10 percent of Part D. State payments comprised 2 percent of the total, 5 percent of Part A, 0 percent of Part B, and 11 percent of Part D, and revenue from interest comprised 4 percent of the total, 8 percent of Part A, 2 percent of Part B, and 0 percent of Part D.

Although Medicare's future is uncertain, it has helped low-income elderly Americans obtain medical care. Most of the controversy is over its funding; the conflict between liberals and conservatives is over the need for quasi-welfare programs such as federally sponsored health care. Conservatives tend to prefer privately run programs, but liberals urge a need for the federal government to help the poor as a last resort. Thus Medicare—like Medicaid—is also a political issue, and its effectiveness depends on the support of political leaders.

See also: Disease and the Poor; Medicaid; Social Security; War on Poverty

Sources: 2005 Annual Report of the Social Security and Medicare Boards of Trustees, Centers for Medicare & Medicaid Services (www.cms.hhs.gov/); Patterson, James T., *America's Struggle against Poverty in the Twentieth Century* (Cambridge, MA: Harvard University Press, 2000); Medicare (www.medicare.gov/).

MINIMUM WAGE. The minimum wage is the lowest wage that an employer may legally pay to employees on an hourly, daily, or monthly basis. Although other nations implemented minimum wages in the nineteenth century, the United States first introduced a nationwide minimum wage in 1938—with the Fair Labor Standards Act (FLSA); at present, the Department of Labor (DOL) oversees the legal aspects of minimum wage requirements. Experts debate the economic and social impact of an institutionalized minimum wage; in theory, establishing a point beneath which no employer can legally pay helps prevent absolute destitution, because all workers earn enough for basic survival. Consequently, some supporters have argued that establishing a minimum wage helps prevent the outright exploitation of workers. In practice, this idea has not always worked, however, and even today many American workers earning minimum wage live below the official poverty line.

One reason for the disconnect between theory and practice is that there is often a difference between the minimum wage and the "living wage"—the wage required for workers to obtain the basic necessities of life. The definition of what constitutes basic necessities likewise varies, and there is no absolute standard on which to judge. In affluent times, such as the 1960s, many Americans came to expect items previously considered luxuries—such as televisions and automobiles—as basic necessities, and even as rights; likewise, the official definition of poverty—the income threshold set by policymakers based on low-cost family food plans—varies significantly as consumer expectations and the economy changes. As the poverty threshold increases, so also does the political pressure to raise the minimum wage. For example, in the 1970s high oil prices and rising inflation lowered the ability of low-wage workers to maintain a normal standard of living.

In the political debate over the impact that the minimum wage has on the economy, supporters deny that the minimum wage adversely impacts employment, arguing that any adverse effect is modest and outweighed by the social benefit derived from higher wages. Those in opposition argue that the minimum wage harms the economy because it increases unemployment among low-wage workers as employers hire fewer workers to compensate for higher costs per worker. The increased burden that the minimum wage places on employers, others argue, slows economic growth, because businesses struggle to maintain artificially high wages. Supporters counter by arguing that the minimum wage increases the overall average standard of living, because all workers with steady employment are guaranteed a specific wage. Business leaders also have some reasons to support the minimum wage; some experts argue that a minimum wage creates an incentive to work, and employers can demand more from the workers they hire. Some policymakers believe the minimum wage is a low-cost alternative to increasing welfare spending, although, of course, the minimum wage does not affect the unemployed.

The minimum wage is an economic strategy to regulate the number of working Americans who live below the official poverty line. However, the concept of an established, federally regulated minimum wage does not meet with universal acceptance; there is substantial criticism of its effects. In general, the minimum wage increases during affluent times—when Americans expect a higher basic standard of life—and during times of significant inflation, when prices for goods rise high enough to lower the buying power of low-paid workers drastically. Since the implementation of the first U.S. minimum wage in 1938, the overall living situation of most American workers has improved, and, even though the minimum wage does not provide protection against inflation, it sets a basic limit, at least, that all workers can expect to earn.

See also: New Deal

Sources: Department of Labor (www.dol.gov); Divine, Robert A., T. H. Breen, et al., *The American Story*, 2nd ed. (New York: Penguin Books, 2005); Iceland, John, *Poverty in America*, 2nd ed. (Berkeley: University of California Press, 2006); Minimum Wage Laws in the States (July 24, 2007) (http://www.dol.gov/esa/minwage/america.htm); Patterson, James T., *America's Struggle against Poverty in the Twentieth Century* (Cambridge, MA: Harvard University Press, 2000).

N

NATIONAL CENTER FOR CHILDREN IN POVERTY. The National Center for Children in Poverty (NCCP) is a nonprofit, nonpartisan research and policy organization based at Columbia University that performs and publishes research on child poverty in America. A major goal of NCCP is to disseminate its research findings to policymakers and the general populace to work for more successful means to prevent child poverty and to improve the ability of low-income families to provide for their children. The NCCP researches child poverty and children's mental health, social security, and welfare.

The NCCP began in 1989 through financial support from the Carnegie Corporation of New York and the Ford Foundation. The NCCP has three primary goals: to secure the economic status of low-income families, to encourage the growth of stable and nurturing families, and to help prepare low-income children for successful school experiences. The family takes the central role in each of these goals: the NCCP focuses on "family-oriented solutions" to achieve its goals. NCCP programs exist at the state, local, and national levels. The NCCP promotes strong communities to support healthy families that foster the growth of successful children. The "Improving the Odds" program, for example, provides a state-by-state picture of policy decisions and public services that affect young children. The collaborative project, "Making 'Work Supports' Work," helps state and national policymakers improve public supports for the families of low-wage workers. "Project THRIVE" analyzes public education policy to support the Early Childhood Comprehensive Systems (ECCS) initiatives funded by the Maternal and Child Health Bureau.

The NCCP looks to the future; its focus is on public policy and providing detailed information to policymakers, teachers, health care workers, and social workers. Several NCCP research themes are specifically aimed at policymakers and relevant public policy issues. For example, the NCCP researches ways to "make work pay" through improved work supports—a phrase used by President Bill Clinton in support of his 1996 Welfare Reform bill. The NCCP also researches ways to provide successful early-learning environments for young children, as well as ways to provide adequate health and mental health care for low-income families. The NCCP focuses on the politically possible solutions: "policymakers need the right information to make good decisions . . . to promote the health and successful development of children." NCCP research seeks to provide the data needed to influence these decisions. The NCCP also provides the media with its findings, thus reaching a more general audience.

See also: Children and Poverty; Clinton Welfare Reform

Sources: Haveman, Robert H., and John Karl Scholz, "The Clinton Welfare Reform Plan: Will It End Poverty as We Know It?" Institute for Research on Poverty Discussion Paper no. 1037–94 (1994); National Center for Children in Poverty (www.nccp.org/); Patterson, James T., *America's Struggle against Poverty in the Twentieth Century* (Cambridge, MA: Harvard University Press, 2000); Transcript of President Clinton's 1997 State of the Union speech, CNN article (http://edition.cnn.com/2005/ALLPOLITICS/01/31/sotu.clinton1997/index.html); Trattner, Walter I., *From Poor Law to Welfare State*, 6th ed. (New York: Free Press, 1999).

NEW DEAL. Initiated by President Franklin Delano Roosevelt in 1933 to correct the problems of the Great Depression, the New Deal marked a profound shift in the way that Americans viewed poverty and the government's role in establishing social order. The New Deal rejected the conservative, individualistic mentality of the Progressives and replaced it with a liberal organized, bureaucratic, planned economy.

During the New Deal, the federal government shifted from the ideology of conservative individualism to an ideology supporting a liberal group orientation. This switch was clearly illustrated in the transition from the Hoover to Roosevelt administrations. Hoover's pro-business policies represented the failure of free-market capitalism to come to terms with the reality of the Great Depression, whereas New Deal policies were an optimistic, if sometimes poorly planned, switch to direct federal relief. There were two main stages of the New Deal: the initial months of Roosevelt's first term in 1933—the "Hundred Days"—when Roosevelt implemented many policies and programs without a comprehensive plan; and the later New Deal of 1935–1936, when Congress fine-tuned older policies—such as the AAA, which had been ruled unconstitutional and needed to be revised. The ideology of Keynesian economics—that the government could spend its way out of the Depression—gained recognition during this second stage. In general, the first stage represented the idealistic period, when Roosevelt implemented innovative policies. The second stage represented a more pragmatic approach that marked the end of idealistic hopes that the New Deal would revolutionize America's social order.

New Deal Programs. The Great Depression began in October 1929 when the stock market crashed, causing economic chaos and forcing many banks and businesses to go bankrupt. Following the precepts of *laissez-faire,* Hoover, a Progressive Republican and self-made businessman, chose not to involve the federal government directly; he hoped that the economy would correct itself. However, the Depression continued to worsen, and many Americans resented Hoover's inaction; for example, the makeshift shantytowns that developed across the nation because of widespread unemployment were referred to as "Hoovervilles." Running against Hoover in the 1932 election, Roosevelt emphasized his willingness to activate the federal government in implementing new approaches in an attempt to correct the Depression, and this new approach, along with his engaging personality, enabled him to defeat Hoover by a huge margin. Attempting to follow up on his varied and often unrealistic campaign promises, Roosevelt took immediate action following his inauguration and, with the help of advisors such as Harry Hopkins and Rexford Tugwell, implemented diverse but often poorly planned programs.

The greatest success of the early New Deal was the way that Roosevelt's optimism and willingness to take action raised morale, even when the actual programs did little to correct the Depression itself. Roosevelt's early New Deal policies ranged from programs such as the Federal Deposit Insurance Corporation (FDIC)—intended to provide greater financial security to banks in order to prevent bank runs, which were common in the early years of the Depression—to work programs such as the Civilian Conservation Corps (CCC), which focused more on keeping men employed than on the worth of the actual projects undertaken. Under the direction of Harry Hopkins, the Reconstruction Finance Corporation (RFC), originally formed under the Hoover Administration in 1932 to loan money to prevent businesses from bankruptcy, began passing out modest relief checks to unemployed Americans in 1933, marking the first outright program of federal welfare.

The immediate results of the first New Deal programs were mixed because the causes of the Great Depression were more complicated than a simple stock market crash. Some long-term causes of the Great Depression were evident in the 1920s: the overproduction and underconsumption of products had a negative impact on the economy because workers' wages lagged at the same time that corporate upper classes reaped greater profits. At the end of the 1920s, 60 percent of Americans lived below the poverty line; and the top 1 percent owned 20 percent of the nation's wealth. The agricultural downturn of the 1920s also foreboded the Great Depression. The 1910s had been a period of vast agricultural growth, fueled in part by the increased demand of wartime production. In the years after World War I, however, American farmers continued to generate high levels of produce, which flooded the market and drove prices and profits down. The result was a crisis in the American agricultural industry, which lasted through the 1930s and only ended with the return to wartime production levels during World War II.

The New Deal's response to the plight of farmers was one of its most ironic and least-thought-out plans. The Agricultural Adjustment Act (AAA) paid farmers to control production levels by restricting the acreage used—and even destroying crops—in an attempt to drive prices up; at the same time many people were starving in American cities. As in many New Deal programs, the AAA did not have the intended effect: rather than helping farmers regain self-sufficiency through increased prices, the acreage limitation forced many sharecroppers from their farms without compensation; most landowners merely pocketed the federal money and farmed the allowed acreage themselves. In short, the AAA harmed both destitute sharecroppers in rural areas and limited the availability of food in urban areas. If Roosevelt and his advisors had spent more time planning their programs, such counterproductive measures might have been avoided. Instead, many New Deal programs were poorly coordinated and did not correspond to an overall plan. Roosevelt's approach to the New Deal was precisely to take action despite the lack of comprehensive planning; rather than overplan, as Hoover did, Roosevelt determined that the best way to increase American morale was to demonstrate that the federal government cared about the situation and was taking direct steps to improve it.

One of the most innovative and best-planned projects was the Tennessee Valley Authority (TVA), established in 1933, which set up an extensive system of dams along the Tennessee River to control floods, facilitate navigation, and provide electricity for several states. The TVA succeeded because it provided employment opportunities and improved essential aspects of the nation's infrastructure. Unlike programs such as the AAA that lacked clear planning and were inefficient, the TVA combined innovative regional planning with the creation of new jobs. The Works Progress Administration (WPA) in 1935 was a later attempt to provide financial assistance and occupations to the unemployed. Directed by Harry Hopkins, the WPA—like the CCC—focused more on relief than on meaningful projects; the program's primary goal was to restore good work ethic and self-respect in American men through employment. One of the more unique aspects of the WPA was its provisions for intellectuals and artists: the WPA also provided assistance to musicians, actors, painters, and writers.

The Impact of the New Deal. Many New Deal programs affected minority groups, sometimes improving their situation. African Americans often participated in New Deal programs, some of which brought hope to the black community, although the New Deal did little to improve the overall situation. Programs such as the Civilian Conservation Corps (CCC) and the National Youth Administration (NYA) did not discriminate against African Americans, who comprised 11 percent of the CCC and 10 percent of the NYA. African American intellectuals also participated in the New Deal: Richard Wright, author of *Native Son*, a 1930s protest novel, worked under the Federal Writer's project. Aubrey Williams, the assistant director of the WPA, worked with the NYA to provide blacks with better education. Despite the efforts of the New Deal to provide African Americans with improved housing, employment, and education, many urban blacks failed to obtain lasting jobs and remained isolated in ghettos. Because of housing programs, such as FHA loans, and the development of public housing, however, the African American mortality rate declined as the average standard of living of urban blacks improved. Overall, the New Deal implemented programs to help African Americans, but the New Deal did not solve many of the most pressing problems, such as racial segregation and the isolation of many blacks in run-down inner-city ghettos. At its best, the New Deal acknowledged that blacks required assistance just as whites did, although racial prejudice remained strong throughout the nation.

Labor and unions benefited during the New Deal. The establishment of the National Recovery Administration (NRA) in 1933 was the first attempt to facilitate industrial recovery through coordinating labor and business with the government. Intended to decrease competition and thus increase efficiency, one measure of the NRA allowed businesses to draft codes of fair conduct, and another gave labor the right to establish maximum hours, minimum wage, and collective bargaining. However, the NRA failed to provide labor with real improvements, because companies ignored the collective bargaining clause, set minimum wages at starvation levels, and negated the power of unions by setting up company-controlled unions. The 1935 National Labor Relations Act, also known as the Wagner Act (having been proposed by New York Senator Robert Wagner), strengthened the federal government's support for unions and allowed unions such as the American Federation of Labor (AFL) and Committee on Industrial Organization (CIO) to win concessions: bargaining rights, an end to company-sponsored unions, and wage-hour protection from large industrial corporations such as General Motors in 1936 and U.S. Steel in 1937. The success of labor unions, not New Deal programs, brought the most direct results for unskilled laborers, minorities, and women; the try-anything approach of the New Deal merely allowed workers a greater political voice in the wake of the Great Depression.

After the initial optimism about the New Deal had faded, Roosevelt courted more pragmatic policies: the most significant of these was Keynesian economics. The basic ideology of this approach, advocated by British economist John Maynard Keynes, is that government spending and investment will improve the economy. Keynesian economics supports deficit spending rather than tax increases. Keynes argued that the economy will correct itself once enough capital is invested and that deficit spending will allow the government to reap the return of the taxes already in place. Although Roosevelt met and corresponded with Keynes, he never fully embraced the idea, and the New Deal never adopted a policy of all-out deficit spending. The New Deal used microeconomics—dealing with segments of the economy—rather than the macroeconomics that Keynes supported, but did not succeed in bringing the nation out of economic recession. In fact, another recession occurred in 1937; only the return to wartime spending, which, ironically, was in accord with Keynes's plan to rejuvenate the economy, ended the Great Depression.

Historians differ in assessing the overall impact of the New Deal—some laud its progressive reforms, some argue that it was too conservative, and some think that it strayed too far from the American ideal of free-market capitalism. The many facets of the New Deal—social, economic, and political—further obscure attempts to analyze its success or failure. Most historians agree, however, that the New Deal was an economic disappointment because Roosevelt's program failed to correct the Great Depression. Despite Roosevelt's optimism and the economy's slow rise during his first term from 1933–1937, the recession of 1937 destroyed the illusion of the New Deal's success. By 1938 the New Deal had lost support in Congress and Roosevelt no longer enjoyed the unquestioning support for new programs that he had had in his first term. The Supreme Court presented another obstacle for the New Deal; the Court ruled programs such as the AAA and the NRA unconstitutional, prompting Roosevelt to ask Congress to pass a provision allowing him to increase the number of Supreme Court justices (to prevent more unfavorable rulings). This proposal failed, however, and opened political rifts that cost Roosevelt the unwavering support of Congress. After 1937 many Democrats in the South no longer felt obliged to support the President's programs, and only the threat of war in Europe restored Roosevelt's influence. By the beginning of 1942, after the United States entered World War II, defense spending and increased agricultural demand raised prices on American goods. The return to wartime production and the rise of nationalism ended the Great Depression, not the New Deal. Roosevelt presented an optimistic public face in the early 1930s when the nation needed it most, but his lack of a concrete goal for the New Deal ensured its failure. However, the New Deal had a lasting impact on American society and politics, despite the return of conservatism in national politics—illustrated by the Republican focus on individual initiative and big business. The legacy of the New Deal is the fundamental assumption that the federal government is responsible for the economy.

See also: CCC (Civilian Conservation Corps); Federal Housing Authority (FHA); Great Depression; Hoovervilles; PWA (Public Works Administration); Social Security; WPA (Works Progress Administration)

Sources: Conkin, Paul, *The New Deal*, 2nd ed. (Arlington Heights, Illinois: Harlan David-son, 1975); Divine, Robert A., T. H. Breen, et al., *The American Story*, 2nd ed. (New York: Penguin Books, 2005); Goldfield, David R., and Blaine A. Brownell, *Urban America: From Downtown to No Town* (Boston: Houghton Mifflin Co., 1979); Link, Arthur S., and William B. Catton, *American Epoch: A History of the United States since 1900, Volume II 1921–1945*, 4th ed. (New York: Alfred E. Knopf, 1973); Litwack, Leon, *North of Slavery: The Negro in the Free States, 1790–1860* (Chicago: University Press, 1971); Patterson, James T., *America's Struggle against Poverty in the Twentieth Century* (Cambridge, MA: Harvard University Press, 2000); Sitkoff, Harvard, *New Deal for Blacks: The Emergence of Civil Rights as a National Issue* (Oxford: University Press, 1981).

NO CHILD LEFT BEHIND. Implemented in January, 2002, the No Child Left Behind (NCLB) Act significantly altered the federal government's education policy. Dissatisfied with the existing Elementary and Secondary Education Act (ESEA)—first implemented in 1965 and revised many times, most recently in 1998—President George W. Bush authorized NCLB as a way to increase the "accountability" of education administrators and teachers to demonstrate real improvement in elementary and secondary education. Education policy has a direct relation to poverty; education is the most common means of economic and social advancement in America. The NCLB Act explicitly linked the success of the public education system with providing disadvantaged groups, such as recent immigrants and the urban poor, with equal educational opportunity.

In some respects, NCLB was a continuation of the ESEA; in other ways, it completely changed federal education policy. Like the ESEA, NCLB policy seeks to make public education more efficient; the primary difference is the new emphasis on accountability, using state-administered standardized testing as the tool to determine the effectiveness of the education system. To encourage state compliance with NCLB measures, which are voluntary, the federal government withholds funding—which in 2007 was $25,000,000,000—from states that fail to implement the required standardized testing or that do not act to increase equality among low-income areas—such as the inner city and depressed rural areas—and more affluent school districts. An additional measure of the NCLB program allows parents greater control over their children's education by giving them the option of sending their children to a public school other than the one in their home district.

Title I of the NCLB Act, "Improving the Academic Achievement of the Disadvantaged," explicitly calls for programs to "ensure that all children have a fair, equal, and significant opportunity to obtain a high-quality education and reach, at a minimum, proficiency on challenging State academic achievement standards and state academic assessments." The Act provides for twelve measures to achieve this goal. For example, the NCLB ensures that

> high-quality academic assessments, accountability systems, teacher preparation and training, curriculum, and instructional materials are aligned with challenging State academic standards so that students, teachers, parents, and administrators can measure progress against common expectations for student academic achievement.

The NCLB seeks to meet "the educational needs of low-achieving children in our Nation's highest-poverty schools, limited English proficient children, migratory children, children with disabilities, Indian children, neglected or delinquent children, and young children in need of reading assistance." Title I of the NCLB Act hopes to close "the achievement gap between high- and low-performing children, especially the achievement gaps between minority and non-minority students, and between disadvantaged children and their more advantaged peers."

Other NCLB programs, such as "Reading First" and "Even Start," work to help at-risk and low-income children adjust to public school. NCLB has also allocated $125,000,000 to School Dropout Prevention and $500,000,000 to improve schools in low-income areas. However, under the NCLB guidelines, state education agencies retain primary responsibility; the federal government allocates funding for set programs, but state officials are the ones who design and implement these programs. States must comply with federal requirements to provide data on schools receiving funding and on the numbers of impoverished children in their districts. The "School Rewards" program gives additional financial grants to schools that have made significant progress in improving the services to low-income children and their achievement. The U.S. Secretary of Education, however, has the authority to reduce funding to areas that do not meet NCLB standards.

Not surprisingly, not all educators or policymakers agree with NCLB measures. The most common area of concern is the emphasis on standardized testing to measure the performance of the students as well as of the schools. Many educators think that good teaching cannot be measured by a test score because children learn in different ways; standardization leads to an oversimplified educational policy. Some educators suggest that the Congress amend NCLB to allow schools to provide a more personalized approach, tailoring education to students' specific needs.

See also: Children and Poverty; Education; Elementary and Secondary School Act

Sources: Bremner, Robert H., Gary W. Reichard, and Richard Hopkins, eds., *American Choices: Social Dilemma and Public Policy since 1960* (Columbus: Ohio State University Press, 1986); Elementary and Secondary School Act of 1965, Higher Education Act of 1965, 1998 Higher Education Act Amendments, at the History of American Education Web Project (http://www.nd.edu/~rbarger/www7/); National Education Association (http://www.nea.org/esea/index.html); No Child Left Behind, Public Law 107–110, 107th Congress; U.S. Department of Education (www.ed.gov/nclb/); the White House, Washington, D.C. (www.whitehouse.gov/news/reports/no-child-left-behind.html).

O

OFFICE OF ECONOMIC OPPORTUNITY. The Office of Economic Opportunity (OEO) was the agency that administered many of the Johnson administration's Great Society programs. The OEO distributed federal money to public and private local agencies in order to establish programs to provide education, job training, and legal services for the poor. OEO programs included VISTA, a domestic version of the Peace Corps; the Job Corps; Community Action; and Head Start. On the vanguard of Johnson's War on Poverty, the OEO had as its intent to attack the "roots" of poverty through a series of economic and educational reforms. The OEO's focus was on removing the barriers—such as racial prejudice, unemployment, and lack of education—that kept the poor from becoming mainstream citizens. VISTA and the Job Corps provided employment and relief; Community Action attempted to bypass administrative "red tape" by involving the poor directly in the policies that affected them; and Head Start provided early education to low-income children, to help them succeed in school.

The director of the OEO was Sargent Shriver, and he took a personal interest in the agency's affairs. A brother-in-law to John F. Kennedy, Shriver was a capable, though controversial, leader. His businesslike attitude and forceful personality allowed him to gain support, but they also angered aides and officials in other government agencies who thought he was too controlling. Shriver had a "structural" view of poverty, believing that the social and cultural environment and circumstances were the cause of poverty. Economic reform was insufficient to end poverty. Shriver believed that the government must give the poor the "opportunity" to better their condition. Under Shriver's direction, the OEO sought to eliminate poverty through education, employment, and instilling "middle-class" values of thrift, industry, and cleanliness, in the hope that the poor would learn to support themselves.

Prior to 1965, the OEO enjoyed Johnson's support; after that point (because of the OEO's support of anti-establishment groups through Community Action) Johnson did not offer public support, although stopping short of dismantling the program entirely. Johnson's decision reflected the larger political shift away from his

Great Society toward more conservative policies. By then, the Vietnam War had drastically reduced Johnson's popularity and support for his domestic reforms in the War on Poverty, of which the OEO was the essential part. Although the OEO's programs remained in effect throughout the 1960s, waning support for its liberal programs led to President Nixon's decision to disband it in early 1973, distributing its surviving programs among other federal agencies such as the Department of Health and Human Services.

See also: Community Action Program; Economic Opportunity Act; Head Start; VISTA; War on Poverty

Sources: Bremner, Robert H., Gary W. Reichard, and Richard Hopkins, eds., *American Choices: Social Dilemma and Public Policy since 1960* (Columbus: Ohio State University Press, 1986); Economic Opportunity Act (http://www2.volstate.edu/geades/FinalDocs/1960s/eoa.htm); Patterson, James T., *America's Struggle against Poverty in the Twentieth Century* (Cambridge, MA: Harvard University Press, 2000).

THE OTHER AMERICA BY MICHAEL HARRINGTON. Michael Harrington's *The Other America: Poverty in the United States*, which appeared in 1963, challenged the idealism of the white middle class that the American Dream was open to all Americans. Harrington revealed that affluent American society had another side. The *other* America was poverty-stricken, segregated, and without hope. Harrington, a journalist and political activist, visited the ghettos, migrant worker camps, nursing homes, and wino haunts to see firsthand the plight of the poor. The other America, according to Harrington, encompassed the elderly, who were forgotten in society; African Americans, suffering from racism and segregation; farm workers, doing the hardest work for the lowest wages; the homeless, often mentally ill; the hopeless, alienated, segregated, voiceless, invisible Americans. "There is, in a sense, a personality of poverty, a type of human being produced by the grinding, wearing life of the slums. The other Americans feel differently than the rest of the nation. They tend to be hopeless and passive, yet prone to bursts of violence; they are lonely and isolated, often rigid and hostile. To be poor is not simply to be deprived of the material things of this world. It is to enter a fatal, futile universe, an America within America with a twisted spirit."

Harrington defined poverty from economic and psychological points of view. "Poverty," he wrote,

> should be defined in terms of those who are denied the minimal levels of health, housing, food, and education that our present stage of scientific knowledge specifies as necessary for life as it is now lived in the United States. Poverty should be defined psychologically in terms of those whose place in the society is such that they are internal exiles who, almost inevitably, develop attitudes of defeat and pessimism and who are therefore excluded from taking advantage of new opportunities.

Harrington distinguished the impoverished from the affluent members of the middle class by noting the latter's complete awareness of emotional and mental illnesses and ability to seek medical counseling and drugs to alleviate their suffering, unlike the poor, who are completely unaware of such illnesses: depression and neurosis are simply facts of life to be endured. Middle-class citizens have a clear sense of the future and can put off pleasure for the moment to enjoy it at a specified time later; saving money or engaging in pleasure is doable. The poor, however, live more for the moment; if pleasure offers itself, the poor take it and enjoy it, rather than waiting and saving it for later.

In a strange twist on the theory of democracy, Harrington argued that poverty equalizes: the inner city

> groups together failures, rootless people, those born in the wrong time, those at the wrong industry, and the minorities. It is 'integrated' in many cases, but in a way that mocks the ideas of equality: the poorest and most miserable are isolated together without consideration of race, creed, or color. They are practically forbidden any real relationship with the rest of society.

The Other America presents some solutions for the problem of poverty. Harrington argued that only the federal government can wage war on and eliminate poverty. Local and state governments and private charity have proven unsuccessful. The federal government has the funds and centralization to fight the War on Poverty; it can take the lead in developing good public housing; it can help create a different environment to alter the "culture of poverty." But, Harrington warned, public housing should be fully integrated into the community, not set aside like a "modern poor farm." Many of the poor, Harrington advised, bring the culture of poverty to the housing projects; hence the poor cannot be relocated and abandoned: continued education and counseling are needed to help integrate them into mainstream society. The poor are so deep in the mire of poverty that simple solutions like education don't work. First, they have to be raised out of the mire, given hope, and integrated to become a part of society, before education will work. The cost of federal government intervention is high, but the cost of poverty is already high, because poverty yields violence and other antisocial behaviors that tax local, state, and federal government.

The Other America had a significant effect on antipoverty programs during the 1960s. Council of Economic Advisors (CEA) economists in the Kennedy administration advocated that the President initiate more aggressive antipoverty programs, which were taken up by the Johnson administration after Kennedy's assassination. Harrington's arguments therefore directly affected the declaration of the War on Poverty of the 1960s.

See also: Culture of Poverty; Urban Poor; War on Poverty

Sources: Harrington, Michael, *The Other America: Poverty in the United States* (New York: Macmillan, 1963); Iceland, John, *Poverty in America: A Handbook*, 2nd ed. (Berkeley: University of California Press, 2006); Isserman, Maurice, *The Other American: The Life of Michael Harrington* (New York: Public Affairs, 2000).

P

PANHANDLERS. A panhandler, or beggar, is someone who approaches a stranger and asks for food or money. There are two general types of panhandlers: persons who are truly needy—those who are disabled or cannot work—and "professional" beggars who panhandle for profit, not because of need. This distinction parallels attitudes about the "deserving" and "undeserving" poor; conservatives often portray all panhandlers as wily good-for-nothings who seek to trick hardworking Americans into giving them money for drugs and alcohol. Despite such stereotypes, however, the majority of panhandlers live in extreme poverty, and many are homeless. Some scholars distinguish panhandlers from other beggars, distinguishing a panhandler as a person who solicits from strangers without offering anything in return. By this definition, a street musician or person performing odd tasks—such as cleaning car windows at an intersection—does not qualify as a panhandler.

Panhandling is also one of the primary ways that affluent Americans come in contact with the very poor. In contemporary American cities, panhandlers often stand near busy intersections, such as near malls or off highway exits, and ask passersby for money, work, or food. Many contemporary panhandlers use signs explaining their needs. This method of "advertising" need is a result of sprawling urban development. In contrast to the compact cities of the eighteenth and nineteenth centuries, where the rich lived near the poor, in contemporary American cities the very poor often live apart from the affluent, limiting everyday contact between the classes. For example, middle-class professionals who work in the city but live in the suburbs may drive on a highway through a poor area, but they have little contact with the poor themselves; before the invention of the automobile, however, suburb dwellers would not have been able to ignore the poor areas they traveled through. Consequently, successful panhandlers place themselves in a prominent or confrontational position to arouse sufficient pity from passersby in a very short time.

Panhandlers attempt to obtain money or goods by emphasizing their pitiable condition—disability, hunger, deformity, or homelessness—in order to disgust or shame passersby into giving support. The more successful panhandlers emphasize their inability to adapt into mainstream society and thus their need for support; panhandlers who blatantly advertise the effects of extreme poverty upset the complacency of affluent Americans. As such, panhandlers have a connection with the underbelly of society, the "underclass," as concerned critics in the 1980s termed it. The many stereotypes about professional panhandlers also connect to panhandlers' conscious attempt to arouse pity: affluent Americans often feel uncomfortable around panhandlers—who are a highly visible reminder of poverty—but they are unable to distinguish between those that are truly in need (the deserving poor) and professional beggars (the undeserving poor) who seek merely to obtain easy money. Consequently, attitudes about panhandlers tend to parallel general attitudes about poverty: most Americans agree that the able-bodied poor should obtain work, but the disabled and truly needy—the group that most panhandlers either mimic or belong to—deserve some sort of relief.

See also: Homelessness; Urban Poor

Sources: Axinn, June, and Mark J. Stern, *Social Welfare: A History of the American Response to Need,* 5th ed. (Boston: Allyn and Bacon, 2001); Bremner, Robert H., Gary W. Reichard, and Richard Hopkins, ed., *American Choices: Social Dilemma and Public Policy since 1960* (Columbus: Ohio State University Press, 1986); Bose, Rohit, and Stephen W. Hwang, "Income and Spending Patterns among Panhandlers," *Canadian Medical Association Journal,* Vol. 167, No. 5 (September 3, 2002); Patterson, James T., *America's Struggle against Poverty in the Twentieth Century* (Cambridge, MA: Harvard University Press, 2000).

POOR LAWS IN ENGLAND AND EARLY AMERICA. As England expanded power overseas, changed landowning patterns, and expanded manufacturing, it experienced the irony of increasing poverty among its lower classes at a time of greater overall wealth in the realm. The greatest political and economic changes came at the end of the Tudor dynasty, during the reign of Elizabeth I (1558–1603). Elizabeth oversaw the English Parliament's creation of a system of national poor relief—replacing the haphazard and sporadic relief of the poor of her predecessors. The Elizabethan poor laws became the standard for English as well as colonial American poor relief.

Tudor–Stuart Poor Laws. A series of poor-relief legislation during Elizabeth's reign established the bases for English and colonial poor relief. Central to the Elizabethan statutes was the assumption of community responsibility for its own poor, where elected and appointed local officers and magistrates oversaw the collection of parish taxes to apply toward poor relief by means of direct aid and the forced employment of the able-bodied poor in workhouses. Initial statutes under Elizabeth in 1562 (the Statute of Artificers) required the payment of a poor tax, to be collected by the parish priest; those who refused came under the jurisdiction of the local justice of the peace, who could threaten imprisonment for evading the tax. Statutes also required employment of the poor, in particular the "sturdy beggar," in agricultural labor and gave the justice of the peace the power to set wages. A statute in 1572 legislated corporal punishment—whipping and branding of the ear—for able-bodied poor who refused to work. In 1581 Parliament legislated the first house of correction (workhouse) to work and punish sturdy beggars. A 1597 statute required local authorities, called "overseers of the poor," to administer the parish poor-relief system: collecting the poor tax, dispensing monies for relief and employment of the poor, administering the houses of correction, and apprenticing homeless boys and girls.

The Stuart kings of the seventeenth century made little change to the outlines of poor relief established under Elizabeth. Under James I and Charles I, the royal councilors, the Privy Council, assumed direct responsibility for administering poor laws. In 1605, the Privy Council directed the limitation of alehouses in the realm so to restrict "the entertainment of lewd and idle people," who "spend and consume their money and their time in lewd and drunken manner." The numbers of the poor, however, increased, such that more houses of correction were ordered built in order to house, work, and correct the idle poor. Landmark legislation under Charles I in 1630, the Book of Orders, established a centralized system of administration and control of poor relief. The Book of Orders required monthly reports by overseers of the poor and constables to the parish justices of the peace, who in turn reported to the high sheriff of the county, who reported to the Justices of the Assize, who reported to the Privy Council. Dereliction of duty by administrators resulted in heavy fines. The Act of Settlement was legislated under Charles II in 1662, which built on medieval parish laws requiring the poor to remain in the parish of their birth. Local authorities were to ensure that the parish poor were truly deserving of community aid by right of birth; if not, they were to be sent back to their native parish. The design of the Act of Settlement was to prevent the poor from constantly moving about, a shiftless people relying on handouts their entire lives.

English poor laws after the Glorious Revolution of 1689 were refinements of the original laws of the Tudor–Stuart period. Under William III, in 1691, newcomers to a parish had to have the financial means, through property or employment, to be contributing taxpayers. During the reign of George II, in 1744, complaints that parish overseers of the poor were extorting and otherwise misusing funds resulted in legislation that required overseers to have their accounts audited to ensure legality and morality. In 1747 justices of the peace were again authorized to set wages in the parish, an authority first granted in 1562, but which had rarely succeeded in preventing poverty. Eighteenth-century commentators also criticized the Act of Settlement for causing more harm than good. "A poor man is no sooner got into a neighborhood," wrote a member of the House of Commons in 1735, and found "employment he likes, but, upon humour or caprice of the parish, he is sent to another place, where he can find none of these conveniences."

Indeed the literature on the English poor laws written during the 1600s and 1700s by justices, members of Parliament, and other English observers brand the English poor laws as a failed system. In a pamphlet written in 1622, "Greevous Grones for the Poore," the author declared that "though the number of the poor do daily increase, there has been no collection for them, no not these seven years, in many parishes of this land, especially in the country towns; but many of those parishes turn forth their poor . . . so that the country is pitifully pestered with them." "Maimed soldiers," the author continued, "are also thus required for when they return home," but "we will not be troubled with their service . . . so they are turned forth to travel in idleness . . . begging . . . and stealing for their maintenance, until the law brings them unto the fearful end of hanging." Another critic echoed these comments in 1673, writing that the legal system does a great hurt rather than good; makes a world of poor men than otherwise would be . . . men and women growing so idle and proud, that they will not work, but lie upon the parish . . . maintenance; applying themselves to . . . begging or pilfering, and breeding up their children accordingly.

Poor Laws in Colonial America. Although local and provincial government authorities in the thirteen American colonies transported the English poor laws to America, making adjustments to fit the colonial situation, failure dogged the poor-relief system in America as in England. American poor relief was like that of the mother country in relying, as Carl Bridenbaugh wrote in *Vexed and Troubled Englishmen,* "upon the character and energies of the local authorities, and . . . upon the resources of the community." The colonists followed the lead of the English in most aspects of local law, and poor relief was no different. Americans transported the essence and stipulations of the poor laws passed under the Tudors and Stuarts. Hence, town constables "warned out" paupers in American communities, sending them back to their home parish. Sturdy beggars and other idle paupers who refused to leave town were often incarcerated in a variety of institutions, especially the workhouse and the house of correction. Towns collected monies for relieving the deserving poor, such as widows, orphans, the disabled, and veterans and their families. A New Hampshire law from 1680, for example, fined innkeepers who sold liquor to servants or children; the proceeds of the fine went to the relief of the poor. Poor relief ranged from tax forgiveness to grants in kind to paying a townsperson to work or care for the pauper. The Dominion of New England, a short-lived government during the 1680s, legislated the appointing of overseers of the poor, who were to solve individual relief problems for the town poor. Overseers had to keep track of their expenses and were frequently audited.

American colonies also passed legislation in an attempt to restrict the transportation of felons. Virginia, Maryland, Pennsylvania, and South Carolina, all of which had received their fill of transported convicts, passed laws in the latter 1600s and early 1700s to prevent their immigration. Parliament nipped such attempts in the bud, however, in 1717, passing "An act for the further preventing robbery, burglary, and other felonies, and for the more effectual transportation of felons." The parliamentary statute negated the colonial laws restricting convict transportation, which forced the exasperated colonists to enact tough measures designed, according to one 1718 law, "for Suppressing and Punishing" the undeserving poor. New Hampshire legislation in 1718 required towns to erect workhouses "to be used and employed, for the Keeping, Correcting, and Setting to Work of Rogues, Vagabonds, and common Beggars, and other Lewd, idle and Disorderly Persons." The same law allowed justices of the peace to commit to work any of these people listed, as well as fortune tellers, jugglers, gamesmen, drunkards, brawlers, fiddlers, and runaway servants. Overseers were given the authority "to punish them with Whip (not more than 10 Stripes at once) and shackle or Fetter them." They were advised that—to keep the poor from idleness and haughtiness—ten stripes should be inflicted on all newcomers and others "from time to time." This included youth who spent "their time in Loitering," avoiding being educated and trained for "Some honest Calling which may be profitable to themselves and the Publick."

The 1562 Statute of Artificers provided the basis for the American system of apprenticeship and servitude. English law allowed for apprenticing poor youth and transportation to America during their term of service. Colonial towns adopted the

English principle of binding impoverished youth and adults to service for a set number of years. The Americans also adopted British statutes requiring the construction of workhouses. The 1581 law mandating the use of houses of correction to work and hold the poor became the model for similar colonial legislation. The Dominion of New England in the 1680s mandated workhouses to employ and keep the poor. Boston constructed a workhouse in 1685; other New England towns followed suit at the turn of the century.

Over the course of the eighteenth century, colonial poor laws tended to be a restatement of the English codes first promulgated under the Tudors and Stuarts. With independence, a slow but constant change occurred in the United States respecting treatment of the poor. Poor relief continued to be the occupation of local government. Upon the inauguration of the Federal Constitution in 1789, states assumed control over local poor relief. Initially, changes in the institutionalization of the poor involved separating the deserving poor from malefactors and ne'er-do-wells in almshouses and workhouses. Increasingly, in the late 1700s and early 1800s, states provided for specific institutions to care for, work, and manage the poor. Penitentiaries incarcerated the criminal adult poor; reform schools housed juvenile delinquents. Insane asylums housed the mentally ill poor. Orphanages cared for poor, parentless youth. Almshouses were restricted to the deserving poor—the aged and disabled. States began during the 1830s to outlaw imprisonment for debt, which had been such a scourge to the poor in England and America during previous years. Before the twentieth century, in short, state and local government legislated and administered public poor relief. Not until the Progressive Era of the early 1900s did the federal government embark on legislation that would change poor relief in America.

See also: British Poor and the Origins of Colonialism; Children and Poverty; Convict Transportation; Indentured Servitude; Institutionalization of the Poor

Sources: Batchellor, Albert S., et al., eds. *Laws of New Hampshire, Provincial Period,* 3 vols. (Manchester, NH: Clarke, 1904–1915); Burn, Richard, *The History of the Poor Laws: With Observations* (London: Woodfall and Strahan, 1764); Eden, Frederic, *The State of the Poor,* 3 vols. (London: Davis, 1797); Haar, Charles M., "White Indentured Servants in Colonial New York," *Americana,* Vol. 34 (1940); Herrick, Cheesman A., *White Servitude in Pennsylvania, Indentured and Redemption Labor in Colony and Commonwealth* (Philadelphia: McVey, 1926); Leonard, E. M., *The Early History of English Poor Law Relief* (Cambridge, UK: Cambridge University Press, 1900); McCormac, E. I., *White Servitude in Maryland, 1634–1820* (Baltimore: Johns Hopkins, 1904); Morse, Richard B., *Government and Labor in Early America* (New York: Harper & Row, 1965); Nicholls, George, *A History of the English Poor Law,* 2 vols. (London: P. S. King and Son, 1904); Smith, Abbot Emerson, *Colonists in Bondage: White Servitude and Convict Labor in America, 1607–1776* (New York: Norton, 1971).

PROGRESSIVES. During the late nineteenth century, American industrialization had resulted in increasing income and wealth disparity. American cities topped a million inhabitants and slums became a blight on the inner city. At the same time, the Republican-led government adopted a laissez-faire approach to the economy, big business, and workers' rights. Opposition to Republican policies developed among the urban proletariat, stimulating the growth of labor unions such as the American Federation of Labor. At the same time, farmers in the Midwest and the

South—protesting the high price railroads charged for transporting grain, among other monopolistic practices—organized the Farmer's Alliance and Grange Movement. By the 1890s farmers organized into a broad national political movement, the Populist Party, which merged with the Democrats in the elections of 1896. The Populists called for government ownership of railroads and other necessary public institutions; a graduated income tax to close the gap between rich and poor; abandonment of the gold standard in American currency and an increase in the circulation of money (to raise prices); and increased participation of the electorate in the political process.

Although Populist ascendancy climaxed in the election of 1896, when William Jennings Bryan was defeated by William McKinley, one group of American reformers of the urban middle class, the Progressives, embraced the Populist agenda. Progressivism was a diverse cultural and political movement. Participants were typically well-educated, affluent city-dwellers worried about the negative consequences of the Industrial Revolution. The increasing poverty, homelessness, and despair among city slum-dwellers threatened to destroy the technological and political progress of late nineteenth- and early twentieth-century America. Progressives wished to preserve traditional community, democratic equality, the promise of liberty, and social and economic opportunity—even as America confronted the increasing disparity between rich and poor, the rapid development of slums, and the fading hopes of immigrants in the American Dream.

Unlike the Populists, the Progressives acquired political power and used it. The Republican Theodore Roosevelt and the Democrat Woodrow Wilson used the office of the presidency to push for progressive reforms, some of which helped the poor directly. Under the Progressives, the income tax became a reality, helping redistribute wealth and even social disparity through taxation. Laws were enacted to raise wages, limit working hours for women, and increase the number of poor children attending school; and the concerns of labor were, for the first time, embraced by the federal government. In 1912 the Federal Children's Bureau was established, after years of lobbying by child advocates and President Roosevelt. The first federal child labor legislation was passed in 1916.

Besides Roosevelt and Wilson, successful Progressive politicians included Robert LaFollette, governor and senator from Wisconsin. As governor, LaFollette fought for the rights of women and labor and worked to limit the influence of big business, particularly railroads. Reformer Jane Addams, founder of Hull House in Chicago, worked tirelessly for the rights of children, labor, and immigrants. Her efforts helped lead to child labor laws in Illinois, the Immigrants' Protective League, and the Juvenile Protective Association. Jane Addams also worked for and on behalf of the National Child Labor Committee (founded 1904), the National Conference of Charities and Corrections, and the National Association for the Advancement of Colored People (NAACP).

Even though the Progressive agenda was eclipsed by Republican dominance in the 1920s, the economic and social misery brought about by the Great Depression led to a resurgence of Progressive ideas during the New Deal of the 1930s.

See also: Addams, Jane; *How the Other Half Lives* by Jacob Riis; Urban Poor

Sources: Hofstadter, Richard, *The Age of Reform: From Bryan to F.D.R.* (New York: Random House, 1955); McGerr, Michael E., *A Fierce Discontent: The Rise and Fall of the Progressive Movement in America, 1870–1920* (New York: Free Press, 2003).

PROTEST MOVEMENTS. In the mid-1960s, a series of "ghetto" riots occurred across the United States, prompting President Lyndon Johnson to appoint the National Advisory Commission on Civil Disorders—the Kerner Commission—in 1967 to investigate the cause of the uprisings. Johnson and many other policymakers expected the Commission to uncover evidence of a vast conspiracy, but they were incorrect. Instead, the Kerner Commission reported that the riots were the result of America's ingrained inequality, which segregated white and blacks so extensively that there were "two" Americas: the affluent society of white middle class and the depressing conditions of African Americans and minorities. To prevent additional riots, the Commission proposed the implementation of additional policies, more comprehensive even than Johnson's Great Society, to change the structure of American society. Johnson refused to accept the Commission's recommendations; like most affluent Americans, the President was unprepared to accept the reality of minority protest.

The ghetto riots began in Los Angeles in 1965, where black anger over the slowness of Civil Rights progress combined with other issues, such as economic inequality and police brutality, to turn the Watts area into a scene of rioting. The Watts revolt demonstrated the willingness of "black power" to use violence, and, although the uprising alarmed whites, it had a more negative effect on blacks, because it fed the white separatist movement to the suburbs and further isolated blacks within the city. Whites who moved to the suburbs blamed the economic decline of the inner city for the rise of black violence and rebelliousness. The Watts riot lessened support for government programs like welfare, because wealthy whites thought welfare recipients (many of whom lived in Watts) were becoming more violent.

In the 1960s there were three major Black Nationalist movements: the Nation of Islam (NOI), the cultural nationalists, and the Black Panthers; a fourth group working for black rights, the less radical NAACP, took a more conservative approach and enjoyed greater political influence. However, the NAACP rejected violence as a means to fight racism and thus had limited influence among increasingly radical blacks in the 1960s. The NOI adopted its own interpretation of Islam to elevate the status of blacks, but it alienated some African Americans by its insistence that blacks had ties to Asia, not Africa. Nationwide, the NOI's image suffered after the assassination of Malcolm X, reputedly under the orders of the group's leader, Elijah Muhammad. By the time of the Watts uprising, the NOI portrayed the white man as a race of "devils," called the Los Angeles Police Department's behavior "satanic," and had decided to separate itself from whites; although this anti-white stance earned it some support in South Los Angeles, the internal divisions and anti-Christian views of the NOI abridged its power. The cultural nationalist movement was more successful, and, like the NOI, emphasized black history in order to create a positive black identity. The Black Panthers, the most radical of the three groups, adopted an image of violent protest and cultivated leftist ideology; it had the least success among these movements.

Compounded racism—prejudice between minority groups—increased competition among impoverished minorities, leading to civil unrest. In large American cities, such as Los Angeles, Detroit, and New York, European Americans, Mexican Americans (Chicanos), Native Americans, Asian Americans, and African Americans shared the same land and fought for the same jobs, exacerbating racial tension. Although African Americans were the most visible—because of the history of enslavement and segregation—they were not the exclusive target of racism, and disparate minority groups often were prejudicial toward others. In 1960s Los Angeles, for example, as noted by historian Gerald Horne, dark-skinned blacks looked down on light-skinned blacks. The rise of Chicano nationalism in the 1960s also affected how policymakers appeased blacks, because officials feared rewarding black violence with concessions and thus encouraging Mexican Americans to use violent measures as well.

Chicano nationalism took many forms, but the most common was increased respect for their Spanish–Mexican heritage. Some Chicano nationalist groups, such as the Community Service Organization (CSO) and the Asociación Nacional México Americana (ANMA), respected America's political system. Prior to the 1960s, most Chicanos believed that they could advance socially and materially through the American system; however, continued social inequality broke down moderate Chicano reform movements and led to more extreme resistance. In 1966 the Chicano movement radicalized, and, for the first time, many Mexican Americans directly blamed the American system for their plight and began to fight back. The best example of the new approach was the Brown Berets, a roughly equivalent Chicano version of the Black Panthers. The Brown Berets published a newsletter, *La Causa*, extolling their "Ten Point Program" to overcome the American system. These Ten Points called for Chicanos to uphold their Mexican traditions and language, for a halt of urban renewal programs (which tended to target minority areas for destruction), and for the election of Mexican American officials in government. The Brown Berets soon adopted an explicitly anti-American stance; the enemy was now the American government, and the Brown Berets lauded any group—including the Vietnamese—that fought against America. Thus the Chicano antiwar effort took on a subversive character, and, unlike many idealistic college student liberals, the Brown Berets saw the Vietnam War as an opportunity to challenge the American government itself rather than its policy in Vietnam. By 1972, after a brief occupation of Santa Catalina Island (meant to symbolize the reclaiming of the Southwest from Anglo American control), the Brown Berets declined as a political force.

In the 1960s and early 1970s, minority groups worked to develop a stronger national voice, and protest movements were one means of achieving that goal. As demonstrated by the Kerner Commission's 1967 Report, the segregation and impoverishment of America's minority groups prepared the way for protest through political, cultural, and even violent means. Despite the bloodshed, however, leftist nationalist groups and ghetto riots failed to garner much support, and political reform groups, such as the NAACP, and government agencies, such the Equal Opportunity Employment Commission (EEOC), were more successful in obtaining material benefits for America's minority groups.

In 1992, minority groups once again turned to violence to express their frustration. Los Angeles was again the site of the most extreme rioting, because of the police beating of Rodney King, an unarmed African American man. Despite video evidence of police brutality, showing several white officers beating King, the policemen were acquitted; as a result, riots broke out across Los Angeles. As in the Watts riot thirty years before, the unrest was not necessarily about the incident that sparked it—although both involved the actions of the Los Angeles police—because minority groups often felt oppressed by the police. The 1992 rioting and looting had scant organization and accomplished little beyond illustrating that racial, ethnic, and class tensions remained high in America, partly because of poverty and its consequences.

Urban riots forced affluent Americans to recognize that society was far from perfect; however, the effects of rioting were not especially positive for low-income minorities. Political activism returns better long-term results for minority groups who want to participate fully in American society. Although protest movements demonstrated that the poor were not meek, violence did little to encourage middle-class Americans to accept low-income minorities; instead, it encouraged social separation: the riots in the 1960s and in 1992 fueled white flight to the suburbs and the increasing isolation of the minority poor in the impoverished old city.

See also: African Americans and Poverty (post-slavery); Hispanic Americans and Poverty; Urban Poor; War on Poverty

Sources: Chávez, Ernesto, *"¡Mi Raza Primero!": Nationalism, Identity, and Insurgency in the Chicano Movement in Los Angeles, 1966–1978* (Berkeley: University of California, 2002); Davis, Mike, *Dead Cities* (New York: The New Press, 2002); Horne, Gerald, *Fire This Time: The Watts Uprising and the 1960s* (New York: University of Virginia Press, 1995); Kerner Commission, *Report of the National Advisory Commission on Civil Disorders* (Washington, D.C.: 1968); Patterson, James T., *America's Struggle against Poverty in the Twentieth Century* (Cambridge, MA: Harvard University Press, 2000); US Equal Employment Opportunity Commission (EEOC) (www.eeoc.gov/).

PRUITT–IGOE. Completed in 1955 in St. Louis, Missouri, the massive Pruitt–Igoe public housing complex included thirty-three buildings of eleven stories each. Despite initial acclaim, the complex quickly devolved to the point that city officials chose to dynamite it from 1972 to 1976, deeming the complex uninhabitable. In addition to architectural style, primary causes of Pruitt–Igoe's destruction were the ghetto unrest of the mid 1960s and the geographical, racial, and economic division of St. Louis. The importance of Pruitt–Igoe was its effect on the way that city planners and architects viewed their role: prior to Pruitt–Igoe's destruction, "big-box" public housing was generally accepted as an efficient and effective way to house the urban poor. By the early 1970s, however, the social and political order of American cities had fundamentally changed: the violent protests of minority residents and the white flight to the suburbs led to a breakdown of policymaking "from above." Thus the 1972 demolition of Pruitt–Igoe symbolized the failure of a decades-long policy of housing the extremely poor.

Conceived in the early 1950s as the remedy for St. Louis's lack of adequate housing and the gritty appearance of poor neighborhoods, Pruitt–Igoe embodied the ideals of modernist social order. The complex relocated the city's most impoverished residents away from the central business district and allowed extensive urban renewal projects in the older areas of the city, where much of St. Louis's minority residents lived. Designed by Minoru Yamasaki, who also designed New York's World Trade Centers, Pruitt–Igoe followed many tenets of the "International Style" championed by French architect Le Corbusier as the high point of modernist architecture. Working with the St. Louis Housing Authority, Yamasaki designed the cheapest possible plan: cost-saving measures, not just aesthetics, influenced the design of Pruitt–Igoe. For example, Yamasaki designed skip-stop elevators, which only stopped at every third floor) to reduce the cost of installing an elevator stop on every floor, and used flimsy, cheap, built-in accessories such as cabinets and doors with latches or knobs that broke off very easily.

Like other twentieth-century public housing complexes, such as Chicago's Robert Taylor Homes, Pruitt–Igoe functioned as a city within a city. Set up on a strict geometrical layout, the buildings reinforced the sense of separateness from the rest of St. Louis felt by residents. The design also limited opportunities for social gathering, because the narrow hallways and skip-stop elevators became havens for drug dealers and vandals. By the mid-1960s, nearly 27 percent of the 2,762 available apartments were vacant; although 86 percent of the residents indicated that they would prefer to live elsewhere, 69 percent (of the total residents) had no plans to move out. Pruitt–Igoe housed St. Louis's most impoverished residents, the displaced African American "underclass" that had nowhere else to go. Racism played a large role in the problems with Pruitt–Igoe; residents felt ignored and mistreated by city officials and the police. Although most residents of Pruitt–Igoe—nearly 88 percent of the men and 92 percent of the women—welcomed police presence in the project as a counter for youth violence and the drug trade, many residents also complained about the way that police treated them. A common complaint was that the police (both the St. Louis police and the project's police force) took too long to respond to calls, acted disrespectfully to residents, and appeared to disbelieve their complaints.

A multitude of social problems doomed Pruitt–Igoe to failure. There was a high prevalence of divorced or single mothers, for example, as well as youth gangs and drug abuse, and a paucity of responsible adult males. Apathy reigned: hazardous materials, such as broken glass, which no one removed, rendered gathering areas unusable. The complex was also plagued by destructive behavior, both criminal and negligent. Criminal acts included mugging and armed robbery, stealing, men molesting women in elevators and hallways, and fighting. Negligent (noncriminal) acts included the common use of foul language near children, people urinating in the halls and elevators, alcoholism, and filth.

In short, Pruitt–Igoe symbolized all that was wrong with American cities and the cultural and social malaise that resulted in the urban ghetto. Other cities, such as Louisville, Chicago, and Newark, had similar big-box housing complexes with similar problems and results.

See also: African Americans and Poverty (post-slavery); Public Housing; Urban Poor

Sources: Lawson, Benjamin A., "The Pruitt-Igoe Projects: Modernism, Social Control, and the Failure of Public Housing, 1954–1976." Master's Thesis (Oklahoma State University Press, 2007); Rainwater, Lee, *Behind Ghetto Walls: Black Families in a Federal Slum* (Chicago: Aldine and Atherton Publishers, 1970); Stromberg, Jerome S., "Private Problems in Public Housing: A Further Report on the Pruitt-Igoe Project." Occasional Paper no. 39 (1968).

PUBLIC HOUSING. Public housing—government-subsidized low-cost housing units—is an offshoot of industrial society: the concept of low-cost housing communes began soon after the rise of industrialization, in response to the problem of providing shelter for the impoverished urban working class. Early examples that indirectly influenced modern, large-scale complexes included the utopian ideals of social reformers in mid-nineteenth century Europe such as Henri Saint-Simon and wealthy industrialists such as Robert Owen, who pioneered the concept of company towns. The American equivalent of Owen's plan was the development of mill towns, such as Slatersville, Rhode Island, which was set up by Samuel Slater to house workers. Although these communities differed from "modernist" large-scale twentieth-century complexes—they were privately financed and the buildings were small—they were precursors to twentieth–century public housing in that they were self-supporting communities that provided basic shelter. These early communities differed significantly from later complexes such as the Pruitt–Igoe complex in St. Louis and the Robert Taylor Homes in Chicago that relocated poor workers away from urban centers. Twentieth-century public housing, however, kept impoverished minority groups in the inner city.

At the end of the nineteenth century, the terrible living conditions of the urban poor—especially the despicable conditions in tenements in large cities such as New York—came to the forefront. Exposés, such as Jacob Riis's *How the Other Half Lives,* led to moral reform movements in cities across the nation and contributed to government involvement in housing reform. Unlike later public housing, late nineteenth-century tenements were privately owned, and, in terms of design, they bore little resemblance to modernist public housing; for example, they lacked the logical format of the Pruitt–Igoe complex. More important, tenement dwellers experienced *de facto* segregation from "mainstream" middle-class society; as in modernist public housing, the impoverished and mostly minority residents were not accepted in middle-class white society. Many tenement dwellers were from immigrant families and bore obvious marks of difference, whether skin color, native language, or religious practices.

During the Progressive Era of the early twentieth century, the modern conception of public housing began to take shape. In 1911 the National Housing Association (NHA), led by Lawrence Veiller, held its first meeting and clarified its "scientific" approach to housing reform. The NHA had five major goals: to prevent the erection of "unfit" housing, to encourage the building of "proper" housing, to ensure proper management and maintenance of existing housing, to attempt to renovate existing structures, and to bring about "scientific," economic, and "reasonable" housing laws.

At the same time that the NHA was clarifying its strategy, the "garden city" movement was in vogue, supported by Herbert Hoover's housing policy that favored the movement to the suburbs. A revamped plan to develop company towns, the garden city movement attempted to develop working-class suburbs with limited population to ensure good living conditions. Popular prior to World War II, the garden city suburbs left behind impoverished minority groups in the inner city, which increased the need for public housing. Meanwhile, the middle class was unwilling to support programs that primarily aided the lowest and most impoverished social and racial groups. Progressive reformers, such as the writer and activist Catherine Bauer argued, in *Modern Housing* (1934), against the construction of large-scale public housing. Bauer emphasized that a top-down approach to public housing (one that focused only on the very poor and did not include mixed-income support) would lead to the failure of public-housing complexes, which could not function if the residents relied on welfare "handouts" to provide for themselves and their family.

The conception of public housing as a high-rise slum supported by the federal government began during the New Deal. Whereas previous housing programs had attempted to improve the plight of the poor through renovating overcrowded tenements and jump-starting community, the switch toward large-scale public-housing complexes of the New Deal signaled the beginning of an explicit top-down housing policy. During the Great Depression, the problem of the urban poor became so large that policymakers were forced to implement a program of large-scale public housing.

These programs never received sufficient financial support, because the middle class was not interested in programs that "benefited" only the very poor. This same problem hindered later complexes such as Pruitt–Igoe—cost-cutting influenced the starkness of the design and increased resident dissatisfaction.

The 1937 United States Housing Act (USHA) led to the popularity of modernist housing, because it encouraged cost-cutting measures in any way necessary to keep expenses down. Early examples of complexes built under the USHA were Brooklyn's Red Hook and Queensbrough housing developments. As in later complexes, such as Pruitt–Igoe and Chicago's Robert Taylor Homes, these complexes were designed on a strict geometrical layout, did not have any design frills, and were generally dirty, unpleasant places to live. Also like Pruitt–Igoe and the Taylor Homes, the enclosed design and large scale of these early modernist complexes led to residents feeling isolated from the rest of the city.

By the 1950s, despite the obvious problems of modernist, big-box public housing, policymakers retained an idealistic attitude toward modernist public housing. Indeed, urban planners and policymakers often had a utopian vision of what public housing could accomplish. This unwarranted idealism—not unlike the visions of nineteenth-century social reformers—set up the big-box projects to fail, because they could not live up to the groundless expectations of the designers and policymakers. From the mid-1970s to 2000, many American cities demolished their big-box projects and switched to mixed-use developments.

The Department of Housing and Urban Development (HUD)'s HOPE VI grants facilitated this transition. In Louisville, Kentucky, for example, the Park Du Valle housing complex was replaced with a lower-density development, featuring a community center that provided access to health care, a laundromat, shopping and dining, and mass transit connections. The Housing Authority of Louisville (HAL) received $31.4 million to revitalize the Park Du Valle area; of this, HOPE VI provided $20 million. The Park Du Valle revitalization effort is a good example of the growing awareness of city officials that housing is not a separate entity, but part of the overall community. Whereas earlier sites, such as the initial Park Du Valle and Pruitt–Igoe, had been isolated from surrounding neighborhoods, the newer developments fit better into the overall urban setting. This switch is partly because of the increased emphasis on community revitalization and comprehensive planning that is an offshoot of recent changes in urban planning—most notably the rise of "New Urbanism" and its emphasis on livable communities. Although it is too early to assess the long-term effectiveness of these lower-density public housing developments, at least they appear to be an improvement over the dehumanizing conditions of big-box public housing.

See also: African Americans and Poverty (post-slavery); Department of Housing and Urban Development (HUD); *How the Other Half Lives* by Jacob Riis; New Deal; Progressives; Pruitt–Igoe; Urban Poor

Sources: Bauman, John F., Roger Biles, and Kristin M. Szylvian, eds., *From the Tenements to the Taylor Homes: In Search of an Urban Housing Policy in Twentieth-Century America* (University Park: The Pennsylvania State University Press, 2000); Lawson, Benjamin A., "The Pruitt-Igoe Projects: Modernism, Social Control, and the Failure of Public Housing, 1954–1976," Master's Thesis (Oklahoma State University Press, 2007); Park Du Valle Revitalization (http://www.hal1.org/hopevi/index.htm); Rainwater, Lee, *Behind Ghetto Walls:*

Black Families in a Federal Slum (Chicago: Aldine and Atherton Publishers, 1970); Riis, Jacob, *How the Other Half Lives* (New York: Charles Scribner's Sons, 1890); Stromberg, Jerome S., "Private Problems in Public Housing: A Further Report on the Pruitt-Igoe Project," Occasional Paper no. 39 (February 1968); The Community Builders. Our Projects: Villages at Park Du Valle (http://www.tcbinc.org/what_we_do/projects/fp_parkduvalle.htm).

PWA (PUBLIC WORKS ADMINISTRATION). Established by the 1933 National Industrial Recovery Act, the Public Works Administration (PWA) was a New Deal government agency that combined two tasks: providing job opportunities and improving the nation's infrastructure. Through construction projects, such as building highways and public buildings, the goal of the PWA was to provide employment to offset the effects of the Great Depression and, at the same time, contribute to a revitalization of American industry. In reality, however, the PWA proceeded too slowly to be of significant impact on either front.

The National Industrial Recovery Act gave the PWA a budget of $3.3 billion. Under the direction of Secretary of the Interior Harold L. Ickes, from 1933 to 1939 the PWA oversaw nearly 34,000 projects of varying sizes. Although it was a government agency, the PWA relied on private contractors to carry out the actual projects, and its primary role was to select suitable projects and provide financial support. Some of the more notable PWA projects were New York's Lincoln Tunnel and Triborough Bridge and the Overseas Highway that connected Key West to mainland Florida. The PWA also oversaw small-scale projects, such as the construction of schools, streets, hospitals, and sidewalks, across the nation. Housing was another focus of the PWA. Under Ickes's direction, the PWA loaned money to private contractors to begin a program of slum clearance and construction of public housing; by 1937, however, only 25,000 units had been completed—much less than what supporters had envisioned.

Overall, the PWA provided limited help for the poor. PWA programs never provided enough jobs to change unemployment levels significantly. Like the New Deal as a whole, the PWA appeared more useful on paper than in practice, because administrative, financial, and political difficulties lessened the program's effectiveness. In 1939, the PWA officially ended because of declining support for the New Deal.

See also: New Deal; WPA (Works Progress Administration)

Sources: Conkin, Paul K., *The New Deal*, 2nd ed. (Arlington Heights, Illinois: Harlan Davidson, 1975); Link, Arthur S., and William B. Catton, *American Epoch: A History of the United States Since 1900, Volume II: 1921–1945*, 4th ed. (New York: Houghton Mifflin Co., 1973); Patterson, James T., *America's Struggle against Poverty in the Twentieth Century* (Cambridge, MA: Harvard University Press, 2000); The Eleanor Roosevelt Papers. "Public Works Administration," *Teaching Eleanor Roosevelt*, edited by Allida Black, June Hopkins, et al. (Hyde Park, New York: Eleanor Roosevelt National Historic Site, 2004).

R

RACE AND ETHNICITY. Americans have often—but not always correctly—identified poverty as synonymous with minority status. According to the structural theory of poverty, social and cultural barriers, rather than the economy, prevent certain people from maintaining an adequate material existence. According to the structural view, minority groups cannot advance through a simple plan of economic reform. Structural barriers, such as racial and ethnic prejudice and its effects (such as lack of education), need to be overcome before minority groups can rise out of poverty. Although many conservatives disagree with the structural interpretation, it is undeniable that nonwhite racial and ethnic groups—African Americans, Eastern European immigrants, Jews, Hispanics, Asians, and Native Americans—have experienced prejudice. The debate is whether or not that prejudice has been strong enough to erect social and cultural barriers that, left unchecked, keep minority groups from ever advancing.

The structural theory of race and poverty formed a cornerstone to Johnson's War on Poverty in the 1960s. President Johnson, in the State of the Union speech in January, 1965, declared that, for the century after the Civil War ended, the United States has "labored to establish a unity of purpose and interest among the many groups which make up the American community. That struggle has often brought pain and violence. It is not yet over." Two months later, Assistant Secretary of Labor Daniel P. Moynihan authored a Department of Labor report, *The Negro Family: The Case for National Action*, which argued that the African American family in the city was crumbling because of centuries of racial prejudice and that it was up to the American people, through the federal government, to bolster and strengthen the African American family. An important part of this federal attempt was the Civil Rights Act of 1964, which outlawed discrimination, thus opening gaps in social and cultural barriers into which education, activism, and healing could be brought. The Civil Rights Act established the Equal Employment Opportunity Commission (EEOC), which worked to expose the widespread discrimination against minorities in the workplace. In 1966 the EEOC handled 8,854 discrimination cases, and by 1970 that number had risen to 20,310. Section 709(c) of Title VII of the 1964 Civil Rights Act gave the Commission the authority to require employers to keep records and submit reports on the employment status of women and minorities. In 1966 the EEOC required large private companies to submit EEO-1 reports demonstrating the ratio of men and women from five racial or ethnic groups in nine job categories that ranged from laborers to supervisory positions.

The data from EEO-1 reports allowed the EEOC to identify possible areas of employment discrimination; these reports allowed the EEOC to discern patterns of racial discrimination within geographic areas and job type. Between 1967 and 1971, the EEOC held public conferences that exposed discrimination in specific industries, including textile factories in the South, corporations in New York, and the service industry in Houston. According to the EEOC's findings, minorities constituted more than 30 percent of the population of South Carolina and 22 percent of North Carolina's population, but African Americans constituted only 8.4 percent of the textile industry employees in these two states. Of these African Americans, over 95 percent were employed in the lowest-paying job categories, and only 2.3 percent were in positions of authority. Likewise, 4,278 companies in New York City submitted EEO-1 reports in 1967, but only 1,827 of these employed a black worker in a white-collar position, and 1,936 of these did not employ any workers with Spanish surnames in white-collar jobs. Finally, EEOC data demonstrated that minorities and women constituted the majority of Houston's lowest-paying unskilled jobs, despite the city's overall rise in employment opportunities. EEOC reports concluded that widespread discriminatory employment practices that contributed to the enduring impoverishment of America's minority groups were common across the nation.

The relative impoverishment of minority groups in America has lessened in recent years, although non-Hispanic whites are still less likely than other groups to live in poverty. In 2005 the poverty rate for non-Hispanic whites was 8.3 percent, and 16.2 million lived in poverty. Overall, non-Hispanic whites accounted for 66.7 percent of the total population, but only 43.9 percent of those below the poverty rate. In comparison, 24.9 percent of blacks—a total of 9.2 million—lived in poverty in 2005; 11.1 percent of Asians, or 1.4 million, lived in poverty; and 21.8 percent of Hispanics, or 9.4 million, were impoverished. In addition, 25.3 percent of American Indians and 12.2 percent of Native Hawaiians and Pacific Islanders lived in poverty in 2005.

These data suggest that race is not a primary determinant of poverty. Although minorities have historically been subject to racial discrimination, low status, and low-paying jobs, it is an oversimplification to assume that racial and ethnic groups constitute the majority of America's poor or that the majority of the racial and ethnic population is poor. Many individuals of nonwhite races are not poor, and whites represent a significant proportion (nearly 44 percent) of America's poor.

See also: Equal Employment Opportunity Commission; Inequality; Racism; War on Poverty; Wealth and Income

Sources: Atkins, Jacqueline M., ed., *Encyclopedia of Social Work*, 18th ed., 2 vols. (Silver Spring, MD: NASW, 1987); Moynihan, Daniel P., *The Negro Family: The Case for National Action*. Office of Policy Planning and Research, U.S. Department of Labor (1965)

(http://www.dol.gov/oasam); Patterson, James T., *America's Struggle against Poverty in the Twentieth Century* (Cambridge, MA: Harvard University Press, 2000); Equal Employment Opportunity Commission (http://www.eeoc.gov/abouteeoc/35th/index.html).

RACISM. Since America was first colonized in the early seventeenth century, racism has influenced social and economic status. The levels of prejudice vary greatly according to time and place, however, and other factors have often obscured the effects of racism on the American poor. In general, in terms of racism in America, the viewpoint of white Americans is assumed to be the dominant point of reference. British colonists were the first and most influential settlers of the area of North America that is now the United States, and their Anglo-Saxon heritage served as the foundation for the early United States. Although racism has been prevalent throughout America's history, particular historical moments most clearly demonstrate the negative effect of racism. Striking examples include black slavery and its aftermath in the rural South; the nineteenth-century immigrant ghetto seen in Chinatowns and Jewtowns (as described by Jacob Riis); tenements; and the twentieth-century African American ghetto, illustrated in public housing, isolation in slums, and spiritualism.

The institutionalization of race-based slavery in the America is one of the earliest and harshest examples of the correlation between racism and poverty. In 1619, soon after the founding of Britain's first permanent colony in Virginia at Jamestown, Africans were brought to North America. Although the influence of racism on the status of these "20 and Odd Negroes" is unclear, it is likely that these blacks were laborers, perhaps slaves, captured in an African war and sold by the victorious tribe. By the mid-seventeenth century, white American colonists specifically imported Africans as slaves because, among other reasons, their race was considered inferior to that of whites. The institutionalization of race-based slavery in America grew rapidly, and, by its eradication at the end of the Civil War in 1865, the states of the South had developed a social and economic hierarchy. At the bottom of this hierarchy were the "Negroes," who, according to the white elites—both the plantation owners (the top of society) and slave-owning yeomen (the middle)—were biologically and spiritually inferior to whites and thus were born to be slaves. Slaves did not own property, often lived in ramshackle huts, did not enjoy legal rights of any kind, and did not even "own" themselves; therefore, black slaves commonly endured the worst conditions of poverty.

After the end of the Civil War, African Americans obtained legal freedom, but many remained in rural areas of the South as sharecroppers because farming was all that they knew. Consequently, emancipation did not immediately change the material prospects of most blacks, even though the moral victory of "owning" oneself may have been a small comfort. Sharecropping required farm tools, however, so poor freedmen were at the mercy of greedy country store proprietors, who gave loans for supplies with very high interest rates that most blacks were unable to pay off. Not surprisingly, most blacks in the South remained very poor. In the late nineteenth and early twentieth centuries, many rural African Americans migrated to northern cities looking for work. Racism was very prevalent in the North as well, and blacks were forced to reside in run-down slum areas—away from the white areas of the city, but still close enough to cause occasional confrontations, such as the 1919 Chicago Riot and the Tulsa Race Riot of 1921.

Although African Americans have experienced the most visible racism, other immigrant groups have faced prejudice. Asians especially experienced strong racism, including laws limiting their immigration to America, and isolation in Chinatowns in American cities. Competition for jobs and housing exacerbated racism, as did "nativism," a WASP (white Anglo Saxon Protestant) point of view that immigrants—especially from Ireland, Eastern Europe, Africa, and Asia—are invaders in an established America, a threat to American ideals. Commercial and military interests also led to openly racist ideals, such as when, during World War II, America launched a propaganda campaign that portrayed Asians as buck-toothed, bespectacled savages in order to raise support for the war against Japan; moreover, the United States government interred Japanese Americans in detention camps. Racism has had a direct influence on poverty levels: most immigrants were already poor, and racism denied them the ability to merge with mainstream society. Forced to congregate in older areas of cities, such as in New York's "Chinatown," "Jewtown," and "Little Italy," or confined to isolated rural areas, as in the case of blacks in the South and Germans in the Midwest, racial minorities had fewer opportunities than whites to benefit materially.

Writers discussing the African American ghetto have often referred to the odd, inferior culture of the ghetto. White perceptions of Harlem in the 1920, as described in Carl Van Vechten's *Nigger Heaven* (1926), for example, illustrate racially biased views that African American neighborhoods are "wide open," that is, strange. Vechten, an affluent white and devotee of the "art for art's sake" school, prided himself on his knowledge and patronage of black artists, writers, and musicians in Harlem. Unable to escape ethnocentric prejudices, however, Vechten superimposed his own psychological darkness onto Harlem—best illustrated in the climax of *Nigger Heaven*, in which the femme fatale black female attempts to lead the WASP-ish black hero back to his cultural roots. Langston Hughes, one of the most famous African American poets, addressed the racist but well-intentioned condescension of his white patrons. In many of his poems, such as his 1959 "Theme for English B," he asked why the color of his skin mattered.

The stigma of the African American ghetto as a dangerous and decrepit area remains strong, and reform measures such as urban renewal and public housing have only increased this perception. The 1960s "ghetto" riots—the most explosive of which was the 1965 Watts riot—also contributed to an increase in racial separation. Since the invention of the automobile in the early twentieth century, affluent and middle-class whites moved away from the central area of cities to the suburbs, leaving a concentration of impoverished minorities in the old urban core. One exception was the town of Watts, south of Los Angeles, which became a black-dominated area, or a "black island" in a "white sea." Pejoratively referred to by locals as "Nigger Heaven" after Van Vechten's novel, Watts suffered economically and became the site of low-cost housing. Ironically, the outbreak of violence in Watts increased white fear of African Americans and acted as a catalyst to increase "white flight" from minority-dominated areas. The backlash was so strong that the mayor of Los Angeles, Sam Yorty, in order to obtain higher office, attempted to manipulate white fears of additional riots. Throughout American history, the incidence of such riots is small, because the effects of racism were deeply ingrained within mainstream American society and largely went ignored. However, racial prejudice has had a profound impact on America's social, economic, and material makeup, and racism has had an even more significant impact on the American poor than the quantifiable data show.

See also: African Americans and Poverty (post-slavery); Protest Movements; Race and Ethnicity

Sources: Atkins, Jacqueline M., ed., *Encyclopedia of Social Work*, 18th ed., 2 vols. (Silver Spring, MD: NASW, 1987); Callow, Alexander B. Jr., ed. *American Urban History: An Interpretive Reader with Commentaries*, 3rd ed. (New York: Oxford University Press, 1982); Goldfield, David R., and Blaine A. Brownell, *Urban America: From Downtown to No Town* (Boston: Houghton Mifflin Co., 1979); Horne, Gerald, *Fire This Time: The Watts Uprising and the 1960s* (New York: University of Virginia Press, 1995); Huggins, Nathan Irvin, *Harlem Renaissance* (New York: Oxford University Press, 1971); Litwack, Leon, *North of Slavery: The Negro in the Free States, 1790–1860* (Chicago: University Press, 1971); Patterson, James T., *America's Struggle against Poverty in the Twentieth Century* (Cambridge, MA: Harvard University Press, 2000); Sitkoff, Harvard, *New Deal for Blacks: The Emergence of Civil Rights as a National Issue* (Oxford: Oxford University Press, 1981); Thornton, John, "The African Experience of the '20 and Odd Negroes' Arriving in Virginia in 1619" in Stanley N. Katz, John M. Murrin, Douglas Greenberg, eds., *Colonial America Essays in Politics and Social Development*, 5th ed. (Boston: McGraw Hill, 2001).

REDEMPTIONERS. Redemptioners (also known as "free-willers") were part of the system of servitude in early America. Whereas indentured servants were typically from the British Isles, redemptioners were from Europe, usually Germany. The system of redemption was the primary method by which non-British Europeans came to America during the seventeenth and eighteenth centuries. Beginning in the late 1600s, but expanding in the 1700s to encompass a majority of servant immigrants to America, few redemptioners immigrated to the South or to New England. Rather, the majority arrived at and labored in the middle colonies, such as Pennsylvania and New York. The system of redemption continued into the early 1800s, which helped ensure a strong presence of German culture in Pennsylvania. Indeed, redemptioners provided so much of the bound labor in Pennsylvania that the colony had few convict servants.

The redemptioner system was very similar to that of indentured servitude. Both systems involved destitute people who voluntarily bound themselves to a merchant or captain for transport to America, agreeing to be auctioned off at arrival to a master whom they would serve for a period of, generally, four to seven years. On signing a contract in England or, in Europe, agreeing to be transported in return for service, both servants and redemptioners retained few rights and crossed the Atlantic packed into ships where disease thrived and mortality was high. Arriving in America, neither servant nor redemptioner quite knew what to expect, even though their shared experience was that the reality of serving a master was far different from the glowing picture of America that the spirit in England or newlander in Germany had painted to solicit their interest. Labor in America was, for any kind of servant, a harsh reality; masters tended to want to get a yield from their investment before the term of service was complete.

The redemptioner was different from the indentured servant not only in the place of origin but also in the time and place where they signed their contracts for service. Indentured servants signed a contract before the voyage, often because they were driven to it as a last resort out of hunger and despair. Once their names were on indentures, the recruiter ensured them of food and shelter as they awaited transport across the Atlantic. Redemptioners, however, usually signed the contract on arriving in America. Initially they planned on paying for their passage, either with funds they brought or that they would acquire from family or friends in America. The funds usually ran out long before arrival, and family and friends were difficult to find when the captain would not allow passengers to disembark until the passage was fully paid for. A more important difference was that indentured servants were usually single, male or female, while the redemptioners traveled with their entire family, bringing along their household goods. Sometimes the entire family was sold into service to pay for the passage; sometimes the parents sold the children; sometimes the head of family sold himself or herself for the sake of the others. Families were easily split up as a result; different masters might purchase the labor of different family members.

The organist and musician Gottlieb Mittelberger, who voyaged from Germany to America in 1750 to deliver an organ to a church congregation, kept a diary of his voyage, in part to record the sufferings of the redemptioners from the Palatine state of Germany and Switzerland with whom he sailed. The experience of redemptioners was to take all of their belongings on board ship, which would make a long and tedious journey down the Rhine—on Mittelberger's voyage it took seven weeks. Once the ship arrived at Rotterdam, at the mouth of the Rhine, there could be other delays before setting sail for England, then on to America. The redemptioners with Mittelberger suffered through a voyage that lasted five months; most who began the voyage in May with some funds for the passage found themselves penniless by the time that they reached Philadelphia. Many died en route. The ship captain crowded 400 passengers on board the boat; there were no comforts or privacy. Disease spread quickly and lethally. The mortality rate was horrendous, especially among children, as well as newborns and their mothers, who on dying were unceremoniously tossed overboard to make room for the others. Water was rancid and ship's biscuit wormy. Even when the ship reached Philadelphia, those who could not make full payment had to wait aboard ship while the captain found a merchant or landowner who wished to purchase the redemptioner's labor. A contract for a period of years would then be signed to pay for the Atlantic passage. Often families were split in the process. The redemptioners were exploited throughout the entire process, first by the Newlander who exaggerated or lied to commit the redemptioner to immigrate; the Rhine merchants who charged exorbitant prices for necessities during the initial voyage; the captain who crowded his ship and otherwise mistreated the passengers; and the merchant who purchased the redemptioner in America. Some "soul drivers" in America made an initial purchase of the redemptioners, only to march them into Pennsylvania and sell them to landowners along the way.

Redemptioners had a reputation for hard work and sacrifice to achieve their goals, even if it meant struggling through several years of servitude. One eighteenth-century observer wrote that

As soon as the time stipulated in their indentures is expired, they immediately quit their masters, and get a small tract of land, in settling which for the first three or four years they lead miserable lives, and in the most abject poverty; but all this is patiently borne and submitted to with the greatest cheerfulness, the satisfaction of being land holders smoothes every difficulty, and makes them prefer this manner of living to that comfortable subsistence which they could procure for themselves and their families by working at the trades in which they were brought up.

See also: Children and Poverty; Indentured Servitude; Spirits (Crimps) and Newlanders

Sources: Hofstadter, Richard, *America at 1750: A Social Portrait* (New York: Random House, 1971); McCormac, E. I., *White Servitude in Maryland, 1634–1820* (Baltimore: Johns Hopkins, 1904); Morse, Richard B., *Government and Labor in Early America* (New York: Harper & Row, 1965); Smith, Abbot Emerson, *Colonists in Bondage: White Servitude and Convict Labor in America, 1607–1776* (New York: Norton, 1971).

S

SHARECROPPING. *See* African Americans and Poverty

SLAVERY. Millions of Americans were impoverished by force during the period from the early 1600s to 1865 in the system of slavery that existed throughout the thirteen American colonies and the first states of the United States of America. The "peculiar institution," as Southern whites called the institution of slavery, expanded particularly during the Antebellum years (1790–1861) to include four million slaves working in Southern states. The majority of these slaves had no civil rights, property, income, or freedom of movement and lived in brutal poverty subject to the whims and generosity of their white masters.

Slavery had a long history by the time it was introduced in North America. The ancient Greeks and Romans enslaved enemy women and children as the spoils of war. During the European Middle Ages, agricultural workers were tied to the land and to permanent poverty in the system of serfdom. The Spanish conquerors of Central and South America enslaved the native peoples. In Africa, warring tribes captured and enslaved each other. African chiefs sold war captives to European traders who packed the holds of their ships with as much human cargo as possible, crossed the Atlantic to the New World, and sold those humans who remained alive to planters of the Caribbean and American South, who were hungry for inexpensive labor.

The majority of slaves in North America worked on southern plantations, engaged in daily, grueling labor tending cash crops such as tobacco, sugar, rice, and cotton. Field hands lived in shacks on plantations, had meager diets, wore rags for clothing, and were subject to malnutrition and disease. Life expectancy was low for these permanently impoverished people, made poor by force rather than by choice. Although in the antebellum north there existed a growing impoverished class of proletariat living in cities and working for low wages in factories, these workers at least had some degree of choice as to where they wished to live and how they wished to earn their money. Few slaves were given those choices, remaining bound to land, work, and poverty their entire lives. Slavery had existed sporadically in the Northern colonies before the Revolutionary War, but upon independence and the end of war, the Northern states outlawed or otherwise limited slavery so that by 1800 slavery was restricted to Southern states. After 1800, as the North went through the Industrial Revolution, finding free wage labor adequate to suit the needs of the factory system, the South continued to depend upon agriculture. Southern plantation owners, responding to increasing demand for cotton fiber coming from Northern factories producing cloth goods, increased the numbers of slaves working on their plantations, making slavery a viable economic—if not moral or social—institution. The Industrial Revolution therefore indirectly contributed to the expansion of slavery in the decades preceding the Civil War.

Notwithstanding the utter poverty of their material existence, slaves worked to enrich their lives in other ways. Although husband and wives and their children were sometimes split up at an auction or sale, this was the exception rather than the rule. Slave families experienced paternal and maternal care, love and passion, and sharing of discomfort, hunger, and humiliation, providing a counter to utter hopelessness. Experiencing not only the poverty of their material lives but also poverty of the spirit—that is, humility and the necessity of relying on God—slaves were very religious, and Christianity came to dominate Southern African American culture.

See also: African Americans and Poverty

Sources: Blassingame, John, *The Slave Community: Plantation Life in the Antebellum South* (New York: Oxford, 1979); Fogel, Robert W., and Stanley L. Engerman, *Time on the Cross: The Economics of American Negro Slavery* (Boston: Little, Brown and Co., 1974); Stampp, Kenneth, *The Peculiar Institution: Slavery in the Ante-Bellum South* (New York: Random House, 1956).

SOCIAL SECURITY. The Social Security program began during the Great Depression. As part of his ambitious New Deal program, President Franklin D. Roosevelt established the Committee on Economic Security (CES) in 1934 to study the problem of poverty and develop a comprehensive report for Congress. The resulting legislation was the 1935 Social Security Act. As part of his message to Congress, Roosevelt stated that the development of "social security" rather than the traditional American reliance on family and community for support was necessary during the 1930s due to the "complexities of great communities and organized industry" of the twentieth century. However, Roosevelt emphasized that increased reliance on the government for security was not a rejection of traditional values; rather, he claimed, the changing face of society necessitated new means of providing for the public welfare.

Despite Roosevelt's early emphasis on security for all, practical considerations and ideological resistance—conservatives believed welfare reduced the will to work—limited the bill's impact to a specialized portion of the population: the elderly and the temporarily unemployed. The focus on the elderly made sense during the Great Depression; at that time, policymakers could justify an old-age program as an effective means to provide for working-age Americans as well. The basic logic was as follows: jobs were limited during the depression, and many able-bodied workers were unemployed; younger workers had more energy and could work better; therefore, providing retirement benefits to older workers freed up jobs for younger workers and allowed more efficient production at the same time. As Roosevelt declared after signing the bill into law, "We can never insure one hundred percent of the population against the hazards and vicissitudes of life," but Social Security at least provided "protection to the average citizen . . . against the loss of a job and against poverty-ridden old age."

The 1935 Social Security Act began the American welfare state. In addition to old-age support, the act established the Aid to Dependent Children (ADC) program—which was renamed Aid to Families with Dependent Children (AFDC) in the 1960s, lasting until 1996. The Social Security old-age social insurance program was the primary focus; however; the act emphasized worker responsibility to earn support, and thus was very moderate. Rather than establish old-age support as a right, social security reinforced the primacy of work and self-sufficiency through the system of contributory funding: workers contributed to their future support by giving up a portion of each paycheck to the social security fund. One consequence of this system was that middle-income workers benefited the most—they, contributing more funds, received larger pensions. In contrast, the poorest workers rarely obtained enough support from social security to alleviate their poverty.

Congress made changes to the social security program over the following decades. Some of the most significant were in the 1960s with the passage of the health insurance programs Medicare and Medicaid in 1965. In 1965, Lyndon Johnson outlined his vision for Social Security's new focus on health, saying that "[s]ince World War II, there has been increasing awareness of the fact that the full value of Social Security would not be realized unless provision were made to deal with the problem of costs of illnesses among our older citizens." Johnson hoped that Medicare would "supply the prudent, feasible, and dignified way to free the aged from the fear of financial hardship in the event of illness," and that Medicaid would provide the same for low-income Americans.

Social Security has continued to evolve since 1965. The creation of the Supplemental Security Income (SSI) program was among the most significant changes of the 1970s, during which time most changes were implemented to cut costs. The SSI combined existing programs that affected adults to simplify administration (even so, by the 1970s, AFDC was the largest welfare program, but the SSI had no effect on it). Also in the 1970s, concerns began over funding Social Security, in part because of the recognition that the "baby boomers" (post–World War II) generation would soon reach retirement age. To address this problem, the 1977 Social Security Amendments raised the payroll tax—taken directly from workers' paychecks—from 6.45% to 7.65% and slightly reduced the program's benefits. The next significant changes occurred in 1996, when President Clinton signed two conservative bills: the Contract with America Advancement Act, which cut disability benefits to persons having a drug or alcohol addiction who did not have documentation of additional medical need, and the 1996 Welfare Reform Act, which ended the AFDC and significantly cut federal welfare-relief funding. This emphasis on work and individual responsibility, rather than on costly social-support systems like Social Security, has continued into the twenty-first century, making the future of Social Security uncertain.

See also: Aid to Families with Dependent Children, Clinton Welfare Reform, Medicaid, Medicare, New Deal, War on Poverty

Sources: Axinn, June, and Mark J. Stern, *Social Welfare: A History of the American Response to Need,* 5th ed. (Allyn and Bacon: Boston, 2001); Social Security Act, 1935 (www.ssa.gov/OP_Home/ssact/comp-toc.htm); Social Security Administration (www.ssa.gov); Social Security, Presidential Statements (http://www.ssa.gov/history/presstmts.html); Patterson, James T., *America's Struggle Against Poverty in the Twentieth Century* (Cambridge, MA: Harvard University Press, 2000).

SPIRITS (CRIMPS) AND NEWLANDERS. The seedy side of colonial immigration of the English and European poor involved the spirits (sometimes called crimps) in England and the newlanders (neülander) in Europe—those who recruited, intimidated, and even kidnapped the poor to get them to America. Some spirits or newlanders were legitimate recruiters who worked as a freelance agents, selling indentures to ship captains, or working for English shipowners seeking to pack a ship outbound for America with willing servants and redemptioners. Others, however, were liars and kidnappers who illegally transported people of all ages against their will.

Such was the excitement over the discovery and colonization of the New World that early promoters painted America in unrealistic and false hues. One mid-seventeenth century English writer, William Bullock, claimed in *Virginia Impartially Examined* that the poor and hungry arriving in America would find that "food shall drop into their mouthes." Such nonsense in the hands of the right crimp convinced the desperately poor, looking for their next meal, that America was the place to find it. William Eddis wrote in *Letters from America* (1770) that "broadsides were posted all over the city of London" that used honeyed words to attract the poor to immigrate to America. The message of the broadside was given verbal support by the crimp, who appeared in towns heralded by drummers and fifers marching through streets attracting an audience to hear of the wonderful opportunity to break from poverty and dependence to become a free landowner in America. The crimp, according to Eddis, offered "the most seducing encouragement to adventurers under every possible description; to those who are disgusted with the frowns of fortune in their native land; and to those of an enterprising disposition, who are tempted to court her smiles in a distant region." Crimps "represent the advantages to be obtained in America, in colours so alluring, that it is almost impossible to resist their artifices. Unwary persons are accordingly induced to enter into articles, by which they engage to become servants, agreeable to their respective qualifications, for the term of five years; every necessary accommodation being found them during the voyage; and every method taken that they may be treated with tenderness and humanity during the period of servitude; at the expiration of which they are taught to expect, that opportunities will assuredly offer to secure to the honest and industrious, a competent provision for the remainder of their days."

Crimps sometimes abused the system, going beyond mere enticement to kidnapping adults and youth. Sometimes crimps and their gangs wandered the streets of London at night looking for drunks who would unwittingly sleep off their hangovers in the holds of transport ships. Reports of crimps kidnapping children to pack a ship for transport led the royal government to impose restrictions on such crimes; a 1670 English law made the kidnapping of children for transport a capital crime. Nevertheless English and colonial court records indicate that the practice continued into the eighteenth century. Robert Louis Stevenson fictionalized the experience of one English lad in *Kidnapped*.

Across the English Channel, especially along the Rhine River, peasants and small farmers driven off their land by conflict, poverty, or images of a new world cast their lot with the newlander, a con man who egged on credulous German, Swiss, or Dutch farm families with vague promises of the rich land of America. Some redemptioners began the trip down the Rhine with money in their pockets, but by the time the voyage ensued across the Atlantic, most were penniless and had to sign an indenture upon arrival in America to even leave the ship.

See also: Children and Poverty, Indentured Servitude, Redemptioners

Sources: Herrick, Cheesman A., *White Servitude in Pennsylvania, Indentured and Redemption Labor in Colony and Commonwealth* (Philadelphia: McVey, 1926); Morse, Richard B., *Government and Labor in Early America* (New York: Harper & Row, 1965); Smith, Abbot Emerson, *Colonists in Bondage: White Servitude and Convict Labor in America, 1607–1776* (New York: Norton, 1971).

U

UNEMPLOYMENT. *See* Department of Labor

URBAN POOR. Throughout American history, the urban poor—those persons living below the poverty threshold in urbanized areas—have been one of the most visible and most misunderstood groups of society. Differences in race and ethnicity, economic impoverishment, and lifestyle traits that did not conform to the white middle-class ideal contributed to the separation of the poor from mainstream society, both hiding and magnifying the experience of the urban poor. Until the mid-twentieth century most academic and professional accounts of the urban poor assumed the viewpoint of the white Anglo-Saxon protestant (WASP) middle class, from which perspective most reformers, critics, and casual observers discussed the social, economic, religious, and cultural "difference" of the poor in urban areas. This perspective obscured the fact that WASP men and women also comprised part of the urban poor. With the rise of immigration from Eastern and Southern Europe in the mid-nineteenth century, however, the majority of the urban poor became of immigrant or nonwhite descent.

The urban poor are a difficult group to identify and understand because of the changing perceptions of poverty. As noted by Michael Harrington in *The Other America*, the urban poor's invisibility and isolation hides the great numbers of impoverished Americans and masks their experiences. Also impeding an understanding of the urban poor are the stereotypes—such as "deserving" and "undeserving" poor—adopted by middle class America to describe the urban poor. The "deserving poor" are those hardworking, sober people who, through ill fortune or incapacitation, have been prevented from achieving the goals of economic success. Those, on the other hand, who did not subscribe to the WASP ideal of hard work were "undeserving." The public perception of the poor was increasingly negative during the course of the nineteenth century, particularly as large numbers of Eastern and Southern European Catholics arrived in America in the late 1800s. At the same time the white middle class was influenced by the ideology of Social Darwinism, which taught that only the fittest (hardest working) survive in the American capitalist system. If economic success is a mark of superiority, then the poor must be inherently inferior—and therefore undeserving of public welfare. The urban poor had to rely on private rather than public welfare until the Great Depression brought massive material suffering even to the middle class, discrediting the idea that poverty is a mark of personal inferiority.

The early Industrial Revolution in America negatively impacted the urban poor. Prior to the rise of the machine and the standardization of production, small local shops were the norm. Artisans learned a trade through an apprenticeship in which tradesmen imparted their trades and provided lodging; thus great emphasis was put on personal relations between masters and their apprentices. Employers had closer relations with their workers, sometimes providing lodging in their own homes. The emphasis on quality workmanship allowed individual craftsmen to gain good reputations, which improved their social and financial situations. Mass production, however, led to the breakdown of the master–worker relationship, and quantity became more important than quality. Machines, with workers performing predefined tasks, produced goods more efficiently than one worker making a finished product; factories could rely on unskilled laborers. Mass production also lowered wages for workers, because special skills were no longer as important. This devaluation of skilled labor led to decreased contact between the affluent part of society—the employers—and the unskilled workers and the unemployed. As a result, the affluent became wealthier and the impoverished became poorer, until by the end of the nineteenth century Jacob Riis could justify the assertion, made in *How the Other Half Lives,* that the affluent not only did not care how the poor—"the other half"—lived, but had willfully forgotten them.

Changing social policy toward the poor clearly illustrates the transition from preindustrial to industrial America. In colonial American towns, members of the community in good standing who through misfortune—illness, disability, age, orphaning, widowing—became poor were cared for by the town through private individuals or the almshouse. As population increased and the numbers of itinerant, undeserving poor grew, American cities constructed workhouses to house, employ, and sometimes punish the poor. By the mid-nineteenth century, however, the numbers of inhabitants in major American cities had reached hundreds of thousands, stretching city infrastructures and making it impossible to care for the deserving poor. American cities no longer assumed responsibility for the poor, causing the creation and expansion of the urban slum. Who was "deserving"—and who was "undeserving"—of public poor relief did not matter, because such relief did not exist.

The increasingly nameless and faceless poor was enlarged by the large numbers of impoverished Irish, Italian, Jewish, and Greek (among others) immigrants. Eastern and Southern European newcomers upset the American middle-class ideal, rarely sharing faith in individual initiative with most WASP Americans. The American middle class grew fearful of the consequences of urbanization. Attempting to retain a semblance of order, city officials placed more reliance on institutions to establish order. Nineteenth-century American cities embraced the idea of the police to catch and incarcerate criminals and nonconformists, many of whom were the poor. Accompanying the white middle-class fear of immigrants was the anxiety about where they lived: the urban ghetto.

The conflict between the WASP middle class and the urban poor often occurred in the workplace. The former, spouting the ideals of Social Darwinism and laissez faire capitalism, were the socialist ideals of organized labor. The development of unions, such as the Knights of Labor and the American Federation of Labor (AFL), allowed workers to voice their discontent through strikes. At times, strikes degenerated into an outright fight between the workers and business and government: the Haymarket Square riot in Chicago (1886) and the Pullman Strike (1894) both resulted in increased federal measures to secure the position of American business. The pro-business stance of the government contributed to the spread of socialist ideology among the urban poor as a means of organizing against and vocalizing discontent about what they believed to be an oppressive system. The popularity of socialism and communism among the urban poor of all races alarmed political and business elites, who renewed their efforts to secure the position of individual initiative and free-market capitalism. But it was not until the stock market crash of October 1929, and the ill-starred response of President Herbert Hoover, that the federal government began to listen to the voice of the poor.

The Great Depression discredited the idea that poverty was a mark of inferiority, because the economic collapse impoverished the business elite and the middle class as well as the laboring class and urban poor; thus began the New Deal, America's entry into welfare statehood. Because mainstream Americans experienced poverty during the depression, New Deal programs such as Social Security implied that individual initiative alone was not a guarantee of prosperity. Other New Deal programs directed toward helping the urban poor included the Civilian Conservation Corps (CCC), which relocated unemployed urban youth to rural work camps, and the Works Project Administration (WPA), which employed men in projects such as building sidewalks. Ideologically, the Great Depression led to the awareness that poverty was not a disease or mark of inborn inferiority, justifying the switch from individualized charity to federal welfare. In the 1930s, poverty was no longer a trait of the "other"—immigrants, blacks, drug addicts, heathens, the indolent poor—but affected a large proportion of middle-class white Americans.

Early twentieth-century reformers attempted to clean up urban tenements, but these efforts were usually not successful; too often the reform efforts were half-hearted and did not get to the root of the problem. Housing programs like the Federal Housing Association (FHA) enabled low-income families to obtain affordable loans, increasing the movement to the suburbs. However, many African Americans and minority groups could not move out of the city and were forced to reside in large-scale public housing complexes, separated from the rest of the city. By 1937, when Congress passed the United States Housing Act (USHA), large-scale public housing complexes seemed to be the answer, as large complexes provided a low-cost and (theoretically) cleaner alternative to tenement housing. Early examples of housing complexes built under the USHA were Brooklyn's Red Hook and Queensbrough housing developments; these complexes were designed on a strict geometrical layout, did not have any design frills, and were generally dirty, unpleasant places to live. The enclosed design and large scale of these "big box" complexes led to a feeling of isolation from the rest of the city.

The isolation of African Americans in public housing led to the downward spiral of the conditions of the inner city, as city officials tended to focus their resources in other areas. The complacency of city officials was shattered in the mid 1960s with the nationwide outbreak of "ghetto" riots: the worst were in Watts (1965), Detroit (1967), and Newark (1967). President Johnson appointed the Kerner Commission to investigate the causes of these disturbances; the Commission's 1967 *Report* clearly identified the racial segregation of blacks into the worst areas of decaying cities as the cause of the violence. The Kerner Commission recommended a comprehensive overhaul of the existing structure of American society, including increasing the work for civil rights and equality, that was more radical and farther-reaching than President Johnson's War on Poverty. Johnson rejected the Kerner Commission's plan, however, so the situation remained unchanged.

Michael Harrington, in *The Other America*, echoed the Kerner Commission's conclusion that the America's poor felt forgotten. Significantly, Harrington's book reported similar findings to Riis's in *How the Other Half Lives*, demonstrating that despite the New Deal, few changes had occurred. In fact, many of the same problems exist today. In 2005, the poverty rate among people who lived in standard metropolitan statistical areas (SMSAs) but outside the city proper—in the suburbs and older towns near large cities—was 9.3 percent, whereas 17 percent of the residents of the principal city area of the SMSA and 14.5 percent of nonurban dwellers lived below the poverty line. Likewise, the most impoverished areas of most cities are the African American or immigrant areas, where there are few jobs, much crime, and little interaction with the rest of the population of the SMSA. Old industrial cities like Camden, New Jersey, and Detroit have large numbers of impoverished minorities in comparison to the more affluent residents living in the outlying suburbs, leaving the principal city with insufficient tax revenue. The problem of the urban poor is presently easy for the middle class to ignore but remains a significant concern for the continued livelihood of America's cities.

Since the Kerner Commission's *Report*, the situation has significantly changed in some ways and remained stagnant in others—somewhat depending on viewpoint and method of analysis. In terms of spatial segregation—the isolation of impoverished minorities in depressed central-city areas—relatively little has changed: central cities across the United States remain underfunded, contested areas; inner-city schools provide substandard education, and the urban poor do not have a strong political voice. However, recent comprehensive urban revitalization campaigns in poverty-stricken cities such as Detroit and Pittsburgh demonstrate that local authorities realize that a functioning central area is a requirement for urban growth. Despite the fact that revitalization leads to "gentrification" and does not often benefit the poorest residents, the spatial isolation of the inner city (a leading cause of ghetto unrest in the 1960s) is less defined. The movement of wealthier persons to revitalized central city areas should provide important information about the state of the urban poor in the twenty-first century but also raises several questions. Will municipal authorities provide adequate housing for the displaced former residents of revitalized areas? Will more attractive urban public space lead to reconciliation of class groups, or will the daily reminder of unattainable affluence goad the poor to renewed unrest?

See also: African Americans and Poverty, Great Depression, Immigrants, Labor, New Deal, Progressives, War on Poverty

Sources: Bauman, John F., Roger Biles, and Kristin M. Szylvian, eds., *From the Tenements to the Taylor Homes: In Search of an Urban Housing Policy in Twentieth-Century America* (University Park: The Pennsylvania State University Press, 2000); Brown, Robert, *Middle Class Democracy and the Revolution in Massachusetts, 1691–1780* (Cornell, New York: Cornell, 1955); Callow, Alexander B., Jr., ed., *American Urban History: An Interpretive*

Reader with Commentaries, 3rd ed. (New York: 1982); Goldfield, David R., and Blaine A. Brownell, *Urban America: From Downtown to No Town* (Boston: Houghton Mifflin Co., 1979); Harrington, Michael, *The Other America: Poverty in the United States* (New York: Macmillan, 1963); Horne, Gerald, *Fire This Time: The Watts Uprising and the 1960s* (New York: University of Virginia Press, 1995); Huggins, Nathan Irvin, *Harlem Renaissance* (New York: Oxford University Press, 1971); Lawson, Benjamin A., "The Pruitt-Igoe Projects: Modernism, Social Control, and the Failure of Public Housing, 1954–1976" (MA thesis: Oklahoma State University Press, 2007); Litwack, Leon, *North of Slavery: The Negro in the Free States, 1790–1860* (Chicago: University Press, 1971); Patterson, James T., *America's Struggle Against Poverty in the Twentieth Century* (Cambridge, MA: Harvard University Press, 2000); Riis, Jacob, *How the Other Half Lives* (New York: 1890); Sitkoff, Harvard, *New Deal for Blacks: The Emergence of Civil Rights as a National Issue* (Oxford: University Press, 1981); Trattner, Walter I., *From Poor Law to Welfare State,* 6th ed. (New York: Simon and Schuster, 1999).

V

VISTA. Established by the 1964 Economic Opportunity Act, VISTA is a domestic version of the Peace Corps. In the early 1960s President John F. Kennedy set up a task force to determine the practicality of a small, low-paying national-service program available to all ages and requiring a short-term commitment. The President's brother, Attorney General Robert F. Kennedy, was the early choice to direct the program, but Congressional delay meant that VISTA did not pass until after Kennedy's assassination, in Lyndon B. Johnson's term as president. Johnson included VISTA as part of his "War on Poverty" program, which he envisioned as a comprehensive plan to eliminate poverty nationwide. The War on Poverty failed, amid the conflict over the Vietnam War, violent minority uprisings, and the rising popularity of conservative politics; but, like many other EOA programs, Congress did not discontinue VISTA, which is still in effect today.

The common goal of EOA-established programs like VISTA, Community Action, Head Start, the Neighborhood Youth Corps, and the Job Corps, was, in President Johnson's words, to give poor Americans "a chance" to share "in the abundance which has been granted to most of us." The 1960s were a time of economic growth—and thus of fiscal and legislative optimism. In this atmosphere of abundance, Congress was willing to try liberal programs such as VISTA that would not necessarily return a direct and timely reward for the time and effort spent. In fact, the likelihood that VISTA would return quantifiable results was low—its focus was more on providing meaningful employment for reform-minded Americans and demonstrating to the poor that they were not forgotten, as several writers—notably Michael Harrington, in his 1963 book *The Other America*—had charged. Johnson's remarks to a group of VISTA volunteers in December of 1964 encapsulated this attitude: "Your pay will be low; the conditions of your labor often will be difficult. But you will have the satisfaction of leading a great national effort and you will have the ultimate reward which comes to those who serve their fellow man."

The first VISTA volunteers trained in Chapel Hill, North Carolina, for six months before beginning their first assignments in the depressed areas of Hartford, in the rural Appalachian hills of Kentucky, and in migrant camps in California. In its first ten years, VISTA programs worked on various projects across the United States, and VISTA's services broadened. VISTA offered basic medical services to impoverished people unable to afford health care, set up child care centers in migrant communities, and established adult-education programs in cities and on Indian reservations. VISTA also recruited local professionals—architects, doctors, lawyers—to volunteer in low-income areas in an effort to build community.

In the over forty years since its founding, VISTA has overcome significant political hardships. Each presidential administration had its own political ideology and program, and VISTA did not always receive unqualified support. President Ronald Reagan, for example, endorsed a strong conservative platform, and during his two terms VISTA was forced to cut back on national recruiting and training and relied instead on grassroots support. In 1993, President Bill Clinton signed the National and Community Service Trust Act of 1993, which relocated VISTA into a new agency, the Corporation for National Service, where it currently remains.

See also: Economic Opportunity Act, War on Poverty

Sources: *Public Papers of the Presidents of the United States, Lyndon B. Johnson, 1965* (Washington, D.C.: Government Printing Office, 1966); Whittlesey, Susan, *VISTA: Challenge to Poverty* (New York: Coward-McCann, 1970); Volunteers in Service to America VISTA (Washington: ACTION [Service Corps], 1980).

WAGES. *See* Minimum Wage

WAR AND POVERTY. The relationship of poverty to war depends on varying factors such as whether conflict is offensive or defensive, whether it takes place on foreign or domestic soil, and whether it occurs before, during, or after industrialization. Prior to the Industrial Revolution, colonial wars, including the Revolutionary War, occurred on American soil and were highly destructive of food production and trade, producing negative economic consequences. The Civil War brought economic destruction and want to the agricultural South, but less to the industrialized North. The wars of the twentieth century, such as World War I and World War II, brought with them many beneficial effects on the American economy.

Warfare before the Industrial Revolution. The wars between empires that involved colonial America, such as King William's War (1689–1697), Queen Anne's War (1703–1712), King George's War (1744–1749), and the French and Indian War (1755–1763), featured sporadic battles that affected particular local populations, not the total war of an industrial society. The small fishing community of Gosport, for example, off the coast of New Hampshire, petitioned the provincial legislature in 1760 for forbearance regarding payments of tax. The colony was involved in war (the French and Indian War), which sufficiently affected local finances that the town struggled to raise the money required. "The said Inhabitants have allways chearfully paid their Province Tax with Great Willingness and pleasure," the town petition read,

> so long as they were of ability and untill the four last years when their Circumstances in life became so low (being only a few poor fishermen) and the necessaries for living being Excessively dearer at the place of their aboad one half more than any other part of the Province . . . together with their other great charge, Supporting the Gospel Ministry among them the fewness of the Inhabitants & their poverty and their few

> within four years last past being Greatly Reduced they having had thirty Two Ratable poles within that time left them to serve the King or Removed to other places.

Individual communities, rather than society as a whole, suffered from reduced manpower (because of militia duty) and disruption of trade. Wealth inequality studies of eighteenth-century America show little change overall because of war.

The Revolutionary War (1775–1783) likewise affected the economies of revolutionary states according to time and circumstance, not America as a whole. Historians have found little evidence of dramatic changes in wealth accumulation and inequality because of this war. There are, of course, isolated instances to the contrary, especially of towns affected by a disruption of overseas trade because of the presence of the British navy off the American coast. The economy of Salem, Massachusetts, for example, suffered from declining trade, causing increasing wealth inequality and social stratification. The fishing community of Gosport continued to experience economic deprivation because of the war. The nearby port city of Portsmouth, New Hampshire, helped the fishers and fishwives even though the war negatively impacted Portsmouth's economy as well. The Portsmouth selectmen petitioned the New Hampshire legislature in 1776, requesting that the "Poor on the Isles of Shoals be relieved out of the Public Treasury, to ease the Burthens of this Town which has been at great Expense on their Account, & at a time when we are unable to Maintain our own." Three years later, in a 1779 "Statement of the Condition of Matters in Town," the town complained of economic deprivation "In Consequence of" supporting the inhabitants of Gosport, "which this Town has been burthen'd with the poorer Sort of them since that Time." Portsmouth trade declined dramatically, such that "Multitudes are reduced from easy Circumstances, to want & beggary, and half the Inhabitants have frequently been without Bread or Fuel." Inflation made the cost of poor relief £30,000 in 1779, which increased to £80,000 in 1780. Other places in Revolutionary America, however, saw little significant change in economic stratification due to the war. In Chester County, Pennsylvania, for example, wealth inequality during the war years was little different from during the previous decades of the eighteenth century. Wealth inequality increased from 1760 to 1780, but little more than in previous decades, an indicator that the county's inequality was a part of the maturing of colonial society rather than because of war. In fact, independence—more than warfare—appears to have had the biggest effect on poverty in Revolutionary America. The haphazard and decentralized trade and currency policies of the new Confederation government caused inflation that brought suffering to the agricultural poor.

Modern Warfare. Industrialization brought increasing wealth inequality to America, a situation only exacerbated during wartime. For example, the top 10 percent of the population owned 43 percent of the wealth from 1750 to 1800, but from 1800 to 1860 this jumped to 61 percent. The percent of the labor force in industry went from 17.5 percent in 1800 to 46.8 percent in 1860. The Civil War in the North continued these trends. Wages (rising 43 percent) lagged behind prices, which rose 117 percent during the war. There were increasing numbers of propertyless living in the growing cities. Meanwhile, those with capital thrived—the rich got richer, and the poor got poorer. The Civil War had the most dramatic impact on the South, where most of the fighting occurred. Before the beginning of the war, there was growing inequality in the South among whites; decline in food production during the war, and the disabled Southern economy, continued this trend. The loss of property because of the emancipation of slaves in 1865 would, perhaps, have leveled wealth inequality in the South if it were not for the millions of freedmen living in the South, most of whom were very poor. The freedmen experienced freedom in all of its forms, including insecurity, hunger, and despair.

The mixed picture of poverty in America during wartime becomes clearer during World War I. Prior to the beginning of the war in 1914, wealth inequality continued to increase in America from the 1800s, and most Americans owned very little of the country's wealth. This trend was not halted during the war, especially during American involvement from 1917 to 1918, as wages lagged behind inflation. But there were more jobs during the war, many of them filled by women, and there was increasing government involvement in the economy during the Progressive era, particularly during the administration of Woodrow Wilson.

After the war, many sectors of the American economy were booming until the onset of the Great Depression. During the 1930s, depression, homelessness, unemployment, bank failures, and insecurity plagued Americans. Franklin Roosevelt's New Deal helped the situation, but full recovery did not occur until the outbreak of World War II. After Roosevelt declared America to be an "Arsenal of Democracy," providing industrial production to countries threatened by the Axis powers—and then in the wake of the bombing of Pearl Harbor—the American economy quickly left the Depression behind. During the war, unemployment dropped from 7 million to less than a million; 6.5 million workers were added to American payrolls. Personal income doubled. War production doubled every two years. Although the number of taxpayers more than quadrupled—from 13 to 59 million—the tax burden fell increasingly upon large corporations and the rich, leading to wealth redistribution. The wealth of the top one percent of the population was cut in half during the war. The post–World War II period in America continued the trend of lessening wealth inequality, in part because of a strong economy and the growth of government programs to help the poor, disabled, unemployed, and elderly.

See also: New Deal, Wealth and Income Inequality

Sources: Ball, Duane E., "Dynamics of Population and Wealth in Eighteenth-Century Chester County, Pennsylvania," *Journal of Interdisciplinary History* 6 (1976): 621–644; Faulkner, Harold U., *American Economic History* (New York: Harper & Row, Publishers, 1960); Lawson, Russell M., *Portsmouth: An Old Town by the Sea* (Charleston: Arcadia Publishing, 2003); Link, Arthur S., and William B. Catton, *American Epoch: A History of the United States since 1900,* Vol. II: The Age of Franklin D. Roosevelt, 1921–1945 (New York: Alfred E. Knopf, 1973); Morris, Richard J., "Wealth Distribution in Salem, Massachusetts, 1759–1799: the Impact of the Revolution and Independence" in *Essex Institute Historical Collections* 114 (1978): 87–102.

WAR ON POVERTY. Part of Lyndon B. Johnson's Great Society program, the War on Poverty began in 1964 with the passage of the Economic Opportunity Act. The 1960s were a time of economic prosperity, which gave liberals the opportunity to allocate surplus funds to improve society. Johnson described his reason for implementing these programs in the 1964 "Great Society" speech given at the University of Michigan. According to Johnson, the success of the "Great Society" depended on "abundance and liberty for all," an ideal that "demands an end to poverty and racial injustice, to which we are totally committed in our time." Johnson saw

America under the Great Society as "a place where every child can find knowledge to enrich his mind and to enlarge his talents" and "where leisure is a welcome chance to build and reflect, not a feared cause of boredom and restlessness." The Great Society programs, including the War on Poverty, were idealistic in that Johnson sought to serve "not only the needs of the body and the demands of commerce but the desire for beauty and the hunger for community." Despite the Great Society's liberal emphasis on the role of the federal government, it had much in common with the Progressive ideals of the early twentieth century. There were three areas in particular in which Johnson sought to implement the Great Society: in the cities, in the countryside, and in the classroom.

Johnson was especially focused on the needs of America's cities, especially impoverished minority areas, where the War on Poverty had the greatest effect. In the 1964 Great Society speech Johnson predicted that "perhaps 50 years from now"—in 2014—"there will be 400 million Americans—four-fifths of them in urban areas." Consequently, the "urban population will double, city land will double, and we will have to build homes, highways, and facilities . . . in the next 40 years we must rebuild the entire urban United States." Central to his plan to ensure that America approached these changes in the correct way was Johnson's plan to eradicate both material and psychological poverty; the War on Poverty was the means for achieving that goal.

In a 1964 speech Johnson outlined his plan, officially declaring "a national war on poverty." Johnson summed up the impact of poverty on the "millions of Americans—one fifth of our people—who have not shared in the abundance" of 1960s America. In contrast to the prosperity enjoyed by the white middle class, the poor, Johnson explained, struggle daily "to secure the necessities for even a meager existence," unable to enjoy the "abundance, the comforts, the opportunities they see all around them." This last statement underlines the primary difference between the New Deal and the Great Society: the poor in the 1960s were more aware of the material goods they were missing, primarily via television, and they expected to take part in consumer society at a much greater level than had the poor in the 1930s. Thus, the poor tended to feel especially marginalized from mainstream society, leading to—according to Johnson—"hopelessness for the young," as the "young man or woman who grows up without a decent education, in a broken home, in a hostile and squalid environment, in ill health or in the face of racial injustice—that young man or woman is often trapped in a life of poverty," without the "skills demanded by a complex society," which leads to "a mounting sense of despair which drains initiative and ambition and energy."

The War on Poverty was also an ideological battle. To justify the need for his War on Poverty, Johnson stated that "We do this, first of all, because it is right, because it is wise, and because, for the first time in our history, it is possible to conquer poverty." Johnson portrayed his program as an "investment" in the American people and economic system, stating that "if we can raise the annual earnings of 10 million among the poor by only $1,000 we will have added $14 billion a year to our national output. In addition we can make important reductions in public assistance payments which now cost us $4 billion a year, and in the large costs of fighting crime and delinquency, disease and hunger." Despite the initial financial commitment, the War on Poverty would lead to increased financial success for all, Johnson argued, as American "history has proved that each time we broaden the base of abundance, giving more people the chance to produce and consume, we create new industry, higher production, increased earnings and better income for all."

Johnson envisioned the War on Poverty as not "a struggle simply to support people, to make them dependent on the generosity of others," but as a politically initiated "struggle to give people a chance." The Johnson administration developed a comprehensive plan to address poverty through economic reform, education, and community building, to "allow [the poor] to develop and use their capacities . . . so that they can share, as others share, in the promise of this nation." The 1964 Economic Opportunity Act was the first official legislation of the War on Poverty, which gave power to the Office of Economic Opportunity (OEO). The OEO established many programs—including the Job Corps, Head Start, Neighborhood Youth Corps (NYC), and the Community Action Program (CAP)—to address the different facets of the nation's poverty. These programs were not very successful. Intended to prepare disadvantaged youth for "the responsibilities of citizenship and to increase the employability of young men and young women aged sixteen through twenty-one by providing them in rural and urban residential centers with education, vocational training, useful work experience, including work directed toward the conservation of natural resources, and other appropriate activities," the Job Corps lacked sufficient financial support and failed. The EOA also established work-training and work-study programs to facilitate educational and vocational training among low-income youth, and the Head Start program spearheaded the OEO's attempt to help low-income children adapt to school and society.

The most infamous aspect of the EOA was the Community Action Program (CAP). Intended to provide "services, assistance, and other activities of sufficient scope and size to give promise of progress toward elimination of poverty or a cause or causes of poverty through developing employment opportunities, improving human performance, motivation, and productivity, or bettering the conditions under which people live, learn, and work," the CAP directly involved the poor in its administration. This policy of "maximum feasible participation" of the poor angered existing policymakers, hampering the CAP's ability to influence the passage of significant legislation. Consequently, the CAP intended to give the poor a political voice, but all it accomplished was to lessen support for the War on Poverty, as it emphasized the political, economic, and cultural split between the middle class and the poor. The 1964 Economic Opportunity Act was the backbone of Johnson's War on Poverty and the Great Society program, so its lack of success placed Johnson's entire domestic-reform plan in jeopardy; when Richard Nixon became president in 1969 he did not support the renewal of many of Johnson's liberal programs.

See also: Community Action Program, Economic Opportunity Act, Job Corps, Office of Economic Opportunity

Sources: Economic Opportunity Act (http://www2.volstate.edu/geades/FinalDocs/1960s/eoa.htm); Bremner, Robert H., Gary W. Reichard, and Richard Hopkins, eds., *American Choices: Social Dilemma and Public Policy since 1960* (Columbus: Ohio State University Press, 1986); Iceland, John, *Poverty in America,* 2nd ed. (Berkeley: University of California Press, 2006); Johnson, Lyndon, "The War on Poverty" (1964), *Public Papers of the Presidents of the United States, Lyndon B. Johnson,* Book II (1965) (Washington, D.C.: Government Printing Office, 1966); Johnson, Lyndon, "Great Society Speech" (1964), *Public Papers of the Presidents of the United States, Lyndon B. Johnson,* Book I (1963–64) (Washington, D.C.:

Government Printing Office, 1965); Patterson, James T., *America's Struggle Against Poverty in the Twentieth Century* (Cambridge, MA: Harvard University Press, 2000).

WARNING OUT. Warning out was the practice by which colonial New Englanders sought to restrict the settlement of paupers in established communities. Warning out was based on the English Act of Settlement, enacted in 1662 under Charles II, which required local magistrates to expel paupers who lived in, but were not natives of, English towns, requiring the paupers to return to the towns of their birth. A 1691 act under William III specified that newcomers to English towns must either own property or be gainfully employed or apprenticed. Settlement legislation in England was primarily directed toward an orderly economic solution to the growing problem of poverty. Warning out in New England was likewise a way "to Keepe the Town harmless from being burthened in way of Charge" but also was a means of preserving community order and cohesion.

Warning out during the seventeenth and eighteenth centuries applied only to towns that were prosperous and expanding in population, experiencing the movement of goods and peoples; typically these were small port cities. The poor, especially newcomers to America, naturally sought out opportunity and often searched extensively in town after town for work and support. As in England, American towns found that frequently they had to help the orphaned, disabled, and elderly poor. Such towns were sufficiently humane to help, but only temporarily, until the pauper found other means. The town felt obliged to support paupers who were longtime members of the community, but recent arrivals ought rather to seek assistance from the communities of their birth. Town constables approached recently arrived newcomers demanding evidence of the means to purchase property or material family support; otherwise the constable warned out the person, declaring that the town would not provide assistance should the need arise. Options for the person so warned were to risk staying, to depart for another town, or to find immediate employment—often by servitude. Boston required newcomers to post a £20 bond. Towns might inquire into the person's character by hearsay or letter before making a judgment. In New Hampshire, even if the pauper stayed, he or she was liable to the town parish tax rate. New Hampshire townspeople who willingly boarded strangers were warned by the town that they assumed responsibility should the person be or become poor.

Contributing to the suspiciousness that gave rise to warning out was the potential that newcomers could bring strange behaviors and beliefs that were neither orthodox nor acceptable. During the eighteenth century, the increasing transportation of convicts to the American colonies brought additional suspicion on the heads of those strangers who were seen on street corners, at the docks, in taverns—even in the meetinghouse—who did not soon depart. Because the colonial American attitude toward the poor held that poverty represented a moral failing, simply too much risk was involved in allowing poor strangers to settle in a town where everything and everyone was familiar and known.

See also: Poor Laws in England and America

Sources: Benton, Josiah H., *Warning Out in New England* (Boston: Clarke, 1911); Burn, Richard, *The History of the Poor Laws: With Observations* (London: Woodfall and Strahan, 1764); Nicholls, George, *A History of the English Poor Law,* 2 vols. (London:

P. S. King and Son, 1904); *Portsmouth New Hampshire Town Records,* typescript, Portsmouth Public Library.

WEALTH AND INCOME INEQUALITY. Poverty in society is the result of wealth inequality—the unequal distribution of wealth in property and capital—which depends upon the basis of production in a society, as well as upon the labor system, mortality rates, fertility rates, age distribution, and wage rates. Industrialization and urbanization in nineteenth-century America brought greater inequality than had existed in the rural, agricultural economy of colonial America. With increasing government intervention in the economy after the 1930s, however, inequality returned to preindustrial, colonial levels.

Surviving tax and probate records of colonial America indicate that towns had greater inequality than the countryside, the South had greater inequality than the North, and as a region's economy grew in sophistication so did its inequality. Examples include Maryland from 1650 to 1720, when the tobacco economy was expanding, relying heavily on white servitude and black slavery. From 1656 to 1683 the top 10% of the population owned 43% of the wealth; but by 1713 to 1719 the top 10% owned 64% of the wealth. Colonial Charleston was little different; the top 10% owned 58% of the wealth. At the same time, in Hartford, Connecticut, a small but growing town, the top 10% of the population owned 34% of the wealth. The richest 10% in the agricultural town of Litchfield, Connecticut, at mid-century, owned 24% of the wealth. But in Boston, by the time of the American Revolution, the top 10% of the population controlled almost two thirds of the wealth.

In short, as the American colonies matured, inequality in growing towns outpaced that in rural districts, and inequality in the South, because of slavery, was greater than that in the North, save in the largest Northern cities, such as Boston. The presence of available land on the frontiers limited inequality in rural areas. Growing commercial wealth in colonial cities ensured that smaller numbers of people controlled larger amounts of wealth. At the same time, fertility patterns had an impact on inequality. Greater numbers of children in farm areas had less effect on family finances than they had in urban areas. As America began to modernize during the late 1700s and early 1800s, increasing fertility resulted in greater net inequality. The younger the population, the greater the inequality; old, established towns with older populations tended to have stable changes in wealth accumulation.

The impact of the Industrial Revolution and the growth of American cities had a huge impact on the growing numbers of poor. In the ten largest American cities in 1860, more than half of the men were proletariat (propertyless), even more had little money, and movement upward on the status ladder was slow. During the process of industrialization during the nineteenth century, skilled laborers displaced unskilled laborers more frequently, leading to increased inequality. This trend continued during the opening decades of the twentieth century, so that as wealth grew in America, so did inequality. During the 1920s, company profits soared, but wages lagged, leading to an increasingly unequal distribution of wealth: the top 1% of the population owned 20% of wealth. This trend was reversed in the 1930s for several reasons. Most important was the New Deal in the 1930s, which inaugurated programs subsidizing farmers, bolster banks, employ youth, and create public works programs. Government spending in the economy in such programs as the Works Progress Administration, the Tennessee Valley Authority, and the Public

Works Administration, provided jobs for unskilled workers, balancing the previous trend of skilled workers displacing unskilled.

Continuing government involvement in the economy, including greater budgets in military production as well as welfare programs such as Medicare and Medicaid, has continued to provide an artificial leveling of wealth distribution in America. Wealth inequality in the past half century is therefore much less than it was in the nineteenth century—more like the relative equality of colonial America. The total percentage of poor in America declined by about ten percent during the 1960s and has remained fairly stable since the 1970s, according to U.S. Census Bureau figures. The biggest decline—twenty percent—in poverty rates during the past half century has occurred in the African American community, although its poverty rate is double (about twenty-five percent) that of the population as a whole.

See also: Measurement of Inequality

Sources: Daniels, Bruce E., "Long Range Trends of Wealth Distribution in Eighteenth-Century New England," *Explorations in Economic History* 11 (1973–1974): 123–135; Iceland, John, *Poverty in America: A Handbook,* 2nd ed. (Berkeley: University of California Press, 2006); Lindert, Peter H., *Fertility and Scarcity in America* (Princeton: Princeton University Press, 1978); Main, Gloria L., *Tobacco Colony: Life in Early Maryland, 1650–1720* (Princeton, 1982); Main, Jackson T., *The Social Structure of Revolutionary America* (Princeton: Princeton University Press, 1965); Williamson, Geoffrey G., and Peter H. Lindert, *American Inequality: A Macroeconomic History* (New York: Academic Press, 1980).

"WELFARE MOMS". "Welfare moms" are single unemployed mothers who cannot support themselves and their children and are thus dependent on government assistance. Welfare moms comprise one of the lowest levels of society, and policymakers have difficulty passing legislation to effectively support them. One of the problems is the stigma surrounding welfare moms, who are often African Americans who became pregnant while teenagers, and never finished high school. Over the years the federal government has tried different programs to limit the dependency of these single mothers, setting up several types of programs to provide money for child-care facilities so that women can find work. Other programs give money to mothers so that they can get an education, and still other programs encourage welfare moms to marry so that they can stay at home with their children while their husbands provide for them. Further contributing to the stigmata surrounding welfare mothers is the fact that many welfare moms are members of minority groups.

Throughout American history, single mothers have been among the most impoverished. Conflict over the "deserving" and "undeserving" poor have seen single mothers at the nexus of the argument. Issues of illegitimate children led Progressive-era reformers to refuse aid on moral grounds: mothers with illegitimate children were not considered morally fit, and these reform efforts were primarily intended as a means to "improve" the spiritual/psychological poverty, regarding material relief as secondary. The New Deal (early welfare state) changed this in some ways. The Social Security Act of 1935 established the Aid to Dependent Children (ADC) program, which allocated $1 of federal funds for each $2 (this was soon changed to equally matching funds, but with a limit of $12 per family) spent locally to aid single mothers. This program, like all New Deal programs, did not provide sufficient support, and had many loopholes for local officials to refuse aid; for example, the local ADC administrators often refused aid to mothers with dependent children who had male friends or relatives even if these men were unemployed. Under the ADC, support was reserved only for the obviously needy, and the government was often very conservative in these estimates of need—and even when funding was available it was rarely sufficient.

In the following decades this situation changed little. Lyndon Johnson's War on Poverty was the first comprehensive attempt to rectify the social and economic division of American society, illustrated by the plight of welfare mothers in urban slums. The Office of Economic Opportunity (OEO), established by the Economic Opportunity Act of 1964, set up programs to help the poor move up in society. The concept of "welfare moms" played an especially significant part in the War on Poverty, combining the stigma of immorality and race: the common (but not necessarily correct) perception of welfare moms was as indolent and immoral. A common theme among sociologists/social reformers in the 1960s was the "culture of poverty," meaning that the impoverished, and especially African Americans, had an entirely separate social system from mainstream America. Both Michael Harrington, who presented his theory in *The Other America,* and Lee Rainwater, who studied the social habits of African American public housing residents, argued that black slums were "matriarchal" because of the lack of a stable adult male presence. Both writers noted the prevalence of unwed mothers and the high incidence of single black mothers. Neither writer was wrong in observing the prevalence of single mothers, but their interpretation that this was a sign of "cultural" difference among the very poor is oversimplified. In part, this reflected the avowedly troublesome straits of black men, an unusually large percentage of whom were unemployed and thus unable to support a family, or in prison. In 1980, 51 percent of black males in large urban areas had been arrested at least once for an "index crime"—murder, aggravated assault, forcible rape, robbery, car theft—compared to 14 percent of white males in the same areas, and blacks comprised 48 percent of all prison inmates while constituting only 12 percent of the nation's population.

Despite the good intentions of liberal policymakers, the economic boom of the 1960s that had raised hopes of eradicating poverty faltered, allowing conservatives to regain control and cut back on welfare programs. In the debates over the future of the American welfare state, welfare moms played a large role: few policymakers could ignore that these mothers needed some kind of support if their children were to develop into functioning citizens. Even conservative administrations did not cut funding to welfare moms, and when Bill Clinton signed the Republican-sponsored 1996 welfare reform bill, he allotted four billion dollars to help single mothers on welfare pay for child- and health care. Clinton placed much of the responsibility on states, emphasizing the need to "make work pay" by improving education systems to reduce the number of dependents. Clinton also sought to improve child support measures through existing programs such as Head Start, hoping to educate and provide job training for the poor. Clinton welfare reform, which aimed to lessen the number of welfare moms by encouraging them to find employment, thereby providing for themselves and their children, was very similar to the New Deal's Aid to Dependent Children program. Notwithstanding the many political solutions tried over the years, policymakers have as yet failed to a suitable method for preventing impoverished single mothers from joining the ranks of the welfare moms.

See also: African Americans and Poverty, Aid to Families with Dependent Children, Children and Poverty, Clinton Welfare Reform, New Deal, Office of Economic Opportunity, *The Other America*, War on Poverty

Sources: Haveman, Robert H., and John Karl Scholz, "The Clinton Welfare Reform Plan: Will It End Poverty as We Know It?" Institute for Research on Poverty Discussion Paper no. 1037–94 (1994); Harrington, Michael, *The Other America: Poverty in the United States* (Baltimore: Penguin, 1963); Patterson, James T., *America's Struggle Against Poverty in the Twentieth Century* (Cambridge, MA: Harvard University Press, 2000); Rainwater, Lee, *Behind Ghetto Walls: Black Families in a Federal Slum* (Chicago: Aldine and Atherton Publishing, 1970).

WELFARE STATE (POST–NEW DEAL). Designed as a safety net to protect people from the economic insecurity of the capitalist system, the American welfare state began with the New Deal, President Franklin Roosevelt's coordinated response to counteract the Great Depression. Despite considerable fluctuations in popularity, the welfare system continues to this day. The 1935 Social Security Act—and the social-relief programs of the following decades, like the Aid to Dependent Children (ADC) program—are the best examples of the early American welfare state; the Great Society—the 1964 Economic Opportunity Act, with its accompanying programs of the Office of Economic Opportunity (OEO)—is the best example of the liberal 1960s welfare state; the 1996 implementation of TANF (Temporary Assistance to Needy Families) is a good example of the recent conservative welfare state. The American welfare state is a fluid system and the subject of much debate and criticism. Nevertheless, the basic idea that the government has a responsibility to prevent reasonably well-intentioned Americans from extreme economic and social debasement meets with enough support to make the welfare state is a significant aspect of American social policy.

Intended as a way to help the poor function within mainstream society, a welfare state is created when the government accepts responsibility for providing support for its citizens. The American concept of the welfare state differs from that of other nations in that the United States continues to promote individual responsibility; America has never adopted a system of federally controlled education or health care (for example) comparable to those of France or Great Britain. In America the conception of a welfare state is less rigid than it is in Europe, and the primary role of the American government is seen as providing aid to both public and private organizations that function on the local level. This decentralized approach ensures that the federal government does not become too domineering, acting, in theory, as a safeguard to protect democracy.

In the days since Roosevelt, many twentieth-century presidents have enacted their own form of social welfare, the collective impact of which amounts to the American welfare state. Harry S. Truman had the "Fair Deal," Dwight D. Eisenhower had the "New Look," John F. Kennedy had the "New Frontier," and Lyndon B. Johnson had the "Great Society." The Great Society, combined with the War on Poverty, was the most comprehensive of these programs. The 1960s were a time of economic prosperity, and Johnson sought to extend the nation's prosperity to all Americans: his Great Society and its War on Poverty first explicitly focused on improving the social and material status of African Americans. Prior to the 1960s, and after the election of Republican Richard Nixon as president in 1968, the federal government assumed a very limited role in poor relief; even during the Johnson Administration's tenure, most Americans viewed welfare as a temporary evil that promoted indolence and which should be avoided whenever possible.

The Proactive 1960s Welfare State. Johnson's 1964 Economic Opportunity Act was the first phase of the Great Society program, designed to help minorities and the impoverished move up into mainstream society through economic, social, and educational reform policies. This act allowed for the formation of several programs administered by the Office of Economic Opportunity, such as the Community Action Program, the Job Corps, and Head Start. The most ambitious and controversial of these was the Community Action Program, which—as outlined in the Economic Opportunity Act—was supposed to provide

> services, assistance, and other activities of sufficient scope and size to give promise of progress toward elimination of poverty or a cause or causes of poverty through developing employment opportunities, improving human performance, motivation, and productivity, or bettering the conditions under which people live, learn, and work.

Unlike the earlier programs of the New Deal and those of following administrations, the CAP attempted to bypass the top-down emphasis of traditional welfare, instead emphasizing the need to directly involve the poor in the development of policies and programs. This ill-defined policy of the "maximum feasible participation" of the poor gained publicity for the CAP but angered the affluent because of the program's inherent ambiguities and propensity to attract anti-establishment activists; because of this, the CAP was not very effective. The structure of the Job Corps was more similar to New Deal programs such as the Civilian Conservation Corps (CCC) in that it provided employment to the nation's poor, but it was plagued by inefficiency and poor funding because of a lack of Congressional support and did not produce significant results. Head Start was one of the longest-lasting programs established under the 1964 Economic Opportunity Act and is still in place today despite research findings ambiguous about whether the program produces long-term results.

Other Influences on Welfare Policy. Other branches of government, most notably the Judiciary, have also had an impact on American welfare; the legal system has not always condoned federal welfare legislation. America, according to some scholars, is committed to equal justice in principle, but not always in practice: the poor and minorities do not have the advantages of the wealthy. In 1964, Attorney General Robert F. Kennedy said that the legal system is a synonym for "technicalities and obstruction" when ruling on welfare legislation; the poor, therefore, see the law as the enemy and not as a protector. At the same time, however, the law protects the existing rights of the poor. In 1970, for example, the Supreme Court ruled that welfare recipients were required to receive due process and proper notification before the government could revoke their benefits, establishing that welfare was not "gratuity" but "property." By this case, the Court ensured that welfare recipients enjoyed the same legal rights extended to owners of private property.

The Civil Rights movement has also been intricately involved in the American welfare state. After the influential 1954 case *Brown v. Board of Education*, and especially in the 1960s, the federal government adopted a liberal "reformist" policy of instigating programs like Affirmative Action to help minorities "catch up." The Johnson Administration in particular realized that ignoring the poor and minorities would hamper the nation's growth; despite the white backlash in the wake of the 1960s urban unrest, under-represented minority groups received federal support under Johnson. One of the best examples of this is the Education Act of 1965, which gave financial support to low-income districts to help offset the unequal funding created by local subsidies of particular schools; this act did not solve the problem, however, as wealthy districts still receive more funding, and most states do not put all tax revenue raised for education in a common fund for equal distribution. The relative amount of funding schools receive provides insight into the economic division of cities.

The rise of conservatism and the Republican Party to prominence has raised many questions about the future of the American welfare state. After the Vietnam War destroyed Johnson's chances for reelection in 1968, Republican president Richard Nixon gave half-hearted support to some Great Society programs like Head Start. Under Nixon the Family Assistance Plan (FAP) scaled back the expensive and outdated Aid to Families with Dependent Children (AFDC) program. Overall, Nixon's administration marked a return to the pro-business, anti-welfare orientation of the Republican Party. Returning to the traditional Progressive mindset touting individual initiative and self-discipline as the means for social advance, conservatives broke from the New Deal assumption that supporting the poor and unemployed was the government's duty. Nixon's policy of revenue sharing gave money to metropolitan areas, spurring the growth of suburban American but harming the inner city, thus exacerbating de facto segregation. Programs such as Affirmative Action also came under fire from conservatives unhappy with the welfare state; they stressed moral reform and character building rather than welfare, which they associated with vice and laziness. Mirroring late–nineteenth-century conservatives, late–twentieth-century conservatives defined poverty as a sign of moral infirmity and not the product of environment. Jimmy Carter, a Southern Democrat, did little to correct the rising conservative outlook of affluent Americans; Carter's unpopularity prepared the way for Ronald Reagan's rise to the presidency on an unabashedly conservative platform.

The Debate over Welfare Reform. In many respects Reagan's presidency marked the end of the American welfare state as a political given, though for political purposes he did not end established programs like Social Security, Medicare or Medicaid. Reagan ran on a conservative platform, directly repudiating the liberal welfare state: while campaigning for the 1980 election, Reagan catered to the conservative "egalitarian" ideology that opposed affirmative action programs that, according to conservatives, gave preferential treatment to minorities at the expense of the white middle class. Instead, Reagan supported the conservative view that self-discipline, personal responsibility, and hard work were the main tenets of social success; though Reagan continued education programs for minorities, he worked to end direct welfare programs. Reagan and his successor George H. W. Bush focused on policies to lessen direct federal control of domestic relief efforts. They advocated, instead, a business-first orientation, arguing that business stimulates the economy, provides jobs, and increases the nation's spending power, which in turn combats poverty, though indirectly.

Though the election of Bill Clinton in 1993 brought the Democrats back in control, the Clinton Administration did not adopt as liberal a stance toward welfare as earlier Democrat administrations. Instead, Clinton signed a Republican-sponsored welfare reform bill in 1996 intending to get people off welfare and into jobs that would help them out of poverty. Clinton's stated purpose was to "end welfare as we know it" by changing federal assistance from a relief handout for people in poverty to a program of financial aid for needy people. The 1996 welfare reform bill allocated more control over welfare to states, limited the maximum benefits to five years of support per family, required able-bodied adults to work after two years of support, abolished the Aid to Families with Dependent Children, and ended welfare assistance to non-U.S. citizens. The reform bill also allocated four billion dollars to assist "welfare moms" in paying for child- and health care to help them get off welfare. Clinton believed that the American welfare system was "broken beyond repair."

The American welfare state remains controversial and is primarily a political—not a social—issue. Liberals and conservatives (and to a certain extent Republicans and Democrats) differ not so much in their assessment that some action should be taken to improve the situation of the poor as in their view of the correct level of federal government influence in these programs. In many ways this is the same fundamental issue that divided Republican Herbert Hoover and his Democratic successor Franklin D. Roosevelt in their approach to the Great Depression. Hoover, a self-made businessman and engineer, implemented polices that emphasized individual charity, personal integrity, and capitalism; Roosevelt, in contrast, implemented the New Deal as a direct federal relief program that took the responsibility of caring for the poor away from individuals and placed their welfare under governmental control. In the early 1930s Roosevelt's direct welfare program garnered great popular support, but Hoover's reliance on businesses and individuals made him seem unconcerned about the consequences of the Great Depression. This same political split continued for decades as Democratic presidents such as Johnson implemented ambitious welfare programs and increased federal government control and Republican presidents such as Reagan lessened federal control and placed more emphasis on the responsibility of businesses and individuals.

Unlike the more rigid European welfare states, the American welfare state continues to promote individual responsibility. Rather than the federal government controlling health care and education, as in France and England, American welfare takes a more decentralized approach, the federal government assuming leadership and providing funding for state and local programs. Even liberal Democratic presidents like Johnson used federal resources more for funding localized programs like CAP and Head Start than for assuming direct federal control. Consequently, the American welfare state is much less liberal than its European counterparts, and the debate over its continued usefulness is primarily a political issue—a question of how much direct federal influence is needed to solve the problems of poverty in America.

See also: Aid to Families with Dependent Children, Clinton Welfare Reform, Community Action Program, Head Start, Job Corps, New Deal, Office of Economic Opportunity, Social Security, War on Poverty

Sources: Bremner, Robert H., Gary W. Reichard, and Richard Hopkins, eds., *American Choices: Social Dilemma and Public Policy since 1960* (Columbus: Ohio State University

Press, 1986); Economic Opportunity Act (http://www2.volstate.edu/geades/FinalDocs/1960s/eoa.htm); Haveman, Robert H., and John Karl Scholz, "The Clinton Welfare Reform Plan: Will It End Poverty as We Know It?" Institute for Research on Poverty Discussion Paper no. 1037-94 (1994); Quadagno, Jill, "Theories of the Welfare State," *Annual Review of Sociology* 13 (1987): 109–128; Patterson, James T., *America's Struggle Against Poverty in the Twentieth Century* (Cambridge, MA: Harvard University Press, 2000); Trattner, Walter I., *From Poor Law to Welfare State,* 6th ed. (New York: Simon and Schuster, 1999).

WIC (WOMEN, INFANTS, AND CHILDREN PROGRAM) *See* Food Stamps and WIC.

WPA (WORKS PROGRESS ADMINISTRATION). Created in 1935 under the Emergency Relief Appropriation, the Works Progress Administration (WPA) was one of the most influential and controversial programs of the New Deal. Under the direction of Harry Hopkins, the WPA became the New Deal's largest welfare–work relief program. The WPA included both white-collar and blue-collar jobs, and its programs were very diverse. The WPA's original budget was $1,500,000,000—extremely large for a New Deal program—the majority of which Hopkins used to provide employment for jobless workers. Nevertheless, the WPA failed to overcome the stigma of public relief, and the program satisfied no one: those employed grumbled about low wages, and more affluent Americans complained that WPA workers were lazy and ungrateful.

From the beginning, the WPA was a relief-oriented program—Hopkins believed that the WPA's role was to lessen the nation's dependency on the federal dole. To discourage workers with means from relying on the WPA, Hopkins set wages lower than those offered by most private companies and limited eligibility only to workers without outside employment. Hopkins emphasized the WPA's role as a relief organization, and though the program performed some useful public-work tasks (similar to those performed by the Public Works Administration) such as building sidewalks, the program's primary focus was on lessening welfare reliance through providing employment to those without jobs. Inefficiency, low wages, and the lack of important projects resulted in internal dissatisfaction as well as outside criticism.

Unlike other New Deal work–relief programs, the WPA included white-collar job opportunities. Artists and intellectuals—writers, painters, actors, musicians, academics—also found employment through the WPA. Though the pay was very low, this was a unique and significant distinction, as the WPA was the first federal program that funded scholarship and creative work. A few examples of WPA-supervised programs were the Federal Writers' Project, the Federal Theatre Project, and the Federal Art Project. A similar program, the National Youth Administration—directed by Hopkins's assistant Audrey Williams—allocated federal scholarship money to help finance creative and scholarly student work.

The WPA also benefited minority groups, such as African Americans and immigrants. Because the WPA did not provide significant material improvement for any of its workers, this program, like the entire New Deal, had very little lasting impact on the situation of minority groups. Moreover, WPA jobs also did little to remove the social stigma of these groups. In 1938, after a period of decline in funding, President Roosevelt allocated a large funding increase to the WPA, but by this time the entire New Deal program was losing Congressional and popular support. In addition, increased defense spending in preparation for World War II lessened the need for work–relief programs like the WPA as wartime production increased the number and availability of jobs.

See also: New Deal, WPA

Sources: Conkin, Paul, *The New Deal,* 2nd ed. (Arlington Heights, IL: Harlan Davidson, 1975); Link, Arthur S., and William B. Catton, *American Epoch: A History of the United States Since 1900, Volume II: 1921–1945,* 4th ed. (New York: Alfred E. Knopf, 1973); Patterson, James T., *America's Struggle Against Poverty in the Twentieth Century* (Cambridge, MA: Harvard University Press, 2000).

Documents in the History of American Poverty

1. GOTTLIEB MITTELBERGER, ON THE MISFORTUNE OF INDENTURED SERVANTS

Gottlieb Mittelberger was a German organist who traveled to Pennsylvania in 1750 to deliver an organ to a German congregation in Pennsylvania. By chance, Mittelberger traveled aboard a ship that carried a large number of redemptioners. Mittelberger witnessed firsthand their various sufferings and other experiences and recorded his observations in 1756.

Both in Rotterdam and in Amsterdam the people are packed densely, like herrings so to say, in the large sea-vessels. One person receives a place of scarcely 2 feet width and 6 feet length in the bedstead, while many a ship carries four to six hundred souls; not to mention the innumerable implements, tools, provisions, water-barrels and other things which likewise occupy much space.

On account of contrary winds it takes the ships sometimes 2, 3 and 4 weeks to make the trip from Holland to . . . England. But when the wind is good, they get there in 8 days or even sooner. Everything is examined there and the custom-duties paid, whence it comes that the ships ride there 8, 10 to 14 days and even longer at anchor, till they have taken in their full cargoes. During that time every one is compelled to spend his last remaining money and to consume his little stock of provisions which had been reserved for the sea; so that most passengers, finding themselves on the ocean where they would be in greater need of them, must greatly suffer from hunger and want. Many suffer want already on the water between Holland and Old England.

When the ships have for the last time weighed their anchors near the city of Kaupp [Cowes] in Old England, the real misery begins with the long voyage. For from there the ships, unless they have good wind, must often sail 8, 9, 10 to 12 weeks before they reach Philadelphia. But even with the best wind the voyage lasts 7 weeks.

But during the voyage there is on board these ships terrible misery, stench, fumes, horror, vomiting, many kinds of sea-sickness, fever, dysentery, headache, heat, constipation, boils, scurvy, cancer, mouth-rot, and the like, all of which come from old and sharply salted food and meat, also from very bad and foul water, so that many die miserably.

Add to this want of provisions, hunger, thirst, frost, heat, dampness, anxiety, want, afflictions and lamentations, together with other trouble, as . . . the lice abound so frightfully, especially on sick people, that they can be scraped off the body. The misery reaches the climax when a gale rages for 2 or 3 nights and days, so that every one believes that the ship will go to the bottom with all human beings on board. In such a visitation the people cry and pray most piteously.

When in such a gale the sea rages and surges, so that the waves rise often like high mountains one above the other, and often tumble over the ship, so that one fears to go down with the ship; when the ship is constantly tossed from side to side by the storm and waves, so that no one can either walk, or sit, or lie, and the closely packed people in the berths are thereby tumbled over each other, both the sick and the well—it will be readily understood that many of these people, none of whom had been prepared for hardships, suffer so terribly from them that they do not survive it.

I myself had to pass through a severe illness at sea, and I best know how I felt at the time. These poor people often long for consolation, and I often entertained and comforted them with singing, praying and exhorting; and whenever it was possible and the winds and waves permitted it, I kept daily prayer-meetings with them on deck. Besides, I baptized five children in distress, because we had no ordained minister on board. I also held divine service every Sunday by reading sermons to the people; and when the dead were sunk in the water, I commended them and our souls to the mercy of God.

Among the healthy, impatience sometimes grows so great and cruel that one curses the other, or himself and the day of his birth, and sometimes come near killing each other. Misery and malice join each other, so that they cheat and rob one another. One always reproaches the other with having persuaded him to undertake the journey. Frequently children cry out against their parents, husbands against their wives and wives against their husbands, brothers and sisters, friends and acquaintances against each other. But most against the soul-traffickers.

Many sigh and cry: *"Oh, that I were at home again, and if I had to lie in my pigsty!"* Or they say: *"O God, if I only had a piece of good bread, or a good fresh drop of water."* Many people whimper, sigh and cry piteously for their homes; most of them get home-sick. Many hundred people necessarily die and perish in such misery, and must be cast into the sea, which drives their relatives, or those who persuaded them to undertake the journey, to such despair that it is almost impossible to pacify and console them.

No one can have an idea of the sufferings which women in confinement have to bear with their innocent children on board these ships. Few of this class escape with their lives; many a mother is cast into the water with her child as soon as she is dead. One day, just as we had a heavy gale, a woman in our ship, who was to give birth and could not give birth under the circumstances, was pushed through a loop-hole [port-hole] in the ship and dropped into the sea, because she was far in the rear of the ship and could not be brought forward.

Children from 1 to 7 years rarely survive the voyage; and many a time parents are compelled to see their children miserably suffer and die from hunger, thirst and sickness, and then to see them cast into the water. I witnessed misery in no less than 32 children in our ship, all of whom were thrown into the sea. The parents grieve all the more since their children find no resting-place in the earth, but are devoured by the monsters of the sea. . . .

That most of the people get sick is not surprising, because, in addition to all other trials and hardships, warm food is served only three times a week, the rations being very poor and very little. Such meals can hardly be eaten, on account of being so unclean. The water which is served out on the ships is often very black, thick and full of worms, so that one cannot drink it without loathing, even with the greatest thirst. . . . Toward the end we were compelled to eat the ship's biscuit which had been spoiled long ago; though in a whole biscuit there was scarcely a piece the size of a dollar that had not been full of red worms and spiders nests. . . .

At length, when, after a long and tedious voyage, the ships come in sight of land, so that the promontories can be seen, which the people were so eager and anxious to see, all creep from below on deck to see the land from afar, and they weep for joy, and pray and sing, thanking and praising God. The sight of the land makes the people on board the ship, especially the sick and the half dead, alive again, so that their hearts leap within them; they shout and rejoice, and are content to bear their misery in patience, in the hope that they may soon reach the land in safety. But alas!

When the ships have landed at Philadelphia after their long voyage, no one is permitted to leave them except those who pay for their passage or can give good security; the others, who cannot pay, must remain on board the ships till they are purchased, and are released from the ships by their purchasers. The sick always fare the worst, for the healthy are naturally preferred and purchased first; and so the sick and wretched must often remain on board in front of the city for 2 or 3 weeks, and frequently die, whereas many a one, if he could pay his debt and were permitted to leave the ship immediately, might recover and remain alive. . . .

The sale of human beings in the market on board the ship is carried on thus: Every day Englishmen, Dutchmen and High-German people come from the city of Philadelphia and other places, in part from a great distance, say 20, 30, or 40 hours away, and go on board the newly arrived ship that has brought and offers for sale passengers from Europe, and select among the healthy persons such as they deem suitable for their business, and bargain with them how long they will serve for their passage money, which most of them are still in debt for. When they have come to an agreement, it happens that adult persons bind themselves in writing to serve 3, 4, 5 or 6 years for the amount due by them, according to their age and strength. But very young people, from 10 to 15 years, must serve till they are 21 years old.

Many parents must sell and trade away their children like so many head of cattle; for if their children take the debt upon themselves, the parents can leave the ship free and unrestrained; but as the parents often do not know where and to what people their children are going, it often happens that such parents and children, after leaving the ship, do not see each other again for many years, perhaps no more in all their lives. . . .

It often happens that whole families, husband, wife, and children, are separated by being sold to different purchasers, especially when they have not paid any part of their passage money.

When a husband or wife has died at sea, when the ship has made more than half of her trip, the survivor must pay or serve not only for himself or herself, but also for the deceased.

When both parents have died over half-way at sea, their children, especially when they are young and have nothing to pawn or to pay, must stand for their own and their parents' passage, and serve till they are 21 years old. When one has served his or her term, he or she is entitled to a new suit of clothes at parting; and if it has been so stipulated, a man gets in addition a horse, a woman, a cow.

When a serf has an opportunity to marry in this country, he or she must pay for each year which he or she would have yet to serve, 5 to 6 pounds. But many a one who has thus purchased and paid for his bride, has subsequently repented his bargain, so that he would gladly have returned his exorbitantly dear ware, and lost the money besides.

If some one in this country runs away from his master, who has treated him harshly, he cannot get far. Good provision has been made for such cases, so that a runaway is soon recovered. He who detains or returns a deserter receives a good reward.

If such a runaway has been away from his master one day, he must serve for it as a punishment a week, for a week a month, and for a month half a year. But if the master will not keep the runaway after he has got him back he may sell him for so many years as he would have to serve him yet.

Source: Mittelberger, Gottlieb, *Journey to Pennsylvania* (Philadelphia: McVey, 1898: 19–29).

2. POOR WHITES IN THE MID-NINETEENTH CENTURY SOUTH

Emily Burke was a schoolteacher in antebellum Georgia who wrote an account of her observations and experiences.

Although praise-worthy attempts have been made in various parts of Georgia, to diffuse the means of education more extensively than was formerly thought necessary, still there is a class of people in that State, as also in the Carolinas, who have never been benefitted by any of these privileges; and these individuals, though degraded and ignorant as the slaves, are, by their little fairer complexions entitled to all the privileges of legal suffrage. These people are known at the South by such names as crackers, clay-eaters, and sand-hillers. I have previously mentioned the circumstance from which they derived the appellation of crackers. They are called clay-eaters, because all this class of people, from the oldest to little children, are as much addicted to the eating of clay as some communities are to the use of tobacco and snuff. This senseless habit is indulged in to such an extent, that when a person has once seen a clay-eater, he can, ever after, instantly recognize any one of their number by their sickly, sallow, and most unnatural complexions, let them be seen in never so large a crowd. Children, by the time they are ten or twelve years of age, begin to look old, their countenances are stupid and heavy and they often become dropsical and loathsome to the sight. Those who survive this practice thirty or forty years, look very wrinkled and withered, their flesh shrunken to their bones like that of very aged people. They are also called sand-hillers from the grounds they usually occupy, which are the barren and sandy districts of Georgia and South Carolina, to which these poor wretched beings have been driven by the powerful and rich planters, who have wealth and avarice sufficient to secure to themselves all the best soil.

This part of the population of Georgia and some of the contiguous States, are the lineal descendents of those paupers from England, whom Gen. Oglethorpe brought to this country and by whom Georgia was first settled. The same crushed spirit that will ever suffer one to accept of a home in an alms house, seems to have been transmitted down to the present posterity of these emigrants, and their situation has always been such, they never have had the power to acquire education or wealth sufficient to raise them above their original degradation or enable them to shake off that odium they have inherited from their pauper ancestry. They have no ambition to do any thing more than just what is necessary to procure food enough of the coarsest kind to supply the wants of the appetite, and a scanty wardrobe of a fabric they manufacture themselves. If they should ever cherish a desire for any other life than such as the brutes might lead, it would be all in vain, for the present institutions and state of society at the South are calculated to paralyze every energy of both body and mind. They are not treated with half the respect by the rich people that the slaves are, and even the slaves themselves look upon them as their inferiors. I have seen the servants when one of these poor women came into a planter's house, dressed in her homespun frock, bonnet and shawl, collect together in an adjoining room or on the piazza and indulge in a fit of laughter and ridicule about her "cracker gown and bonnet," as they would call them.

Slavery renders labor so disreputable, and wages of slave labor so low, that if places could be found where they might hire out to service, there would be but little inducement to do so. Sometimes a young man who has a little more ambition than usual falls to the lot of his people, will succeed in obtaining a situation as overseer on a plantation. As such an office is to them quite honorable, they will almost give their services for it. I knew one young man about the age of nineteen who took the entire charge of a large plantation, and even labored with his own hands in the time of preparing the cotton for market, for the paltry sum of fifty dollars per year besides his board.

The sand-hillers usually cultivate a few acres of that barren land they are allowed to live upon, in the labor of which the females are obliged to take a part as well as the man. In this way they raise their corn, vegetables, and cotton, sufficient for domestic manufacture and sometimes a small quantity for market. When they do this, they can provide themselves with such luxuries as coffee, tea, sugar, etc., though besides coffee they seldom use any thing that is not the product of their own industry.

While I was residing in the interior of Georgia, one of these women sent her little daughter for me on horseback to go and make her a visit. I returned with the child on the beast with her; in the evening she carried me home in the same way. I found this woman living in a small log house, very neat, but there was nothing belonging to it, to which the term comfortable could be applied. She had a bed, a table, two or three benches that were used instead of chairs and a very little crockery. The kitchen was a separate little building, of course scantily supplied with cooking utensils. The entertainment she prepared for me, while I sat with her in her little kitchen on a stool, consisted of coffee without sugar, fried bacon and corn bread mixed with water only. She had neither vegetables, or butter, or any other condiment we consider essential to any repast. In the course of the afternoon she showed me a roll of cloth she had just taken from the loom, which she told me, was all the product of her own hard labor, commencing with the cotton seed. On inquiring if she could not purchase cloth much cheaper than she could manufacture it, she replied, "she could if her time was worth any thing, but there was no labor she could perform that would bring her any money."

At that age when the youth of the North are confined at hard lessons for six hours a day from one season to another, these children are wasting the spring time of their lives, in the fields and woods, climbing trees, robbing bird's nests, or breaking up the haunts of squirrels, and engaged in every such kind of mischief, enough of which is always to be found for idle hands to do. These are the children and youth that the advantages of education which some enjoy at the South, have never yet reached, and probably never will, till some special effort is made in their behalf by missionary labor. As long as the present feeling between the rich and poor exists, they can never be brought together into the same schools and if this could be effected it would not be expedient. I have seen the results of such an experiment in my own school. While I was teaching in the north part of Georgia, I gave two little girls belonging to one of these poor families, their tuition for the purpose of encouraging them to come to school, but the neglect and scornful treatment they received from those who considered themselves their superiors, because they had wealthy parents and servants and could dress fashionably while they were obliged to wear their coarse homespun dresses, contributed to make them so miserable they could derive but little advantage from their instruction, and such will always be the case if attempts are made to bring them into the schools of the wealthy.

Efforts have been made to persuade these parents to put their sons to useful trades, but if they do this they are obliged to labor in the shops with the slaves, and this being placed on a level with the colored people, they feel is a degradation they can not submit to, therefore they choose to bring up their sons to hunting and fishing.

I have been thus particular in my account of these oppressed people, with the hope, that this little book may fall into the hands of some philanthropic person who may, in the hands of God, be instrumental in educating and elevating a class of people now surrounded by all the intellectual and religious privileges of our boasted free and happy land, who might almost be termed heathen.

Source: Burke, Emily P., *Reminiscences of Georgia* (James Fitch, 1850: 205–211).

3. PENNSYLVANIA, THE HOPE OF THE POOR IMMIGRANT

> Quaker Gabriel Thomas wrote this account of the natural environment of Pennsylvania, which would allow for the poorest man to find plentiful sustenance with which to make a new life.

I must needs say, even the Present Encouragements are very great and inviting, for Poor People (both Men and Women) of all kinds, can here get three times the Wages for their Labour they can in England or Wales.

I shall instance in a few, which may serve; nay, and will hold in all the rest. The first was a Black-Smith, (my next Neighbour) who himself and one Negro Man he had, got Fifty Shillings in one Day, by working up a Hundred Pound Weight of Iron, which at Six Pence per Pound (and that is the common Price in that Countrey) amounts to that Summ. . . .

Labouring-Men have commonly here, between 14 and 15 Pounds a Year, and their Meat, Drink, Washing and Lodging; and by the Day their Wages is generally between Eighteen Pence and Half a Crown, and Diet also; But in Harvest they have usually between Three and Four Shilling each Day, and Diet. The Maid Servants Wages is commonly betwixt Six and Ten Pounds per Annum, with very good Accommodation. And for the Women who get their Livelihood by their own Industry, their Labour is very dear, for I can buy in London a Cheese-Cake for Two Pence, bigger than theirs at that price when at the same time their Milk is as cheap as we can buy it in London, and their Flour cheaper by one half.

Corn and Flesh, and what else serves Man for Drink, Food and Rayment, is much cheaper here than in England, or elsewhere; but the chief reason why Wages of Servants of all sorts is much higher here than there, arises from the great Fertility and Produce of the Place; besides, if these large Stipends were refused them, they would quickly set up for themselves, for they can have Provision very cheap, and Land for a very small matter, or next to nothing in comparison of the Purchace of Lands in England; and the Farmers there, can better afford to give that great Wages than the Farmers in England can, for several Reasons very obvious.

As First, their Land costs them (as I said but just now) little or nothing in comparison, of which the Farmers commonly will get twice the encrease of Corn for every Bushel they sow, that the Farmers in England can from the richest Land they have.

In the Second place, they have constantly good price for their Corn, by reason of the great and quick vent into Barbadoes and other Islands; through which means Silver is become more plentiful than here in England, considering the Number of People, and that causes a quick Trade for both Corn and Cattle; and that is the reason that Corn differs now from the Price formerly, else it would be at half the Price it was at then; for a Brother of mine (to my own particular knowledge) sold within the compass of one Week, about One Hundred and Twenty fat Beasts, most of them good handsom large Oxen.

Thirdly, They pay no Tithes, and their Taxes are inconsiderable; the Place is free for all Persuasions, in a Sober and Civil way; for the Church of England and the Quakers bear equal Share in the Government. They live Friendly and Well together; there is no Persecution for Religion, nor ever like to be; 'tis this that knocks all Commerce on the Head, together with high Imposts, strict Laws, and cramping Orders. Before I end this Paragraph, I shall add another Reason why Womens Wages are so exorbitant; they are not yet very numerous, which makes them stand upon high Terms for their several Services, in Sempstering, Washing, Spinning, Knitting, Sewing, and in all the other parts of their Imployments; for they have for Spinning either Worsted or Linen, Two Shillings a Pound, and commonly for Knitting a very Course pair of Yarn Stockings, they have half a Crown a pair; moreover they are usually Marry'd before they are Twenty Years of Age, and when once in that Noose, are for the most part a little uneasie, and make their Husbands so too, till they procure them a Maid Servant to bear the burden of the Work, as also in some measure to wait on them too. . . .

Reader, what I have here written, is not a Fiction, Flam, Whim, or any sinister Design, either to impose upon the Ignorant, or Credulous, or to curry Favour with the Rich and Mighty, but in meer Pity and pure Compassion to the Numbers of Poor Labouring Men, Women, and Children in England, half starv'd, visible in their meagre looks, that are continually wandering up and down looking for Employment without rinding any, who here need not lie idle a moment, nor want due Encouragement or Reward for their Work, much less Vagabond or Drone it about. Here are no Beggars to be seen (it is a Shame and Disgrace to the State that there are so many in England) nor indeed have any here the least Occasion or Temptation to take up that Scandalous Lazy Life. . . .

What I have deliver'd concerning this Province, is indisputably true, I was an Eye-Witness to it all, for I went in the first Ship that was bound from England for that Countrey, since it received the Name of Pensilvania, which was in the Year 1681. The Ship's Name was the John and Sarah of London, Henry Smith Commander. I have declin'd giving any Account of several things which I have only heard others speak of, because I did not see them my self, for I never held that way infallible, to make Reports from Hear-say. I saw the first Cellar when it was digging for the use of our Governour Will. Penn.

Source: Thomas, Gabriel, *An Historical and Geographical Account of Pensilvania and of West-New-Jersey*, 1698, in *Narratives of Early Pennsylvania West New Jersey and Delaware*, ed. Albert C. Meyers (New York: Charles Scribner's Sons, 1912: 326–329, 332–333).

4. THE WRETCHEDNESS OF WHITE SERVANTS, BY WILLIAM EDDIS

William Eddis, the customs agent at Annapolis, Maryland, wrote this account of indentured servants in 1770.

Persons in a state of servitude are under four distinct denominations: negroes, who are the entire property of their respective owners: convicts, who are transported from the mother country for a limited term: indentured servants, who are engaged for five years previous to their leaving England; and free-willers, who are supposed, from their situation, to possess superior advantages. . . .

Persons convicted of felony, and in consequence transported to this continent, if they are able to pay the expence of passage, are free to pursue their fortune agreeably to their inclinations or abilities. Few, however, have means to avail themselves of this advantage. These unhappy beings are, generally, consigned to an agent, who classes them suitably to their real or supposed qualifications; advertises them for sale, and disposes of them, for seven years, to planters, to mechanics, and to such as choose to retain them for domestic service. Those who survive the term of servitude, seldom establish their residence in this country: the stamp of infamy is too strong upon them to be easily erased: they either return to Europe, and renew their former practices; or, if they have fortunately imbibed habits of honesty and industry, they remove to a distant situation, where they may hope to remain unknown, and be enabled to pursue with credit every possible method of becoming useful members of society. . . .

The generality of the inhabitants in this province are very little acquainted with those fallacious pretences, by which numbers are continually induced to embark for this continent. On the contrary, they too generally conceive an opinion that the difference is merely nominal between the indented servant and the convicted felon: nor will they readily believe that people, who had the least experience in life, and whose characters were unexceptionable, would abandon their friends and families, and their ancient connexions, for a servile situation, in a remote appendage to the British Empire. From this persuasion they rather consider the convict as the more profitable servant, his term being for seven, the latter only for five years; and, I am sorry to observe, that there are but few instances wherein they experience different treatment. Negroes, being a property for life, the death of slaves, in the prime of youth or strength, is a material loss to the proprietor; they are, therefore, almost in every instance, under more comfortable circumstances than the miserable European, over whom the rigid planter exercises an inflexible severity. They are strained to the utmost to perform their allotted labour; and, from a prepossession in many cases too justly founded, they are supposed to be receiving only the just reward which is due to repeated offences. . . .

The situation of the free-willer is, in almost every instance, more to be lamented than either that of the convict or the indented servant; the deception which is practised on those of this description being attended with circumstances of greater duplicity and cruelty. Persons under this denomination are received under express conditions that, on their arrival in America, they are to be allowed a stipulated number of days to dispose of themselves to the greatest advantage. They are told, that their services will be eagerly solicited, in proportion to their abilities; that their reward will be adequate to the hazard they encounter by courting fortune in a distant region; and that the parties with whom they engage will readily advance the sum agreed on for their passage; which, being averaged at about nine pounds sterling, they will speedily be enabled to repay, and to enjoy, in a state of liberty, a comparative situation of ease and affluence. . . . It is, therefore, an article of agreement with these deluded victims, that if they are not successful in obtaining situations, on their own terms, within a certain number of days after their arrival in the country, they are then to be sold, in order to defray the charges of passage, at the discretion of the master of the vessel, or the agent to whom he is consigned in the province.

You are also to observe, that servants imported, even under this favourable description, are rarely permitted to set their feet on shore, until they have absolutely formed their respective engagements. As soon as the ship is stationed in her birth, planters, mechanics, and others, repair on board; the adventurers of both sexes are exposed to view, and very few are happy enough to make their own stipulations, some very extraordinary qualifications being absolutely requisite to obtain this distinction; and even when this is obtained, the advantages are by no means equivalent to their sanguine expectations. The residue, stung with disappointment and vexation, meet with horror the moment which dooms them, under an appearance of equity, to a limited term of slavery. Character is of little importance; their abilities not being found of a superior nature, they are sold as soon as their term of election is expired, apparel and provision being their only compensation; till, on the expiration of five tedious laborious years, they are restored to a dearly purchased freedom.

Source: Eddis, William, *Letters from America, Historical and Descriptive* (London, 1792: 63–64, 66–67, 69–72, 74–75).

5. GEORGE WASHINGTON AND THE REDEMPTIONERS

Virginia plantation owner George Washington wrote this account of Palatine servants in 1774.

Mr. Young, hearing me express a desire of importing Palatines to settle on my lands on the Ohio, tells me, that, in discoursing of this matter in your company, you suggested an expedient, which might probably be attended with success; and that if I inclined to adopt it, you wished to be informed before the sailing of your ship.

The desire of seating and improving my lands on the Ohio, is founded on interested as well as political views. But the intention of importing Palatines for the purpose was more the effect of sudden thought, than mature consideration, because I am totally unacquainted with the manner, as well as the expense of doing it; and I was led into the notion principally from a report of either this or some other ship of yours being blamed, for not taking an offered freight of these Germans at forty shillings sterling. I was thus induced to think if this charge was not much accumulated by other expenses, that I could fall on no better expedient to settle my lands with industrious people, than by such an importation.

The terms upon which I have thought of importing Palatines, or people from Ireland, or Scotland, are these; to import them at my expense, where they are unable to transport themselves, into the Potomac River, and from hence to the Ohio; to have them, in the first case, engaged to me under indenture; in the second, by some other contract equally valid, to become tenants upon the terms hereafter mentioned; as without these securities, I would not encounter the expense, trouble, and hazard of such an importation.

But to make matters as easy and agreeable as possible to these emigrants, I will engage, on my part, that the indentures shall be considered in no other light, than as a security for reimbursing to me every expense I am under, with interest, in importing them, removing them to the land, and supporting them there, till they can raise a crop for their own subsistence . . . I must, for my own safety, consider them as jointly bound for this payment, till the expiration of the indented terms, otherwise I must be an inevitable loser by every death or other accident; whilst they cannot, in the worst light, be considered as more than servants at large during the indented term. . . .

Having thus exhibited a general view of my design, I shall now be obliged to you, Sir, to inform me with as much precision as you can, what certainty there is that your ship will go to Holland; what probability there is of her getting Palatines, if she does go; when they may be expected in this country; what would be the freight; and, as near as you can judge, the whole incidental expense attending each person delivered at Alexandria; and, moreover, whether it would be expected, that the whole of these charges, including freight, should be paid down immediately on the arrival of the ship here, as it must appear rather hard to make a certain provision for an uncertain event.

It may not be amiss further to observe, that I see no prospect of these people being restrained in the smallest degree, either in their civil or religious principles; which I take notice of, because these are privileges, which mankind are solicitous to enjoy, and upon which emigrants must be anxious to be informed.

Source: Sparks, Jared, *The Writings of George Washington*, Vol. 2. (Boston: Little, Brown, and Co., 1855: 383–386).

6. HOW THE OTHER HALF LIVES

Jacob Riis wrote an account of New York City poor in 1890; this excerpt examines slum life in the city.

In the dull content of life bred on the tenement-house dead level there is little to redeem it, or to calm apprehension for a society that has nothing better to offer its toilers; while the patient efforts of the lives finally attuned to it to render the situation tolerable, and the very success of these efforts, serve only to bring out in stronger contrast the general gloom of the picture by showing how much farther they might have gone with half a chance. Go into any of the "respectable" tenement neighborhoods—the fact that there are not more than two saloons on the corner, nor over three or four in the block will serve as a fair guide—where live the great body of hard-working Irish and German immigrants and their descendants, who accept naturally the conditions of tenement life, because for them there is nothing else in New York; be with and among its people until you understand their ways, their aims, and the quality of their ambitions, and unless you can content yourself with the scriptural promise that the poor we shall have always with us, or with the menagerie view that, if fed, they have no cause of complaint, you shall come away agreeing with me that, humanly speaking, life there does not seem worth the living. Take at random one of these uptown tenement blocks, not of the worst nor yet of the most prosperous kind, within hail of what the newspapers would call a "fine residential section." These houses were built since the last cholera scare made people willing to listen to reason. The block is not like the one over on the East Side in which I actually lost my way once. There were thirty or forty rear houses in the heart of it, three or four on every lot, set at all sorts of angles, with odd, winding passages, or no passage at all, only "runways" for the thieves and toughs of the neighborhood. These yards are clear. There is air there, and it is about all there is. The view between brick walls outside is that of a stony street; inside, of rows of unpainted board fences, a bewildering maze of clothes-posts and lines; underfoot, a desert of brown, hard-baked soil from which every blade of grass, every stray weed, every speck of green, has been trodden out, as must inevitably be every gentle thought and aspiration above the mere wants of the body in those whose moral natures such home surroundings are to nourish. In self-defence, you know, all life eventually accommodates itself to its environment, and human life is no exception. Within the house there is nothing to supply the want thus left unsatisfied. Tenement-houses have no aesthetic resources. If any are to be brought to bear on them, they must come from the outside. There is the common hall with doors opening softly on every landing as the strange step is heard on the stairs, the air-shaft that seems always so busy letting out foul stenches from below that it has no time to earn its name by bringing down fresh air, the squeaking pumps that hold no water, and the rent that is never less than one week's wages out of the four, quite as often half of the family earnings.

Why complete the sketch? It is drearily familiar already. Such as it is, it is the frame in which are set days, weeks, months, and years of unceasing toil, just able to fill the mouth and clothe the back. Such as it is, it is the world, and all of it, to which these weary workers return nightly to feed heart and brain after wearing out the body at the bench, or in the shop. To it come the young with their restless yearnings. . . . These in their coarse garment—girls with the love of youth for beautiful things, with this hard life before them—who shall save them from the tempter? Down in the street the saloon, always bright and gay, gathering to itself all the cheer of the block, beckons the boys. In many such blocks the census-taker found two thousand men, women, and children, and over, who called them home. . . .

With the first hot nights in June police despatches, that record the killing of men and women by rolling off roofs and window-sills while asleep, announce that the time of greatest suffering among the poor is at hand. It is in hot weather, when life indoors is well-nigh unbearable with cooking, sleeping, and working, all crowded into the small rooms together, that the tenement expands, reckless of all restraint. Then a strange and picturesque life moves upon the flat roofs. In the day and early evening mothers air their babies there, the boys fly their kites from the house-tops, undismayed by police regulations, and the young men and girls court and pass the growler. In the stifling July nights, when the big barracks are like fiery furnaces, their very walls giving out absorbed heat, men and women lie in restless, sweltering rows, panting for air and sleep. Then every truck in the street, every crowded fire-escape, becomes a bedroom, infinitely preferable to any the house affords. A cooling shower on such a night is hailed as a heaven-sent blessing in a hundred thousand homes.

Life in the tenements in July and August spells death to an army of little ones whom the doctor's skill is powerless to save. When the white badge of mourning flutters from every second door, sleepless mothers walk the streets in the gray of the early dawn, trying to stir a cooling breeze to fan the brow of the sick baby. There is no sadder sight than this patient devotion striving against fearfully hopeless odds. Fifty "summer doctors," especially trained to this work, are then sent into the tenements by the Board of Health, with free advice and medicine for the poor. Devoted women follow in their track with care and nursing for the sick. Fresh-air excursions run daily out of New York on land and water; but despite all efforts the grave-diggers in Calvary work overtime, and little coffins are stacked mountains high on the deck of the Charity Commissioners' boat when it makes its semi-weekly trips to the city cemetery. . . .

A single factor, the scandalous scarcity of water in the hot summer when the thirst of the million tenants must be quenched, if not in that in something else, has in the past years more than all other causes encouraged drunkenness among the poor. But to my mind there is a closer connection between the wages of the tenements and the vices and improvidence of those who dwell in them than, with the guilt of the tenement upon our heads, we are willing to admit even to ourselves. . . .

Perhaps of all the disheartening experiences of those who have devoted lives of unselfish thought and effort, and their number is not so small as often supposed, to the lifting of this great load, the indifference of those they would help is the most puzzling. They will not be helped. Dragged by main force out of their misery, they slip back again on the first opportunity, seemingly content only in the old rut. The explanation was supplied by two women of my acquaintance in an Elizabeth Street tenement, whom the city missionaries had taken from their wretched hovel and provided with work and a decent home somewhere in New Jersey. In three weeks they were back, saying that they preferred their dark rear room to the stumps out in the country. But to me the oldest, the mother, . . . made the bitter confession: "We do get so kind o' downhearted living this way, that we have to be where something is going on, or we just can't stand it." And there was sadder pathos to me in her words than in the whole long story of their struggle with poverty; for unconsciously she voiced the sufferings of thousands, misjudged by a happier world, deemed vicious because they are human and unfortunate.

Source: Riis, Jacob A., *How the Other Half Lives: Studies Among the Tenements of New York* (New York, Charles Scribner's Sons, 1890: 162–167, 172–175).

7. WILLIAM JENNINGS BRYAN'S DEFENSE OF SILVER COINAGE

William Jennings Bryan, Democratic nominee for President of the United States, was an advocate of increased money circulation in the economy, as he declared in this speech in 1896.

The man who is employed for wages is as much a business man as his employer; the attorney in a country town is as much a business man as the corporation counsel in a great metropolis; the merchant at the cross-roads store is as much a business man as the merchant of New York; the farmer who goes forth in the morning and toils all day who begins in the spring and toils all summer and who by the application of brain and muscle to the natural resources of the country creates wealth, is as much a business man as the man who goes upon the board of trade and bets upon the price of grain; the miners who go down a thousand feet into the earth, or climb two thousand feet upon the cliffs, and bring forth from their hiding places the precious metals to be poured into the channels of trade are as much business men as the few financial magnates who, in a back room, corner the money of the world. We come to speak for this broader class of business men.

. . . We do not come as aggressors. Our war is not a war of conquest; we are fighting in the defense of our homes, our families, and posterity. We have petitioned, and our petitions have been scorned; we have entreated, and our entreaties have been disregarded; we have begged, and they have mocked when our calamity came. We beg no longer; we entreat no more; we petition no more. We defy them. . . .

I shall not slander the inhabitants of the fair State of Massachusetts nor the inhabitants of the State of New York by saying that, when they are confronted with the proposition, they will declare that this nation is not able to attend to its own business. It is the issue of 1776 over again. Our ancestors, when but three millions in number, had the courage to declare their political independence of every other nation; shall we, their descendants, when we have grown to seventy millions, declare that we are less independent than our forefathers? No, my friends, that will never be the verdict of our people. Therefore, we care not upon what lines the battle is fought. If they say bimetallism is good, but that we cannot have it until other nations help us, we reply that, instead of having a gold standard because England has, we will restore bimetallism, and then let England have bimetallism because the United States has it. If they dare to come out in the open field and defend the gold standard as a good thing, we will fight them to the uttermost. Having behind us the producing masses of this nation and the world, supported by the commercial interests, the laboring interests, and the toilers everywhere, we will answer their demand for a gold standard by saying to them: You shall not press down upon the brow of labor this crown of thorns, you shall not crucify mankind upon a cross of gold.

Source: Bryan, William J., *The First Battle: A Story of the Campaign* (Chicago: W. B. Conkey Co., 1896: 200, 206).

8. JANE ADDAMS'S AUTOBIOGRAPHY

Jane Addams wrote about poverty in Chicago in her autobiography, *Twenty Years at Hull House.*

That neglected and forlorn old age is daily brought to the attention of a Settlement which undertakes to bear its share of the neighborhood burden imposed by poverty, was pathetically clear to us during our first months of residence at Hull-House. One day a boy of ten led a tottering old lady into the House, saying that she had slept for six weeks in their kitchen on a bed made up next to the stove; that she had come when her son died, although none of them had ever seen her before; but because her son had "once worked in the same shop with Pa she thought of him when she had nowhere to go." The little fellow concluded by saying that our house was so much bigger than theirs that he thought we would have more room for beds. The old woman herself said absolutely nothing, but looking on with that gripping fear of the poorhouse in her eyes, she was a living embodiment of that dread which is so heartbreaking that the occupants of the County Infirmary themselves seem scarcely less wretched than those who are making their last stand against it.

This look was almost more than I could bear for only a few days before some frightened women had bidden me come quickly to the house of an old German woman, whom two men from the county agent's office were attempting to remove to the County Infirmary. The poor old creature had thrown herself bodily upon a small and battered chest of drawers and clung there, clutching it so firmly that it would have been impossible to remove her without also taking the piece of furniture. She did not weep nor moan nor indeed make any human sound, but between her broken gasps for breath she squealed shrilly like a frightened animal caught in a trap. The little group of women and children gathered at her door stood aghast at this realization of the black dread which always clouds the lives of the very poor when work is slack, but which constantly grows more imminent and threatening as old age approaches. The neighborhood women and I hastened to make all sorts of promises as to the support of the old woman and the county officials, only too glad to be rid of their unhappy duty, left her to our ministrations. This dread of the poorhouse, the result of centuries of deterrent Poor Law administration, seemed to me not without some justification one summer when I found myself perpetually distressed by the unnecessary idleness and forlornness of the old women in the Cook County Infirmary, many of whom I had known in the years when activity was still a necessity, and when they yet felt bustlingly important. To take away from an old woman whose life has been spent in household cares all the foolish little belongings to which her affections cling and to which her very fingers have become accustomed, is to take away her last incentive to activity, almost to life itself. To give an old woman only a chair and a bed, to leave her no cupboard in which her treasures may be stowed, not only that she may take them out when she desires occupation, but that their mind may dwell upon them in moments of revery, is to reduce living almost beyond the limit of human endurance.

The poor creature who clung so desperately to her chest of drawers was really clinging to the last remnant of normal living—a symbol of all she was asked to renounce. For several years after this summer I invited five or six old women to take a two weeks' vacation from the poorhouse which was eagerly and even gayly accepted. Almost all the old men in the County Infirmary wander away each summer taking their chances for finding food or shelter and return much refreshed by the little "tramp," but the old women cannot do this unless they have some help from the outside, and yet the expenditure of a very little money secures for them the coveted vacation. I found that a few pennies paid their car fare into town, a dollar a week procured lodging with an old acquaintance; assured of two good meals a day in the Hull-House coffee-house they could count upon numerous cups of tea among old friends to whom they would airily state that they had "come out for a little change" and hadn't yet made up their minds about "going in again for the winter." They thus enjoyed a two weeks' vacation to the top of their bent and returned with wondrous tales of their adventures, with which they regaled the other paupers during the long winter.

The reminiscences of these old women, their shrewd comments upon life, their sense of having reached a point where they may at last speak freely with nothing to lose because of their frankness, makes them often the most delightful of companions. I recall one of my guests, the mother of many scattered children, whose one bright spot through all the dreary years had been the wedding feast of her son Mike,—a feast which had become transformed through long meditation into the nectar and ambrosia of the very gods. As a farewell fling before she went "in" again, we dined together upon chicken pie, but it did not taste like the "the chicken pie at Mike's wedding" and she was disappointed after all.

Even death itself sometimes fails to bring the dignity and serenity which one would fain associate with old age. I recall the dying hour of one old Scotchwoman whose long struggle to "keep respectable" had so embittered her that her last words were gibes and taunts for those who were trying to minister to her. "So you came in yourself this morning, did you? You only sent things yesterday. I guess you knew when the doctor was coming. Don't try to warm my feet with anything but that old jacket that I've got there; it belonged to my boy who was drowned at sea nigh thirty years ago, but it's warmer yet with human feelings than any of your damned charity hot-water bottles." Suddenly the harsh gasping voice was stilled in death and I awaited the doctor's coming shaken and horrified.

The lack of municipal regulation already referred to was, in the early days of Hull-House, paralleled by the inadequacy of the charitable efforts of the city and an unfounded optimism that there was no real poverty among us. Twenty years ago there was no Charity Organization Society in Chicago and the Visiting Nurse Association had not yet begun its beneficial work, while the relief societies, although conscientiously administered, were inadequate in extent and antiquated in method.

As social reformers gave themselves over to discussion of general principles, so the poor invariably accused poverty itself of their destruction. I recall a certain Mrs. Moran, who was returning one rainy day from the office of the county agent with her arms full of paper bags containing beans and flour which alone lay between her children and starvation. Although she had no money she boarded a street car in order to save her booty from complete destruction by the rain, and as the burst bags dropped "flour on the ladies' dresses" and "beans all over the place," she was sharply reprimanded by the conductor, who was the further exasperated when he discovered she had no fare. He put her off, as she had hoped he would, almost in front of Hull-House. She related to us her state of mind as she stepped off the car and saw the last of her wares disappearing; she admitted she forgot the proprieties and "cursed a little," but, curiously enough, she pronounced her malediction, not against the rain nor the conductor, nor yet against the worthless husband who had been sent up to the city prison, but, true to the Chicago spirit of the moment, went to the root of the matter and roundly "cursed poverty."

This spirit of generalization and lack of organization among the charitable forces of the city was painfully revealed in that terrible winter after the World's Fair, when the general financial depression throughout the country was much intensified in Chicago by the numbers of unemployed stranded at the close of the exposition. When the first cold weather came the police stations and the very corridors of the city hall were crowded by men who could afford no other lodging. They made huge demonstrations on the lake front, reminding one of the London gatherings in Trafalgar Square.

It was the winter in which Mr. Stead wrote his indictment of Chicago. I can vividly recall his visits to Hull-House, some of them between eleven and twelve o'clock at night, when he would come in wet and hungry from an investigation of the levee district, and while he was drinking hot chocolate before an open fire, would relate in one of his curious monologues, his experience as an out-of-door laborer standing in line without an overcoat for two hours in the sleet, that he might have a chance to sweep the streets; or his adventures with a crook, who mistook him for one of this own kind and offered him a place as an agent for a gambling house, which he promptly accepted. Mr. Stead was much impressed with the mixed goodness in Chicago, the lack of rectitude in many high places, the simple kindness of the most wretched to each other. Before he published "If Christ Came to Chicago" he made his attempt to rally the diverse moral forces of the city in a huge mass meeting, which resulted in a temporary organization, later developing into the Civic Federation. I was a member of the committee of five appointed to carry out the suggestions made in this remarkable meeting, and our first concern was to appoint a committee to deal with the unemployed. But when has a committee ever dealt satisfactorily with the unemployed? Relief stations were opened in various part of the city, temporary lodging houses were established, Hull-House undertaking to lodge the homeless women who could be received nowhere else; employment stations were opened giving sewing to the women, and street sweeping for the men was organized. It was in connection with the latter that the perplexing question of the danger of permanently lowering wages at such a crisis, in the praiseworthy effort to bring speedy relief, was brought home to me. I insisted that it was better to have the men work half a day for seventy-five cents than a whole day for a dollar, better that they should earn three dollars in two days than in three days. I resigned from the street-cleaning committee in despair of making the rest of the committee understand that, as our real object was not street cleaning but the help of the unemployed, we must treat the situation in such wise that the men would not be worse off when they returned to their normal occupations. The discussion opened up situations new to me and carried me far afield in perhaps the most serious economic reading I have ever done.

A beginning also was then made toward a Bureau of Organized Charities, the main office being put in charge of a young man recently come from Boston, who lived at Hull-House. But to employ scientific methods for the first time at such a moment involved difficulties, and the most painful episode of the winter came for me from an attempt on my part to conform to carefully received instructions. A shipping clerk whom I had known for a long time had lost his place, as so many people had that year, and came to the relief station established at Hull-House four or five times to secure help for his family. I told him one day of the opportunity for work on the drainage canal and intimated that if any employment were obtainable, he ought to exhaust that possibility before asking for help. The man replied that he had always worked indoors and that he could not endure outside work in winter. I am grateful to remember that I was too uncertain to be severe, although I held to my instructions. He did not come again for relief, but worked for two days digging on the canal, where he contracted pneumonia and died a week later. I have never lost trace of the two little children he left behind him, although I cannot see them without a bitter consciousness that it was at their expense I learned that life cannot be administered by definite rules and regulations; that wisdom to deal with a man's difficulties comes only through some knowledge of his life and habits as a whole; and that to treat an isolated episode is almost sure to invite blundering.

It was also during this winter that I became permanently impressed with the kindness of the poor to each other; the woman who lives upstairs will willingly share her breakfast with the family below because she knows they "are hard up"; the man who boarded with them last winter will give a month's rent because he knows the father of the family is out of work; the baker across the street, who is fast being pushed to the wall by his downtown competitors, will send across three loaves of stale bread because he has seen the children looking longingly into his window and suspects they are hungry. There are also the families who, during times of business depression, are obliged to seek help from the county or some benevolent society, but who are themselves most anxious not to be confounded with the pauper class, with whom indeed they do not in the least belong. Charles Booth, in his brilliant chapter on the unemployed, expresses regret that the problems of the working class are so often confounded with the problems of the inefficient and the idle, that although working people live in the same street with those in need of charity, to thus confound two problems is to render the solution of both impossible.

I remember one family in which the father had been out of work for this same winter, most of the furniture had been pawned, and as the worn-out shoes could not be replaced the children could not go to school. The mother was ill and barely able to come for the supplies and medicines. Two years later she invited me to supper one Sunday evening in the little home which had been completely restored, and she gave as a reason for the invitation that she couldn't bear to have me remember them as they had been during that one winter, which she insisted had been unique in her twelve years of married life. She said that it was as if she had met me, not as I am ordinarily, but as I should appear misshapen with rheumatism or with a face distorted by neuralgic pain; that it was not fair to judge poor people that way. She perhaps unconsciously illustrated the difference between the relief-station relation to the poor and the Settlement relation to its neighbors, the latter wishing to know them through all the varying conditions of life, to stand by when they are in distress, but by no means to drop intercourse with them when normal prosperity has returned, enabling the relation to become more social and free from economic disturbance.

Possibly something of the same effort has to be made within the Settlement itself to keep its own sense of proportion in regard to the relation of the crowded city quarter to the rest of the country. It was in the spring following this terrible winter, during a journey to meet lecture engagements in California, that I found myself amazed at the large stretches of open country and prosperous towns through which we passed day by day, whose existence I had quite forgotten.

In the latter part of the summer of 1895, I served as a member on a commission appointed by the mayor of Chicago, to investigate conditions in the county poorhouse, public attention having become centered on it through one of those distressing stories, which exaggerates the wrong in a public institution while at the same time it reveals conditions which need to be rectified. However necessary publicity is for securing reformed administration, however useful such exposures may be for political purposes, the whole is attended by such a waste of the most precious human emotions, by such a tearing of living tissue, that it can scarcely be endured. Every time I entered Hull-House during the days of the investigation, I would find waiting for me from twenty to thirty people whose friends and relatives were in the suspected institution, all in such acute distress of mind that to see them was to look upon the victims of deliberate torture. In most cases my visitor would state that it seemed impossible to put their invalids in any other place, but if these stories were true, something must be done. Many of the patients were taken out only to be returned after a few days or weeks to meet the sullen hostility of their attendants and with their own attitude changed from confidence to timidity and alarm.

This piteous dependence of the poor upon the good will of public officials was made clear to us in an early experience with a peasant woman straight from the fields of Germany, whom we met during our first six months at Hull-House. Her four years in America had been spent in patiently carrying water up and down two flights of stairs, and in washing the heavy flannel suits of iron foundry workers. For this her pay had averaged thirty-five cents a day. Three of her daughters had fallen victims to the vice of the city. The mother was bewildered and distressed, but understood nothing. We were able to induce the betrayer of one daughter to marry her; the second, after a tedious lawsuit, supported his child; with the third we were able to do nothing. This woman is now living with her family in a little house seventeen miles from the city. She has made two payments on her land and is a lesson to all beholders as she pastures her cow up and down the railroad tracks and makes money from her ten acres. She did not need charity for she had an immense capacity for hard work, but she sadly needed the service of the State's Attorney office, enforcing the laws designed for the protection of such girls as her daughters.

We early found ourselves spending many hours in efforts to secure support for deserted women, insurance for bewildered widows, damages for injured operators, furniture from the clutches of the installment store. The Settlement is valuable as an information and interpretation bureau. It constantly acts between the various institutions of the city and the people for whose benefit these institutions were erected. The hospitals, the county agencies, and State asylums are often but vague rumors to the people who need them most. Another function of the Settlement to its neighborhood resembles that of the big brother whose mere presence on the playground protects the little one from bullies.

We early learned to know the children of hard-driven mothers who went out to work all day, sometimes leaving the little things in the casual care of a neighbor, but often locking them into their tenement rooms. The first three crippled children we encountered in the neighborhood had all been injured while their mothers were at work: one had fallen out of a third-story window, another had been burned, and the third had a curved spine due to the fact that for three years he had been tied all day long to the leg of the kitchen table, only released at noon by his older brother who hastily ran in from a neighboring factory to share his lunch with him. When the hot weather came the restless children could not brook the confinement of the stuffy rooms, and, as it was not considered safe to leave the doors open because of sneak thieves, many of the children were locked out. During our first summer an increasing number of these poor little mites would wander into the cool hallway of Hull-House. We kept them there and fed them at noon, in return for which we were sometimes offered a hot penny which had been held in a tight little fist "ever since mother left this morning, to buy something to eat with." Out of kindergarten hours our little guests noisily enjoyed the hospitality of our bedrooms under the so-called care of any resident who volunteered to keep an eye on them, but later they were moved into a neighboring apartment under more systematic supervision.

Hull-House was thus committed to a day nursery which we sustained for sixteen years first in a little cottage on a side street and then in a building designed for its use called the Children's House. It is now carried on by the United Charities of Chicago in a finely equipped building on our block, where the immigrant mothers are cared for as well as the children, and where they are taught the things which will make life in America more possible. Our early day nursery brought us into natural relations with the poorest women of the neighborhood, many of whom were bearing the burden of dissolute and incompetent husbands in addition to the support of their children. Some of them presented an impressive manifestation of that miracle of affection which outlives abuse, neglect, and crime—the affection which cannot be plucked from the heart where it has lived, although it may serve only to torture and torment. "Has your husband come back?" you inquire of Mrs. S., whom you have known for eight years as an overworked woman bringing her three delicate children every morning to the nursery; she is bent under the double burden of earning the money which supports them and giving them the tender care which alone keeps them alive. The oldest two children have at last gone to work, and Mrs. S. has allowed herself the luxury of staying at home two days a week. And now the worthless husband is back again—the "gentlemanly gambler" type who, through all vicissitudes, manages to present a white shirtfront and a gold watch to the world, but who is dissolute, idle and extravagant. You dread to think how much his presence will increase the drain upon the family exchequer, and you know that he stayed away until he was certain that the children were old enough to earn money for his luxuries. Mrs. S. does not pretend to take his return lightly, but she replies in all seriousness and simplicity, "You know my feeling for him has never changed. You may think me foolish, but I was always proud of his good looks and educated appearance. I was lonely and homesick during those eight years when the children were little and needed so much doctoring, but I could never bring myself to feel hard toward him, and I used to pray the good Lord to keep him from harm and bring him back to us; so, of course, I'm thankful now." She passes on with a dignity which gives one a new sense of the security of affection.

I recall a similar case of a woman who had supported her three children for five years, during which time her dissolute husband constantly demanded money for drink and kept her perpetually worried and intimidated. One Saturday, before the "blessed Easter," he came back from a long debauch, ragged and filthy, but in a state of lachrymose repentance. The poor wife received him as a returned prodigal, believed that his remorse would prove lasting, and felt sure that if she and the children went to church with him on Easter Sunday and he could be induced to take the pledge before the priest, all their troubles would be ended. After hours of vigorous effort and the expenditure of all her savings, he finally sat on the front doorstep the morning of Easter Sunday, bathed, shaved and arrayed in a fine new suit of clothes. She left him sitting there in the reluctant spring sunshine while she finished washing and dressing the children. When she finally opened the front door with the three shining children that they might all set forth together, the returned prodigal had disappeared, and was not seen again until midnight, when he came back in a glorious state of intoxication from the proceeds of his pawned clothes and clad once more in the dingiest attire. She took him in without comment, only to begin again the wretched cycle. There were of course instances of the criminal husband as well as of the merely vicious. I recall one woman who, during seven years, never missed a visiting day at the penitentiary when she might see her husband, and whose little children in the nursery proudly reported the messages from father with no notion that he was in disgrace, so absolutely did they reflect the gallant spirit of their mother.

While one was filled with admiration for these heroic women, something was also to be said for some of the husbands, for the sorry men who, for one reason or another, had failed in the struggle of life. Sometimes this failure was purely economic and the men were competent to give the children, whom they were not able to support, the care and guidance and even education which were of the highest value. Only a few months ago I met upon the street one of the early nursery mothers who for five years had been living in another part of the city, and in response to my query as to the welfare of her five children, she bitterly replied, "All of them except Mary have been arrested at one time or another, thank you." In reply to my remark that I thought her husband had always had such admirable control over them, she burst out, "That has been the whole trouble. I got tired taking care of him and didn't believe that his laziness was all due to his health, as he said, so I left him and said that I would support the children, but not him. From that minute the trouble with the four boys began. I never knew what they were doing, and after every sort of a scrape I finally put Jack and the twins into institutions where I pay for them. Joe has gone to work at last, but with a disgraceful record behind him. I tell you I ain't so sure that because a woman can make big money that she can be both father and mother to her children."

As I walked on, I could but wonder in which particular we are most stupid—to judge a man's worth so solely by his wage-earning capacity that a good wife feels justified in leaving him, or in holding fast to that wretched delusion that a woman can both support and nurture her children.

One of the most piteous revelations of the futility of the latter attempt came to me through the mother of "Goosie," as the children for years called a little boy who, because he was brought to the nursery wrapped up in his mother's shawl, always had his hair filled with the down and small feathers from the feather brush factory where she worked. One March morning, Goosie's mother was hanging out the washing on a shed roof before she left for the factory. Five-year-old Goosie was trotting at her heels handing her clothes pins, when he was suddenly blown off the roof by the high wind into the alley below. His neck was broken by the fall, and as he lay piteous and limp on a pile of frozen refuse, his mother cheerily called him to "climb up again," so confident do overworked mothers become that their children cannot get hurt. After the funeral, as the poor mother sat in the nursery postponing the moment when she must go back to her empty rooms, I asked her, in a futile effort to be of comfort, if there was anything more we could do for her. The overworked, sorrow-stricken woman looked up and replied, "If you could give me my wages for to-morrow, I would not go to work in the factory at all. I would like to stay at home all day and hold the baby. Goosie was always asking me to take him and I never had any time." This statement revealed the condition of many nursery mothers who are obliged to forego the joys and solaces which belong to even the most poverty-stricken. The long hours of factory labor necessary for earning the support of a child leave no time for the tender care and caressing which may enrich the life of the most piteous baby.

With all of the efforts made by modern society to nurture and educate the young, how stupid it is to permit the mothers of young children to spend themselves in the coarser work of the world! It is curiously inconsistent that with the emphasis which this generation has placed upon the mother and upon the prolongation of infancy, we constantly allow the waste of this most precious material. I cannot recall without indignation a recent experience. I was detained late one evening in an office building by a prolonged committee meeting of the Board of Education. As I came out at eleven o'clock, I met in the corridor of the fourteenth floor a woman whom I knew, on her knees scrubbing the marble tiling. As she straightened up to greet me, she seemed so wet from her feet up to her chin, that I hastily inquired the cause. Her reply was that she left home at five o'clock every night and had no opportunity for six hours to nurse her baby. Her mother's milk mingled with the very water with which she scrubbed the floors until she should return at midnight, heated and exhausted, to feed her screaming child with what remained within her breasts.

These are only a few of the problems connected with the lives of the poorest people with whom the residents in a Settlement are constantly brought in contact.

I cannot close this chapter without a reference to that gallant company of men and women among whom my acquaintance is so large, who are fairly indifferent to starvation itself because of their preoccupation with higher ends. Among them are visionaries and enthusiasts, unsuccessful artists, writers, and reformers. For many years at Hull-House, we knew a well-bred German woman who was completely absorbed in the experiment of expressing musical phrases and melodies by means of colors. Because she was small and deformed, she stowed herself into her trunk every night, where she slept on a canvas stretched hammock-wise from the four corners and her food was of the meagerest; nevertheless if a visitor left an offering upon her table, it was largely spent for apparatus or delicately colored silk floss, with which to pursue the fascinating experiment. Another sadly crippled old woman, the widow of a sea captain, although living almost exclusively upon malted milk tablets as affording a cheap form of prepared food, was always eager to talk of the beautiful illuminated manuscripts she had sought out in her travels and to show specimens of her own work as an illuminator. Still another of these impressive old women was an inveterate inventor. Although she had seen prosperous days in England, when we knew her, she subsisted largely upon the samples given away at the demonstration counters of the department stores, and on bits of food which she cooked on a coal shovel in the furnace of the apartment house whose basement back room she occupied. Although her inventions were not practicable, various experts to whom they were submitted always pronounced them suggestive and ingenious. I once saw her receive this complimentary verdict—"this ribbon to stick in her coat"—with such dignity and gravity that the words of condolence for her financial disappointment, died upon my lips.

These indomitable souls are but three out of many whom I might instance to prove that those who are handicapped in the race for life's goods, sometimes play a magnificent trick upon the jade, life herself, by ceasing to know whether or not they possess any of her tawdry goods and chattels.

Source: Addams, Jane, *Twenty Years at Hull House with Autobiographical Notes* (New York: The Macmillan Company, 1910: 154–176).

9. HERBERT HOOVER'S STATE OF THE UNION ADDRESS, 1929

The Great Depression began in late October 1929, when the stock market crashed, but in his December 1929 State of the Union speech, President Herbert Hoover emphasized that there was no cause for long-term alarm. The economy, he mistakenly believed, would recover; this speech thus takes a confident tone. Of special note are Hoover's assertions that the banking system and the agricultural system remained structurally sound: soon afterward, the banking system collapsed, leading to bank runs in which banks nationwide went under; Hoover's optimistic view of agriculture proved similarly unfounded. The final irony of this speech was Hoover's praise of the veterans: in 1932, a crowd of angry and impoverished World War One veterans, nicknamed the "Bonus Army," gathered in Washington to demand early payment of promised service benefits. After violence broke out, Hoover called for federal troops to disperse the Bonus Army, destroying what little credibility he had left.

Herbert Hoover
State of the Union
December 3rd, 1929

To the Senate and House of Representatives:

The Constitution requires that the President "shall, from time to time, give to the Congress information of the state of the Union, and recommend to their consideration such measures as he shall judge necessary and expedient." In complying with that requirement I wish to emphasize that during the past year the Nation has continued to grow in strength; our people have advanced in comfort; we have gained in knowledge; the education of youth has been more widely spread; moral and spiritual forces have been maintained; peace has become more assured. The problems with which we are confronted are the problems of growth and of progress. In their solution we have to determine the facts, to develop the relative importance to be assigned to such facts, to formulate a common judgment upon them, and to realize solutions in a spirit of conciliation. . . .

Finances of the Government

The finances of the Government are in sound condition. I shall submit the detailed evidences and the usual recommendations in the special Budget message. I may, however, summarize our position. The public debt on June 30 this year stood at $16,931,000,000, compared to the maximum in August, 1919, of $26,596,000,000. Since June 30 it has been reduced by a further $238,000,000. In the Budget to be submitted the total appropriations recommended for the fiscal year 1931 are $3,830,445,231, as compared to $3,976,141,651 for the present fiscal year. The present fiscal year, however, includes $150,000,000 for the Federal Farm Board, as to which no estimate can as yet be determined for 1931.

Owing to the many necessary burdens assumed by Congress in previous years which now require large outlays, it is with extreme difficulty that we shall be able to keep the expenditures for the next fiscal year within the bounds of the present year. Economies in many directions have permitted some accommodation of pressing needs, the net result being an increase, as shown above, of about one-tenth of 1 per cent above the present fiscal year. We can not fail to recognize the obligations of the Government in support of the public welfare but we must coincidentally bear in mind the burden of taxes and strive to find relief through some tax reduction. Every dollar so returned fertilizes the soil of prosperity.

Tax Reduction

The estimate submitted to me by the Secretary of the Treasury and the Budget Director indicates that the Government will close the fiscal year 1930 with a surplus of about $225,000,000 and the fiscal year 1931 with a surplus of about $123,000,000. Owing to unusual circumstances, it has been extremely difficult to estimate future revenues with accuracy.

I believe, however, that the Congress will be fully justified in giving the benefits of the prospective surpluses to the taxpayers, particularly as ample provision for debt reduction has been made in both years through the form of debt retirement from ordinary revenues. In view of the uncertainty in respect of future revenues and the comparatively small size of the indicated surplus in 1931, relief should take the form of a provisional revision of tax rates.

I recommend that the normal income tax rates applicable to the incomes of individuals for the calendar year 1929 be reduced from 5, 3, and $1\frac{1}{2}$ per cent, to

4, 2, and $^1/_2$ per cent, and that the tax on the income of corporations for the calendar year 1929 be reduced from 12 to 11 per cent. It is estimated that this will result in a reduction of $160,000,000 in income taxes to be collected during the calendar year 1930. The loss in revenue will be divided approximately equally between the fiscal years 1930 and 1931. Such a program will give a measure of tax relief to the maximum number of taxpayers, with relatively larger benefits to taxpayers with small or moderate incomes. . . .

General Economic Situation

The country has enjoyed a large degree of prosperity and sound progress during the past year with a steady improvement in methods of production and distribution and consequent advancement in standards of living. Progress has, of course, been unequal among industries, and some, such as coal, lumber, leather, and textiles, still lag behind. The long upward trend of fundamental progress, however, gave rise to over-optimism as to profits, which translated itself into a wave of uncontrolled speculation in securities, resulting in the diversion of capital from business to the stock market and the inevitable crash. The natural consequences have been a reduction in the consumption of luxuries and semi-necessities by those who have met with losses, and a number of persons thrown temporarily out of employment. Prices of agricultural products dealt in upon the great markets have been affected in sympathy with the stock crash.

Fortunately, the Federal Reserve system had taken measures to strengthen the position against the day when speculation would break, which together with the strong position of the banks has carried the whole credit system through the crisis without impairment. The capital which has been hitherto absorbed in stock-market loans for speculative purposes is now returning to the normal channels of business. There has been no inflation in the prices of commodities; there has been no undue accumulation of goods, and foreign trade has expanded to a magnitude which exerts a steadying influence upon activity in industry and employment.

The sudden threat of unemployment and especially the recollection of the economic consequences of previous crashes under a much less secured financial system created unwarranted pessimism and fear. It was recalled that past storms of similar character had resulted in retrenchment of construction, reduction of wages, and laying off of workers. The natural result was the tendency of business agencies throughout the country to pause in their plans and proposals for continuation and extension of their businesses, and this hesitation unchecked could in itself intensify into a depression with widespread unemployment and suffering.

I have, therefore, instituted systematic, voluntary measures of cooperation with the business institutions and with State and municipal authorities to make certain that fundamental businesses of the country shall continue as usual, that wages and therefore consuming power shall not be reduced, and that a special effort shall be made to expand construction work in order to assist in equalizing other deficits in employment. Due to the enlarged sense of cooperation and responsibility which has grown in the business world during the past few years the response has been remarkable and satisfactory. We have canvassed the Federal Government and instituted measures of prudent expansion in such work that should be helpful, and upon which the different departments will make some early recommendations to Congress.

I am convinced that through these measures we have reestablished confidence. Wages should remain stable. A very large degree of industrial unemployment and suffering which would otherwise have occurred has been prevented. Agricultural prices have reflected the returning confidence. The measures taken must be vigorously pursued until normal conditions are restored.

Agriculture

The agricultural situation is improving. The gross farm income as estimated by the Department of Agriculture for the crop season 1926–27 was $12,100,000,000; for 1927–28 it was $12,300,000,000; for 1928–29 it was $12,500,000,000; and estimated on the basis of prices since the last harvest the value of the 1929–30 crop would be over $12,650,000,000. The slight decline in general commodity prices during the past few years naturally assists the farmers' buying power.

The number of farmer bankruptcies is very materially decreased below previous years. The decline in land values now seems to be arrested and rate of movement from the farm to the city has been reduced. Not all sections of agriculture, of course, have fared equally, and some areas have suffered from drought. Responsible farm leaders have assured me that a large measure of confidence is returning to agriculture and that a feeling of optimism pervades that industry.

The most extensive action for strengthening the agricultural industry ever taken by any government was inaugurated through the farm marketing act of June 15 last. Under its provisions the Federal Farm Board has been established, comprised of men long and widely experienced in agriculture and sponsored by the farm organizations of the country. During its short period of existence the board has taken definite steps toward a more efficient organization of agriculture, toward the elimination of waste in marketing, and toward the upbuilding of farmers' marketing organizations on sounder and more efficient lines. Substantial headway has been made in the organization of four of the basic commodities—grain, cotton, livestock, and wool. Support by the board to cooperative marketing organizations and other board activities undoubtedly have served to steady the farmers' market during the recent crisis and have operated also as a great stimulus to the cooperative organization of agriculture. The problems of the industry are most complex, and the need for sound organization is imperative. Yet the board is moving rapidly along the lines laid out for it in the act, facilitating the creation by farmers of farmer-owned and farmer-controlled organizations and federating them into central institutions, with a view to increasing the bargaining power of agriculture, preventing and controlling surpluses, and mobilizing the economic power of agriculture. . . .

The Banking System

It is desirable that Congress should consider the revision of some portions of the banking law.

The development of "group" and "chain" banking presents many new problems. The question naturally arises as to whether if allowed to expand without restraint these methods would dangerously concentrate control of credit, and whether they would not in any event seriously threaten one of the fundamentals of the American credit system—which is that credit which is based upon banking deposits should be controlled by persons within those areas which furnish these deposits and thus be subject to the restraints of local interest and public opinion in those areas. To some degree, however, this movement of chain or group banking is a groping for stronger support to the banks and a more secure basis for these institutions.

The growth in size and stability of the metropolitan banks is in marked contrast to the trend in the country districts, with its many failures and the losses these failures have imposed upon the agricultural community.

The relinquishment of charters of national banks in great commercial centers in favor of State charters indicates that some conditions surround the national banks which render them unable to compete with State banks; and their withdrawal results in weakening our national banking system.

It has been proposed that permission should be granted to national banks to engage in branch banking of a nature that would preserve within limited regions the local responsibility and the control of such credit institutions.

All these subjects, however, require careful investigation, and it might be found advantageous to create a joint commission embracing Members of the Congress and other appropriate Federal officials for subsequent report. . . .

Social Service

The Federal Government provides for an extensive and valuable program of constructive social service, in education, home building, protection to women and children, employment, public health, recreation, and many other directions.

In a broad sense Federal activity in these directions has been confined to research and dissemination of information and experience, and at most to temporary subsidies to the States in order to secure uniform advancement in practice and methods. Any other attitude by the Federal Government will undermine one of the most precious possessions of the American people; that is, local and individual responsibility. We should adhere to this policy.

Federal officials can, however, make a further and most important contribution by leadership in stimulation of the community and voluntary agencies, and by extending Federal assistance in organization of these forces and bringing about cooperation among them.

As an instance of this character, I have recently, in cooperation with the Secretaries of Interior and Labor, laid the foundations of an exhaustive inquiry into the facts precedent to a nation-wide White House conference on child health and protection. This cooperative movement among interested agencies will impose no expense upon the Government. Similar nation-wide conferences will be called in connection with better housing and recreation at a later date.

In view of the considerable difference of opinion as to the policies which should be pursued by the Federal Government with respect to education, I have appointed a committee representative of the important educational associations and others to investigate and present recommendations. In cooperation with the Secretary of the Interior, I have also appointed a voluntary committee of distinguished membership to assist in a nation-wide movement for abolition of illiteracy.

I have recommended additional appropriations for the Federal employment service in order that it may more fully cover its cooperative work with State and local services. I have also recommended additional appropriations for the Women's and Children's Bureaus for much needed research as to facts which I feel will prove most helpful. . . .

Veterans

It has been the policy of our Government almost from its inception to make provision for the men who have been disabled in defense of our country. This policy should be maintained. Originally it took the form of land grants and pensions. This system continued until our entry into the World War. The Congress at that time inaugurated a new plan of compensation, rehabilitation, hospitalization, medical care and treatment, and insurance, whereby benefits were awarded to those veterans and their immediate dependents whose disabilities were attributable to their war service. The basic principle in this legislation is sound.

In a desire to eliminate all possibilities of injustice due to difficulties in establishing service connection of disabilities, these principles have been to some degree extended. Veterans whose diseases or injuries have become apparent within a brief period after the war are now receiving compensation; insurance benefits have been liberalized. Emergency officers are now receiving additional benefits. The doors of the Government's hospitals have been opened to all veterans, even though their diseases or injuries were not the result of their war service. In addition adjusted service certificates have been issued to 3,433,300 veterans. This in itself will mean an expenditure of nearly $3,500,000,000 before 1945, in addition to the $600,000,000 which we are now appropriating annually for our veterans' relief.

The administration of all laws concerning the veterans and their dependents has been upon the basis of dealing generously, humanely, and justly. While some inequalities have arisen, substantial and adequate care has been given and justice administered. Further improvement in administration may require some amendment from time to time to the law, but care should be taken to see that such changes conform to the basic principles of the legislation.

I am convinced that we will gain in efficiency, economy, and more uniform administration and better definition of national policies if the Pension Bureau, the National Home for Volunteer Soldiers, and the Veterans' Bureau are brought together under a single agency. The total appropriations to these agencies now exceed $800,000,000 per annum. . . .

Conclusion

The test of the rightfulness of our decisions must be whether we have sustained and advanced the ideals of the American people; self-government in its foundations of local government; justice whether to the individual or to the group; ordered liberty; freedom from domination; open opportunity and equality of opportunity; the initiative and individuality of our people; prosperity and the lessening of poverty; freedom of public opinion; education; advancement of knowledge; the growth of religious spirit; the tolerance of all faiths; the foundations of the home and the advancement of peace.

Source: Woolley, John T., and Gerhard Peters, *The American Presidency Project* [online] (Santa Barbara: University of California [hosted], Gerhard Peters [database]) (http://www. presidency.ucsb.edu/ws/?pid=22021).

10. FRANKLIN DELANO ROOSEVELT'S FIRESIDE CHAT, 1937

In 1933, when Franklin D. Roosevelt began his first term as president, he enjoyed strong support for his "New Deal," intended to counteract the Great Depression. The first year of his term was especially productive; Roosevelt had little difficulty implementing significant programs such as the Agricultural

Adjustment Act (AAA) and the National Recovery Administration (NRA), both of which served as powerful symbols that the federal government was taking corrective action. By 1937, however, that initial optimism had faded, and Roosevelt faced opposition to his New Deal from Congress and the Supreme Court. In fact, the Court declared both the AAA and the NRA unconstitutional, leading Roosevelt to search for ways to circumvent the Court's power to nullify his policies. In this 1937 radio address, Roosevelt outlined his plan to increase the number of Supreme Court justices, which would have allowed him to nominate enough justices to tip the balance in his favor. This proposal failed, however, and support for the New Deal dwindled in the years prior to the United States' entrance into the Second World War.

Franklin D. Roosevelt
Fireside Chat,
March 9th, 1937

Last Thursday I described in detail certain economic problems which everyone admits now face the Nation. For the many messages which have come to me after that speech, and which it is physically impossible to answer individually, I take this means of saying "thank you."

Tonight, sitting at my desk in the White House, I make my first radio report to the people in my second term of office.

I am reminded of that evening in March, four years ago, when I made my first radio report to you. We were then in the midst of the great banking crisis.

Soon after, with the authority of the Congress, we asked the Nation to turn over all of its privately held gold, dollar for dollar, to the Government of the United States.

Today's recovery proves how right that policy was.

But when, almost two years later, it came before the Supreme Court its constitutionality was upheld only by a five-to-four vote. The change of one vote would have thrown all the affairs of this great Nation back into hopeless chaos. In effect, four Justices ruled that the right under a private contract to exact a pound of flesh was more sacred than the main objectives of the Constitution to establish an enduring Nation.

In 1933 you and I knew that we must never let our economic system get completely out of joint again—that we could not afford to take the risk of another great depression.

We also became convinced that the only way to avoid a repetition of those dark days was to have a government with power to prevent and to cure the abuses and the inequalities which had thrown that system out of joint.

We then began a program of remedying those abuses and inequalities—to give balance and stability to our economic system to make it bomb-proof against the causes of 1929.

Today we are only part-way through that program—and recovery is speeding up to a point where the dangers of 1929 are again becoming possible, not this week or month perhaps, but within a year or two.

National laws are needed to complete that program. Individual or local or state effort alone cannot protect us in 1937 any better than ten years ago.

It will take time—and plenty of time—to work out our remedies administratively even after legislation is passed. To complete our program of protection in time, therefore, we cannot delay one moment in making certain that our National Government has power to carry through.

Four years ago action did not come until the eleventh hour. It was almost too late.

If we learned anything from the depression we will not allow ourselves to run around in new circles of futile discussion and debate, always postponing the day of decision.

The American people have learned from the depression. For in the last three national elections an overwhelming majority of them voted a mandate that the Congress and the President begin the task of providing that protection—not after long years of debate, but now.

The Courts, however, have cast doubts on the ability of the elected Congress to protect us against catastrophe by meeting squarely our modern social and economic conditions.

We are at a crisis in our ability to proceed with that protection. It is a quiet crisis. There are no lines of depositors outside closed banks. But to the far-sighted it is far-reaching in its possibilities of injury to America.

I want to talk with you very simply about the need for present action in this crisis—the need to meet the unanswered challenge of one-third of a Nation ill-nourished, ill-clad, ill-housed.

Last Thursday I described the American form of Government as a three horse team provided by the Constitution to the American people so that their field might be plowed. The three horses are, of course, the three branches of government—the Congress, the Executive and the Courts. Two of the horses are pulling in unison today; the third is not. Those who have intimated that the President of the United States is trying to drive that team, overlook the simple fact that the President, as Chief Executive, is himself one of the three horses.

It is the American people themselves who are in the driver's seat. It is the American people themselves who want the furrow plowed.

It is the American people themselves who expect the third horse to pull in unison with the other two.

I hope that you have re-read the Constitution of the United States in these past few weeks. Like the Bible, it ought to be read again and again.

It is an easy document to understand when you remember that it was called into being because the Articles of Confederation under which the original thirteen States tried to operate after the Revolution showed the need of a National Government with power enough to handle national problems. In its Preamble, the Constitution states that it was intended to form a more perfect Union and promote the general welfare; and the powers given to the Congress to carry out those purposes can be best described by saying that they were all the powers needed to meet each and every problem which then had a national character and which could not be met by merely local action.

But the framers went further. Having in mind that in succeeding generations many other problems then undreamed of would become national problems, they gave to the Congress the ample broad powers "to levy taxes . . . and provide for the common defense and general welfare of the United States."

That, my friends, is what I honestly believe to have been the clear and underlying purpose of the patriots who wrote a Federal Constitution to create a National Government with national power, intended as they said, "to form a more perfect union for ourselves and our posterity."

For nearly twenty years there was no conflict between the Congress and the Court. Then Congress passed a statute which, in 1803, the Court said violated an express provision of the Constitution. The Court claimed the power to declare it unconstitutional and did so declare it. But a little later the Court itself admitted that it was an extraordinary power to exercise and through Mr. Justice Washington laid down this limitation upon it: "It is but a decent respect due to the wisdom, the integrity and the patriotism of the legislative body, by which any law is passed, to presume in favor of its validity until its violation of the Constitution is proved beyond all reasonable doubt."

But since the rise of the modern movement for social and economic progress through legislation, the Court has more and more often and more and more boldly asserted a power to veto laws passed by the Congress and State Legislatures in complete disregard of this original limitation.

In the last four years the sound rule of giving statutes the benefit of all reasonable doubt has been cast aside. The Court has been acting not as a judicial body, but as a policy-making body.

When the Congress has sought to stabilize national agriculture, to improve the conditions of labor, to safeguard business against unfair competition, to protect our national resources, and in many other ways, to serve our clearly national needs, the majority of the Court has been assuming the power to pass on the wisdom of these Acts of the Congress—and to approve or disapprove the public policy written into these laws.

That is not only my accusation. It is the accusation of most distinguished Justices of the present Supreme Court. I have not the time to quote to you all the language used by dissenting Justices in many of these cases. But in the case holding the Railroad Retirement Act unconstitutional, for instance, Chief Justice Hughes said in a dissenting opinion that the majority opinion was "a departure from sound principles," and placed "an unwarranted limitation upon the commerce clause." And three other Justices agreed with him.

In the case holding the A.A.A. unconstitutional, Justice Stone said of the majority opinion that it was a "tortured construction of the Constitution." And two other Justices agreed with him.

In the case holding the New York Minimum Wage Law unconstitutional, Justice Stone said that the majority were actually reading-into the Constitution their own "personal economic predilections," and that if the legislative power is not left free to choose the methods of solving the problems of poverty, subsistence and health of large numbers in the community, then "government is to be rendered impotent." And two other Justices agreed with him.

In the face of these dissenting opinions, there is no basis for the claim made by some members of the Court that something in the Constitution has compelled them regretfully to thwart the will of the people.

In the face of such dissenting opinions, it is perfectly clear, that as Chief Justice Hughes has said: "We are under a Constitution, but the Constitution is what the Judges say it is."

The Court in addition to the proper use of its judicial functions has improperly set itself up as a third House of the Congress—a super-legislature, as one of the justices has called it—reading into the Constitution words and implications which are not there, and which were never intended to be there.

We have, therefore, reached the point as a Nation where we must take action to save the Constitution from the Court and the Court from itself. We must find a way to take an appeal from the Supreme Court to the Constitution itself. We want a

Supreme Court which will do justice under the Constitution—not over it. In our Courts we want a government of laws and not of men.

I want—as all Americans want—an independent judiciary as proposed by the framers of the Constitution. That means a Supreme Court that will enforce the Constitution as written—that will refuse to amend the Constitution by the arbitrary exercise of judicial power—amendment by judicial say-so. It does not mean a judiciary so independent that it can deny the existence of facts universally recognized.

How then could we proceed to perform the mandate given us? It was said in last year's Democratic platform, "If these problems cannot be effectively solved within the Constitution, we shall seek such clarifying amendment as will assure the power to enact those laws, adequately to regulate commerce, protect public health and safety, and safeguard economic security." In other words, we said we would seek an amendment only if every other possible means by legislation were to fail.

When I commenced to review the situation with the problem squarely before me, I came by a process of elimination to the conclusion that, short of amendments, the only method which was clearly constitutional, and would at the same time carry out other much needed reforms, was to infuse new blood into all our Courts. We must have men worthy and equipped to carry out impartial justice. But, at the same time, we must have Judges who will bring to the Courts a present-day sense of the Constitution—Judges who will retain in the Courts the judicial functions of a court, and reject the legislative powers which the courts have today assumed.

In forty-five out of the forty-eight States of the Union, Judges are chosen not for life but for a period of years. In many States Judges must retire at the age of seventy. Congress has provided financial security by offering life pensions at full pay for Federal Judges on all Courts who are willing to retire at seventy. In the case of Supreme Court Justices, that pension is $20,000 a year. But all Federal Judges, once appointed, can, if they choose, hold office for life, no matter how old they may get to be.

What is my proposal? It is simply this: whenever a Judge or Justice of any Federal Court has reached the age of seventy and does not avail himself of the opportunity to retire on a pension, a new member shall be appointed by the President then in office, with the approval, as required by the Constitution, of the Senate of the United States.

That plan has two chief purposes. By bringing into the judicial system a steady and continuing stream of new and younger blood, I hope, first, to make the administration of all Federal justice speedier and, therefore, less costly; secondly, to bring to the decision of social and economic problems younger men who have had personal experience and contact with modern facts and circumstances under which average men have to live and work. This plan will save our national Constitution from hardening of the judicial arteries.

The number of Judges to be appointed would depend wholly on the decision of present Judges now over seventy, or those who would subsequently reach the age of seventy.

If, for instance, any one of the six Justices of the Supreme Court now over the age of seventy should retire as provided under the plan, no additional place would be created. Consequently, although there never can be more than fifteen, there may be only fourteen, or thirteen, or twelve. And there may be only nine.

There is nothing novel or radical about this idea. It seeks to maintain the Federal bench in full vigor. It has been discussed and approved by many persons of high authority ever since a similar proposal passed the House of Representatives in 1869.

Why was the age fixed at seventy? Because the laws of many States, the practice of the Civil Service, the regulations of the Army and Navy, and the rules of many of our Universities and of almost every great private business enterprise, commonly fix the retirement age at seventy years or less.

The statute would apply to all the courts in the Federal system. There is general approval so far as the lower Federal courts are concerned. The plan has met opposition only so far as the Supreme Court of the United States itself is concerned. If such a plan is good for the lower courts it certainly ought to be equally good for the highest Court from which there is no appeal.

Those opposing this plan have sought to arouse prejudice and fear by crying that I am seeking to "pack" the Supreme Court and that a baneful precedent will be established.

What do they mean by the words "packing the Court"?

Let me answer this question with a bluntness that will end all honest misunderstanding of my purposes.

If by that phrase "packing the Court" it is charged that I wish to place on the bench spineless puppets who would disregard the law and would decide specific cases as I wished them to be decided, I make this answer: that no President fit for his office would appoint, and no Senate of honorable men fit for their office would confirm, that kind of appointees to the Supreme Court.

But if by that phrase the charge is made that I would appoint and the Senate would confirm Justices worthy to sit beside present members of the Court who understand those modern conditions, that I will appoint Justices who will not undertake to override the judgment of the Congress on legislative policy, that I will appoint Justices who will act as Justices and not as legislators—if the appointment of such Justices can be called "packing the Courts," then I say that I and with me the vast majority of the American people favor doing just that thing—now.

Is it a dangerous precedent for the Congress to change the number of the Justices? The Congress has always had, and will have, that power. The number of Justices has been changed several times before, in the Administrations of John Adams and Thomas Jefferson—both signers of the Declaration of Independence—Andrew Jackson, Abraham Lincoln and Ulysses S. Grant.

I suggest only the addition of Justices to the bench in accordance with a clearly defined principle relating to a clearly defined age limit. Fundamentally, if in the future, America cannot trust the Congress it elects to refrain from abuse of our Constitutional usages, democracy will have failed far beyond the importance to it of any kind of precedent concerning the Judiciary.

We think it so much in the public interest to maintain a vigorous judiciary that we encourage the retirement of elderly Judges by offering them a life pension at full salary. Why then should we leave the fulfillment of this public policy to chance or make it dependent upon the desire or prejudice of any individual Justice?

It is the clear intention of our public policy to provide for a constant flow of new and younger blood into the Judiciary. Normally every President appoints a large number of District and Circuit Judges and a few members of the Supreme Court. Until my first term practically every President of the United States had appointed at least one member of the Supreme Court. President Taft appointed five members and named a Chief Justice; President Wilson, three; President Harding, four, including a Chief Justice; President Coolidge, one; President Hoover, three, including a Chief Justice.

Such a succession of appointments should have provided a Court well-balanced as to age. But chance and the disinclination of individuals to leave the Supreme bench have now given us a Court in which five Justices will be over seventy-five years of age before next June and one over seventy. Thus a sound public policy has been defeated.

I now propose that we establish by law an assurance against any such ill-balanced Court in the future. I propose that hereafter, when a Judge reaches the age of seventy, a new and younger Judge shall be added to the Court automatically. In this way I propose to enforce a sound public policy by law instead of leaving the composition of our Federal Courts, including the highest, to be determined by chance or the personal decision of individuals.

If such a law as I propose is regarded as establishing a new precedent, is it not a most desirable precedent?

Like all lawyers, like all Americans, I regret the necessity of this controversy. But the welfare of the United States, and indeed of the Constitution itself, is what we all must think about first. Our difficulty with the Court today rises not from the Court as an institution but from human beings within it. But we cannot yield our constitutional destiny to the personal judgment of a few men who, being fearful of the future, would deny us the necessary means of dealing with the present.

This plan of mine is no attack on the Court; it seeks to restore the Court to its rightful and historic place in our system of Constitutional Government and to have it resume its high task of building anew on the Constitution "a system of living law." The Court itself can best undo what the Court has done.

I have thus explained to you the reasons that lie behind our efforts to secure results by legislation within the Constitution. I hope that thereby the difficult process of constitutional amendment may be rendered unnecessary. But let us examine that process.

There are many types of amendment proposed. Each one is radically different from the other. There is no substantial group within the Congress or outside it who are agreed on any single amendment.

It would take months or years to get substantial agreement upon the type and language of an amendment. It would take months and years thereafter to get a two-thirds majority in favor of that amendment in both Houses of the Congress.

Then would come the long course of ratification by three-fourths of all the States. No amendment which any powerful economic interests or the leaders of any powerful political party have had reason to oppose has ever been ratified within anything like a reasonable time. And thirteen States which contain only five percent of the voting population can block ratification even though the thirty-five States with ninety-five percent of the population are in favor of it.

A very large percentage of newspaper publishers, Chambers of Commerce, Bar Associations, Manufacturers' Associations, who are trying to give the impression that they really do want a constitutional amendment would be the first to exclaim as soon as an amendment was proposed, "Oh! I was for an amendment all right, but this amendment that you have proposed is not the kind of an amendment that I was thinking about. I am, therefore, going to spend my time, my efforts and my money to block that amendment, although I would be awfully glad to help get some other kind of amendment ratified."

Two groups oppose my plan on the ground that they favor a constitutional amendment. The first includes those who fundamentally object to social and economic legislation along modern lines. This is the same group who during the campaign last Fall tried to block the mandate of the people.

Now they are making a last stand. And the strategy of that last stand is to suggest the time-consuming process of amendment in order to kill off by delay the legislation demanded by the mandate.

To them I say: I do not think you will be able long to fool the American people as to your purposes.

The other group is composed of those who honestly believe the amendment process is the best and who would be willing to support a reasonable amendment if they could agree on one.

To them I say: we cannot rely on an amendment as the immediate or only answer to our present difficulties. When the time comes for action, you will find that many of those who pretend to support you will sabotage any constructive amendment which is proposed. Look at these strange bed-fellows of yours. When before have you found them really at your side in your fights for progress?

And remember one thing more. Even if an amendment were passed, and even if in the years to come it were to be ratified, its meaning would depend upon the kind of Justices who would be sitting on the Supreme Court bench. An amendment, like the rest of the Constitution, is what the Justices say it is rather than what its framers or you might hope it is.

This proposal of mine will not infringe in the slightest upon the civil or religious liberties so dear to every American.

My record as Governor and as President proves my devotion to those liberties. You who know me can have no fear that I would tolerate the destruction by any branch of government of any part of Our heritage of freedom.

The present attempt by those opposed to progress to play upon the fears of danger to personal liberty brings again to mind that crude and cruel strategy tried by the same opposition to frighten the workers of America in a pay-envelope propaganda against the Social Security Law. The workers were not fooled by that propaganda then. The people of America will not be fooled by such propaganda now.

I am in favor of action through legislation:

First, because I believe that it can be passed at this session of the Congress.

Second, because it will provide a reinvigorated, liberal-minded Judiciary necessary to furnish quicker and cheaper justice from bottom to top.

Third, because it will provide a series of Federal Courts willing to enforce the Constitution as written, and unwilling to assert legislative powers by writing into it their own political and economic policies.

During the past half century the balance of power between the three great branches of the Federal Government, has been tipped out of balance by the Courts in direct contradiction of the high purposes of the framers of the Constitution. It is my purpose to restore that balance. You who know me will accept my solemn assurance that in a world in which democracy is under attack, I seek to make American democracy succeed. You and I will do our part.

Source: Woolley, John T., and Gerhard Peters, *The American Presidency Project* [online] (Santa Barbara: University of California [hosted], Gerhard Peters [database]) (http://www. presidency.ucsb.edu/ws/?pid=15381)

11. JOHN F. KENNEDY'S SPEECH TO CONGRESS, 1962

In this speech President Kennedy outlined his plan to make America's welfare-relief programs more comprehensive. In fact, Kennedy's awareness of and willingness to address domestic poverty issues was the forerunner of Lyndon Johnson's War on Poverty: Johnson took over as president when Kennedy was assassinated in 1963.

John F. Kennedy
Special Message to the Congress on Public Welfare Programs.
February 1st, 1962

To the Congress of the United States:

Few nations do more than the United States to assist their least fortunate citizens—to make certain that no child, no elderly or handicapped citizen, no family in any circumstances in any State, is left without the essential needs for a decent and healthy existence. In too few nations, I might add, are the people aware of the progressive strides this country has taken in demonstrating the humanitarian side of freedom. Our record is a proud one—and it sharply refutes those who accuse us of thinking only in the materialistic terms of cash registers and calculating machines.

Our basic public welfare programs were enacted more than a quarter century ago. Their contribution to our national strength and well-being in the intervening years has been remarkable.

But the times, the conditions, the problems have changed—and the nature and objectives of our public assistance and child welfare programs must be changed, also, if they are to meet our current needs.

The impact of these changes should not be underestimated:

- People move more often—from the farm to the city, from urban centers to the suburbs, from the East to the West, from the South to the North and Midwest.

- Living costs, and especially medical costs, have spiraled.

- The pattern of our population has changed. There are more older people, more children, more young marriages, divorces, desertions and separations.

- Our system of social insurance and related programs has grown greatly: in 1940 less than 1% of the aged were receiving monthly old age insurance benefits; today over 2/3rds of our aged are receiving these benefits. In 1940 only 21,000 children, in families where the breadwinner had died, were getting survivor insurance benefits; today such monthly benefits are being paid to about 2 million children.

All of these changes affect the problems public welfare was intended to relieve as well as its ability to relieve it. Moreover, even the nature and causes of poverty have changed. At the time the Social Security Act established our present basic framework for public aid, the major cause of poverty was unemployment and economic depression. Today, in a year of relative prosperity and high employment, we are more concerned about the poverty that persists in the midst of abundance.

The reasons are often more social than economic, more often subtle than simple. Some are in need because they are untrained for work—some because they cannot work, because they are too young or too old, blind or crippled. Some are in need because they are discriminated against for reasons they cannot help. Responding to their ills with scorn or suspicion is inconsistent with our moral precepts and inconsistent with their nearly universal preference to be independent. But merely responding with a "relief check" to complicated social or personal problems—such as ill health, faulty education, domestic discord, racial discrimination, or inadequate skills—is not likely to provide a lasting solution. Such a check must be supplemented, or in some cases made unnecessary, by positive services and solutions, offering the total resources of the community to meet the total needs of the family to help our less fortunate citizens help themselves.

Public welfare, in short, must be more than a salvage operation, picking up the debris from the wreckage of human lives. Its emphasis must be directed increasingly toward prevention and rehabilitation—on reducing not only the long-range cost in budgetary terms but the long-range cost in human terms as well. Poverty weakens individuals and nations. Sounder public welfare policies will benefit the nation, its economy, its morale, and, most importantly, its people.

Under the various titles of the Social Security Act, funds are available to help the States provide assistance and other social services to the needy, aged and blind, to the needy disabled, and to dependent children. In addition, grants are available to assist the States to expand and strengthen their programs of child welfare services. These programs are essentially State programs. But the Federal Government, by its substantial financial contribution, its leadership, and the standards it sets, bears a major responsibility. To better fulfill this responsibility, the Secretary of Health, Education, and Welfare recently introduced a number of administrative changes designed to get people off assistance and back into useful, productive roles in society.

These changes provided for:

- the more effective location of deserting parents;
- an effort to reduce that proportion of persons receiving assistance through willful misrepresentation, although that proportion is only a small part of the 1.5% of persons on the rolls found to be ineligible;
- allowing dependent children to save money for educational, employment or medical needs without having that amount deducted from their public assistance grants;
- providing special services and safeguards to children in families of unmarried parents, in families where the father has deserted, or in homes in danger of becoming morally or physically unsuitable; and—an improvement in the training of personnel, the development of services and the coordination of agency efforts.

In keeping with this new emphasis, the name of the Bureau of Public Assistance has been changed to the Bureau of Family Services.

But only so much can be done by administrative changes. New legislation is required if our State-operated programs are to be fully able to meet modern needs.

I. Prevention and Rehabilitation

As already mentioned, we must place more stress on services instead of relief.

I recommend that the States be encouraged by the offer of additional Federal funds to strengthen and broaden the rehabilitative and preventive services they offer to persons who are dependent or who would otherwise become dependent. Additional Federal funds would induce and assist the States to establish or augment their rehabilitation services, strengthen their child welfare services, and add to their number of competent public welfare personnel. At the present time, the cost of these essential services is lumped with all administrative costs—routine clerical and office functions—and the Federal Government pays one-half of the total of all such costs incurred by the States. By separating out and identifying the cost of these essential rehabilitation, social work and other service costs, and paying the States three-fourths of such services—a step I earnestly recommend for your consideration—the Federal Government will enable and encourage the States to provide more comprehensive and effective services to rehabilitate those on welfare. The existing law should also be amended to permit the use of Federal funds for utilization by the State welfare agency of specialists from other State agencies who can help mount a concerted attack on the problems of dependency.

There are other steps we can take which will have an important effect on this effort. One of these is to expand and improve the Federal-State program of vocational rehabilitation for disabled people. Among the 92,500 disabled men and women successfully rehabilitated into employment through this program last year were about 15,000 who had formerly been receiving public assistance. Let me repeat this figure: 15,000 people, formerly supported by the taxpayers through welfare, are now back at work as self-supporting taxpayers. Much more of this must be done—until we are restoring to employment every disabled person who can benefit from these rehabilitation services.

The prevention of future adult poverty and dependency must begin with the care of dependent children—those who must receive public welfare by virtue of a parent's death, disability, desertion or unemployment. Our society not only refuses to leave such children hungry, cold, and devoid of opportunity—we are insistent that such children not be community liabilities throughout their lives. Yet children who grow up in deprivation, without adequate protection, may be poorly equipped to meet adult responsibilities.

The Congress last year approved, on a temporary basis, aid for the dependent children of the unemployed as a part of the permanent Aid to Dependent Children program. This legislation also included temporary provisions for foster care where the child has been removed from his home, and an increase in Federal financial assistance to the aged, blind and disabled. The need for these temporary improvements has not abated, and their merit is clear. I recommend that these temporary provisions be made permanent.

But children need more than aid when they are destitute. We need to improve our preventive and protective services for children as well as adults. I recommend that the present ceiling of $25,000,000 authorized for annual appropriations for grants to the States for child welfare services be gradually raised, beginning with $30,000,000 for 1963, up to $50,000,000 for the fiscal year ending June 30, 1969, and succeeding years.

Finally, many women now on assistance rolls could obtain jobs and become self-supporting if local day care programs for their young children were available. The need for such programs for the children of working mothers has been increasing rapidly. Of the 22 million women now working, about 3 million have children under 6, and another $4^{1}/_{2}$ million have school-age children between 6 and 17. Adequate care for these children during their most formative years is essential to their proper growth and training. Therefore, I recommend that the child welfare provisions of the Social Security Act be changed to authorize earmarking up to $5,000,000 of grants to the States in 1963 and $10,000,000 a year thereafter for aid in establishing local programs for the day care of young children of working mothers.

II. Promoting New Skills and Independence

We must find ways of returning far more of our dependent people to independence. We must find ways of returning them to a participating and productive role in the community.

One sure way is by providing the opportunity every American cherishes to do sound and useful work. For this reason, I am, recommending a change in the law to permit States to maintain with Federal financial help community work and training projects for unemployed people receiving welfare payments. Under such a program, unemployed people on welfare would be helped to retain their work skills or learn new ones; and the local community would obtain additional manpower on public projects.

But earning one's welfare payment through required participation in a community work or training project must be an opportunity for the individual on welfare, not a penalty. Federal financial participation will be conditioned upon proof that the work will serve a useful community or public purpose, will not displace regular employees, will not impair prevailing wages and working conditions, and will be accompanied by certain basic health and safety protections. Provisions must also be made to assure appropriate arrangements for the care and protection of children during the absence from home of any parent performing work or undergoing training.

Moreover, systematic encouragement would be given all welfare recipients to obtain vocational counseling, testing, and placement services from the United States Employment Service and to secure useful training wherever new job skills would be helpful. Close cooperative arrangements would be established with existing training and vocational education programs, and with the vocational and on-the-job training opportunities to be created under the Manpower Development and Training and Youth Employment Opportunities programs previously proposed.

III. More Skilled Personnel

It is essential that state and local welfare agencies be staffed with enough qualified personnel to insure constructive and adequate attention to the problems of needy individuals—to take the time to help them find and hold a job—to prevent public dependency and to strive, where that is not possible, for rehabilitation—and to ascertain promptly whether any individual is receiving aid for which he does not qualify, so that aid can be promptly withdrawn.

Unfortunately, there is an acute shortage of trained personnel in all our welfare programs. The lack of experienced social workers for programs dealing with children and their families is especially critical.

At the present time, when States expend funds for the training of personnel for the administration of these programs, they receive Federal grants on a dollar-for-dollar basis. This arrangement has failed to produce a sufficient number of trained staff, especially social workers. I recommend, therefore, that Federal assistance to the States for training additional welfare personnel be increased; and that in addition, the Secretary of Health, Education, and Welfare be authorized to make special arrangements for the training of family welfare personnel to work with those children whose parents have deserted, whose parents are unmarried, or who have other serious problems.

IV. Fitting General Conditions or Safeguards to Individual Needs

In order to make certain that welfare funds go only to needy people, the Social Security Act requires the States to take all income and resources of the applicant into consideration in determining need. Although Federal law permits, it does not require States to take into full account the full expenses individuals have in earning income. This is not consistent with equity, common sense or other Federal laws such as our tax code. It only discourages the will to earn. In order to encourage assistance recipients to find and retain employment, I therefore recommend that the Act be amended to require the States to take into account the expenses of earning income.

Among relatives caring for dependent children are a few who do not properly handle their assistance payments—some to the extent that the well-being of the child is adversely affected. Where the State determines that a relative's ability to manage money is contrary to the welfare of the child, Federal law presently requires payments to be made to a legal guardian or representative, if Federal funds are to be used. But this general requirement may sometimes block progress in particular situations. In order to recognize the necessity for each State to make exceptions to this rule in a very limited number of cases, I recommend that the law be amended to permit Federal sharing to continue even though protective payments in behalf of children—not to exceed $1/2$ of 1% of ADC recipients in each State—are made to other persons concerned with the welfare of the family. The States would be required to reexamine these exceptions at intervals to determine whether a more permanent arrangement such as guardianship is required.

When first enacted, the aid to dependent children program provided for Federal sharing in assistance payments only to the child. Since 1951, there has been Federal sharing in any assistance given to one adult in the household as well as to the child or children. Inasmuch as under current law there may be two parents in homes covered by this program, one incapacitated or unemployed, I recommend in the interest of equity the extension of Federal sharing in assistance payments both to the needy relative and to his or her spouse when both are living in the home with the child.

V. More Efficient Administration

Under present public assistance provisions, States may impose residence requirements up to five of the last nine years for the aged, blind and disabled. Increased mobility, as previously mentioned, is a hallmark of our times. It should not operate unfairly on either an individual State or an individual family. I recommend that the Social Security Act be amended so as to provide that States receiving Federal funds not exclude any otherwise eligible persons who have been residents of the State for one year immediately preceding their application for assistance. I also recommend that the law be amended to provide a small increase in assistance funds to those States which simplify their laws by removing all residence requirements in any of their Federally aided programs.

In view of the changing nature of the economic and social problems of the country, the desirability of a periodic review of our public welfare programs is obvious. For that purpose I propose that the Secretary of Health, Education, and Welfare be authorized to appoint an Advisory Council on Public Welfare representing broad community interests and concerns, and such other advisory committees as he deems necessary to advise and consult with him in the administration of the Social Security Act.

No study of the public welfare program can fail to note the difficulty of the problems faced or the need to be imaginative in dealing with them. Accordingly, I recommend that amendments be made to encourage experimental, pilot or demonstration projects that would promote the objectives of the assistance titles and help make our welfare programs more flexible and adaptable to local needs.

The simplification and coordination of administration and operation would greatly improve the adequacy and consistency of assistance and related services. As a step in that direction, I recommend that a new title to the Social Security Act be enacted which would give to States the option of submitting a single, unified State plan combining their assistance programs for aged, blind and disabled, and their medical assistance programs for the aged, granting to such States additional Federal matching for medical payments on behalf of the blind and disabled.

These proposed far-reaching changes—aimed at far-reaching problems—are in the public interest and in keeping with our finest traditions. The goals of our public welfare programs must be positive and constructive—to create economic and social opportunities for the less fortunate—to help them find productive, happy and independent lives. It must stress the integrity and preservation of the family unit. It must contribute to the attack on dependency, juvenile delinquency, family breakdown, illegitimacy, ill health and disability. It must reduce the incidence of these problems, prevent their occurrence and recurrence, and strengthen and protect the vulnerable in a highly competitive world.

Unless such problems are dealt with effectively, they fester and grow, sapping the strength of society as a whole and extending their consequences in troubled families from one generation to the next.

The steps I recommend to you today to alleviate these problems will not come cheaply. They will cost more money when first enacted. But they will restore human dignity; and in the long run, they will save money. I have recommended in the Budget submitted for fiscal year 1963 sufficient funds to cover the extension of existing programs and the new legislation here proposed.

Communities which have—for whatever motives—attempted to save money through ruthless and arbitrary cutbacks in their welfare rolls have found their efforts to little avail. The root problems remained.

But communities which have tried the rehabilitative road—the road I have recommended today—have demonstrated what can be done with creative, thoughtfully conceived, and properly managed programs of prevention and social rehabilitation. In those communities, families have been restored to self-reliance, and relief rolls have been reduced.

To strengthen our human resources—to demonstrate the compassion of free men, and in the light of our own constructive self-interest—we must bring our welfare programs up to date. I urge that the Congress do so without delay.

JOHN F. KENNEDY

Source: Woolley, John T., and Gerhard Peters, *The American Presidency Project* [online] (Santa Barbara: University of California [hosted], Gerhard Peters [database]) (http://www. presidency.ucsb.edu/ws/?pid=8758).

12. LYNDON B. JOHNSON'S STATE OF THE UNION ADDRESS, 1964

In his State of the Union address on January 8, 1964, President Lyndon B. John-son outlined his proposal for the War on Poverty. Later that year, in response to Johnson's speech, Congress passed the Economic Opportunity Act, which established the Office of Economic Opportunity to oversee the new liberal programs—like the Job Corps and Community Action—that formed the basis of the War on Poverty.

President Lyndon B. Johnson's
Annual Message to the Congress on the State of the Union
January 8, 1964

. . .

Unfortunately, many Americans live on the outskirts of hope—some because of their poverty, and some because of their color, and all too many because of both. Our task is to help replace their despair with opportunity.

This administration today, here and now, declares unconditional war on poverty in America. I urge this Congress and all Americans to join with me in that effort.

It will not be a short or easy struggle, no single weapon or strategy will suffice, but we shall not rest until that war is won. The richest Nation on earth can afford to win it. We cannot afford to lose it. One thousand dollars invested in salvaging an unemployable youth today can return $40,000 or more in his lifetime.

Poverty is a national problem, requiring improved national organization and sup-port. But this attack, to be effective, must also be organized at the State and the local level and must be supported and directed by State and local efforts.

For the war against poverty will not be won here in Washington. It must be won in the field, in every private home, in every public office, from the courthouse to the White House.

The program I shall propose will emphasize this cooperative approach to help that one-fifth of all American families with incomes too small to even meet their basic needs.

Our chief weapons in a more pinpointed attack will be better schools, and better health, and better homes, and better training, and better job opportunities to help more Americans, especially young Americans, escape from squalor and misery and unemployment rolls where other citizens help to carry them.

Very often a lack of jobs and money is not the cause of poverty, but the symptom. The cause may lie deeper in our failure to give our fellow citizens a fair chance to develop their own capacities, in a lack of education and training, in a lack of med-ical care and housing, in a lack of decent communities in which to live and bring up their children.

But whatever the cause, our joint Federal-local effort must pursue poverty, pur-sue it wherever it exists—in city slums and small towns, in sharecropper shacks or in migrant worker camps, on Indian Reservations, among whites as well as Negroes, among the young as well as the aged, in the boom towns and in the depressed areas.

Our aim is not only to relieve the symptom of poverty, but to cure it and, above all, to prevent it. No single piece of legislation, however, is going to suffice.

We will launch a special effort in the chronically distressed areas of Appalachia.

We must expand our small but our successful area redevelopment program.

We must enact youth employment legislation to put jobless, aimless, hopeless youngsters to work on useful projects.

We must distribute more food to the needy through a broader food stamp program.

We must create a National Service Corps to help the economically handicapped of our own country as the Peace Corps now helps those abroad.

We must modernize our unemployment insurance and establish a high-level commission on automation. If we have the brain power to invent these machines, we have the brain power to make certain that they are a boon and not a bane to humanity.

We must extend the coverage of our minimum wage laws to more than 2 million workers now lacking this basic protection of purchasing power.

We must, by including special school aid funds as part of our education program, improve the quality of teaching, training, and counseling in our hardest hit areas.

We must build more libraries in every area and more hospitals and nursing homes under the Hill-Burton Act, and train more nurses to staff them.

We must provide hospital insurance for our older citizens financed by every worker and his employer under Social Security, contributing no more than $1 a month during the employee's working career to protect him in his old age in a dignified manner without cost to the Treasury, against the devastating hardship of prolonged or repeated illness.

We must, as a part of a revised housing and urban renewal program, give more help to those displaced by slum clearance, provide more housing for our poor and our elderly, and seek as our ultimate goal in our free enterprise system a decent home for every American family.

We must help obtain more modern mass transit within our communities as well as low-cost transportation between them.

Above all, we must release $11 billion of tax reduction into the private spending stream to create new jobs and new markets in every area of this land.

. . .

These programs are obviously not for the poor or the underprivileged alone. Every American will benefit by the extension of Social Security to cover the hospital costs of their aged parents. Every American community will benefit from the construction or modernization of schools, libraries, hospitals, and nursing homes, from the training of more nurses and from the improvement of urban renewal in public transit. And every individual American taxpayer and every corporate taxpayer will benefit from the earliest possible passage of the pending tax bill from both the new investment it will bring and the new jobs that it will create.

For our goal is not merely to spread the work. Our goal is to create more jobs. I believe the enactment of a 35-hour week would sharply increase costs, would invite inflation, would impair our ability to compete, and merely share instead of creating employment. But I am equally opposed to the 45- or 50-hour week in those industries where consistently excessive use of overtime causes increased unemployment.

So, therefore, I recommend legislation authorizing the creation of a tripartite industry committee to determine on an industry-by-industry basis as to where a higher penalty rate for overtime would increase job openings without unduly increasing costs, and authorizing the establishment of such higher rates.

. . .

Let me make one principle of this administration abundantly clear: All of these increased opportunities—in employment, in education, in housing, and in every field—must be open to Americans of every color. As far as the writ of Federal law will run, we must abolish not some, but all racial discrimination. For this is not merely an economic issue, or a social, political, or international issue. It is a moral issue, and it must be met by the passage this session of the bill now pending in the House.

All members of the public should have equal access to facilities open to the public. All members of the public should be equally eligible for Federal benefits that are financed by the public. All members of the public should have an equal chance to vote for public officials and to send their children to good public schools and to contribute their talents to the public good.

. . .

So I ask you now in the Congress and in the country to join with me in expressing and fulfilling that faith in working for a nation, a nation that is free from want and a world that is free from hate—a world of peace and justice, and freedom and abundance, for our time and for all time to come.

Source: Woolley, John T., and Gerhard Peters, *The American Presidency Project* [online] (Santa Barbara: University of California [hosted], Gerhard Peters [database]) (http://www.presidency.ucsb.edu/ws/?pid=26787).

13. LYNDON B. JOHNSON'S GREAT SOCIETY SPEECH, 1964

Lyndon B. Johnson's Great Society program, of which the War on Poverty was the most visible part, was the federal government's most comprehensive plan to address domestic poverty since the New Deal. In this speech, Johnson very clearly outlined the main tenets of his vision for the Great Society.

President Lyndon B. Johnson's
Remarks at the University of Michigan
May 22, 1964

For a century we labored to settle and to subdue a continent. For half a century we called upon unbounded invention and untiring industry to create an order of plenty for all of our people.

The challenge of the next half century is whether we have the wisdom to use that wealth to enrich and elevate our national life, and to advance the quality of our American civilization.

Your imagination, your initiative, and your indignation will determine whether we build a society where progress is the servant of our needs, or a society where old values and new visions are buried under unbridled growth. For in your time we have the opportunity to move not only toward the rich society and the powerful society, but upward to the Great Society.

The Great Society rests on abundance and liberty for all. It demands an end to poverty and racial injustice, to which we are totally committed in our time. But that is just the beginning.

The Great Society is a place where every child can find knowledge to enrich his mind and to enlarge his talents. It is a place where leisure is a welcome chance to build and reflect, not a feared cause of boredom and restlessness. It is a place where the city of man serves not only the needs of the body and the demands of commerce but the desire for beauty and the hunger for community.

It is a place where man can renew contact with nature. It is a place which honors creation for its own sake and for what it adds to the understanding of the race. It is a place where men are more concerned with the quality of their goals than the quantity of their goods.

But most of all, the Great Society is not a safe harbor, a resting place, a final objective, a finished work. It is a challenge constantly renewed, beckoning us toward a destiny where the meaning of our lives matches the marvelous products of our labor.

So I want to talk to you today about three places where we begin to build the Great Society—in our cities, in our countryside, and in our classrooms.

Many of you will live to see the day, perhaps 50 years from now, when there will be 400 million Americans—four-fifths of them in urban areas. In the remainder of this century urban population will double, city land will double, and we will have to build homes, highways, and facilities equal to all those built since this country was first settled. So in the next 40 years we must rebuild the entire urban United States.

Aristotle said: "Men come together in cities in order to live, but they remain together in order to live the good life." It is harder and harder to live the good life in American cities today.

The catalog of ills is long: there is the decay of the centers and the despoiling of the suburbs. There is not enough housing for our people or transportation for our traffic. Open land is vanishing and old landmarks are violated.

Worst of all expansion is eroding the precious and time honored values of community with neighbors and communion with nature. The loss of these values breeds loneliness and boredom and indifference.

Our society will never be great until our cities are great. Today the frontier of imagination and innovation is inside those cities and not beyond their borders.

New experiments are already going on. It will be the task of your generation to make the American city a place where future generations will come, not only to live but to live the good life.

. . .

A second place where we begin to build the Great Society is in our countryside. We have always prided ourselves on being not only America the strong and America the free, but America the beautiful. Today that beauty is in danger. The water we drink, the food we eat, the very air that we breathe, are threatened with pollution. Our parks are overcrowded, our seashores overburdened. Green fields and dense forests are disappearing.

A few years ago we were greatly concerned about the "Ugly American." Today we must act to prevent an ugly America.

For once the battle is lost, once our natural splendor is destroyed, it can never be recaptured. And once man can no longer walk with beauty or wonder at nature his spirit will wither and his sustenance be wasted.

A third place to build the Great Society is in the classrooms of America. There your children's lives will be shaped. Our society will not be great until every young mind is set free to scan the farthest reaches of thought and imagination. We are still far from that goal.

Today, 8 million adult Americans, more than the entire population of Michigan, have not finished 5 years of school. Nearly 20 million have not finished 8 years of school. Nearly 54 million—more than one-quarter of all America—have not even finished high school.

Each year more than 100,000 high school graduates, with proved ability, do not enter college because they cannot afford it. And if we cannot educate today's youth, what will we do in 1970 when elementary school enrollment will be 5 million greater than 1960? And high school enrollment will rise by 5 million. College enrollment will increase by more than 3 million.

In many places, classrooms are overcrowded and curricula are outdated. Most of our qualified teachers are underpaid, and many of our paid teachers are unqualified. So we must give every child a place to sit and a teacher to learn from. Poverty must not be a bar to learning, and learning must offer an escape from poverty.

But more classrooms and more teachers are not enough. We must seek an educational system which grows in excellence as it grows in size. This means better training for our teachers. It means preparing youth to enjoy their hours of leisure as well as their hours of labor. It means exploring new techniques of teaching, to find new ways to stimulate the love of learning and the capacity for creation.

These are three of the central issues of the Great Society. While our Government has many programs directed at those issues, I do not pretend that we have the full answer to those problems.

But I do promise this: We are going to assemble the best thought and the broadest knowledge from all over the world to find those answers for America. I intend to establish working groups to prepare a series of White House conferences and meetings—on the cities, on natural beauty, on the quality of education, and on other emerging challenges. And from these meetings and from this inspiration and from these studies we will begin to set our course toward the Great Society.

Source: *Public Papers of the Presidents of the United States: Lyndon B. Johnson, 1963–64, Volume I*, entry 357, 704–707. Washington, D.C.: Government Printing Office, 1965. (www.lbjlib.utexas.edu/johnson/archives.hom/speeches.hom/selected_speeches.asp)

14. LYNDON B. JOHNSON'S WAR ON POVERTY SPEECH, 1965

In this letter, Lyndon Johnson emphasized the need to step up the War on Poverty. In 1964 Congress passed the Economic Opportunity Act, which implemented many of the programs Johnson discussed in the letter, such as the Job Corps, VISTA, Community Action Programs, and the Neighborhood Youth Corps. Johnson's tone in this letter was positive about the results, but in the following years race riots and dissention over the Vietnam War undermined these programs.

Lyndon B. Johnson
Letter to the President of the Senate and to the Speaker of the House on
Stepping Up the War on Poverty.
February 17th, 1965

Dear Mr. President: (Dear Mr. Speaker:)
I request the doubling of the War Against Poverty.
In addition I request legislation to improve our ability to conduct that war.

We reaffirm our faith that poverty can be eliminated from this country, and our solemn commitment to prosecute the war against poverty to a successful conclusion. For that struggle is not only for the liberation of those imprisoned in poverty, but for the conscience and the values of a prosperous and free nation.

From the very beginning, this country, the idea of America itself, was the promise that all would have an equal chance to share in the fruits of our society.

As long as children are untrained, men without work, and families shut in gateless poverty, that promise is unkept. New resources and knowledge, our achievements and our growth, have given us the resources to meet this pledge. Not meanly or grudgingly, but in obedience to an old and generous faith, let us make a place for all at the table of American abundance.

Our objective was stated by the Congress in the Economic Opportunity Act of 1964: "to eliminate the paradox of poverty in the midst of plenty in this Nation by opening to everyone, the opportunity for education and training, the opportunity to work, and the opportunity to live in decency and dignity."

The Page of Progress

We have already begun to move toward this objective:

Local anti-poverty programs have been approved in 44 of the 50 states, and by June every state will be taking part.

Work is now underway on 53 Job Corps Centers. Seven are already in operation and 15 will be completed each month. Each will be filled with young men or women anxious to learn and work, and to give themselves a new and often unexpected opportunity for a productive life.

We will, this year, provide a school readiness program for 100,000 children about to enter kindergarten. This will help them overcome the handicaps of experience and feeling which flow from poverty and permit them to receive the full advantages of school experience.

By July, 3,500 VISTA Volunteers, aged 18–82, will be working to help their fellow Americans in communities across the country.

25,000 families, eligible for public assistance, are now enrolled in a work-experience program which provides jobs and skills for the family breadwinners, giving them a new prospect of emerging from a poverty which often reaches back through three generations.

We have established procedures, processed applications, and begun to make loans to thousands of struggling rural families and to small businesses.

In 49 cities and 11 rural communities, Neighborhood Youth Corps have been established. In these Corps, young men and women between 16 and 21 can work to keep themselves in school, to return if they have dropped out, or to prepare for permanent jobs.

35,000 college level students can now continue their education through the income provided by part-time jobs. And 35,000 adults will be taught to read and write this year.

The Rise of National Concern

All of these programs—the accomplishments of the first year and the hopes of the future—depend upon the concern and initiative of local communities. It is now clear that the war against poverty has touched the hearts and the sense of duty of the American people. This cause has truly become their cause.

Community action organizations, planning and organizing the local effort to end poverty, have sprung up in communities in every part of the country. Over 5,000 prominent citizens are serving, without pay, on such organizations. National groups, such as the American Bar Association, have pledged their special resources to the plight of the poor. And 75 national organizations have banded together in a Citizens Crusade Against Poverty to begin specific projects.

And the response of the American nation is growing each day. New community action proposals from local groups are coming in at a rate of 130 a month. We have already received 750 applications.

Applications for the Job Corps are arriving at a rate of nearly 6,000 a day.

8,000 men and women have volunteered to serve their fellow citizens in the VISTA program.

We estimate that at least 90,000 adults will be ready to enroll in adult basic education programs during the coming year.

And the same steady rise of interest and hope can be seen in every part of our program. We cannot afford, in conscience or in the national interest, to disappoint these hopes or to waste the valuable resources of human skill and energy which we are now beginning to tap.

Recommendations

Therefore I am requesting the Congress to authorize the continuation of these programs for the next two years, and to authorize and appropriate 1.5 billion dollars to conduct them during the fiscal year.

I am also asking Congress to extend for ten months, to June 30, 1967, the period during which certain programs may be funded with 90 percent federal assistance. If we do not do this, then many communities, especially those in rural or isolated areas and which lack the resources to get underway quickly, will be unable to qualify before the cutoff date.

In addition I recommend transfer of the work-study program to the Office of Education in the Department of Health, Education, and Welfare, as well as a series of technical amendments.

Last year Congress and my administration took a step unparalleled in the history of any nation. We pledged ourselves to the elimination of poverty in America. That was our commitment to the people we serve, and it reflected not only our own intentions but the will of the American people. We knew, and said then, that this battle would not be easily or swiftly won. But we began. Today we can take together another step along the path to the fulfillment of the American dream for all our citizens.

Sincerely,

LYNDON B. JOHNSON

Source: Woolley, John T., and Gerhard Peters, *The American Presidency Project* [online] (Santa Barbara: University of California [hosted], Gerhard Peters [database]) (http://www.presidency.ucsb.edu/ws/?pid=27432).

15. RICHARD M. NIXON'S SPECIAL MESSAGE TO CONGRESS ON POVERTY, 1969

After his election as president in 1968, Richard Nixon emphasized economic and legal solutions to poverty as part of his plan to curtail Lyndon Johnson's liberal Great Society and War on Poverty program. However, as this document shows, Nixon did not reject completely Johnson's policies; instead, he called for revisions to lessen direct federal control. In this sense, Nixon adopted a more conservative stance than Johnson, but, compared to later Republicans like Ronald Reagan, retained a somewhat liberal approach to welfare.

Richard Nixon
Special Message to the Congress on the Nation's Antipoverty Programs.
February 19th, 1969

To the Congress of the United States:

The blight of poverty requires priority attention. It engages our hearts and challenges our intelligence. It cannot and will not be treated lightly or indifferently, or without the most searching examination of how best to marshal the resources available to the Federal Government for combating it.

At my direction, the Urban Affairs Council has been conducting an intensive study of the nation's anti-poverty programs, of the way the anti-poverty effort is organized and administered, and of ways in which it might be made more effective.

That study is continuing. However, I can now announce a number of steps I intend to take, as well as spelling out some of the considerations that will guide my future recommendations.

The Economic Opportunity Act of 1964 is now scheduled to expire on June 30, 1970. The present authorization for appropriations for the Office of Economic Opportunity runs only until June 30, 1969.

I will ask Congress that this authorization for appropriations be extended for another year. Prior to the end of the Fiscal Year, I will send Congress a comprehensive proposal for the future of the poverty program, including recommendations for revising and extending the Act itself beyond its scheduled 1970 expiration.

How the work begun by OEO can best be carried forward is a subject on which many views deserve to be heard—both from within Congress, and among those many others who are interested or affected, including especially the poor themselves. By sending my proposals well before the Act's 1970 expiration, I intend to provide time for full debate and discussion.

In the maze of anti-poverty efforts, precedents are weak and knowledge uncertain. These past years of increasing Federal involvement have begun to make clear how vast is the range of what we do not yet know, and how fragile are projections based on partial understanding. But we have learned some lessons about what works and what does not. The changes I propose will be based on those lessons and those discoveries, and rooted in a determination to press ahead with anti-poverty efforts even though individual experiments have ended in disappointment.

From the experience of OEO, we have learned the value of having in the Federal Government an agency whose special concern is the poor. We have learned the need for flexibility, responsiveness, and continuing innovation. We have learned the need for management effectiveness. Even those most thoroughly committed to the goals of the anti-poverty effort recognize now that much that has been tried has not worked.

The OEO has been a valuable fount of ideas and enthusiasm, but it has suffered from a confusion of roles.

OEO's greatest value is as an initiating agency—devising new programs to help the poor, and serving as an "incubator" for these programs during their initial, experimental phases. One of my aims is to free OEO itself to perform these functions more effectively, by providing for a greater concentration of its energies on its innovative role.

Last year, Congress directed that special studies be made by the Executive Branch of whether Head Start and the Job Corps should continue to be administered directly by OEO, or whether responsibility should be otherwise assigned.

Section 309 of the Vocational Education Amendments of 1968 provides:

"The President shall make a special study of whether the responsibility for administering the Head Start program established under the Economic Opportunity Act of 1964 should continue to be vested in the Director of the Office of Economic Opportunity, should be transferred to another agency of the Government, or should be delegated to another such agency pursuant to the provisions of section 602(d) of the aforementioned Economic Opportunity Act of 1964, and shall submit the findings of this study to the Congress not later than March 1, 1969."

I have today submitted this study to the Congress. Meanwhile, under the Executive authority provided by the Economic Opportunity Act, I have directed that preparations be made for the delegation of Head Start to the Department of Health, Education, and Welfare. Whether it should be actually transferred is a question I will take up in my later, comprehensive message, along with my proposals for a permanent status and organizational structure for OEO. Pending a final decision by the Secretary of HEW on where within the department responsibility for Head Start would be lodged, it will be located directly within the Office of the Secretary.

In order to provide for orderly preparation, and to ensure that there is no interruption of programs, I have directed that this delegation be made effective July 1, 1969. By then the summer programs for 1969 will all have been funded, and a new cycle will be beginning.

I see this delegation as an important element in a new national commitment to the crucial early years of life.

Head Start is still experimental. Its effects are simply not known—save of course where medical care and similar services are involved. The results of a major national evaluation of the program will be available this Spring. It must be said, however, that preliminary reports on this study confirm what many have feared: the long-term effect of Head Start appears to be extremely weak. This must not discourage us. To the contrary it only demonstrates the immense contribution the Head Start program has made simply by having raised to prominence on the national agenda the fact—known for some time, but never widely recognized—that the children of the poor mostly arrive at school age seriously deficient in the ability to profit from formal education, and already significantly behind their contemporaries. It also has been made abundantly clear that our schools as they now exist are unable to overcome this deficiency.

In this context, the Head Start Follow-Through Program already delegated to HEW by OEO, assumes an even greater importance.

In recent years, enormous advances have been made in the understanding of human development. We have learned that intelligence is not fixed at birth, but is largely formed by the environmental influences of the early formative years. It develops rapidly at first, and then more slowly; as much of that development takes place in the first four years as in the next thirteen. We have learned further that environment has its greatest impact on the development of intelligence when that development is proceeding most rapidly—that is, in those earliest years.

This means that many of the problems of poverty are traceable directly to early childhood experience—and that if we are to make genuine, long-range progress, we must focus our efforts much more than heretofore on those few years which may determine how far, throughout his later life, the child can reach.

Recent scientific developments have shown that this process of early childhood development poses more difficult problems than had earlier been recognized—but they also promise a real possibility of major breakthroughs soon in our understanding of this process. By placing Head Start in the Department of HEW, it will be possible to strengthen it by association with a wide range of other early development programs within the department, and also with the research programs of the National Institutes of Health, the National Institute of Mental Health, and the National Institute of Child Health and Human Development.

Much of our knowledge is new. But we are not on that ground absolved from the responsibility to respond to it. So crucial is the matter of early growth that we must make a national commitment to providing all American children an opportunity for healthful and stimulating development during the first five years of life. In delegating Head Start to the Department of HEW, I pledge myself to that commitment.

The Vocational Education Amendments of 1968 directed the Commissioner of Education to study the Job Corps in relation to state vocational education programs. I have directed the Secretaries of Labor and of Health, Education, and Welfare, and the Assistant Secretary of Labor for Manpower, to work with the Acting Commissioner of Education in preparing such a report for submission to Congress at the earliest opportunity.

One of the priority aims of the new Administration is the development by the Department of Labor of a comprehensive manpower program, designed to make centrally available to the unemployed and the underemployed a full range of Federal job training and placement services. Toward this end, it is essential that the many Federal manpower programs be integrated and coordinated.

Therefore, as a first step toward better program management, the Job Corps will be delegated to the Department of Labor.

For the Department, this will add another important manpower service component. For the Job Corpsmen, it will make available additional training and service opportunities. From the standpoint of program management, it makes it possible to coordinate the Job Corps with other manpower services, especially vocational education, at the point of delivery.

The Department of Labor already is deeply involved in the recruitment, counseling and placement of Job Corpsmen. It refers 80 percent of all male and 45 percent of all female enrollees; it provides job market information, and helps locate Job Corpsmen in the areas of greatest opportunity.

This delegation will also be made effective on July 1, 1969; and the Departments of Interior and Agriculture will continue to have operating responsibility for the Job Corps centers concerned primarily with conservation.

I have directed that preparations be made for the transfer of two other programs from OEO to the Department of Health, Education, and Welfare: Comprehensive Health Centers, which provide health service to the residents of poor neighborhoods, and the Foster Grandparents program. In my judgment, these can be better administered at present, or in the near future, within the structure of the Department.

In making these changes, I recognize that innovation costs money—and that if OEO is to continue its effectiveness as an innovating agency, adequate funds must be made available on a continuing basis. Moreover, it is my intent that Community Action Agencies can continue to be involved in the operation of programs such as Head Start at the local level, even though an agency other than OEO has received such programs, by delegation, at the national level. It also is my intent that the vital Community Action Programs will be pressed forward, and that in the area of economic development OEO will have an important role to play, in cooperation with other agencies, in fostering community-based business development.

One of the principal aims of the Administration's continuing study of the anti-poverty effort will be to improve its management effectiveness. When poverty fund monies are stolen, those hurt most are the poor—whom the monies were meant to help. When programs are inefficiently administered, those hurt most again are the poor. The public generally, and the poor especially, have a right to demand effective and efficient management. I intend to provide it.

I expect that important economies will result from the delegation of the Job Corps to the Department of Labor, and we shall continue to strive for greater efficiency, and especially for greater effectiveness in Head Start.

A Concentrated Management Improvement Program initiated in OEO will be intensified. Under this program, selected Community Action Agencies will be required to take steps to devise improvements in such areas as organizational structure, financial and accounting systems, personnel training and work scheduling. Standards will be applied under the "management improvement program" to evaluate the operations of Community Action Agencies. We intend to monitor these programs actively in order to insure that they are achieving high-level effectiveness and that they are being administered on an orderly basis.

In the past, problems have often arisen over the relationship of State, county and local governments to programs administered by OEO. This has particularly been the case where the State and local officials have wanted to assume greater responsibility for the implementation of the programs but for various reasons have been prevented from doing so. I have assigned special responsibility for working out these problems to the newly-created Office of Intergovernmental Relations, under the supervision of the Vice President.

I have directed the Urban Affairs Council to keep the anti-poverty effort under constant review and evaluation, seeking new ways in which the various departments can help and better ways in which their efforts can be coordinated.

My comprehensive recommendations for the future of the poverty program will be made after the Urban Affairs Council's own initial study is completed, and after I have reviewed the Comptroller General's study of OEO ordered by Congress in 1967 and due for submission next month.

Meanwhile, I would stress this final thought: If we are to make the most of experimental programs, we must frankly recognize their experimental nature and frankly acknowledge whatever shortcomings they develop. To do so is not to belittle the experiment, but to advance its essential purpose: that of finding new ways, better ways, of making progress in areas still inadequately understood.

We often can learn more from a program that fails to achieve its purpose than from one that succeeds. If we apply those lessons, then even the "failure" will have made a significant contribution to our larger purposes.

I urge all those involved in these experimental programs to bear this in mind—and to remember that one of the primary goals of this Administration is to expand our knowledge of how best to make real progress against those social ills that have so stubbornly defied solution. We do not pretend to have all the answers. We are determined to find as many as we can.

The men and women who will be valued most in this administration will be those who understand that not every experiment succeeds, who do not cover up failures but rather lay open problems, frankly and constructively, so that next time we will know how to do better.

In this spirit, I am confident that we can place our anti-poverty efforts on a secure footing—and that as we continue to gain in understanding of how to master the difficulties, we can move forward at an accelerating pace.

Source: Woolley, John T., and Gerhard Peters, *The American Presidency Project* [online] (Santa Barbara: University of California [hosted], Gerhard Peters [database]) (http://www. presidency.ucsb.edu/ws/?pid=2397).

16. RICHARD M. NIXON'S STATEMENT ON WELFARE, 1970

In this statement Richard Nixon outlined the need to reform the programs enacted as part of Lyndon Johnson's War on Poverty. The Family Assistance Plan (FAP), which Nixon discussed here, was the most significant of his proposed reforms. Intended to reform the Aid to Families with Dependent Children (AFDC) program, FAP provoked a bitter struggle in Congress between liberals and conservatives about whether the poor were to blame for their situation or whether society as a whole was responsible for their care. FAP was a compromise that did not satisfy either Republicans or Democrats, and Congress never implemented it.

Richard Nixon
Statement Announcing Extensions of Welfare Reform Proposals
June 10th, 1970

Past programs to aid the poor have failed. They have degraded the poor and defrauded the taxpayer. The family assistance plan represents the most comprehensive and far-reaching effort to reform social welfare in nearly four decades. Today, I am announcing significant extensions of the administration's welfare reform proposals.

Basic Principles

The family assistance plan is based on four fundamental principles:

- Strong incentives to encourage work and training;
- Equity to provide assistance to working poor families;
- Respect for individual choice and family responsibility; and
- Administrative efficiency to earn the trust of the taxpayer.

Administration officials have worked recently to identify ways to extend the principles of this income strategy to other domestic programs such as Medicaid, food stamps, and public housing.

On the basis of this review, I have made my decision to propose basic amendments to the Family Assistance Act of 1970.

Health Insurance for Poor Families

The most important proposal I make today is to reform the Medicaid program.

Medicaid is plagued by serious faults. Costs are mounting beyond reason. Services vary considerably from State to State. Benefits are only remotely related to family resources. Eligibility may terminate abruptly as a family moves off, often losing more in medical benefits than it gains in income.

In short—just like the existing welfare system—Medicaid is inefficient, inequitably excludes the working poor, and often provides an incentive for people to stay on welfare.

I will propose legislation at the beginning of the next Congress to establish a family health insurance program for all poor families with children. This insurance would provide a comprehensive package of health services, including both hospital and outpatient care.

Final decisions on the specifications of the family health insurance proposal must await further review by the new Domestic Council. We are satisfied that the basic principles will work. This proposal will constitute the second legislative stage of the administration's income strategy against poverty.

Unified Administration of Food Stamps and Family Assistance

The administration has already made extensive changes in the food stamp program to improve benefits, make them more equitable, and help even the very poorest families to receive assistance. We will propose that the Congress build on these executive reforms to integrate food stamps with family assistance and other income support programs.

Therefore, I plan to:

- Submit a reorganization plan at the beginning of the next Congress to transfer the food stamp program from the Department of Agriculture to the Department of Health, Education, and Welfare;

- Make it possible for a family to "check off" its food stamp purchase and receive its stamp allotment automatically with its family assistance check; and

- Revise the food stamp price schedule to make it rise evenly with increases in income.

Assisted Housing

Present subsidized housing programs are marked by inconsistencies and inequities. Many families pay the same rent despite wide differences in income. A small increase in earnings may force the family to move, losing much more housing assistance than is gained in income.

We have proposed a solution to many of these problems in the Housing Act of 1970. Rents would vary directly with income. A family would not be forced to move at some arbitrary income limit. We will offer this provision of the Housing Act to the Senate Finance Committee for its consideration.

Reform of Individual and Family Services

In other amendments, we are proposing significant changes in social services for the poor. This proposal has been developed in recent months and will be ready for submission to the Congress next week. These amendments will:

- Encourage accountability and program results;
- Strengthen the role of Governors, mayors, and county executives;
- Seek to eliminate duplication and overlap.

Other Major Changes

Other administration amendments to the Family Assistance Act make important changes. For example:

- Phasing out the special program for unemployed fathers, thus eliminating one of the most serious disincentives noted by the Senate Finance Committee;
- Limiting the welfare burden of the States by placing a ceiling on their financial obligations under the program;
- Strengthening the work requirement; and
- Reducing areas of administrative discretion.

Nowhere has the failure of government been more tragically apparent in past years than in its efforts to help the poor. The 91st Congress has an historic but rapidly vanishing opportunity to reverse that record by enacting the Family Assistance Act of 1970. Let there be no mistake about this administration's total commitment to passage of this legislative milestone this year.

Source: Woolley, John T., and Gerhard Peters, *The American Presidency Project* [online] (Santa Barbara: University of California [hosted], Gerhard Peters [database]) (http://www.presidency.ucsb.edu/ws/?pid=2539).

17. RONALD REAGAN'S SPEECH AT THE REPUBLICAN NATIONAL CONVENTION, 1984

In this speech, Ronald Reagan clearly defined the difference between liberal, often Democratic, pro-welfare policies and conservative, often Republican, anti-welfare policies. A conservative, Reagan presented this conflict in black and white terms: the liberal pro-welfare stance led to "pessimism, fear, and limits," but Reagan's stance engendered "hope, confidence, and growth." Reagan also explained his plan to cut back on the welfare state as a simplification process that would stress the benefits of work, economic growth, and the traditional family.

Ronald Reagan
Remarks Accepting the Presidential Nomination at the
Republican National Convention
August 23, 1984

. . .

America is presented with the clearest political choice of half a century. The distinction between our two parties and the different philosophy of our political opponents are at the heart of this campaign and America's future.

. . .

The choices this year are not just between two different personalities or between two political parties. They're between two different visions of the future, two fundamentally different ways of governing—their government of pessimism, fear, and limits, or ours of hope, confidence, and growth.

Their [the Democrats'] government sees people only as members of groups; ours serves all the people of America as individuals. Theirs lives in the past, seeking to apply the old and failed policies to an era that has passed them by. Ours learns from the past and strives to change by boldly charting a new course for the future. Theirs lives by promises, the bigger, the better. We offer proven, workable answers.

Our opponents [the Democrats] began this campaign hoping that America has a poor memory. Well, let's take them on a little stroll down memory lane. Let's remind them of how a 4.8-percent inflation rate in 1976 became back-to-back years of double-digit inflation—the worst since World War I—punishing the poor and the elderly, young couples striving to start their new lives, and working people struggling to make ends meet.

Inflation was not some plague borne on the wind; it was a deliberate part of their official economic policy, needed, they said, to maintain prosperity. They didn't tell us that with it would come the highest interest rates since the Civil War. As average monthly mortgage payments more than doubled, home building nearly ground to a halt; tens of thousands of carpenters and others were thrown out of work. And who controlled both Houses of the Congress and the executive branch at that time? Not us, not us.

Campaigning across America in 1980, we saw evidence everywhere of industrial decline. And in rural America, farmers' costs were driven up by inflation. They were devastated by a wrongheaded grain embargo and were forced to borrow money at exorbitant interest rates just to get by. And many of them didn't get by. Farmers have to fight insects, weather, and the marketplace; they shouldn't have to fight their own government.

. . . Under their policies, tax rates have gone up three times as much for families with children as they have for everyone else over these past three decades. In just the 5 years before we came into office, taxes roughly doubled.

. . . The Census Bureau confirms that, because of the tax laws we inherited, the number of households at or below the poverty level paying Federal income tax more than doubled between 1980 and 1982. Well, they received some relief in 1983, when our across-the-board tax cut was fully in place. And they'll get more help when indexing goes into effect this January.

Our opponents have repeatedly advocated eliminating indexing. Would that really hurt the rich? No, because the rich are already in the top brackets. But those working men and women who depend on a cost-of-living adjustment just to keep abreast of inflation would find themselves pushed into higher tax brackets and wouldn't even be able to keep even with inflation because they'd be paying a higher income tax. That's bracket creep; and our opponents are for it, and we're against it.

It's up to us to see that all our fellow citizens understand that confiscatory taxes, costly social experiments, and economic tinkering were not just the policies of a single administration. For the 26 years prior to January of 1981, the opposition party controlled both Houses of Congress. Every spending bill and every tax for more than a quarter of a century has been of their doing.

. . . By nearly every measure, the position of poor Americans worsened under the leadership of our opponents. Teenage drug use, out-of-wedlock births, and crime increased dramatically. Urban neighborhoods and schools deteriorated. Those whom government intended to help discovered a cycle of dependency that could not be broken. Government became a drug, providing temporary relief, but addiction as well.

And let's get some facts on the table that our opponents don't want to hear. The biggest annual increase in poverty took place between 1978 and 1981—over 9 percent each year, in the first 2 years of our administration. Well, I should—pardon me—I didn't put a period in there. In the first 2 years of our administration, that annual increase fell to 5.3 percent. And 1983 was the first year since 1978 that there was no appreciable increase in poverty at all.

Pouring hundreds of billions of dollars into programs in order to make people worse off was irrational and unfair. It was time we ended this reliance on the government process and renewed our faith in the human process.

In 1980 the people decided with us that the economic crisis was not caused by the fact that they lived too well. Government lived too well. It was time for tax increases to be an act of last resort, not of first resort.

. . . But worst of all, Americans were losing the confidence and optimism about the future that has made us unique in the world. Parents were beginning to doubt that their children would have the better life that has been the dream of every American generation.

We can all be proud that pessimism is ended. America is coming back and is more confident than ever about the future. Tonight, we thank the citizens of the United States whose faith and unwillingness to give up on themselves or this country saved us all.

Together, we began the task of controlling the size and activities of the government by reducing the growth of its spending while passing a tax program to provide incentives to increase productivity for both workers and industry. Today, a working family earning $25,000 has about $2,900 more in purchasing power than if tax and inflation rates were still at the 1980 level.

Today, of all the major industrial nations of the world, America has the strongest economic growth; one of the lowest inflation rates; the fastest rate of job creation—$6\frac{1}{2}$ million jobs in the last year and a half—a record 600,000 business incorporations in 1983; and the largest increase in real, after-tax personal income since World War II. We're enjoying the highest level of business investment in history, and America has renewed its leadership in developing the vast new opportunities in science and high technology. America is on the move again and expanding toward new eras of opportunity for everyone.

. . . Our [the Reagan Administration's] tax policies are and will remain pro-work, pro-growth, and pro-family. We intend to simplify the entire tax system—to make taxes more fair, easier to understand, and, most important, to bring the tax rates of every American further down, not up. Now, if we bring them down far enough, growth will continue strong; the underground economy will shrink; the world will beat a path to our door; and no one will be able to hold America back; and the future will be ours.

Source: Woolley, John T., and Gerhard Peters, *The American Presidency Project* [online] (Santa Barbara: University of California [hosted], Gerhard Peters [database]) (http://www. presidency.ucsb.edu/ws/?pid=40290).

18. RONALD REAGAN'S RADIO ADDRESS ON WELFARE, 1987

When Ronald Reagan became president in 1981, he pushed for a conservative approach to the welfare state. This speech, from the latter part of his second term in office, illustrates his emphasis on education, work, and "self-reliance" over welfare handouts. Reagan's proposed reforms to the Aid to Families with

Dependent Children (AFDC) were a forerunner to the more drastic reforms of 1996, when Bill Clinton signed a comprehensive reform that abolished the AFDC and echoed Reagan's emphasis on work and individual initiative as the means to overcome poverty.

Ronald Reagan
Radio Address to the Nation on Welfare Reform
August 1st, 1987

My fellow Americans:

Americans always have cared about the less fortunate, and I'm sure it'll deeply gladden the hearts of many of you to know the kind of progress we've made during the past $6\frac{1}{2}$ years in helping the poor. We have between 4 and 6 million fewer low-income families on the Federal income tax rolls. We've tamed inflation rates that were devastating the purchasing power of those least able to afford the basic necessities of life and reversed an upward spiral in the number of poor people that began in 1979. The official statistics released on Thursday show that the poverty rate is down for the third year in a row. The 1.6-percentage drop in poverty over the last 3 years is the largest sustained improvement since 1970. And median family income, adjusted for inflation, rose by 4.2 percent in 1986—the largest increase since 1972.

All of us can be pleased with this progress; pleased but not satisfied. More must be done to reduce poverty and dependency and, believe me, nothing is more important than welfare reform. It's now common knowledge that our welfare system has itself become a poverty trap—a creator and reinforcer of dependency—and that's why last year, in my State of the Union Message, I called for an overhaul of our welfare system.

Since that time, I've sent to Congress a carefully designed package of proposals that rejects the old Federal approach of sweeping solutions dictated from Washington. The central point of our new proposal—as outlined in our earlier study "Up From Dependency" and now embodied in our legislative proposal, the Low-Income Opportunity Improvement Act—is a provision that will allow States and localities to test new ideas for reducing welfare dependency. Through experimental changes, through carefully tested and evaluated demonstrations, this new approach can determine what does work in reducing welfare dependency. When the National Governors' Association met last weekend in Michigan, they gave substantial support to our plans to give them greater flexibility and they promised to work closely with us and the Congress.

But, while we must let loose the creative energies of our States and localities, I think there are some critical improvements we can make at the Federal level. Under the laws now in place, all mothers who have children under age 6 are exempt from participating in work activities that—as several demonstration projects have shown—can help Aid For Dependent Children (AFDC) recipients become more self-reliant. Fewer than one-fifth of all recipients now participate in work activities. We must lift this counterproductive exemption and thereby get early help to these women and their children before they become chronically dependent on welfare. We must also reform work requirements so that long gaps in school or in other work-related experiences no longer occur—and so too, work opportunities for AFDC recipients must be expanded. We must give teenagers on AFDC who have not completed high school the opportunity to continue their schooling and older recipients to participate in employment and training activities. Two proposals we've sent to the Congress—GROW, or Greater Opportunities Through Work, in AFDC and the AFDC Youth Training Initiative—will allow us to do all of these things.

So too, changes in our child support enforcement system can reduce welfare dependency. Parents who bring children into the world have a responsibility for these children, whether they live with them or not. The administration is taking steps to ensure that States are able to do a better job in locating absent parents, establishing paternity, and collecting child support on behalf of AFDC recipients. We also have asked the Congress for new laws that would increase child support award amounts for both welfare and nonwelfare families.

Now the question I ask about any welfare reform proposal is: Will it help people become self-sufficient and lead a full life, or will it keep them down in a state of dependency? I'm afraid that several Members of Congress have suggested some proposals that, while claiming to require work-related activities, would make staying on welfare more attractive. Their misguided compassion would only bring more people into the welfare system, encourage them to stay on the welfare rolls longer, and discourage work. For example, the Democratic House bill contains no demonstration authority at all and another Senate bill only a very limited one.

AFDC work program reforms that emphasize early intervention to prevent welfare dependency, child support enforcement improvements to provide children the help that they need, and demonstration projects that give us the information necessary to make changes in the national welfare system: that is my welfare reform strategy; I hope it has your support.

Until next week, thanks for listening, and God bless you.

Source: Woolley, John T., and Gerhard Peters, *The American Presidency Project* [online] (Santa Barbara: University of California [hosted], Gerhard Peters [database]) (http://www. presidency.ucsb.edu/ws/?pid=34638).

19. BILL CLINTON'S STATE OF THE UNION ADDRESS, 1997

> In 1996, President Bill Clinton signed a Republican-sponsored welfare reform bill intended to "end welfare as we know it." In his 1997 State of the Union speech, Clinton described this bill as a way to get needy people off welfare and into jobs that would enable them to become self-reliant citizens. Clinton's emphasis on traditional family and work over welfare was in the conservative tradition of Republican presidents such as Ronald Reagan, whose anti-welfare ideas found fruition in the 1996 Welfare Reform Act.

President Bill Clinton
State of the Union address to Congress
February 4, 1997

Mr. Speaker, Mr. Vice President, Members of the 105th Congress, distinguished guests, and my fellow Americans. I think I should start by saying, thanks for inviting me back. I come before you tonight with a challenge as great as any in our peacetime history and a plan of action to meet that challenge, to prepare our people for the bold new world of the 21st century. We have much to be thankful for. With four years of growth, we have won back the basic strength of our economy. With crime and welfare rolls declining, we are winning back our optimism, the enduring faith that we can master any difficulty. With the Cold War receding and global commerce at record levels, we are helping to win an unrivaled peace and prosperity all across the world.

My fellow Americans, the state of our Union is strong. But now we must rise to the decisive moment, to make a nation and a world better than any we have ever known. The new promise of the global economy, the information age, unimagined new work, life-enhancing technology, all these are ours to seize. That is our honor and our challenge. We must be shapers of events, not observers. For if we do not act, the moment will pass, and we will lose the best possibilities of our future.

We face no imminent threat, but we do have an enemy. The enemy of our time is inaction. So tonight I issue a call to action: action by this Congress, action by our States, by our people, to prepare America for the 21st century; action to keep our economy and our democracy strong and working for all our people; action to strengthen education and harness the forces of technology and science; action to build stronger families and stronger communities and a safer environment; action to keep America the world's strongest force for peace, freedom, and prosperity; and above all, action to build a more perfect Union here at home.

The spirit we bring to our work will make all the difference. We must be committed to the pursuit of opportunity for all Americans, responsibility from all Americans, in a community of all Americans. And we must be committed to a new kind of Government, not to solve all our problems for us but to give our people, all our people, the tools they need to make the most of their own lives.

And we must work together. The people of this nation elected us all. They want us to be partners, not partisans. They put us all right here in the same boat, they gave us all oars, and they told us to row. Now, here is the direction I believe we should take. First, we must move quickly to complete the unfinished business of our country, to balance the budget, renew our democracy, and finish the job of welfare reform.

. . .

Over the last four years, we moved a record 2.25 million people off the welfare rolls. Then last year, Congress enacted landmark welfare reform legislation, demanding that all able-bodied recipients assume the responsibility of moving from welfare to work. Now each and every one of us has to fulfill our responsibility, indeed, our moral obligation, to make sure that people who now must work, can work.

Now we must act to meet a new goal: 2 million more people off the welfare rolls by the year 2000. Here is my plan: Tax credits and other incentives for businesses that hire people off welfare; incentives for job placement firms and states to create more jobs for welfare recipients; training, transportation, and child care to help people go to work.

Now I challenge every state: Turn those welfare checks into private sector paychecks. I challenge every religious congregation, every community nonprofit, every business to hire someone off welfare. And I'd like to say especially to every employer in our country who ever criticized the old welfare system, you can't blame that old system anymore. We have torn it down. Now do your part. Give someone on welfare the chance to go to work.

Tonight I am pleased to announce that five major corporations—Sprint, Monsanto, UPS, Burger King, and United Airlines—will be the first to join in a new national effort to marshal America's businesses, large and small, to create jobs so that people can move from welfare to work. We passed welfare reform. All of you know I believe we were right to do it. But no one can walk out of this chamber with a clear conscience unless you are prepared to finish the job.

. . .

To prepare America for the 21st century, we must build stronger families. Over the past 4 years, the Family and Medical Leave law has helped millions of Americans to take time off to be with their families. With new pressures on people in the way they work and live, I believe we must expand family leave so that workers can take time off for teacher conferences and a child's medical checkup. We should pass flex-time, so workers can choose to be paid for overtime in income or trade it in for time off to be with their families.

We must continue, step by step, to give more families access to affordable, quality health care. Forty million Americans still lack health insurance. Ten million children still lack health insurance; 80 percent of them have working parents who pay taxes. That is wrong. My balanced budget will extend health coverage to up to 5 million of those children. Since nearly half of all children who lose their insurance do so because their parents lose or change a job, my budget will also ensure that people who temporarily lose their jobs can still afford to keep their health insurance. No child should be without a doctor just because a parent is without a job.

My Medicare plan modernizes Medicare, increases the life of the trust fund to 10 years, provides support for respite care for the many families with loved ones afflicted with Alzheimer's, and for the first time, it would fully pay for annual mammograms.

Just as we ended drive-through deliveries of babies last year, we must now end the dangerous and demeaning practice of forcing women home from the hospital only hours after a mastectomy. I ask your support for bipartisan legislation to guarantee that a woman can stay in the hospital for 48 hours after a mastectomy. With us tonight is Dr. Kristen Zarfos, a Connecticut surgeon whose outrage at this practice spurred a national movement and inspired this legislation. I'd like her to stand so we can thank her for her efforts. Dr. Zarfos, thank you.

In the last four years, we have increased child support collections by 50 percent. Now we should go further and do better by making it a felony for any parent to cross a state line in an attempt to flee from this, his or her most sacred obligation.

Finally, we must also protect our children by standing firm in our determination to ban the advertising and marketing of cigarettes that endanger their lives.

. . .

America is far more than a place. It is an idea, the most powerful idea in the history of nations. And all of us in this Chamber, we are now the bearers of that idea, leading a great people into a new world. A child born tonight will have almost no memory of the 20th century. Everything that child will know about America will be because of what we do now to build a new century. We don't have a moment to waste. Tomorrow there will be just over 1,000 days until the year 2000; 1,000 days to prepare our people; 1,000 days to work together; 1,000 days to build a bridge to a land of new promise. My fellow Americans, we have work to do. Let us seize those days and the century.

Thank you, God bless you, and God bless America.

Source: Woolley, John T., and Gerhard Peters, *The American Presidency Project* [online] (Santa Barbara: University of California [hosted], Gerhard Peters [database]) (http://www. presidency.ucsb.edu/ws/?pid=53358).

Bibliography

GOVERNMENT REPORTS

Bartlett, Susan, Ellen Bobronnikov, Nicole Pacheco, et al.; Fred Lesnett, project officer. *WIC Participant and Program Characteristics 2004, WIC-04-PC.* Alexandria, VA: U.S. Department of Agriculture, Food and Nutrition Service, Office of Analysis, Nutrition and Evaluation, 2006. (http://www.fns.usda.gov/oane/MENU/Published/WIC/FILES/pc2004.pdf)

Characteristics of Food Stamp Households, Fiscal Year 2005. U.S. Department of Agriculture, Food and Nutrition Service, Office of Analysis, Nutrition and Evaluation, 2006. (http://www.fns.usda.gov/oane/MENU/published/FSP/FILES/Participation/2005Characteristics.pdf)

Children's Health Insurance Program. "2006 Status Report." Texas Health and Human Services Commission: 2006. (http://www.hhsc.state.tx.us/reports/CHIP_Status_Report_2006.pdf)

DeNavas-Walt, Carmen, Bernadette D. Proctor, and Cheryl Hill Lee. "Income, Poverty, and Health Insurance Coverage in the United States: 2005." U.S. Census Bureau: 2006.

Gibson, Campbell, and Kay Jung. *Historical Census Statistics on Population Totals by Race, 1790 to 1990, and by Hispanic Origin, 1970 to 1990, for Large Cities and Other Urban Places in the United States.* U.S. Census Bureau, Population Division, Working Paper No. 76, February 2005. (http://www.census.gov/population/www/documentation/twps0076.html)

Gibson, Campbell, and Kay Jung. "Historical Census Statistics on Population Totals by Race, 1790 to 1990, and by Hispanic Origin, 1790 to 1990, for the United States, Regions, Divisions, and States." U.S. Census Bureau, *Population Division Working Paper 87 No. 56,* 2002.

Kerner Commission, *Report of the National Advisory Commission on Civil Disorders.* Washington, D.C.: Government Printing Office, 1968. (http://www.eisenhowerfoundation.org/docs/kerner.pdf)

Volunteers in Service to America VISTA. Washington: ACTION (Service Corps), Volunteers in Service to America, 1980.

WIC Program Coverage: How Many Eligible Individuals Participated in the Special Supplemental Nutrition Program for Women, Infants, and Children (WIC): 1994 to 2003?

Alexandria, VA: U.S. Department of Agriculture, Food and Nutrition Services, Office of Analysis, Nutrition, and Evaluation, 2006. (http://www.fns.usda.gov/oane/MENU/Published/WIC/WIC.htm)

PUBLISHED AND UNPUBLISHED DOCUMENTS

Batchellor, Albert S. et al., eds. *Laws of New Hampshire, Provincial Period*, 3 vols. Manchester, NH: Clarke, 1904–1915.

The Eleanor Roosevelt Papers. "Public Works Administration." *Teaching Eleanor Roosevelt*, edited by Allida Black, June Hopkins, et al. Hyde Park, NY: Eleanor Roosevelt National Historic Site, 2004. (http://www.nps.gov/archive/elro/teaching.htm)

Johnson, Lyndon B. "The War on Poverty." 1964. *Public Papers of the Presidents of the United States, Lyndon B. Johnson, Book II: 1965*. Washington, D.C.: Government Printing Office, 1966.

Johnson, Lyndon B. "Great Society Speech." 1964. *Public Papers of the Presidents of the United States, Lyndon B. Johnson, Book I: 1963–64*. Washington, D.C.: Government Printing Office, 1965. (http://www.lbjlib.utexas.edu/johnson/archives.hom/speeches.hom/selected_speeches.asp)

Portsmouth New Hampshire Town Records. Typescript. Portsmouth Public Library.

President Clinton's 1997 State of the Union speech. Transcript. CNN article. (http://edition.cnn.com/2005/ALLPOLITICS/01/31/sotu.clinton1997/index.html)

Woolley, John T., and Gerhard Peters, The American Presidency Project [online]. Santa Barbara: University of California (hosted), Gerhard Peters (database). (http://www.presidency.ucsb.edu/ws/?pid=27432)

PERIODICALS

Atkinson, Anthony R. "On the Measurement of Inequality." *Journal of Economic Theory* 2 (1970).

Ball, Duane E. "Dynamics of Population and Wealth in Eighteenth-Century Chester County, Pennsylvania." *Journal of Interdisciplinary History* 6 (1976).

Bose, Rohit, and Stephen W. Hwang. "Income and Spending Patterns Among Panhandlers," *Canadian Medical Association Journal*. Sept. 3, 2002. 167 (5).

Bowman, Mary Jean. "A Graphical Analysis of Personal Income Distribution in the United States." *American Economic Review* 35 (1945).

Butler, James D. "British Convicts Shipped to American Colonies." *American Historical Review* 2 (1896).

Dalton, Hugh. "The Measurement of the Inequality of Incomes." *Economic Journal* 30 (1920).

Daniels, Bruce E. "Long Range Trends of Wealth Distribution in Eighteenth-Century New England." *Explorations in Economic History* 11 (1973–1974).

Gillian, Charles E. "Jail Bird Immigrants to Virginia." *Virginia Historical Magazine* Vol. 52 (1944).

Haar, Charles M. "White Indentured Servants in Colonial New York." *Americana* 34 (1940).

Haveman, Robert H., and John Karl Scholz. "The Clinton Welfare Reform Plan: Will It End Poverty as We Know It?" Institute for Research on Poverty Discussion Paper no. 1037–94, 1994.

Hoffman, Alexander von. "The Origins of American Housing Reform." Joint Center for Housing Studies, Harvard University, 1998.

Hwang, Stephen W. "Homelessness and Health." *Canadian Medical Association Journal*. Jan. 23, 2001. 164 (2).

Morris, Richard J. "Wealth Distribution in Salem, Massachusetts, 1759–1799: the Impact of the Revolution and Independence." In *Essex Institute Historical Collections*. 114 (1978).

Quadagno, Jill. "Theories of the Welfare State." *Annual Review of Sociology* 13 (1987).

Schutz, Robert R. "On the Measurement of Income Inequality," *American Economic Review* 41 (1951).

Stromberg, Jerome S. "Private Problems in Public Housing: A Further Report on the Pruitt-Igoe Project." *Occasional Paper #39,* 1968.

"The Town Records of Gosport, New Hampshire." *New England Historical and Genealogical Society.* 1913–1914.

BOOKS

Addams, Jane. *Twenty Years at Hull House.* Chicago: The Macmillan Co., 1910.

Atkins, Jacqueline M., ed. *Encyclopedia of Social Work,* 18th ed., 2 vols. Silver Spring, MD: NASW, 1987.

Axinn, June, and Mark J. Stern. *Social Welfare: A History of the American Response to Need.* 5th ed. Allyn and Bacon: Boston, 2001.

Bauman, John F., Roger Biles, and Kristin M. Szylvian, eds. *From the Tenements to the Taylor Homes: In Search of an Urban Housing Policy in Twentieth-Century America.* University Park, PA: Pennsylvania State University Press, 2000.

Beer, George Louis. *The Old Colonial System: 1660–1754.* New York: Peter Smith, 1958.

Benson, Jackson. *John Steinbeck, Writer: A Biography.* New York: Penguin Books, 1990.

Benton, Josiah H. *Warning Out in New England.* Boston: W. B. Clarke, 1911.

Blassingame, John. *The Slave Community: Plantation Life in the Antebellum South.* New York: Oxford University Press, 1979.

Boyer, Paul. *Urban Masses and Moral Order in America, 1820–1920.* Cambridge, MA: Harvard University Press, 1978.

Brace, Charles Loring. *The Dangerous Classes of New York, and Twenty Years' Work Among Them.* New York: Wynkoop and Hallenbeck, 1872.

Bremner, Robert H., Gary W. Reichard, and Richard Hopkins, ed. *American Choices: Social Dilemma and Public Policy since 1960.* Columbus: Ohio State University Press, 1986.

Bridenbaugh, Carl. *Cities in Revolt.* New York: Oxford University Press, 1955.

Bridenbaugh, Carl. *Cities in the Wilderness.* New York: Oxford University Press, 1938.

Brown, Alexander. *The Genesis of the United States.* London: Boston and New York: Houghton Mifflin, 1890.

Brown, Robert. *Middle Class Democracy and the Revolution in Massachusetts, 1691–1780.* Cornell, NY: Cornell University Press, 1955.

Burn, Richard. *The History of the Poor Laws: With Observations.* London: Woodfall and Strahan,1764.

Bushman, Richard L. *From Puritan to Yankee: Character and the Social Order in Connecticut, 1690–1765.* Cambridge, MA: Harvard University Press, 1967.

Callow, Alexander B., Jr., ed. *American Urban History: An Interpretive Reader with Commentaries,* 3rd ed. New York: Oxford University Press, 1982.

Chávez, Ernesto. *"¡Mi Raza Primero!": Nationalism, Identity, and Insurgency in the Chicano Movement in Los Angeles, 1966–1978.* Berkeley: University of California Press, 2002.

Clarkson, L. A. *The Pre-Industrial Economy in England, 1500–1750.* New York: Schocken Books, 1972.

Conkin, Paul. *The New Deal,* 2nd ed. Arlington Heights, IL: Harlan Davidson Inc, 1975.

Crane, Stephen. *Maggie: A Girl of the Streets.* New York: Appleton, 1896.

Davis, Allen. *American Heroine: The Life and Legend of Jane Addams.* New York: Oxford University Press, 1973.

Davis, Mike. *City of Quartz.* New York: Vintage Books, 1992.

Davis, Mike. *Dead Cities.* New York: New Press, 2002.

Divine, Robert A., T. H. Breen, et al. *The American Story,* 2nd ed. New York: Penguin Books, 2005.

Eden, Frederic. *The State of the Poor,* 3 vols. London: Davis, 1797.

Ekelund, Robert B., Jr., and Robert F. Hebert. *A History of Economic Theory and Method.* NewYork: McGraw-Hill, 1975.

Ellman, Richard, and Robert O'Clair, eds. *The Norton Anthology of Modern Poetry,* 2nd edition. New York: W. W. Norton, 1973.

Faulkner, Harold U. *American Economic History.* 8th ed. New York: Harper & Row, Publishers, 1960.

Fogel, Robert W., and Stanley L. Engerman. *Time on the Cross: The Economics of American Negro Slavery.* Boston: Little, Brown and Company, 1974.

Ford, Worthington C. *Washington as an Employer and Importer of Labor.* Brooklyn: Privately Printed, 1889.

Galbraith, John Kenneth. *The Affluent Society.* New York: Boston: Houghton Mifflin Co., 1958.

Goldfield, David R., and Blaine A. Brownell. *Urban America: From Downtown to No Town.* Boston: Houghton Mifflin Co., 1979.

Grob, Gerald N. *The Deadly Truth: A History of Disease in America.* Cambridge, MA: Harvard University Press, 2002.

Handlin, Oscar. *The Uprooted: The Epic Story of the Great Migrations that Made the American People,* 2nd ed. Boston: Little, Brown and Company, 1973.

Harrington, Michael. *The Other America: Poverty in the United States.* New York: Macmillan, 1963.

Heilbroner, Robert L. *The Worldly Philosophers: The Lives, Times, and Ideas of the Great Economic Thinkers.* New York: Time Incorporated, 1961.

Herrick, Cheesman A. *White Servitude in Pennsylvania, Indentured and Redemption Labor in Colony and Commonwealth.* Philadelphia: McVey, 1926.

Hofstadter, Richard. *America at 1750: A Social Portrait.* New York: Alfred E. Knopf, 1971.

Hofstadter, Richard. *The Age of Reform: From Bryan to F.D.R.* New York: Random House, 1955.

Horne, Gerald. *Fire This Time: The Watts Uprising and the 1960s.* Charlottesville, VA: University Press of Virginia, 1995.

Huggins, Nathan Irvin. *Harlem Renaissance.* New York: Oxford University Press, 1971.

Iceland, John. *Poverty in America,* 2nd ed. Berkeley: University of California Press, 2006.

Isserman, Maurice. *The Other American: The Life of Michael Harrington.* New York: Public Affairs, 2000.

Katz, Michael B. *Poverty and Policy in American History.* New York: Academic Press, 1983.

Katz, Stanley N., John M. Murrin, Douglas Greenberg, eds. *Colonial America: Essays in Politics and Social Development,* 5th edition. Boston: McGraw Hill, 2001.

Knorr, Klaus. *British Colonial Theories, 1570–1850.* Toronto: University of Toronto Press, 1968.

Lawson, Benjamin A. "The Pruitt-Igoe Projects: Modernism, Social Control, and the Failure of Public Housing, 1954–1976." MA Thesis: Oklahoma State University, 2007.

Lawson, Russell M. *Portsmouth: An Old Town by the Sea.* Charleston: Arcadia Publishing, 2003.

Lawson, Russell M. *The American Plutarch: Jeremy Belknap and the Historian's Dialogue with the Past.* Westport, CT: Praeger Publishers, 1998.

Leonard, E. M. *The Early History of English Poor Law Relief.* Cambridge, MA: Cambridge University Press, 1900.

Lindert, Peter H. *Fertility and Scarcity in America.* Princeton: Princeton University Press, 1978.

Link, Arthur S., and William B. Catton. *American Epoch: A History of the United States Since 1900, Volume II: 1921–1945,* 4th ed. New York: Alfred E. Knopf, 1973.

Litwack, Leon. *North of Slavery: The Negro in the Free States, 1790–1860.* Chicago: University of Chicago Press, 1971.

McCormac, E. I. *White Servitude in Maryland, 1634–1820*. Baltimore: Johns Hopkins Press, 1904.

McGerr, Michael E. *A Fierce Discontent: The Rise and Fall of the Progressive Movement in America, 1870–1920*. New York: Free Press, 2003.

Main, Gloria L. *Tobacco Colony: Life in Early Maryland, 1650–1720*. Princeton: Princeton University Press, 1982.

Main, Jackson T. *The Social Structure of Revolutionary America*. Princeton: Princeton University Press, 1965.

Mazzari, Louis. "Child Health." In *Encyclopedia of New England*. New Haven: Yale University Press, 2005.

Morse, Richard B. *Government and Labor in Early America*. New York: Harper & Row, Publishers, 1965.

Moynihan, Daniel P., ed. *Toward a National Urban Policy*. New York: Basic Books, 1970.

Mumford, Lewis. *Technics and Civilization*. New York: Harcourt Brace and World, 1963.

Nash, Gary B. *The Urban Crucible: Social Change, Political Consciousness, and the Origins of the American Revolution*. Cambridge, MA: Harvard University Press, 1979.

Nicholls, George. *A History of the English Poor Law*, 2 vols. London: P. S. King and Son, 1904.

Patterson, James T. *America's Struggle Against Poverty in the Twentieth Century*. Cambridge, MA: Harvard University Press, 2000.

Rainwater, Lee. *Behind Ghetto Walls: Black Families in a Federal Slum*. Chicago: Aldine and Atherton Publishers, 1970.

Richards, Eugene. *Cocaine True Cocaine Blue*. New York: Aperture, 1994.

Riis, Jacob. *How the Other Half Lives*. New York: Charles Scribner's Sons, 1890.

Rogers, James. *A History of Agriculture and Prices in England*, 6 vols. Oxford: Clarendon Press 1887.

Rosen, George. *A History of Public Health*. Baltimore: Johns Hopkins University Press, 1993.

Sitkoff, Harvard. *New Deal for Blacks: The Emergence of Civil Rights as a National Issue*. Oxford: Oxford University Press, 1981.

Smith, Abbot Emerson. *Colonists in Bondage: White Servitude and Convict Labor in America, 1607–1776*. New York: W. W. Norton, 1971.

Smith, James D. *The Personal Distribution of Income and Wealth*. New York: National Bureau of Economic Research, 1975.

Stampp, Kenneth. *The Peculiar Institution: Slavery in the Ante-Bellum South*. New York: Random House, 1956.

Steinbeck, John. *The Grapes of Wrath*. New York: Viking Press, 1939.

Stevens, Rosemary. *In Sickness and Wealth: American Hospitals in the Twentieth Century*. Baltimore: Johns Hopkins University Press, 1999.

Stromberg, Jerome S. "Private Problems in Public Housing: A Further Report on the Pruitt-Igoe Project." *Occasional Paper #39*. February 1968.

The Constitution and By-Laws of the Scots' Charitable Society of Boston. Cambridge, MA: Wilson, 1878.

The Rules, Regulations, &c. of the Portsmouth Female Asylum, with the Act of Incorporation. Portsmouth, NH: 1815.

Thernstrom, Stephan. *Poverty and Progress: Social Mobility in a Nineteenth Century City*. Cambridge, MA: Harvard University Press, 1964.

Trattner, Walter I. *From Poor Law to Welfare State*, 6th ed. New York: Simon and Schuster, 2007, 1999.

Vergara, Camillo. *The New American Ghetto*. New Brunswick, NJ: Rutgers University Press, 1995.

Weber, Max. *The Protestant Ethic and the Spirit of Capitalism*. Translated by Talcott Parsons. New York: Charles Scribners and Sons, 1958.

Whittlesey, Susan. *VISTA: Challenge to Poverty*. New York: Coward-McCann Inc., 1970.

Williamson, Jeffrey G., and Peter H. Lindert. *American Inequality: A Macroeconomic History.* New York: Academic Press, 1980.

Wright, Louis B. *The Cultural Life of the American Colonies.* New York: Harper & Row Publishers, 1957.

Zinn, Howard. *A People's History of the United States,* rev. ed. New York: Harper Collins, 2003, 1995.

WEB SITES

ACF Head Start Office. (http://eclkc.ohs.acf.hhs.gov/hslc/HeadStartOffices)

Administration for Children and Families (ACF). (www.acf.hhs.gov/index.html)

The Annie E. Casey Foundation. *KIDS COUNT Retrospective Study 1996.* (www.kidscount.org)

Centers for Medicare & Medicaid Services. (www.cms.hhs.gov)

Children's Bureau. (www.acf.hhs.gov)

Children's Defense Fund Action Council. (www.cdfactioncouncil.org/stateandlocal/default.asp)

Children's Defense Fund. (www.childrensdefense.org)

CHIP. (www.cms.hhs.gov)

Christian Churches Together. (www.christianchurchestogether.org)

Civilian Conservation Corps. (http://arcweb.sos.state.or.us/50th/ccc/cccintro.html)

The Civilian Conservation Corps and the National Park Service. (www.nps.gov/history/history/online_books/ccc/)

The Community Builders. Our Projects: Villages at Park Du Valle. (www.tcbinc.org/what_we_do/projects/fp_parkduvalle.htm)

Council of Economic Advisors. "What is Poverty." (www.whitehouse.gov/cea)

Department of Education. (www.ed.gov)

Department of Health and Human Services. (www.hhs.gov/children/index.shtml)

Department of Housing and Urban Development. (www.hud.gov)

Department of Labor. (www.dol.gov)

Economic Opportunity Act. (www2.volstate.edu/geades/FinalDocs/1960s/eoa.htm)

EEOC History, 35th Anniversary: 1965–2000. (www.eeoc.gov/abouteeoc/35th/index.html)

Equal Employment Opportunity Commission (EEOC). (www.eeoc.gov)

History of American Education Web Project. (www.nd.edu/~rbarger/www7/)

HUD, The Annual Homeless Assessment Report to Congress, February 2007. (www.huduser.org/publications/povsoc/annual_assess.html)

Minimum Wage Laws in the States, July 24, 2007. (www.dol.gov/esa/minwage/america.htm)

National Center for Children in Poverty. (www.nccp.org)

National Education Association. (www.nea.org/esea/index.html)

No Child Left Behind. Public Law 107–110 107th Congress. (http://www.ed.gov/nclb/landing.jhtml)

Office of Family Assistance. (www.acf.hhs.gov/programs/ofa/)

Office of Head Start. (www.acf.hhs.gov/programs/hsb/)

Park Du Vall Revitalization. (www.hal1.org/hopevi/index.htm)

Social Security Act, 1935. (www.ssa.gov/OP_Home/ssact/comp-toc.htm)

Social Security Administration. (www.ssa.gov)

Social Security Administration. *Food Stamp Facts.* (www.socialsecurity.gov)

Social Security Online—Medicaid Information. (www.socialsecurity.gov/disabilityresearch/wi/medicaid.htm)

Social Security, Presidential Statements. (www.ssa.gov/history/presstmts.html)

The White House. (www.whitehouse.gov/news/reports/no-child-left-behind.html)

Index

About the Authors

RUSSELL M. LAWSON holds a Ph.D. in history from the University of New Hampshire. He is Associate Professor of History at Bacone College in Muskogee, Oklahoma. He has written numerous works in American and European history. He is editor of *Research and Discovery: Landmarks and Pioneers in American Science*, 3 vols. (2008). Other recent works include *The Isles of Shoals in the Age of Sail: A Brief History* and *The Piscataqua Valley in the Age of Sail: A Brief History*, both published in 2007. He was an editor and contributor to *Dictionary of United States History, New England States* (2005), *Encyclopedia of New England Culture* (2005), and *The American Years: Chronologies of American History and Experience* (2003).

BENJAMIN A. LAWSON is currently working on a Ph.D. in recent American urban and social history at the University of Iowa, where he serves as a Graduate Instructor. He has previously published entries in *Research and Discovery: Landmarks and Pioneers in American Science*, 3 vols. (2008) and has had original maps, drawings, and photographs published in several books. Benjamin also has a BFA in studio art and a BA in art history from Oklahoma State University.